THE ORIGIN OF CONCURRENT PROGRAMMING

From Semaphores to Remote Procedure Calls

Springer Science+Business Media, LLC

THE ORIGIN OF CONCURRENT PROGRAMMING

From Semaphores to Remote Procedure Calls

Edited by PER BRINCH HANSEN

Springer

Per Brinch Hansen
Center for Science and Technology
Syracuse University
Syracuse, NY 13244
USA
pbh@top.cis.syr.edu

Library of Congress Cataloging-in-Publication Data
The origin of concurrent programming: from semaphores to remote procedure calls/
editor, Per Brinch Hansen.
p. cm.
Includes bibliographical references.
1. Parallel programming (Computer science) I. Brinch Hansen, Per, 1938-
QA76.642.O75 2002
005.2′.75–dc21

2002016002

Printed on acid-free paper

ISBN 978-1-4419-2986-0 ISBN 978-1-4757-3472-0 (eBook)
DOI 10.1007/978-1-4757-3472-0

9 8 7 6 5 4 3 2 1 SPIN 10860478

www.springer-ny.com

FOR JONATHAN GREENFIELD

PREFACE

If you want to discover new ideas in computing, textbooks won't help you. You need to find out how the masters of the field did it. You need to read their original papers!

That's why I put twenty-four papers together in a previous volume called *Classic Operating Systems: From Batch Processing to Distributed Systems* (Springer-Verlag, 2001).

But there is another side to this story. *You cannot build (or understand) a modern operating system unless you know the principles of concurrent programming.* The classic papers in the present book cover *the major breakthroughs in concurrent programming from the mid 1960s to the late 1970s.* These pioneering contributions have remained the foundation of concurrent programming in operating systems and parallel computing.

All the papers were written by the computer scientists who invented these ideas. Apart from a brief summary, I let the papers speak for themselves.

This book is for programmers, researchers, and students of electrical engineering and computer science. I assume that you are familiar with operating system principles.

I thank the copyright owners for permission to reprint these papers. A footnote on the title page of each paper gives full credit to the publication in which the work first appeared, including the name of the copyright holder.

PER BRINCH HANSEN
Syracuse University

CONTENTS

OVERVIEW

THE INVENTION OF CONCURRENT PROGRAMMING

PER BRINCH HANSEN

(2001)

The author selects classic papers written by the computer scientists who made the major breakthroughs in concurrent programming. These papers cover the pioneering era of the field from the semaphores of the mid 1960s to the remote procedure calls of the late 1970s. The author summarizes the classic papers and puts them in historical perspective.

A PROGRAMMING REVOLUTION

This is the story of one of the major revolutions in computer programming: *the invention of concurrent programming.*

Tom Kilburn and David Howarth pioneered the use of interrupts to simulate concurrent execution of several programs on the *Atlas computer* (Kilburn 1961). This programming technique became known as *multiprogramming.*

The early multiprogramming systems were programmed in assembly language without any conceptual foundation. The slightest programming mistake could make these systems behave in a completely erratic manner that made program testing nearly impossible.

By the end of the 1960s multiprogrammed operating systems had become so huge and unreliable that their designers spoke openly of a *software crisis* (Naur 1969).

As J. M. Havender (1968) recalled:

P. Brinch Hansen, The invention of concurrent programming. In *The Origin of Concurrent Programming: From Semaphores to Remote Procedure Calls*, P. Brinch Hansen, Ed.,

> The original multitasking concept of the [*IBM OS/360*] envisioned relatively unrestrained competion for resources to perform a number of tasks concurrently ... But as the system evolved many instances of task deadlock were uncovered.

Elliott Organick (1973) pointed out that the termination of a task in the *Burroughs B6700* system might cause its offspring tasks to lose their stack space!

In the mid 1960s computer scientists took the first steps towards a deeper understanding of concurrent programming. In less than fifteen years, they discovered *fundamental concepts*, expressed them by *programming notation*, included them in *programming languages*, and used these languages to write *model operating systems*. In the 1970s the new programming concepts were used to write the first *concise textbooks* on the principles of *operating systems* and *concurrent programming*.

The development of concurrent programming was originally motivated by the desire to develop reliable operating systems. From the beginning, however, it was recognized that principles of concurrent programming "have a general utility that goes beyond operating systems"—they apply to *any* form of parallel computing (Brinch Hansen 1971a).

I would like to share the excitement of these discoveries with you by offering my own assessment of the classic papers in concurrent programming.

This essay is not just an editorial overview of the selected papers. It is also my personal reflections on the major contributions, which inspired me (and others) in our common search for simplicity in concurrent programming.

If you compare my early papers with this essay, you will notice an occasional change of perspective. With thirty years of hindsight, that is inevitable.

I have made an honest attempt to rely only on the *publication record* to document historic events and settle issues of priority. However, as a contributor to these ideas I cannot claim to have written an unbiased account of these events. That can only be done by a professional historian.

THE CLASSIC PAPERS

Choosing the *classic papers* was easier than I thought:

- *First I made a short list of fundamental contributions to abstract concurrent programming of major and lasting technical importance.*

- *Then I selected the original papers in which computer scientists first introduced these ideas.*
- *I added a few papers that illustrate the influence of concurrent programming concepts on operating system principles and programming language implementation.*
- *Finally I put the papers in chronological order to illustrate how each new idea was motivated by earlier successes and failures.*

Fundamental Concepts

Asynchronous processes
Speed independence
Fair scheduling
Mutual exclusion
Deadlock prevention
Process communication
Hierarchical structure
Extensible system kernels

Programming Language Concepts

Concurrent statements
Critical regions
Semaphores
Message buffers
Conditional critical regions
Secure queueing variables
Monitors
Synchronous message communication
Remote procedure calls

Classic Papers

1. *E. W. Dijkstra, Cooperating Sequential Processes (1965).*
2. *E. W. Dijkstra, The Structure of the THE Multiprogramming System (1968).*
3. *P. Brinch Hansen, RC 4000 Software: Multiprogramming System (1969).*
4. *E. W. Dijkstra, Hierarchical Ordering of Sequential Processes (1971).*
5. *C. A. R. Hoare, Towards a Theory of Parallel Programming (1971).*
6. *P. Brinch Hansen, An Outline of a Course on Operating System Principles (1971).*
7. *P. Brinch Hansen, Structured Multiprogramming (1972).*
8. *P. Brinch Hansen, Shared Classes (1973).*
9. *C. A. R. Hoare, Monitors: An Operating System Structuring Concept (1974).*
10. *P. Brinch Hansen, The Programming Language Concurrent Pascal (1975).*
11. *P. Brinch Hansen, The Solo Operating System: A Concurrent Pascal Program (1976).*
12. *P. Brinch Hansen, The Solo Operating System: Processes, Monitors and Classes (1976).*
13. *P. Brinch Hansen, Design Principles (1977).*
14. *E. W. Dijkstra, A Synthesis Emerging? (1975).*
15. *C. A. R. Hoare, Communicating Sequential Processes (1978).*
16. *P. Brinch Hansen, Distributed Processes: A Concurrent Programming Concept (1978).*
17. *P. Brinch Hansen, Joyce—A Programming Language for Distributed Systems (1987).*
18. *P. Brinch Hansen, SuperPascal: A Publication Language for Parallel Scientific Computing (1994).*
19. *P. Brinch Hansen, Efficient Parallel Recursion (1995).*

After following this selection procedure rigorously, I was surprised to see that *every* single paper turned out to have been written by either Edsger Dijkstra, Tony Hoare or me. In retrospect, this was, perhaps, not so surprising.

In Judy Bishop's (1986) view:

> The swing away from assembly language which gained genuine momentum during the seventies was slow to affect the area of concurrent systems—operating systems, embedded control systems and the like. What happened was that three people—Edsger Dijkstra, Tony

Hoare and Per Brinch Hansen—independently developed key abstractions which were taken up by researchers worldwide, realized in experimental languages, reported on, adapted and refined. In this way, the problems of concurrency could be expressed in well understood notation, and solutions and principles gradually evolved.

To produce an anthology of reasonable size (about 500 pages) *I omitted*:

- Subsequent work that built on the seminal papers without adding anything fundamentally new.
- Survey papers and assessments of ideas.
- Implementation details (except in outline).
- Testing, verification, and formal theory.
- Functional multiprogramming and data parallel languages.

These guidelines eliminated many valuable contributions to concurrent programming (as well as two dozen of my own papers). Some of them are listed as recommended *further reading* in the *bibliography* at the end of this essay.

PART I CONCEPTUAL INNOVATION

It is difficult for students today to imagine how little anyone knew about systematic programming in the early 1960s. Let me illustrate this by telling you about my first modest experience with multiprogramming.

In 1963 I graduated from the Technical University of Denmark without any programming experience (it was not yet being taught). There were (as far as I remember) no textbooks available on programming languages, compilers or operating systems.

After graduating I joined the Danish computer company Regnecentralen. Working on a Cobol compiler project, headed by Peter Naur and Jørn Jensen, I taught myself to program.

In 1966 Peter Kraft and I were asked to design a real-time system for supervising a large ammonia nitrate plant in Poland. A small computer would be used to perform a fixed number of cyclical tasks simultaneously. These tasks would share data tables and peripherals. Since plant operators could change the frequencies of individual tasks (and stop some of them indefinitely), we could not make any assumptions about the relative (or absolute) speeds of the tasks.

It was obvious that we needed multiprogramming with process synchronization. But what kind of synchronization?

A common technique at the time was to *suspend* a process in a queue until it was *resumed* by another process. The trouble was that resumption had no effect if the queue was empty. This happened if resumption was attempted *before* a process was suspended. (This pitfall reminds me of a mailman who throws away your letters if you are not at home when he attempts to deliver them!)

This mechanism is unreliable because it makes a seemingly innocent assumption about the relative timing of parallel events: A process must *never* attempt to resume another process that is not suspended. However, since the timing of events is unpredictable in a real-time system, this would have been a disastrous choice for our real-time system.[1]

Regnecentralen had no experience with multiprogramming. Fortunately, Edsger Dijkstra was kind enough to send me a copy of his 1965 monograph "Cooperating Sequential Processes," with a personal dedication: "Especially made for graceful reading!" (I still have it.)

Using Dijkstra's semaphores, Peter Kraft, Charles Simonyi and I were able to implement the *RC 4000 real-time control system* on the prototype of Regnecentralen's RC 4000 computer with only 4K words of memory (without a drum or disk) (Brinch Hansen 1967a, 1967b).

1 *Cooperating Sequential Processes*

The first classic is one of the great works in computer programming:

E. W. Dijkstra, Cooperating Sequential Processes (1965)

Here Dijkstra lays the *conceptual foundation* for *abstract concurrent programming.* He begins by making the crucial assumption about *speed independence*:

> We have stipulated that processes should be connected loosely; by this we mean that apart from the (rare) moments of explicit intercommunication, the individual processes themselves are to be regarded as

[1] Around 1965 IBM's *PL/I* language included queueing variables of this kind known as *events.* Surprisingly, the *suspend* and *resume* primitives are also included in the recent *Java* language (Doug Lea 1997).

completely independent of each other. In particular, we disallow any assumption about the relative speeds of the different processes.

Indivisible operations were well-known in multiprogramming systems, in the form of *supervisor calls* (Kilburn 1961). Dijkstra's contribution was to make explicit assumptions about these *critical sections* (as he calls them).[2]

For pedagogical reasons, Dijkstra first attempts to program critical sections using assignments and inspection of simple variables only.

Through a carefully presented sequence of rejected solutions, Dijkstra arrives at the following *correctness criteria* for cyclical processes cooperating by means of common variables and critical sections:

1. *Mutual exclusion*: "At any moment at most one of the processes is engaged in its critical section."
2. *Fairness*: "The decision which of the processes is the first to enter its critical section cannot be postponed to eternity."
3. *Speed independence*: "Stopping a process in its 'remainder of cycle' [that is, outside its critical region] has no effect upon the others."

The Dutch mathematician T. J. Dekker found a general solution to the mutual exclusion problem without synchronizing primitives. For single-processor systems, I have always viewed this as an ingenious, academic exercise. Computer designers had solved the problem (in a restricted way) by the simple technique of *disabling interrupts*.

As a more realistic solution, Dijkstra introduces *binary semaphores*, which make the mutual exclusion problem trivial.[3]

Using *general semaphores* (due to Carel Scholten), Dijkstra implements message communication through a *bounded buffer*.[4] He achieves a pleasing *symmetric behavior* of communicating processes by viewing senders as processes that consume empty buffer slots and produce full slots. Similarly, receivers consume full slots and produce empty ones.

Dijkstra also presents an ingenious method of *deadlock prevention*, known as *the banker's algorithm*.

---

[2]Hoare (1971) renamed them *critical regions*.

[3]Dijkstra used Dutch *acronyms*, *P* and *V*, for the semaphore operations. Being allergic to acronyms in any language, I renamed them *wait* and *signal* (Brinch Hansen 1971a).

[4]The *bounded buffer* is used as a programming example throughout this essay.

```
begin integer number of queuing portions,
              number of empty positions,
              buffer manipulation;
      number of queuing portions:= 0;
      number of empty positions:= N;
      buffer manipulation:= 1;
      parbegin
      producer: begin
             again 1: produce next portion;
                      P(number of empty positions);
                      P(buffer manipulation);
                      add portion to buffer;
                      V(buffer manipulation);
                      V(number of queuing portions);
                      goto again 1
                end;
      consumer: begin
             again 2: P(number of queuing portions);
                      P(buffer manipulation);
                      take portion from buffer;
                      V(buffer manipulation);
                      V(number of empty positions);
                      process portion taken;
                      goto again 2
                end
      parend
end
```

The Bounded Buffer with Semaphores

In the 1960s Alan Perlis noticed that Regnecentralen's compiler group discussed programming problems by writing *Algol 60* statements on a blackboard. This was unusual at a time when systems programs were still being written in assembly language.

Edsger Dijkstra was also firmly in the Algol 60 tradition (Naur 1960). He writes parallel algorithms in Algol extended with a *parallel statement:*[5]

$$\textbf{parbegin } S_1;\ S_2;\ \ldots\ S_n \textbf{ parend}$$

As Dijkstra defines it:

> Initiation of a parallel compound implies simultaneous initiation of all

[5] Also known as a *concurrent statement* (Brinch Hansen 1972b).

its constituent statements, its execution is completed after the completion of the execution of all its constituent statements.

This modest proposal is one of the first published examples of an *abstract programming notation* for concurrent processes.

2 THE Multiprogramming System

Dijkstra demonstrated the depth of his ideas in the construction of an elegant *model operating system*:

E. W. Dijkstra, The Structure of the THE Multiprogramming System (1968)

This was a spooling system that compiled and executed a stream of Algol 60 programs with paper tape input and printer output. It used software-implemented demand paging between a 512K word drum and a 32K word memory. There were five user processes and ten input/output processes, one for each peripheral device. The system used *semaphores* for process synchronization and communication.

Dijkstra's multiprogramming system illustrated the conceptual clarity of *hierarchical ordering*. His system consisted of several *program layers*, which gradually transform the physical machine into a more pleasant *abstract machine*:

Level 0: Processor allocation.
Level 1: Demand paging ("segment controller").
Level 2: Operator console ("message interpreter").
Level 3: Virtual devices ("input/output streams").
Level 4: User processes.
Level 5: System operator.

Apart from the operator, these program layers could be designed and tested one at a time.

This short paper concentrates on Dijkstra's most startling claim:

> We have found that it is possible to design a refined multiprogramming system in such a way that its logical soundness can be proved a priori and its implementation can admit exhaustive testing. The only errors that showed up during testing were trivial coding errors ... the resulting system is guaranteed to be flawless.

The hierarchical structure was used to prove the following properties of *harmoniously cooperating processes*:

1. "Although a process performing a task may in so doing generate a finite number of tasks for other processes, a single initial task cannot give rise to an infinite number of task generations."
2. "It is impossible that all processes have returned to their homing position while somewhere in the system there is still pending a generated but unaccepted task."
3. "After the acceptance of an initial task all processes eventually will be (again) in their homing position."

Software managers continue to believe that software design is based on a magical discipline, called "software engineering," which can be mastered by average programmers. Dijkstra explained that the truth of the matter is simply that

> the intellectual level needed for system design is in general grossly underestimated. I am convinced more than ever that this type of work is very difficult, and that every effort to do it with other than the best people is doomed to either failure or moderate success at enormous expense.

Nico Habermann (1967), Edsger Dijkstra (1971), Coen Bron (1972) and Mike McKeag (1976) described the THE system in more detail.

3 RC 4000 Multiprogramming System

In 1974 Alan Shaw wrote:

> There exist many approaches to multiprogramming system design, but we are aware of only two that are *systematic* and *manageable* and at the same time have been *validated* by producing real working operating systems. These are the hierarchical abstract machine approach developed by Dijkstra (1968a) and the nucleus methods of Brinch Hansen (1969) ... The nucleus and basic multiprogramming system for the RC 4000 is one of the most elegant existing systems.

The *RC 4000 multiprogramming system* was not a complete operating system, but *a small kernel upon which operating systems for different purposes could be built* in an orderly manner:

P. Brinch Hansen, RC 4000 Software: Multiprogramming System (1969)

The kernel provided the basic mechanisms for creating a *tree of parallel processes* that communicated by messages. Jørn Jensen, Søren Lauesen and I designed it for Regnecentralen's *RC 4000 computer.* We started working on the system in the fall of 1967. A well-documented reliable version was running in the spring of 1969.

Before the RC 4000 multiprogramming system was programmed, I described a *design philosophy* that drastically generalized the concept of an operating system (Brinch Hansen 1968):

> The system has no built-in assumptions about program scheduling and resource allocation; it allows any program to initiate other programs in a hierarchal manner.[6] Thus, the system provides a general frame[work] for different scheduling strategies, such as batch processing, multiple console conversation, real-time scheduling, etc.

This radical idea was probably the most important contribution of the RC 4000 system to operating system technology. If the kernel concept seems obvious today, it is only because it has passed into the general stock of knowledge about system design. It is now commonly referred to as the principle of *separation of mechanism and policy* (Wulf 1974).

The RC 4000 system was also noteworthy for its *message communication. Every communication consisted of an exchange of a message and an answer between two processes.* This protocol was inspired by an early decision to treat peripheral devices as processes, which receive input/output commands as messages and return acknowledgements as answers. In distributed systems this form of communication is now known as *remote procedure calls.*

The system also enabled a server process to be engaged in *nondeterministic communication* with several client processes at a time. This was known as a *conversational process.*

The RC 4000 system was programmed in assembly language. As a purely academic exercise for this essay, I have used an informal Pascal notation (Wirth 1971) to outline a conversational process that implements a *bounded buffer* used by client processes. In retrospect, such a process is equivalent to the "secretary" concept that Dijkstra (1971) would sketch two years later (in very preliminary form).

In the RC 4000 system, the *initial process* was a conversational process that spawned other processes in response to messages from console processes.

[6] Here I obviously meant "processes" rather than "programs."

```
{ The buffer process receives messages from client processes
  requesting it to accept or return data items. The messages
  arrive in buffer elements, which are linked to a message
  queue. The buffer process receives a message in a buffer
  element and uses the same buffer element to return an
  answer to the client process. }
number of items := 0;
{ Inspect the message queue from the beginning }
current buffer := nil;
cycle
  { Postpone receipt of the current buffer element (if any) }
  previous buffer := current buffer;
  { Wait for the next buffer element in the queue (which
    may already have arrived) }
  wait event(previous buffer, current buffer);
  case current buffer.request of
    accept item:
      if number of items < N then
        begin
          take a data item from the current buffer element
            and store it within the buffer process;
          number of items := number of items + 1;
          { Remove the current buffer element from the queue }
          get event(current buffer);
          { Use the same buffer element to return an
            acknowledgment to the client process }
          send answer(acknowledgment, current buffer);
          { Reinspect the queue from the beginning }
          current buffer := nil;
        end;
    return item:
      if number of items > 0 then
        begin
          select a data item stored within the buffer process;
          number of items := number of items - 1;
          { Remove the current buffer element from the queue }
          get event(current buffer);
          { Use the same buffer element to return the
            data item to the client process }
          send answer(data item, current buffer);
          { Reinspect the queue from the beginning }
          current buffer := nil;
        end
  end
end
```

The Bounded Buffer as a Conversational Process

If this *basic operating system* temporarily was unable to honor a request, it would postpone the action by delaying its receipt of the message. In the meantime, it would attempt to serve other clients.

According to Søren Lauesen (1975):

> The RC 4000 software was extremely reliable. In a university environment, the system typically ran under the simple operating system for three months without crashes ... The crashes present were possibly due to transient hardware errors.

When the RC 4000 system was finished I described it in a 5-page journal paper (Brinch Hansen 1970). I then used this paper as an outline of the 160-page system manual (Brinch Hansen 1969) by expanding each section of the paper.[7] The third article in this book is a reprint of the most important part of the original manual, which has been out of print for decades.[8]

As usual, Niklaus Wirth (1969) immediately recognized the advantages and limitations of the system:

> I am much impressed by the clarity of the multiple process concept, and even more so by the fact that a computer manufacturer adopts it as the basis of one of his products. I have come to the same conclusion with regard to semaphores, namely that they are not suitable for higher level languages. Instead, the natural synchronization events are exchanges of messages.
>
> What does not satisfy me completely at your scheme is that a specific mechanism of dynamic buffer space allocation is inextricably connected with the problem of process synchronization, I would prefer a scheme where the programmer himself declares such buffers in his programs (which of course requires an appropriate language).

4 Hierarchical Ordering of Sequential Processes

E. W. Dijkstra, Hierarchical Ordering of Sequential Processes (1971)

[7] In May 1968 I outlined these ideas in a panel discussion on Operating Systems at the Tenth Anniversary Algol Colloquium in Zurich, Switzerland. The panelists included Edsger Dijkstra and Niklaus Wirth, both of whom received copies of the RC 4000 system manual in July 1969.

[8] My operating system book (Brinch Hansen 1973b) includes a slightly different version of the original manual supplemented with abstract (untested) Pascal algorithms.

With deep insight, Dijkstra explains his *layered approach* to operating system design in greater detail. This time he proves the correctness of critical sections and the bounded buffer implemented with *semaphores.* He also introduces and solves the scheduling problem of the *dining philosophers*, which poses subtle dangers of *deadlock* and *unfairness* (described in flamboyant terminology as "deadly embrace" and "starvation").

The THE multiprogramming system was implemented in assembly language without memory protection. Every process could potentially access and change *any* variable in the system. However, using well-defined programming rules and systematic testing, Dijkstra and his students were able to verify that *all processes cooperated harmoniously.*

At the end of the paper, Dijkstra briefly sketches an alternative scenario of *secretaries* and *directors:*[9]

> Instead of N sequential processes cooperating in critical sections via common variables, we take out the critical sections and combine them into a N+1st process, called a "secretary"; the remaining N processes are called "directors". Instead of N equivalent processes, we now have N directors served by a common secretary.
>
> What used to be critical sections in the N processes are in the directors "calls upon the secretary".
>
> A secretary presents itself primarily as a bunch of non-reentrant routines with a common state space.
>
> When a director calls a secretary ... the secretary may decide to keep him asleep, a decision that implies that she should wake him up in one of her later activities. As a result the identity of the calling program cannot remain anonymous as in the case of the normal subroutine. The secretaries must have variables of type "process identity".
>
> In general, a director will like to send a message to his secretary when calling her ... and will require an answer back from his secretary when she has released his call.

On the basis of this proposal, Greg Andrews (1991) credits Dijkstra with being "the first to advocate using data encapsulation to control access to shared variables in a concurrent program." Twenty-five years ago, I repeated the prevailing opinion that "Dijkstra (1971) suggested the idea of monitors" (Brinch Hansen 1975a). Today, after reading the classic papers again, I find this claim (which Dijkstra never made) debatable.

[9]The gender bias in the terminology was not considered unusual thirty years ago.

Dijkstra had implemented his multiprogramming system as cooperating processes communicating through *common variables* in *unprotected memory*. From his point of view, the idea of combining critical regions and common variables into server processes ("secretaries") was a new approach to resource scheduling.

However, this idea was obvious to the designers of the RC 4000 multiprogramming system, based, as it was, on a paradigm of processes with *disjoint memories* communicating through *messages* only. There was simply no other way of using the RC 4000 system!

The "secretaries," which Dijkstra described informally, had already been implemented as "conversational processes" in the RC 4000 system. Mike McKeag (1972) demonstrated the similarity of these ideas by using the RC 4000 message primitives to outline simple secretaries for well-known synchronization problems, such as the *bounded buffer*, the *dining philosophers*, and a *readers and writers* problem.

I am not suggesting that the RC 4000 primitives would have been a good choice for a programming language. They would not. They lacked a crucial element of language design: notational elegance. And I certainly did not view conversational processes (or "secretaries") as the inspiration for the future monitor concept.

I am simply pointing out that the *idea* of a *resource manager* was already known by 1969, in the form of a *basic monitor*, invoked by supervisor calls, or a *conversational process* (a "secretary"), invoked by message passing.

What was new, was the goal of extending programming languages with this paradigm (Discussions 1971). And that had not been done yet.

PART II PROGRAMMING LANGUAGE CONCEPTS

The invention of *precise terminology* and *notation* plays a major role not only in the sciences but in all creative endeavors.

When a *programming concept* is understood informally it would seem to be a trivial matter to invent a *programming notation* for it. But in practice this is hard to do. The main problem is to replace an intuitive, vague idea with a precise, unambiguous definition of its meaning and restrictions. The mathematician George Pólya (1957) was well aware of this difficulty:

> An important step in solving a problem is to choose the notation. It should be done carefully. The time we spend now on choosing the notation may well be repaid by the time we save later by avoiding

> hesitation and confusion. Moreover, choosing the notation carefully, we have to think sharply of the elements of the problem which must be denoted. Thus, choosing a suitable notation may contribute essentially to understanding the problem.

A *programming language concept* must represent a *general idea* that is used often. Otherwise, it will just increase the complexity of the language at no apparent gain. The meaning and rules of a programming concept must be *precisely defined.* Otherwise, the concept is meaningless to a programmer. The concept must be represented by a *concise notation* that makes it easy to recognize the elements of the concept and their relationships. Finally, it should be possible by simple techniques to obtain a *secure, efficient implementation* of the concept. A compiler should be able to check that the rules governing the use of the concept are satisfied, and the programmer should be able to predict the speed and size of any program that uses the concept by means of performance measurements of its implementation.

As long as nobody studies your programs, their *readability* may not seem to be much of a problem. But as soon as you write a description for a wider audience, the usefulness of an *abstract notation* that suppresses irrelevant detail becomes obvious. So, although Dijkstra's THE system was implemented in assembly language, he found it helpful to introduce a programming notation for parallel statements in his description (Dijkstra 1965).

5 Conditional Critical Regions

In the fall of 1971, Tony Hoare enters the arena at a Symposium on Operating Systems Techniques at Queen's University of Belfast:

C. A. R. Hoare, Towards a Theory of Parallel Programming (1971)

This is *the first notable attempt to extend programming languages with abstract features for parallel programming.* Hoare points out that the search for parallel language features is "one of the major challenges to the invention, imagination and intellect of computer scientists of the present day."

Hoare boldly formulates *design principles* for *parallel programming languages*:

1. *Interference control.* The idea of preventing time-dependent errors by compile-time checking was novel at a time when multiprogramming systems relied exclusively on run-time checking of variable access:

> Parallel programs are particularly prone to time-dependent errors, which either cannot be detected by program testing nor by run-time checks. It is therefore very important that a high-level language designed for this purpose should provide complete security against time-dependent errors by means of a *compile-time check.*

2. *Disjoint processes.* Dijkstra's parallel statement `{Q1//Q2//...//Qn}` is used to indicate that the program statements Q_1, Q_2, ..., Q_n define disjoint processes to be executed in parallel. According to Hoare:

> It is expected that the compiler will check the disjointness of the processes by ensuring that no variable subject to change in any of the Q_j is referred to at all in any Q_i for $i \neq j$. Thus it can be guaranteed by a compile-time check that no time-dependent errors could ever occur at run time.

3. *Resources.* The programming language *Pascal* is extended with a notation indicating that a variable r of some type T is a resource shared by parallel processes:

```
r: T; ... {resource r; Q1//Q2//...//Qn}
```

4. *Critical regions.* Inside the process statements Q_1, Q_2, ..., Q_n a critical region `C` on the resource `r` is expressed by the structured notation

```
with r do C
```

A compiler is expected to check that the resource is neither used nor referred to outside its critical regions.

5. *Conditional critical regions.* Sometimes the execution of a critical region `C` must be delayed until a resource `r` satisfies a condition, defined by a Boolean expression `B`:

```
with r when B do C
```

The conditional form of a critical region is the most original language feature proposed in Hoare's paper.[10]

[10] *Simula I* and *SOL* also included statements for waiting on Boolean conditions (later removed from Simula). However, these were simulation languages without any concept (or need) of critical regions (Dahl 1963, Knuth 1964).

```
B: record inpointer, outpointer, count: Integer;
   buffer: array 0...N-1 of T end;
 with B do
      begin inpointer:= 0; outpointer:= 0;
            count:= 0;
      end;
{resource B;
 ...
 with B when count < N do
      begin buffer[inpointer]:= next value;
            inpointer:= (inpointer + 1) mod N;
            count:= count + 1
      end
 //
 ...
 with B when count > 0 do
      begin this value:= buffer[outpointer];
            outpointer:= (outpointer + 1) mod N;
            count:=count - 1
      end
}
```

The Bounded Buffer with Conditional Critical Regions

Hoare emphasized that "The solutions proposed in this paper cannot claim to be final, but it is believed that they form a sound basis for further advance."

At the Belfast symposium (Brinch Hansen 1971a), I expressed some reservations from a software designer's point of view:

> The conceptual simplicity of simple and conditional critical regions is achieved by ignoring the sequence in which waiting processes enter these regions. This abstraction is unrealistic for heavily used resources. In such cases, the operating system must be able to identify competing processes and control the scheduling of resources among them. This can be done by means of a *monitor*—a set of shared procedures which can delay and activate individual processes and perform operations on shared data.

Hoare's response (Discussions 1971):

> As a result of discussions with Brinch Hansen and Dijkstra, I feel that this proposal is not suitable for operating system implementation ...

> My proposed method encourages the programmer to ignore the question of which of several outstanding requests for a resource should be granted.
>
> A year ago I would have said that this was a very serious criticism indeed of a language proposal that it encouraged the programmer to ignore certain essential problems. I now believe that a language should be usable at a high level of abstraction, and at high levels of abstraction it is an excellent thing to encourage the programmer to ignore certain types of problems, in particular scheduling problems.

Hoare's paper was as an eye-opener for me: It was my introduction to *the difficult art of language design.* The idea of checking interference during scope analysis struck me as magical!

Years later, I included variants of conditional critical regions in two programming languages, *Distributed Processes* (Brinch Hansen 1978) and *Edison* (Brinch Hansen 1981).

6 Operating System Principles

Abstract concurrent programming had an immediate and dramatic impact on our fundamental understanding of computer operating systems.

The implementation techniques of operating systems were reasonably well understood in the late 1960s. But most systems were too large and poorly described to be studied in detail. All of them were written either in assembly language or in sequential programming languages extended with assembly language features. Most of the literature on operating systems emphasized low-level implementation details of particular systems rather than general concepts. The terminology was unsystematic and incomplete (Brinch Hansen 2000).

Before the invention of abstract concurrent programming, it was impractical to include algorithms in operating system descriptions. Technical writers mixed informal prose with unstructured flowcharts and complicated pictures of linked lists and state transitions.[11]

In its Cosine Report (1971), the National Academy of Engineering summarized the state of affairs at the time [with emphasis added]:

[11]See, for example, IBM (1965), Elliott Organick (1972), and Stuart Madnick (1974).

> The subject of computer operating systems, if taught at all, is typically a descriptive study of some specific operating system, with little attention being given to emphasizing the relevant basic concepts and principles. To worsen matters, *it has been difficult for most university departments to develop a new course stressing operating systems principles ... There are essentially no suitable textbooks on the subject.*

I consider myself lucky to have started in industry. The RC 4000 project convinced me that a fundamental understanding of operating systems would change computer programming radically. I was so certain of this that I decided to leave industry and become a researcher.

In November 1970 I became a research associate at Carnegie-Mellon University, where I wrote *the first comprehensive textbook on operating system principles*:

P. Brinch Hansen, An Outline of a Course on Operating System Principles (1971)

While writing the book I reached the conclusion that *operating systems are not radically different from other programs. They are just large programs based on the principles of a more fundamental subject: parallel programming.*

Starting from a concise definition of the purpose of an operating system, I divided the subject into five major areas. First, I presented the principles of parallel programming as the essence of operating systems. Then I described processor management, memory management, scheduling algorithms and resource protection as techniques for implementing parallel processes.

I defined operating system concepts by abstract algorithms written in Pascal extended with a notation for structured multiprogramming. My (unimplemented) programming notation included *concurrent statements*, *semaphores*, *conditional critical regions*, *message buffers*, and *monitors*. These programming concepts are now discussed in all operating system texts.

The book includes a concise vocabulary of *operating system terminology*, which is used consistently throughout the text. The vocabulary includes the following terms:

concurrent processes, *processes* that overlap in time; concurrent processes are called **disjoint** if each of them only refers to **private data**; they are called **interacting** if they refer to **common data**.

synchronization, a general term for any constraint on the order in which *operations* are carried out; a synchronization rule can, for example, specify the precedence, priority, or mutual exclusion in time of operations.

> **monitor**, a *common data* structure and a set of meaningful *operations* on it that exclude one another in time and control the *synchronization* of *concurrent processes.*

My book *Operating System Principles* was published in July 1973. Peter Naur (1975) reviewed it:

> The presentation is generally at a very high level of clarity, and gives evidence of deep insight. In pursuing his general aim, the establishment of a coherent set of basic principles for the field, the author is highly successful. The principles are supported by algorithms written in Pascal, extended where necessary with carefully described primitives. Close attention is paid to the thorny question of terminology.

In my outline of the book I made a prediction that would guide my future research:

> So far nearly all operating systems have been written partly or completely in machine language. This makes them unnecessarily difficult to understand, test and modify. I believe it is desirable and possible to write efficient operating systems almost entirely in a *high-level language.* This language must permit *hierarchal structuring* of data and program, extensive *error checking* at compile time, and production of *efficient machine code.*

7 *Structured Multiprogramming*

P. Brinch Hansen, Structured Multiprogramming (1972)

The conditional critical region, proposed by Hoare (1971), had minor notational limitations and a potentially serious implementation problem:

1. A shared variable is declared as both a *variable* and a *resource.* The textual separation of these declarations can be misused to treat the same variable as a scheduled resource in some contexts and as an ordinary variable in other contexts. This would enable a process to refer directly to a variable while another process is within a "critical" region on the same variable.

I closed this loophole by using a single declaration to introduce a *shared variable* (of some type T):

var v: **shared** T

2. When a process is delayed by a Boolean expression without side effects, it cannot indicate the urgency of its request to other processes. This complicates the programming of *priority scheduling.*

It was an obvious remedy to permit a conditional *await statement* to appear anywhere within a critical region:

region v **do**
begin ... **await** B; ... **end**

3. The major concern was that *it did not seem possible to implement conditional critical regions efficiently.* The root of the problem is the unbounded reevaluation of Boolean expressions until they are true.

Many years later, Charles Reynolds (1993) asked:

> How does a process wait for some condition to be true? It seems to me that the critical insight occurred in realizing that the responsibility for determining an awaited event has occurred must lie with the application programmer and not with the underlying run-time support. The awakening of processes awaiting events is part of the application algorithm and must be indicated by explicit announcement of the events by means of "signal" or "cause" commands present in the application algorithm. This idea is clearly present as early as Brinch Hansen (1972b).

I suggested that programmers should be able to *associate secure queueing variables with shared data structures and control the transfers of processes to and from them.*

In my proposal, the declaration

var e: **event** v;

associates a queuing variable *e* of type *event* with a shared variable *v*.

A process can leave a critical region associated with *v* and join the queue *e* by executing the standard procedure

await(e)

```
var B: shared record
              buffer: array 0..max-1 of T;
              p, c: 0..max-1;
              full: 0..max;
              nonempty, nonfull: event B;
            end;
procedure send(m: T);
region B do
begin
  while full = max do await(nonfull);
  buffer[p] := m;
  p := (p + 1) mod max;
  full := full + 1;
  cause(nonempty);
end
procedure receive(var m: T);
region B do
begin
  while full = 0 do await(nonempty);
  m := buffer[c];
  c := (c + 1) mod max;
  full := full - 1;
  cause(nonfull);
end
```

The Bounded Buffer with Secure Events

Another process can enable all processes in the queue *e* to reenter their critical regions by executing the standard procedure

cause(e)

If several processes are waiting in the same queue, a *cause* operation on the queue will (eventually) enable *all* of them to resume their critical regions (one at a time). Mutual exclusion is still maintained, and processes waiting to resume critical regions have priority over processes that are waiting to enter the beginning of critical regions.

In this situation, a resumed process may find that another process has made its scheduling condition *B* false again. Consequently, processes must use *waiting loops* of the form[12]

[12] *Mesa* (Lampson 1980) and *Java* (Lea 1997) would also require waiting loops on Boolean conditions.

while not B **do** await(e)

My proposal was completely unrelated to the unpredictable event queues of the 1960s, which caused the programmer to lose control over scheduling. The crucial difference was that the new queues were associated with a shared variable, so that all scheduling operations were mutually exclusive operations. The programmer could control the scheduling of processes to any degree desired by associating each queue with a *group* of processes or an *individual* process.

The idea of associating secure scheduling queues with a shared data structure to enable processes to delay and resume critical regions has been used in all monitor proposals. In an unpublished draft, Hoare (1973a) proposed *wait* and *signal* operations on *condition variables*, which, he says, "are very similar to Brinch Hansen's await and cause operations." In the following I will call all these kinds of queues *secure queueing variables.*

Secure queueing variables were an efficient solution to the problem of process scheduling within critical regions. However, like semaphores, queueing variables always struck me (and others) as *somewhat too primitive* for abstract concurrent programming. To this day nobody has found a better compromise between notational elegance and efficient implementation. Still, I cannot help feeling that we somehow looked at the scheduling problem from the wrong point of view.

We now had all the pieces of the monitor puzzle, and I had adopted a programming style that combined shared variables, critical regions, secure queueing variables, and procedures in a manner that closely resembled monitors. But we still did *not* have an abstract monitor notation.

8 Shared Classes

The missing element in conditional critical regions was a concise representation of *data abstraction.* The declaration of a resource and the operations associated with it were not combined into a single syntactical form, but were distributed throughout the program text.

In the spring of 1972 I read two papers by Dahl (1972) and Hoare (1972) on the *class* concept of the programming language *Simula 67.* Although Simula is *not* a concurrent programming language, it inspired me in the following way: So far I had thought of a monitor as a program module that defines all operations on a *single* instance of a data structure. From Simula

I learned to regard a program module as the definition of a *class* of data structures accessed by the same procedures.

This was a moment of truth for me. Within a few days I wrote a chapter on resource protection for my operating system book:

P. Brinch Hansen, Shared Classes (1973)

I proposed to *represent monitors by shared classes* and pointed out that *resource protection* and *type checking* are part of the same problem: to verify automatically that all operations on data structures maintain certain properties (called *invariants*).

My book includes a single monitor for a *bounded buffer*. The shared class defines a data structure of type B, two procedures that can operate on the data structure, and a statement that defines its initial state.

```
shared class B =
  buffer: array 0..max-1 of T;
  p, c: 0..max-1;
  full: 0..max;
procedure send(m: T);
begin
  await full < max;
  buffer[p] := m;
  p := (p + 1) mod max;
  full := full + 1;
end
procedure receive(var m: T);
begin
  await full > 0;
  m := buffer[c];
  c := (c + 1) mod max;
  full := full - 1;
end
begin p := 0; c := 0; full := 0 end
```

The Bounded Buffer as a Shared Class

The shared class notation permits *multiple instances* of the same *monitor type*. A buffer variable b of type B is declared as

var b: B

Upon entry to the block in which the buffer variable is declared, storage is allocated for its data components, and the buffer is initialized by executing the statement at the end of the class definition.

Send and *receive* operations on a buffer *b* are denoted

b.send(x)   b.receive(y)

A shared class is a notation that explicitly restricts the operations on an *abstract data type* and enables a compiler to check that these restrictions are obeyed. It also indicates that all operations on a particular instance must be executed as *critical regions.* In short, *a shared class is a monitor type.*

My decision to use *await statements* in the first monitor proposal was a matter of taste. I might just as well have used *secure queueing variables.*

You might well ask why after inventing shared classes with secure queueing variables I published my original ideas in a textbook, instead of a professional journal. Well, I was young and idealistic. I felt that my first book should include at least one original idea. It did not occur to me that researchers rarely look for original ideas in undergraduate textbooks.[13]

Why didn't I publish a tutorial on the monitor concept? My professional standards were deeply influenced by the *Gier Algol compiler* (Naur 1963), the *THE multiprogramming system* (Dijkstra 1968), the *RC 4000 multiprogramming system* (Brinch Hansen 1969), and the *Pascal compiler* (Wirth 1971). Every one of these systems had been implemented *before* it was described in a professional journal.

Since this was my standard of software research, I decided to implement monitors in a programming language before writing more about it.

9 Monitor Papers

In his first paper on monitors, Hoare (1973b) used my shared classes and secure queueing variables (with minor changes) to outline an unimplemented paging system. A year later, he published a second paper on monitors (Hoare 1974b). He acknowledged that "This paper develops Brinch Hansen's concept of a monitor."

Avi Silberschatz (1992) concluded that "The monitor concept was developed by Brinch Hansen (1973b). A complete description of the monitor was given by Hoare (1974b)."

---

[13] I did, however, send the complete manuscript of *Operating System Principles*, which included my monitor concept, to Edsger Dijkstra and Tony Hoare in May 1972 (Horning 1972).

C. A. R. Hoare, Monitors: An Operating System Structuring Concept (1974)

Hoare's contribution to the monitor concept was to *refine* the rules of *process resumption*:

1. He replaced the "resume-all, one-at-a-time" policy of secure event variables with the more convenient "first-come, first-served" policy of condition variables.

2. He decreed "that a signal operation be followed immediately by resumption of a waiting program, without possibility of an intervening procedure call from yet a third program." This eliminated the need for waiting loops.

3. He advocated Ole-Johan Dahl's simplifying suggestion that a signal operation should terminate a monitor call (Hoare 1973c).

```
bounded buffer: monitor
  begin buffer: array 0..N-1 of portion;
        lastpointer: 0..N-1;
        count: 0..N;
        nonempty, nonfull: condition;
    procedure append(x: portion);
      begin if count = N then nonfull.wait;
            note 0 ≤ count < N;
            buffer[lastpointer] := x;
            lastpointer := lastpointer ⊕ 1;
            count := count + 1;
            nonempty.signal
      end append;
    procedure remove(result x: portion);
      begin if count = 0 then nonempty.wait;
            note 0 < count ≤ N;
            x := buffer[lastpoint ⊖ count];
            count := count - 1;
            nonfull.signal
      end remove;
    count := 0; lastpointer := 0
  end bounded buffer;
```

The Bounded Buffer as a Monitor

This influential paper deserves a place in the history of concurrent programming as *the first monitor tutorial*:

1. The monitor concept is illustrated by solutions to familiar *programming exercises*: a single resource scheduler, a bounded buffer, an alarm clock, a buffer pool, a disk head optimizer, and a readers and writers problem.

2. As an academic exercise he presents a *semaphore implementation* of monitors. (In practice, monitors would, of course, be implemented by uninterruptible operations in assembly language.)

3. Finally, he defines simple *proof rules* for condition variables.

PART III CONCURRENT PROGRAMMING LANGUAGES

Hoare (1974a) introduced the essential requirement that *a programming language must be secure* in the following sense: A language should enable its compiler and run-time system to detect as many cases as possible in which the language concepts break down and produce meaningless results.[14]

For a parallel programming language the most important security measure is to check that processes access disjoint sets of variables only and do not interfere with each other in time-dependent ways.

Unless the parallel features of a programming language are secure in this sense, the effects of parallel programs are generally both unpredictable and time-dependent and may therefore be meaningless. This does not necessarily prevent you from writing correct parallel programs. It does, however, force you to use a low-level, error-prone notation that precludes effective error checking during compilation and execution.

The only secret about secure concurrent languages was that they could be designed at all. Once you have seen that this is possible, it is not so difficult to invent other concurrent languages. That is why I have included only *the first secure concurrent language, Concurrent Pascal.*

In the first survey paper on concurrent programming I cited 11 papers only, written by four researchers. None of them described a concurrent programming language (Brinch Hansen 1973e). The development of monitors and Concurrent Pascal started a wave of research in concurrent programming languages. A more recent survey of the field includes over 200 references to nearly 100 languages (Bal 1989).

Concurrent Pascal had obvious limitations by today's standards. But in 1975 it laid the foundation for the development of *secure programming languages with abstract concepts for parallelism.*

---

[14]This definition of *security* differs somewhat from its usual meaning of "the ability of a system to withstand attacks from adversaries" (Naur 1974).

10 Concurrent Pascal

On July 1, 1972, I became associate professor of computer science at California Institute of Technology. During my first academic year I prepared three new courses and introduced Pascal on campus. These tasks kept me busy for a while.

I also started thinking about designing a programming language with concurrent processes and monitors. To reduce the effort, I decided to include these concepts in an existing sequential language. Since I had used the language in my operating system book, Pascal was an obvious choice for me.

In September 1973, I sent Mike McKeag "a copy of a preliminary working document that describes my suggestion for an extension of Pascal with concurrent processes and monitors" (Brinch Hansen 1973d). This is the earliest evidence of *Concurrent Pascal.*

By January 1975, the Concurrent Pascal compiler and its run-time support were running on a PDP 11/45 minicomputer at Caltech (Hartmann 1975, Brinch Hansen 1975f).

In May 1975, I published a paper on the new language:

P. Brinch Hansen, The Programming Language Concurrent Pascal (1975)

Concurrent Pascal extends Pascal with abstract data types known as processes, monitors, and classes. Each type module defines the representation and possible transformations of a single data structure. The syntax clearly shows that each module consists of a set of variable declarations, a set of procedures, and an initial statement.

A module cannot access the variables of another module. *The compiler uses this scope rule to detect synchronization errors before a program is executed.* The run-time synchronization of monitor calls prevents other race conditions.

A process can *delay* itself in a monitor variable of type *queue.* When another process performs a *continue* operation on the same queue, the delayed process (if any) immediately resumes execution of its monitor procedure. In any case, the process performing the continue operation immediately returns from its monitor procedure.

A queue is either empty or holds a single process. A multiprocess queue can be implemented as an array of single-process queues.

As a language designer, I have always felt that one should experiment with the simplest possible ideas before adopting more complicated ones. This led me to use *single-process queues* and *combine process continuation with*

```
type buffer =
monitor
var contents: array [1..max] of T;
    head, tail, length: integer;
    sender, receiver: queue;
procedure entry send(x: T);
begin
  if length = max then delay(sender);
  contents[tail] := x;
  tail := tail mod max + 1;
  length := length + 1;
  continue(receiver)
end;
procedure entry receive(var x: T);
begin
  if length = 0 then delay(receiver);
  x := contents[head];
  head := head mod max + 1;
  length := length - 1;
  continue(sender)
end;

begin head := 1; tail := 1; full := 0 end
```

The Bounded Buffer in Concurrent Pascal

monitor exit.

I felt that the merits of a signaling scheme could be established only by designing real operating systems (but not by looking at small programming exercises). Since Concurrent Pascal was the first monitor language, I was unable to benefit from the practical experience of others. After designing small operating systems, I concluded that first-in, first-out queues are indeed somewhat more convenient to use.

In any case, the virtues of different signaling mechanisms still strike me as being only mildly interesting. In most cases, any one of them will do, and all of them (including my own) are slightly complicated. Fortunately, *monitors have the marvelous property of hiding the details of scheduling from concurrent processes.*

The programming tricks of assembly language were impossible in Concurrent Pascal: there were no typeless memory words, registers, and addresses in the language. The programmer was not even aware of the existence of physical processors and interrupts. *The language was so secure that concur-*

rent processes ran without any form of memory protection.

The portable compiler (written in Sequential Pascal) *generated platform-independent code, which was executed by a small kernel written in assembly language* (Hartmann 1975, Brinch Hansen 1975e). The language was moved from one computer to another by rewriting the kernel of 4K words in the assembly language of the target computer (Brinch Hansen 1975f).[15]

Greg Andrews (1993) felt that:

> The contribution of Concurrent Pascal was indeed that it added a new dimension to programming languages: modular concurrency. Monitors (and classes) were essential to this contribution. And the modularization they introduced has greatly influenced most subsequent concurrent language proposals.

In a later essay on language description (Brinch Hansen 1981), I said:

> The task of writing a language report that explains a programming language with complete clarity to its implementors and users may look deceptively easy to someone who hasn't done it before. But in reality it is one the most difficult intellectual tasks in the field of programming.

Well, I was someone who hadn't done it before, and the Concurrent Pascal report (Brinch Hansen 1975d) suffered from all the problems I mentioned in the essay. I added, "I am particularly uncomfortable with the many *ad hoc* restrictions in the language."

Ole-Johan Dahl (1993) disagreed:

> I take issue with some of your reservations about Concurrent Pascal. Of course a language built around a small number of mechanisms used orthogonally is an ideal worth striving for. Still, when I read your 1977 book my reaction was that the art of imposing the right restrictions may be as important from an engineering point of view. So, here for once was a language, beautiful by its orthogonal design, which at the same time was the product of a competent engineer by the restrictions imposed in order to achieve implementation and execution efficiency. The adequacy of the language as a practical tool has been amply demonstrated.

[15] Twenty years later, the designers of the *Java* language resurrected the idea of platform-independent parallel programming (Gosling 1996). Unfortunately, they replaced the secure monitor concept of Concurrent Pascal with *insecure* shortcuts (Brinch Hansen 1999).

Concurrent Pascal was followed by more than a dozen *monitor languages*, listed in Brinch Hansen (1993a), among them *Modula* (Wirth 1977a), *Pascal Plus* (Welsh 1979), and *Mesa* (Lampson 1980).

PART IV MODEL OPERATING SYSTEMS

By the end of 1975, I had used Concurrent Pascal to implement three small operating systems of 600–1400 lines each:

- *The single-user operating system Solo*
- *A job stream system*
- *A real-time scheduler*

The development and documentation effort of each system took a few months (or weeks) only.

11 Solo Operating System

As a realistic test of the new programming language, I used Concurrent Pascal to program a small operating system:

P. Brinch Hansen, The Solo Operating System: A Concurrent Pascal Program (1976)

Solo was a portable single-user operating system for the development of Sequential and Concurrent Pascal programs. It was implemented on a PDP 11/45 minicomputer with removable disk packs. Every user disk was organized as a single-level file system. The heart of Solo was a job process that compiled and ran programs stored on the disk. Two additional processes performed input/output spooling simultaneously.

Al Hartmann (1975) had already written the Concurrent Pascal compiler. I wrote the operating system and its utility programs in three months. Wolfgang Franzen measured and improved the performance of the disk allocation algorithm.

The Solo system demonstrated that it is possible to write small operating systems in a secure programming language without machine-dependent features. The discovery that this was indeed possible for small operating systems was more important (I think) than the invention of monitors.

12 Solo Program Text

Solo was *the first modular operating system implemented by means of abstract data types (classes, monitors and processes) with compile-time checking of access rights.* The most significant contribution of Solo was undoubtedly that the program text was short enough to be *published in its entirety* in a computer journal:

> *P. Brinch Hansen, The Solo Operating System: Processes, Monitors and Classes (1976)*

The new programming language had a dramatic (and unexpected) impact on my programming style. It was the first time I had programmed in a language that enabled me to divide programs into modules that could be programmed and tested separately. The creative part was clearly the initial selection of modules and *the combination of modules into hierarchical structures.* The programming of each module was often trivial. I soon adopted the rule that *each module should consist of no more than one page of text.* Since each module defined all the meaningful operations on a single data type (private or shared), the modules could be studied and tested one at a time. As a result these *concurrent programs became more reliable than the hardware they ran on.*

In July 1975, when the Solo operating system had been working for three months, I described it at the International Summer School in Marktoberdorf, Germany. Hoare presented an outline of an unimplemented operating system (Hoare 1976a).

At Caltech we prepared a *distribution tape* with the source text and portable code of the Solo system, including the Concurrent and Sequential Pascal compilers. The system reports were supplemented by *implementation notes* (Brinch Hansen 1976b). By the spring of 1976 we had distributed the system to 75 companies and 100 universities in 21 countries.

In a guest editorial on the Solo papers (Brinch Hansen 1976a), I wrote:

> It is not uncommon for a computer scientist to make a proposal without testing whether it is any good in practice. After spending 3 days writing up the monitor proposal and 3 years implementing it, I can very well understand this temptation. It is perhaps also sometimes a human response to the tremendous pressure on university professors to get funding and recognition fast.
>
> Nevertheless, we must remember that only one thing counts in engineering: Does it work (not "might it work" or "wouldn't it be nice

> if it did")? What would we think of mathematicians if most of their papers contained conjectures only? Sometimes an educated guess can be a great source of inspiration. But we must surely hope that the editors of computer journals will reject most proposals until they have been tried at least experimentally.
>
> All reviewers of my [operating system] book correctly pointed out that the chapter on resource protection [introducing shared classes] was highly speculative. The Solo operating system described here is an attempt to set the record straight by putting monitors to a realistic test.

13 The Architecture of Concurrent Programs

In July 1976 I joined University of Southern California as professor and chair of computer science. Now that Concurrent Pascal was running I knew that the time was ripe for a book on the principles of abstract parallel programming.

My second book, *The Architecture of Concurrent Programs*, includes the complete text of the model operating systems written in Concurrent Pascal (Brinch Hansen 1977b).

In a book review, Roy Maddux and Harlan Mills (1979) wrote: "This is, as far as we know, the first book published on concurrent programming." They were particularly pleased with the Solo system:

> Here, an entire operating system is visible, with every line of program open to scrutiny. There is no hidden mystery, and after studying such extensive examples, the reader feels that he could tackle similar jobs and that he could change the system at will. Never before have we seen an operating system shown in such detail and in a manner so amenable to modification.

Twenty years later, two of my former Ph.D. students recalled their experience of working with Concurrent Pascal:

> *Jon Fellows* (1993): "The beauty of the structures you created using Concurrent Pascal created an aura of magical simplicity. While working with my own programs and those of other graduate students, I soon learned that ordinary, even ugly, programs could also be written in Concurrent Pascal ... My current feeling is that the level of intellectual effort required to create a beautiful program structure cannot

be reduced by programming language features, but that these features can more easily reveal a program's beauty to others who need to understand it."

Charles Hayden (1993): "I think the significance of the system was ... that one could provide a protected environment for concurrent programming—a high-level language environment which could maintain the illusion that there was no "machine" level. It was remarkable that through compile time restrictions and virtual machine error checking ... you could understand the program behavior by looking at the Pascal, not at the machine's registers and memory. It was remarkable that the machine could retain its integrity while programs were being developed, without hardware memory protection."

In designing Concurrent Pascal and the model operating systems written in the language I followed a consistent set of programming principles. These principles carried *structured programming* (Dijkstra 1972a) into the realm of *modular, concurrent programming*:

P. Brinch Hansen, Design Principles (1977)

Roy Maddux and Harlan Mills (1979) agreed that:

> An author does well to start by stating those beliefs and biases he holds that are relevant to his work so that the reader is forewarned about what will follow and can understand the motivation behind subsequent decisions and choices. Brinch Hansen's opening chapter—a reasoned essay on the fundamental principles of programming today—does this remarkably well. The quotations at the end of the chapter are particularly well-chosen and make delightful reading.

PART V DISTRIBUTED COMPUTING

In the late 1970s, parallel computing was moving from multiprocessors with shared memory towards *multicomputers* with *distributed memory.* For microcomputer networks, Dijkstra, Hoare and I suggested different programming models. Although our ideas opened the way for *abstract distributed computing*, they clearly needed further refinement before they could be incorporated into programming languages.

14 A Synthesis Emerging?

Edsger Dijkstra led the way. In a brief note he gave a personal account of a discussion with Tony Hoare at the International Summer School in Marktoberdorf, Germany, in July 1975:

E. W. Dijkstra, A Synthesis Emerging? (1975)

Hoare was trying to explain the class concept of Simula 67, when Dijkstra began to:

> change terminology, notation and a way of looking at it, things I had to do in order to make it all fit within my frame of mind. To begin with, I shall record how our discussions struck root in my mind. I don't know whether a real Simula fan will still recognize the class-concept; he may get the impression that I am writing about something totally different.

Indeed! What emerges is the exciting possibility of *modular programs with nondeterministic process types* (called *generators*). In his usual colorful terminology, Dijkstra calls these programs "elephants built from mosquitoes."

His simplest example is a generator, named *nn*, for *natural numbers*:

```
nn gen begin privar x; x virint := 0;
             do ?inc → x := x + 1
              [] x > 0 cand ?dec → x := x − 1
             od
       end
```

(The notational details are not important here.)

The main program can declare a variable y as a natural number:

privar y; y **vir** nn;

The *generator instance* y keeps a natural number in a *private variable* x. After initializing its value to zero, the generator is ready to perform an endless series of *increase* and *decrease* operations on x in response to *commands* from the main program:

y.inc y.dec

The generator defines the increment operation as a *guarded command*

$$?\text{inc} \rightarrow \text{x} := \text{x} + 1$$

When the main program issues an increment command, the *guard*

$$?\text{inc}$$

is regarded as being true (once), enabling the generator to execute the *guarded statement*

$$\text{x} := \text{x} + 1$$

However, if the main program issues a decrement command, the guard

$$\text{x} > 0 \ \textbf{cand} \ ?\text{dec}$$

does not become true until $x > 0$.

So far, the generator looks very much like a *monitor* implementation of a *semaphore*, but there are subtle differences:

- *Dijkstra views the main program and its generators as processes that are synchronized during the execution of guarded commands.*

- *When the main program terminates, all guards within its local generators become false, and the generator loops terminate too.*

Dijkstra emphasizes that:

> [In the past] it was the purpose of our programs to instruct our machines: now it is the purpose of the machines to execute our programs. Whether the machine does so sequentially, one thing at a time, or with a considerable amount of concurrency, is a matter of implementation and should *not* be regarded as a property of the programming language.

This viewpoint naturally leads him to conclude that

- If the main program is *concurrent*, the generator does indeed implement a *semaphore* that *delays* a decrement operation until $x > 0$.

- However, if the main program is *sequential*, an attempt to decrement a natural number equal to zero will cause the main program to get *stuck.*

At this point Dijkstra introduces the powerful concept of *recursive nondeterministic processes.* He programs a generator that defines a *sequence of integers* recursively. A parallel execution of this program can be visualized as *a pipeline of processes.* Each process accepts commands from its predecessor (which is either another pipeline process or the main program).

An *insert command,* issued by the main program, *propagates* to the end of the chain, where the last process *extends the pipeline* with another process.

A *membership query* moves down the pipeline until it either reaches a process that holds the desired element or is absorbed at the end of the pipeline. In a parallel implementation, a *wave of queries* can move down the pipeline simultaneously.

Edsger Dijkstra called it "A surprising discovery, the depth of which is as far as I am concerned still unfathomed." In 1982 he added a final remark:

> In retrospect this text is not without historical interest: it records the highlights of a discussion mentioned [as "Verbal communication" (Dijkstra 1975)] in C. A. R. Hoare's "Communicating sequential processes", Comm. ACM 21, 8 (Aug. 1978), 666-677. The text was evidently written in a state of some excitement; in retrospect we may conclude that this excitement was not entirely unjustified. Seeing Hoare keenly interested in the topic, I left that arena.

15 Communicating Sequential Processes

Three years after his discussion with Edsger Dijkstra in Marktoberdorf, Tony Hoare publishes a paper on *communicating sequential processes* (also known as *CSP*):

C. A. R. Hoare, Communicating Sequential Processes (1978)

This classic paper develops Dijkstra's (1975a) vision of nondeterministic processes communicating by means of guarded commands (but *without recursion*).

The *bounded buffer,* shown here, is a CSP *process,* named `X`, that can hold up to ten buffer portions. After making the buffer empty to begin with, the process executes a *repetitive command* (prefixed by an asterisk `*`). In each cycle, the buffer process is delayed until one of two possible communications takes place:

1. A process named `producer` is ready to execute an *output command* `X!e`. In that case, the buffer process inputs the value of the expression

```
X::
buffer:(0..9)portion;
in,out:integer; in:= 0; out:= 0;
comment 0 ≤ out ≤ in ≤ out + 10;
  *[in < out + 10; producer?buffer(in mod 10) → in:= in + 1
   □out < in; consumer?more() → consumer!buffer(out mod 10);
    out := out + 1
  ]
```

The Bounded Buffer in CSP

e in the last buffer element, provided that there is room for it in the buffer. This is the effect of the *guarded input command*:

```
in < out + 10; producer?buffer(in mod 10) → in:= in + 1
```

2. A process named consumer outputs a request for more input, X!more(), and inputs the next buffer portion in a local variable v by executing the command X?v. When the buffer is nonempty, it accepts the request before outputting the first portion:

```
out < in; consumer?more() →
  consumer!buffer(out mod 10); out:= out + 1
```

This paper describes *highly original ideas*:

1. *Synchronous communication.* Hoare introduces this idea, which was well-known in computer architectures but novel in programming languages:

> Communication occurs when one process names another as destination for output *and* the second process names the first as source for input. In this case, the value to be output is copied from the first process to the second. There is *no* automatic buffering: In general, an input or output command is delayed until the other process is ready with the corresponding output or input. Such delay is invisible to the delayed process.

2. *Input guards.* CSP incorporates Dijkstra's (1975a) concept of nondeterministic process interactions controlled by guarded commands:

> A guarded command with an input guard is selected for execution only if and when the source named in the input command is ready to execute the corresponding output command. If several input guards of a set of alternatives have ready destinations, only one is selected and the others have *no* effect; but the choice between them is arbitrary.

3. *Coincidence of events.* In 1965, Dijkstra demonstrated that *mutual exclusion* of events is a fundamental programming concept. In 1975, he showed that the opposite idea, the *coincidence* of events, is just as important! This strikes me as the most profound idea incorporated in CSP.

4. *Programming examples.* The CSP paper includes solutions to a wide variety of interesting problems.

However, the CSP proposal also has some *awkward details*:

1. *Direct process naming.* One of the major advantages of monitors is their ability to communicate with processes and schedule them without being aware of process identities. In CSP, an input/output command must name the source or destination process directly. The text of a process must therefore be modified when it is used in different contexts. This complicates the examples in Hoare's paper: the user of a process array `S(1..n)` is itself named `S(0)`. And the prime sieve is composed of three different kinds of processes to satisfy the naming rules.

2. *Pattern matching.* The CSP notation does not include type declarations of communication channels, but depends (conceptually) on *dynamic checking* to recognize matching input and output commands in parallel processes.

3. *Conditional input.* Hoare mentions that:

> conditions can be used to delay acceptance of inputs which would violate scheduling constraints—postponing them until some later occasion when some other process has brought the monitor into a state in which the input can validly be accepted. This technique is similar to a conditional critical region (Hoare 1971) and it obviates the need for special synchronizing variables such as events, queues, or conditions. However, the absence of these special facilities certainly makes it more difficult or less efficient to solve problems involving priorities.[16]

[16]Notice, however, that a *monitor* with *await statements* on Boolean conditions does not require queueing variables either (Brinch Hansen 1973c).

4. *No output guards.* This restriction forces Hoare to publish a CSP version of the bounded buffer with *asymmetric input/output operations.* For aesthetic reasons, I find this lack of elegance regrettable.

5. *Process termination.* CSP uses Dijkstra's (1975a) termination rule:

> A repetitive command may have input guards. If all the sources named by them have terminated, then the repetitive command also terminates.

Hoare maintains that:

> The automatic termination of a repetitive command on termination of the sources of all its input guards is an extremely powerful and convenient feature but it also involves some subtlety of specification to ensure that it is implementable; and it is certainly not primitive, since the required effect can be achieved (with considerable inconvenience) by explicit exchange of "end()" signals.

Seven years later, Hoare (1985) realizes that:

> The trouble with this convention is that it is complicated to define and implement; and methods of proving program correctness seem no simpler with it than without.

6. *No recursion.* The most obvious weakness of CSP is the *omission of* Dijkstra's beautiful concept of *recursive nondeterministic processes.* A CSP process cannot activate itself recursively. It is, however, possible to activate *fixed-length process arrays,* which can imitate the behavior (but not the elegance) of recursive processes.[17]

CSP was a major achievement and the inspiration for a new generation of concurrent programming languages, including the nonrecursive language *occam* for the *transputer* (Inmos 1989a, 1989b) and the recursive language *Joyce* (Brinch Hansen 1987a).

Seven years later Hoare (1985) published a *mathematical theory of communicating sequential processes* using a recursive variant of CSP. This notation has played a significant role in research on the mathematical foundations of concurrency. Hoare (1981) is an early example of this theoretical work (which is beyond the scope of this essay).

---

[17]My alternative programming model, *Distributed Processes,* is also nonrecursive (Brinch Hansen 1978c).

16 Distributed Processes

For microcomputer networks with distributed memory I introduced the idea of *a synchronized procedure that can be called by one process and executed by another process.* This proposal *combines processes and monitors into a single concept*, called *distributed processes.* In distributed operating systems, this communication paradigm is known as *remote procedure calls.*

P. Brinch Hansen, Distributed Processes: A Concurrent Programming Concept (1978)

Distributed Processes have the following properties:

- A real-time program consists of a fixed number of concurrent processes that are started simultaneously and exist forever. Each process can access its *own variables* only. There are no common variables.
- A process can call *common procedures* defined within other processes. These procedures are executed when the other processes are waiting for some conditions to become true. A procedure call from one process to another is called an *external request.* This is the only form of process communication.
- Processes are synchronized by means of nondeterministic *guarded regions* (Hoare 1971, Dijkstra 1975b, Brinch Hansen 1978c).

The *bounded buffer*, shown here, is a process that stores a sequence of characters transmitted between processes by means of *send* and *receive* procedures.

```
process buffer
s: seq[n]char
proc send(c: char) when not s.full: s.put(c) end
proc rec(#v: char) when not s.empty: s.get(v) end
s := [ ]
```

The Bounded Buffer with Distributed Processes

The initial statement makes the buffer empty and terminates. The buffer process, however, continues to exist and can now be called by other processes:

call buffer.send(e)   **call** buffer.rec(v)

After initialization, the buffer process is idle between *external calls.* This process is similar to a *monitor* (Brinch Hansen 1973c) with *conditional critical regions* (Hoare 1971).

In general, an external call of a procedure R, declared in a process Q, may include both *value* and *result parameters*:

call $Q.R$(expressions, variables)

The *parameter passing* between two distributed processes requires a single *input* operation when an external procedure is activated, followed by a single *output* operation when it terminates.

The relationship between two communicating processes is *asymmetrical* and requires only that the caller of a procedure name the process that performs it. This asymmetry is useful in *hierarchical systems*, in which *server processes* should be unaware of the identities of *client processes.*

Every process is *quasiparallel* in the following sense:

- A process begins by executing its initial statement. This continues until the statement either terminates or waits for a condition to become true. Then another operation is started (as the result of an external request). When this operation in turn terminates or waits the process will either begin yet another operation (requested by another process) or it will resume an earlier operation (as the result of a condition becoming true). This interleaving of the initial statement and the external requests continues forever. If the initial statement terminates, the process continues to exist and will still accept external statements.
- In a microprocessor network where each processor is dedicated to a single process it is an attractive possibility to let a process carry out computations *between* external calls of its procedures. The *shortest job next scheduler* (shown in the paper) takes advantage of this capability by selecting the next user while the resource is being used by the present user.

The major *weaknesses* of distributed processes are (1) the implicit *waiting loops* on Boolean conditions and (2) the *absence of parallel recursion.*

It was Jim White (1976) who first proposed remote procedure calls, as an *informal programming style.* However, White did not explain how to prevent *race conditions* between unsynchronized remote calls and local processes that are being executed by the same processor. This flaw potentially made remote procedure calls as unsafe as interrupts that cannot be disabled! Nevertheless, the original idea was his.

My Ph.D. student Charles Hayden (1979) implemented an experimental language with distributed processes on an LSI-11 microcomputer and evaluated the new paradigm by writing small simulation programs.

Greg Andrews (1991) acknowledged that:

> Per Brinch Hansen (1978) developed the first programming language based on [remote procedure calls] RPC. His language is called Distributed Processes (DP).[18]

According to Olivier Roubine (1980), my proposal was "a source of inspiration in the design of the Ada tasking facilities." The *rendezvous* concept in the language *Ada* combines the remote procedure calls of distributed processes with the selection of alternative interactions in CSP.

Since then, operating system designers have turned remote procedure calls into an *unreliable mechanism* of *surprising complexity.* In their present form, remote procedure calls are an attempt to use *unreliable message passing* to invoke procedures through local area networks.

Tay (1990) admits that "Currently, there are no agreed definition on the semantics of RPC." Leach (1983) goes one step further and advocates that "each remote operation implements a protocol tailored to its need." Since it can be both *system-dependent* and *application-dependent*, a remote procedure call is no longer an abstract concept.

After implementing a remote procedure call mechanism for the distributed operating system *Unix United*, Santosh Shrivastava and Fabio Panzieri (1982) concluded:

> At a superficial level it would seem that to design a program that provides a remote procedure call abstraction would be a straightforward exercise. Surprisingly, this is not so. We have found the problem of the design of the RPC to be rather intricate.

[18]Rarely does anyone replace single words, like "Pascal," "Monitor," "Solo" or "Joyce," by baffling acronyms—P, M, S or J. But carefully chosen longer names, like "Conditional Critical Region," "Concurrent Pascal," "Communicating Sequential Processes," "Distributed Processes" and "Remote Procedure Call," are doomed to be abbreviated as CCR, CP, CSP, DP and RPC. *If you believe that papers should be easy to read (but not necessarily easy to write), the lesson is clear: Always use single words to name your concepts!*

17 Joyce

The most surprising idea in Dijkstra's "Emerging Synthesis" (1975a) was his introduction of *recursive nondeterministic processes.* This idea was clearly ahead of its time. Some ten years would pass before Hoare (1985) published a theoretical recursive variant of CSP.

Two years later, I published the first *recursive CSP language* implemented on a computer:

P. Brinch Hansen, Joyce—A Programming Language for Distributed Systems (1987)

Joyce is a secure CSP language based on a minimal subset of Pascal. A Joyce program activates *recursive processes,* known as *agents.* These agents communicate through *synchronous channels.* A channel can transfer messages of different (but fixed) types between two or more agents. The compiler checks *message types* and ensures that agents use *disjoint variables* only.

```
type stream = [int(integer)];

agent buffer(inp, out: stream);
const n = 10;
type contents = array [1..n] of integer;
var head, tail, length: integer;
  ring: contents;
begin
  head := 1; tail := 1; length := 0;
  while true do
    poll
      inp?int(ring[tail]) & length < n ->
        tail := tail mod n + 1;
        length := length + 1|
      out!int(ring[head]) & length > 0 ->
        head := head mod n + 1;
        length := length - 1
    end
end;
```

The Bounded Buffer in Joyce

The *bounded buffer,* shown here, is defined by an *agent procedure.* A buffer agent uses two channels of type *stream.* Every communication through a stream channel transmits a single *symbol,* named *int,* from one agent to another. The symbol carries a *message* of type integer.

A buffer agent transmits an endless stream of symbols from one channel to another in response to *input/output commands* from other agents. In each cycle, a buffer agent executes a *polling statement* that delays it until a *conditional communication* takes place through one of its channels.

In general:

> A Joyce program consists of nested procedures which define communicating agents. Joyce permits unbounded (recursive) activation of agents. The execution of a program activates an initial agent. Agents may dynamically activate subagents which run concurrently with their creators. The variables of an agent are inaccessible to other agents.
>
> Agents communicate by means of symbols transmitted through channels. Every channel has an alphabet—a fixed set of symbols that can be transmitted through the channel. A symbol has a name and may carry a message of a fixed type.
>
> Two agents match when one of them is ready to output a symbol to a channel and the other is ready to input the same symbol from the same channel. When this happens, a communication takes place in which a message from the sending agent is assigned to a variable of the receiving agent.
>
> The communications on a channel take place one at a time. A channel can transfer symbols in both directions between two agents.
>
> A channel may be used by two or more agents. If more than two agents are ready to communicate on the same channel, it may be possible to match them in several different ways. The channel arbitrarily selects two matching agents at a time and lets them communicate.
>
> A polling statement enables an agent to examine one or more channels until it finds a matching agent. Both sending and receiving agents may be polled.
>
> Agents create channels dynamically and access them through local port variables. When an agent creates a channel, a channel pointer is assigned to a port variable. The agent may pass the pointer as a parameter to subagents.
>
> When an agent reaches the end of its defining procedure, it waits until all its subagents have terminated before terminating itself. At this point, the local variables and any channels created by the agent cease to exist.

Hoare (1978) emphasized that CSP should not be regarded as suitable for use as a programming language but only as a partial solution to the problems tackled.

Joyce removed unnecessary limitations of CSP by introducing:

- Recursive agent procedures.
- Simple agent termination.
- Typed channel alphabets.
- Typed port variables.
- Bidirectional synchronous channels.
- Nondeterministic shared channels.
- Symmetric input/output polling.

To be able to experiment with parallel recursion, I developed *portable implementations* of Joyce for a *personal computer* and a *multiprocessor* (Brinch Hansen 1987b, 1989b).

I still marvel at the beauty of recursive agents, such as the *bounded buffer*, the *sorting array*, the *prime sieve*, the *integer set*, and the *Fibonacci tree* (shown in the paper).

How can I explain the joy of being able, for the first time, to explore this new class of algorithms in a concise, executable language? The experience reminds me of the wise observation by the logician Susanne K. Langer (1967):

> There is something uncanny about the power of a happily chosen ideographic language; for it often allows one to express relations which have no names in natural language and therefore have never been noticed by anyone. Symbolism, then, becomes an organ of discovery rather than mere notation.

PART VI IMPLEMENTATION ISSUES

I promised to omit "Implementation details (except in outline)." Parallel programming languages do, however, pose special implementation problems that deserve your attention:

- *Interference control during compilation.*
- *Memory allocation of parallel recursion.*

18 SuperPascal

When Hoare (1971) published his paper on conditional critical regions, we did not fully appreciate the complexity of checking interference in a block-structured parallel language. You see, the subsequent invention of *modular parallelism* made interference checking so simple that we hardly noticed how hard it could have been!

Out of curiosity I asked myself twenty-three years later, *Is it feasible to detect process interference in a block-structured language with nonmodular parallelism?*

> *P. Brinch Hansen, SuperPascal—A Publication Language for Parallel Scientific Computing (1994)*

The parallel features of *SuperPascal* are a subset of *occam 2* with the added generality of *dynamic process arrays* and *recursive parallel processes* (Inmos 1988b, Cok 1991). SuperPascal omits ambiguous and insecure features of Pascal. *Restrictions on the use of variables enable a single-pass compiler to check that parallel processes are disjoint, even if the processes use procedures with global variables.*[19]

When you have read this paper, you can judge for yourself how complicated concurrent programming would have been without some form of modularity, such as the process and monitor types of Concurrent Pascal.

After reading the paper, Dave Parnas (1993) felt that "Some might suggest that nobody would be able to build practical programs in a language with so many restrictions." I answered (Brinch Hansen 1993d):

> I too was surprised at the restrictions required to make parallelism secure in a block-structured language. However, I think that the exercise merely forced me explicitly to recognize the complexity of the procedure concept in our programming languages (such as Pascal). SuperPascal forced me to use a more restricted procedure concept. So far, I have found that the rules enforced by the compiler contribute to program clarity.

After developing a portable implementation of SuperPascal on a Sun workstation:

[19]Since the language does not support conditional communication, a bounded buffer cannot be programmed in SuperPascal.

> [I used] the SuperPascal notation to write portable programs for regular problems in computational science (Brinch Hansen 1995). I found it easy to express these programs in three different programming languages (SuperPascal, Joyce,[20] and occam 2) and run them on three different architectures (a Unix workstation, an Encore Multimax, and a Meiko Computing Surface).[21]

19 Efficient Parallel Recursion

In *CSP* and *Distributed Processes*, Hoare and I shied away from parallel recursion because of the difficulty of *implementing an unbounded tree-structured stack without using garbage collection.*

Dijkstra (1975a) was well aware of this stumbling block:

> the storage requirements for a sequence are very simple, viz. a stack. (In our rejected example of the binary tree, although lifetimes are, in a fashion, nested, life is not so simple.)

After using static memory allocation in Concurrent Pascal, it took me twenty years to discover a simple method for *efficient parallel recursion* (which I used to implement *SuperPascal*):

P. Brinch Hansen, Efficient Parallel Recursion (1995)

I now believe that *we should have used parallel recursion from the beginning, even though we didn't know how to implement it.*[22] This kind of intellectual courage paid off handsomely when Peter Naur (1960) included *sequential recursion* in his famous *Algol 60* report, *before* Dijkstra (1960) had shown how to implement it efficiently using a run-time stack.

THE END OF AN ERA

The development of *abstract language notation for concurrent programming* started in 1965. Twenty years later Judy Bishop (1986) concluded:

---

[20]Brinch Hansen (1988).

[21]The Encore Multimax was a *multiprocessor* with 18 processors sharing a memory of 128 MB (Trew 1991). The Computing Surface was a *multicomputer* with 48 transputers, each with 1 MB of local memory (Inmos 1988a, Trew 1991).

[22]As you can tell, I am now a middle-aged idealist.

> *It is evident that the realm of concurrency is now firmly within the ambit of reliable languages and that future designs will provide for concurrent processing as a matter of course.*

So passed an exciting era.

Acknowledgements

It is a pleasure to acknowledge the perceptive comments of Charles Hayden, Henk Kruijer, Peter O'Hearn and Charles Reynolds.

I thank the Association for Computing Machinery, the Institute of Electrical and Electronics Engineers, and Springer-Verlag for permission to include parts of my earlier essays:

- P. Brinch Hansen, A keynote address on concurrent programming. *Computer 12*, 5 (May 1979), 50–56. Copyright © 1979, Institute of Electrical and Electronics Engineers, Inc.
- P. Brinch Hansen, Monitors and Concurrent Pascal: A personal history. *2nd ACM Conference on the History of Programming Languages*, Cambridge, MA, April 1993. In *SIGPLAN Notices 28*, 3 (March 1993), 1–35. Copyright © 1993, Association for Computing Machinery, Inc.
- P. Brinch Hansen, The evolution of operating systems. In P. Brinch Hansen Ed., *Classic Operating Systems: From Batch Processing to Distributed Systems*. Springer-Verlag, New York, 2001, 1–34. Copyright © 2001, Springer-Verlag New York, Inc.

BIBLIOGRAPHY

⋆ *Classic* papers included in this book.
• *Recommended* for further reading.
◦ *Cited* for historical reasons.

1. • G. R. Andrews and F. B. Schneider 1983. Concepts and notations for concurrent programming. *Computing Surveys 15*, 1 (March), 3–43.
2. • G. R. Andrews 1991. *Concurrent Programming: Principles and Practice.* Benjamin/Cummings, Redwood City, CA.
3. ◦ G. R. Andrews 1993. Reviewers' comments. In P. Brinch Hansen, Monitors and Concurrent Pascal: a personal history. *SIGPLAN Notices 28*, 3 (March 1993), 1–35.
4. • H. E. Bal, J. G. Steiner and A. S. Tanenbaum 1989. Programming languages for distributed computing systems. *ACM Computing Surveys 21*, (September), 261–322.
5. • J. Bishop 1986. *Data Abstraction in Programming Languages.* Addison-Wesley, Reading, MA.

6. • J. Boyle, R. Butler, Terrence Disz, Barnett Glickfeld, Ewing Lusk, Ross Overbeek, James Patterson and Rick Stevens 1987. *Portable Programs for Parallel Processors.* Holt, Rinehart and Winston, New York.

7. ∘ P. Brinch Hansen 1967a. The logical structure of the RC 4000 computer. *BIT 7*, 3, 191–199.

8. ∘ P. Brinch Hansen 1967b. The RC 4000 real-time control system at Pulawy. *BIT 7*, 4. 279–288.

9. ∘ P. Brinch Hansen 1968. *The Structure of the RC 4000 Monitor.* Regnecentralen, Copenhagen, Denmark (February).

10. ⋆ P. Brinch Hansen 1969. *RC 4000 Software: Multiprogramming System.* Regnecentralen, Copenhagen, Denmark, (April). *Article 3.*

11. • P. Brinch Hansen 1970. The nucleus of a multiprogramming system. *Communications of the ACM 13*, 4 (April), 238–241, 250.

12. ⋆ P. Brinch Hansen 1971a. An outline of a course on operating system principles. In C. A. R. Hoare and R. H. Perrott Eds. 1972, *Operating Systems Techniques*, Proceedings of a Seminar at Queen's University, Belfast, Northern Ireland, August–September 1971, Academic Press, New York, 29–36. *Article 6.*

13. • P. Brinch Hansen 1972a. A comparison of two synchronizing concepts. *Acta Informatica* **1**, 3 (1972), 190–199.

14. ⋆ P. Brinch Hansen 1972b. Structured multiprogramming. *Communications of the ACM 15*, 7 (July), 574–578. *Article 7.*

15. • P. Brinch Hansen 1973a. Testing a multiprogramming system. *Software—Practice and Experience 3*, 2 (April–June), 145–150.

16. • P. Brinch Hansen 1973b. *Operating System Principles.* Prentice-Hall, Englewood Cliffs, NJ (May)..

17. ⋆ P. Brinch Hansen 1973c. Class Concept. In *Operating System Principles*, P. Brinch Hansen, Prentice Hall, Englewood Cliffs, NJ, (July 1973), 226–232. *Article 8.*

18. ∘ P. Brinch Hansen 1973d. On September 6, 1973, I sent Mike McKeag "a copy of a preliminary document that describes my suggestion for an extension of Pascal with concurrent processes and monitors" (R. M. McKeag, letter to P. Brinch Hansen, July 3, 1991). No longer available.

19. ∘ P. Brinch Hansen 1973e. Concurrent programming concepts. *ACM Computing Surveys 5*, 4, (December), 223–245.

20. ∘ P. Brinch Hansen 1974a. Concurrent Pascal: a programming language for operating system design. Information Science, California Institute of Technology, Pasadena, CA, (April). (Referenced in A. Silberschatz, R. B. Kieburtz and A. J. Bernstein 1977. Extending Concurrent Pascal to allow dynamic resource management. *IEEE Transactions on Software Engineering 3*, (May), 210–217.)

21. ⋆ P. Brinch Hansen 1975a. The programming language Concurrent Pascal. *IEEE Transactions on Software Engineering 1*, 2 (June), 199–207. Original version: Information Science, California Institute of Technology, Pasadena, CA, (November 1974). *Article 10.*

22. ⋆ P. Brinch Hansen 1975b. The Solo operating system: a Concurrent Pascal program. Information Science, California Institute of Technology, Pasadena, CA, (June–July). Also in *Software—Practice and Experience 6*, 2 (April–June 1976), 141–149. *Article 11.*

23. ⋆ P. Brinch Hansen 1975c. The Solo operating system: processes, monitors and classes. Information Science, California Institute of Technology, Pasadena, CA, (June–July). Also in *Software—Practice and Experience 6*, 2 (April–June 1976), 165–200. *Article 12.*

24. ∘ P. Brinch Hansen 1975d. Concurrent Pascal report. Information science, California Institute of Technology, Pasadena, CA, (June). Also in P. Brinch Hansen 1977b, *The Architecture of Concurrent Programs*, Prentice-Hall, Englewood Cliffs, NJ, (July), 231–270.

25. ∘ P. Brinch Hansen and A. C. Hartmann 1975e. Sequential Pascal report. Information science, California Institute of Technology, Pasadena, CA, (July).

26. ∘ P. Brinch Hansen 1975f. Concurrent Pascal machine. Information Science, California Institute of Technology, Pasadena, CA, (October). Also in P. Brinch Hansen 1977b, *The Architecture of Concurrent Programs*, Prentice-Hall, Englewood Cliffs, NJ, (July), 271–297.

27. ∘ P. Brinch Hansen 1976a. Innovation and trivia in program engineering. Guest Editorial, *Software—Practice and Experience 6*, 2 (April–June), 139–140.

28. ∘ P. Brinch Hansen 1976b. Concurrent Pascal implementation notes. Information Science, California Institute of Technology, Pasadena, CA. No longer available. (Referenced in M. S. Powell, Experience of transporting and using the Solo operating system. *Software—Practice and Experience 9*, 7 (July 1979), 561–570.)

29. • P. Brinch Hansen 1977a. Experience with modular concurrent programming, *IEEE Transactions on Software Engineering 3*, 2 (March), 156–159.

30. • P. Brinch Hansen 1977b. *The Architecture of Concurrent Programs.* Prentice-Hall, Englewood Cliffs, NJ, (July).

31. ⋆ P. Brinch Hansen 1977c. Design Principles. In P. Brinch Hansen, *The Architecture of Concurrent Programs*, Prentice Hall, Englewood Cliffs, NJ, (July), 3–14. *Article 13.*

32. • P. Brinch Hansen 1978a. Network: A multiprocessor program. *IEEE Transactions on Software Engineering 4*, 3 (May), 194–199.

33. • P. Brinch Hansen and J. Staunstrup 1978b. Specification and implementation of mutual exclusion. *IEEE Transactions on Software Engineering 4*, 4 (September), 365–370.

34. ⋆ P. Brinch Hansen 1978c. Distributed Processes: a concurrent programming concept. *Communications of the ACM 21*, 11 (November), 934–941. *Article 16.*

35. • P. Brinch Hansen 1978d. A keynote address on concurrent programming. *IEEE Computer Software and Applications Conference*, Chicago, IL, (November), 1–6. Also in *Computer 12*, 5 (May 1979), 50–56.

36. • P. Brinch Hansen 1978e. Reproducible testing of monitors. *Software—Practice and Experience 8*, 6 (November–December), 721–729.

37. • P. Brinch Hansen 1979. The end of a heroic era. In P. Wegner Ed. *Research Directions in Software Technology*, MIT Press, Cambridge, MA, 646–649.

38. • P. Brinch Hansen and J. A. Fellows 1980. The Trio operating system. *Software—Practice and Experience 10*, 11 (November), 943–948.

39. • P. Brinch Hansen 1981. The design of Edison. *Software—Practice and Experience 11*, 4 (April), 363–396.

40. ⋆ P. Brinch Hansen 1987a. Joyce—A programming language for distributed systems. *Software—Practice and Experience 17* , 1 (January), 29–50. *Article 17.*

41. • P. Brinch Hansen 1987b. A Joyce implementation. *Software—Practice and Experience 17*, 4 (April 1987), 267–276.

42. ∘ P. Brinch Hansen and A. Rangachari 1988. Joyce performance on a multiprocessor. School of Computer and Information Science. Syracuse University, NY, (September).

43. • P. Brinch Hansen 1989a. The Joyce language report. *Software—Practice and Experience 19*, 6 (June), 553–578.

44. • P. Brinch Hansen 1989b. A multiprocessor implementation of Joyce. *Software—Practice and Experience 19*, 6 (June), 579–592.

45. • P. Brinch Hansen 1990. The nature of parallel programming. In M. A. Arbib and J. A. Robinson Eds., *Natural and Artificial Parallel Computation*, MIT Press, Cambridge, MA, 31–46.

46. • P. Brinch Hansen 1993a. Monitors and Concurrent Pascal: a personal history. *SIGPLAN Notices 28*, 3 (March), 1–35. Also in T. J. Bergin and R. G. Gibson Eds. 1996, *History of Programming Languages II*, Addison-Wesley Publishing, Reading, MA, 121–172.

47. • P. Brinch Hansen 1993b. Model programs for computational science: a programming methodology for multicomputers. *Concurrency—Practice and Experience 5*, 5 (August), 407–423.

48. • P. Brinch Hansen 1993c. Parallel cellular automata: a model program for computational science. *Concurrency—Practice and Experience 5*, 5 (August), 425–448.

49. ∘ P. Brinch Hansen 1993d. Letter to D. L. Parnas, (December 17).

50. • P. Brinch Hansen 1994a. Do hypercubes sort faster than tree machines? *Concurrency—Practice and Experience 6*, 2 (April), 143–151.

51. • P. Brinch Hansen 1994b. The programming language SuperPascal. *Software—Practice and Experience 24*, 5 (May), 467–483.

52. ⋆ P. Brinch Hansen 1994c. SuperPascal—A publication language for parallel scientific computing. *Concurrency—Practice and Experience 6*, 5 (August), 461–483. *Article 18.*

53. • P. Brinch Hansen 1994d. Interference control in SuperPascal—a block-structured parallel language. *The Computer Journal 37*, 5, 399–406.

54. • P. Brinch Hansen 1995a. *Studies in Computational Science: Parallel Programming Paradigms.* Prentice Hall, Englewood Cliffs, NJ, (March).

55. ⋆ P. Brinch Hansen 1995b. Efficient parallel recursion, *SIGPLAN Notices 30*, 12 (December), 9–16. *Article 19.*

56. • P. Brinch Hansen 1996. *The Search for Simplicity: Essays in Parallel Programming.* IEEE Computer Society Press, Los Alamitos, CA, (April).

57. • P. Brinch Hansen 1999. Java's insecure parallelism. *SIGPLAN Notices 34*, 4 (April), 38–45.

58. • P. Brinch Hansen 2000. The evolution of operating systems. In P. Brinch Hansen Ed. 2001, *Classic Operating Systems: From Batch Processing to Distributed Systems*, Springer-Verlag, New York, (January), 1–34.

59. • P. Brinch Hansen Ed. 2001. *Classic Operating Systems: From Batch Processing to Distributed Systems.* Springer-Verlag, New York, (January).

60. • C. Bron 1972. Allocation of virtual store in the THE multiprogramming system. In C. A. R. Hoare and R. H. Perrott Eds., *Operating Systems Techniques*, Academic Press, New York, 168–184.

61. • R. H. Campbell and A. N. Habermann 1974. The specification of process synchronization by path expressions. *Lecture Notes in Computer Science 16*, Springer-Verlag, New York, 89–102.

62. • N. Carriero and D. Gelernter 1989. Linda in context. *Communications of the ACM 32*, 4 (April), 444–458.

63. • R. S. Cok 1991. *Parallel Programs for the Transputer.* Prentice Hall, Englewood Cliffs, NJ.

64. • M. I. Cole 1989. *Algorithmic Skeletons: Structured Management of Parallel Computation.* MIT Press, Cambridge, MA.

65. • D. Coleman 1980. Concurrent Pascal—an appraisal. In R. M. McKeag and A. M. Macnaghten Eds., *On the Construction of Programs*, Cambridge University Press, New York, 213–227.

66. ∘ Cosine Report 1971, *An Undergraduate Course on Operating Systems Principles*, P. J. Denning, J. B. Dennis, B. Lampson, A. N. Haberman, R. R. Muntz and D. Tsichritzis Eds., Commission on Education, National Academy of Engineering, Washington, DC, (June).

67. • P. J. Courtois, F. Heymans and D. L. Parnas 1971. Concurrent control with "readers" and "writers." *Communications of the ACM 14*, 10 (October), 667–668.

68. ∘ O.-J. Dahl and K. Nygaard 1963. Preliminary presentation of the Simula language (as of May 18, 1963) and some examples of network descriptions. Norwegian Computing Center, Oslo, Norway.

69. • O.-J. Dahl and C. A. R. Hoare 1972. Hierarchical program structures. In O.-J. Dahl, E. W. Dijkstra and C. A. R. Hoare, Eds., *Structured Programming*, Academic Press, New York, 175–220.

70. ∘ O.-J. Dahl 1993. Reviewers' comments. In P. Brinch Hansen, Monitors and Concurrent Pascal: a personal history. *SIGPLAN Notices 28*, 3 (March), 1–35.

71. ∘ E. W. Dijkstra 1960. Recursive programming. *Numerische Mathematik 2*, 312–318.

72. ⋆ E. W. Dijkstra 1965. Cooperating sequential processes. Technological University, Eindhoven, The Netherlands, (September). Also in F. Genuys Ed. 1968. *Programming Languages*, Academic Press, New York, 43–112. *Article 1.*

73. ⋆ E. W. Dijkstra 1968. The structure of the THE multiprogramming system. *Communications of the ACM 11*, 5 (May), 341–346. *Article 2.*

74. ⋆ E. W. Dijkstra 1971. Hierarchical ordering of sequential processes. *Acta Informatica 1*, 2 (October), 115–138. *Article 4.*

75. • E. W. Dijkstra 1972a. Notes on structured programming, In O.-J. Dahl, E. W. Dijkstra and C. A. R. Hoare, Eds., *Structured Programming*, Academic Press, New York, 1–82.

76. • E. W. Dijkstra 1972b. Information streams sharing a finite buffer. *Information Processing Letters 1*, 5 (October), 179–180.

77. ⋆ E. W. Dijkstra 1975a. A synthesis emerging?, (July). In E. W. Dijkstra 1982, *Selected Writings on Computing: A Personal Perspective*, Springer-Verlag, New York, 147–160. *Article 14.*

78. • E. W. Dijkstra 1975b. Guarded commands, nondeterminacy and formal derivation of programs. *Commmunication of the ACM 18*, 8 (August), 453–457.

79. • E. W. Dijkstra and C. S. Scholten 1982. A class of simple communication patterns. In E. W. Dijkstra, *Selected Writings on Computing: A Personal Perspective*, Springer-Verlag, New York, 334–337.

80. ◦ Discussions 1971. Discussions of conditional critical regions and monitors. In C. A. R. Hoare and R. H. Perrott Eds. 1972, *Operating Systems Techniques*, Proceedings of a Seminar at Queen's University, Belfast, Northern Ireland, August–September 1971. Academic Press, New York, 100–113.

81. ◦ J. A. Fellows 1993. Reviewers' comments. In P. Brinch Hansen, Monitors and Concurrent Pascal: a personal history. *SIGPLAN Notices 28*, 3 (March), 1–35.

82. ◦ J. Gosling, B. Joy and G. Steele 1996. *The Java Language Specification*. Addison-Wesley, Reading, MA.

83. • J. S. Greenfield 1991. Distributed programming with cryptography applications. *Lecture Notes in Computer Science 870*, Springer-Verlag, New York.

84. ◦ A. N. Habermann 1967. On the harmonious cooperation of abstract machines. Ph.D. thesis. Technological University, Eindhoven, The Netherlands.

85. • A. N. Habermann 1972. Synchronization of communicating processes. *Communications of the ACM 15*, 3 (March), 171–176.

86. • A. C. Hartmann 1975. A Concurrent Pascal compiler for minicomputers. Ph.D. thesis, Information Science, California Institute of Technology, Pasadena, CA, (September). Also published as *Lecture Notes in Computer Science 50*, (1977), Springer-Verlag, New York.

87. ◦ J. M. Havender 1968. Avoiding deadlock in multitasking systems. *IBM Systems Journal 7*, 2, 74–88.

88. • C. C. Hayden 1979. Distributed processes: experience and architectures. Ph.D. thesis, Computer Science Department, University of Southern California, Los Angeles, CA.

89. ○ C. C. Hayden 1993. Reviewers' comments. In P. Brinch Hansen, Monitors and Concurrent Pascal: a personal history. *SIGPLAN Notices 28*, 3 (March), 1–35.

90. ⋆ C. A. R. Hoare 1971. Towards a theory of parallel programming. In C. A. R. Hoare and R. H. Perrott Eds. 1972, *Operating Systems Techniques*, Proceedings of a Seminar at Queen's University, Belfast, Northern Ireland, August–September 1971. Academic Press, New York, 61–71. *Article 5.*

91. • C. A. R. Hoare 1972. Proof of correctness of data representations. *Acta Informatica 1*, 271–281.

92. ○ C. A. R. Hoare 1973a. A pair of synchronising primitives. On January 11, 1973, Hoare gave Jim Horning a copy of this undated, unpublished draft (J. J. Horning, personal communication, May 1991).

93. • C. A. R. Hoare 1973b. A structured paging system. *Computer Journal 16*, (August), 209–214.

94. ○ C. A. R. Hoare 1973c. Letter to R. M. McKeag, (October 10).

95. • C. A. R. Hoare 1974a. Hints on programming language design. In C. Bunyan Ed., *Computer Systems Reliability*, Infotech International, Berkshire, England, 505–534.

96. ⋆ C. A. R. Hoare 1974b. Monitors: an operating system structuring concept. *Communications of the ACM 17*, 10 (October), 549–557. *Article 9.*

97. ○ C. A. R. Hoare 1976a. The structure of an operating system. In *Language Hierarchies and Interfaces*, Springer-Verlag, 1976, 242–265.

98. • C. A. R. Hoare 1976b. Hints on the design of a programming language for real-time command and control. In J. P. Spencer Ed., *Real-time Software: International State of the Art Report*, Infotech International, Berkshire, England, 685–699.

99. ⋆ C. A. R. Hoare 1978. Communicating sequential processes. *Communications of the ACM 21*, 8 (August) 1978, 666–677. *Article 15.*

100. ○ C. A. R. Hoare 1981. A calculus of total correctness for communicating sequential processes. *The Science of Computer Programming 1*, 1–2 (October), 49–72.

101. • C. A. R. Hoare 1985. *Communicating Sequential Processes.* Prentice-Hall, Englewood Cliffs, NJ.

102. ○ J. J. Horning 1972. Preliminary report to Karl Karlstrom, computer science editor, Prentice-Hall, on the manuscript of "Operating System Principles" by P. Brinch Hansen, (May 1).

103. • J. H. Howard 1976. Proving monitors. *Communications of the ACM 19*, 5 (May), 273–274.

104. • M. E. C. Hull 1987. occam—a programming language for multiprocessor systems. *Computer Languages 12*, 1, 27–37.

105. ○ IBM 1965. IBM operating system/360 concepts and facilities. In S. Rosen, Ed., *Programming Systems and Languages*, McGraw-Hill, New York, 598–646.

106. ○ Inmos 1988a. *Transputer Reference Manual.* Prentice Hall, Englewood Cliffs, NJ.

107. • Inmos 1988b. *occam 2 Reference Manual*, Prentice Hall, Englewood Cliffs, NJ.

108. • G. Kahn and D. B. McQueen 1977. Coroutines and networks of parallel processes. In B. Gilchrist Ed., *Information Processing 77*, North-Holland Publishing, Ansterdam, The Netherlands, 993–998.

109. • W. H. Kaubisch, R. H. Perrott and C. A. R. Hoare 1976. Quasiparallel programming. *Software—Practice and Experience 6*, (July–September), 341–356.

110. • J. M. Kerridge 1982. A Fortran implementation of Concurrent Pascal. *Software—Practice and Experience 12*, 1 (January), 45–55.

111. • J. L. W. Kessels 1977. An alternative to event queues for synchronization in monitors. *Communications of the ACM 20*, 7 (July), 500–503.

112. ○ T. Kilburn, R. B. Payne and D. J. Howarth 1961. The Atlas supervisor. *AFIPS Computer Conference 20*, 279–294.

113. ○ D. Knuth and J. L. McNeley 1964. SOL—A symbolic language for general-purpose systems simulation. *IEEE Transactions on Electronic Computers 13*, 8 (August), 401–408.

114. • H. S. M. Kruijer 1982. A multi-user operating system for transaction processing written in Concurrent Pascal. *Software—Practice and Experience 12*, 5 (May), 445–454.

115. • B. W. Lampson and D. D. Redell 1980. Experience with processes and monitors in Mesa. *Communications of the ACM 23*, 2 (February), 105–117.

116. ○ S. K. Langer 1967. *An Introduction to Symbolic Logic.* Dover Publications, New York.

117. • S. Lauesen 1975. A large semaphore based operating system. *Communications of the ACM 18*, 7 (July), 377–389.

118. ○ D. Lea 1997. *Concurrent Programming in Java: Design Principles and Patterns.* Addison-Wesley, Reading, MA.

119. ○ P. J. Leach, P. H. Levine, B. P. Douros, J. A. Hamilton, D. L. Nelson and B. L. Stumpf 1983. The architecture of an integrated local network. *IEEE Journal on Selected Areas in Communications 1*, 5, 842–856.

120. • B. H. Liskov 1972. The design of the Venus operating system. *Communications of the ACM 15*, 3 (March), 144–149.

121. ○ R. A. Maddux and H. D. Mills 1979. Review of "The Architecture of Concurrent Programs." *IEEE Computer 12*, (May), 102–103.

122. ○ R. M. McKeag 1972. A survey of system structure and synchronization techniques. Department of Computer Science, Queen's University of Belfast, Northern Ireland, (October). (Supplemented January 1973.)

123. • R. M. McKeag 1976. THE multiprogramming system. In R. M. McKeag and R. Wilson Eds., *Studies in Operating Systems*, Academic Press, New York, 145–184.

124. • R, M. McKeag 1980. A structured operating system. In J. Welsh and R. M. McKeag, *Structured System Programming*, Prentice Hall, Englewood Cliffs, NY, 229–315.

125. ○ S. E. Madnick and J. J. Donovan 1974. *Operating Systems.* McGraw-Hill, New York.

126. • D. May 1989. The influence of VLSI technology on computer architecture. In R. Elliott and C. A. R. Hoare Eds., *Scientific Applications of Multiprocessors*, Prentice-Hall, Englewood Cliffs, NJ, 21–36.

127. ∘ P. Naur Ed. 1960. Report on the algorithmic language Algol 60. *Communications of the ACM 3*, 5 (May), 299–314.

128. • P. Naur Ed. 1963a. Revised report on the algorithmic language Algol 60. *Communications of the ACM 6*, 1 (January), 1–17.

129. • P. Naur 1963b. The design of the Gier Algol compiler. *BIT 3*, 2–3, 123–140 and 145–166.

130. ∘ P. Naur and B. Randell Eds. 1969. *Software Engineering.* NATO Scientific Affairs Division. Brussels, Belgium (October).

131. • P. Naur 1974. *Concise Survey of Computer Methods.* Studentlitteratur, Lund, Sweden.

132. ∘ P. Naur 1975. Review of "Operating System Principles." *BIT 15*, 455–457.

133. • D. Neal and V. Wallentine 1978. Experiences with the portability of Concurrent Pascal. *Software—Practice and Experience 8*, 3 (May–June), 341–354.

134. ∘ E. I. Organick 1972. *The Multics System: An Examination of Its Structure.* MIT Press, Cambridge, MA.

135. ∘ E. I. Organick 1973. *Computer System Organization: The B5700/B6700 Series.* Academic Press, New York.

136. ∘ D. L. Parnas 1993. Letter to P. Brinch Hansen, November 23.

137. • R. H. Perrott 1987. *Parallel Programming.* Addison-Wesley, Reading, MA.

138. ∘ G. Pólya 1957. *How to Solve It.* Doubleday, Garden City, NY.

139. • M. S. Powell 1979. Experience of transporting and using the Solo operating system. *Software—Practice and Experience 9*, 7 (July), 561–570.

140. • C. W. Reynolds 1988. The historical evolution of monitors and their languages. Department of Mathematics and Computer Science, James Madison University, Harrisonburg, VA, (August).

141. • C. W. Reynolds 1990. Signalling regions: multiprocessing in a shared memory reconsidered. *Software—Practice and Experience 20*, 4 (April), 325–356.

142. ∘ C. W. Reynolds 1993. Reviewers' comments. In P. Brinch Hansen, Monitors and Concurrent Pascal: a personal history. *SIGPLAN Notices 28*, 3 (March 1993), 1–35.

143. ∘ D. T. Ross 1974. In search of harmony: After-dinner talk. In W. L. van der Poel and L. A. Maarssen Eds., *Machine Oriented Higher Level Languages.* North-Holland Publishing Company, Amsterdam, The Netherlands, 445–447.

144. • O. Roubine and J.-C. Heliard 1980. Parallel processing in Ada. In R. M. McKeag and A. M. Macnaghten Eds., *On the Construction of Programs*, Cambridge University Press, New York, 193–212.

145. ∘ A. C. Shaw 1974. *The Logical Design of Operating Systems.* Prentice-Hall, Englewood Cliffs, NJ.

146. ○ S. K. Shrivastava and F. Panzieri 1982. The design of a reliable remote procedure call mechanism. *IEEE Transactions on Computers 31*, 7 (July), 692–697.

147. • A. Silberschatz, J. Peterson and P. Galvin 1992. *Operating System Concepts* (third edition). Addison-Wesley Publishing, Reading, MA, 1992.

148. • C. R. Snow 1992. *Concurrent Programming.* Cambridge University Press, New York.

149. • F. Stepczyk and D. Heimbigner 1979. Application of a concurrent programming language. In P. Wegner Ed., *Research Directions in Software Technology*, MIT Press, Cambridge, MA, 666–671.

150. • A. S. Tanenbaum and R. van Renesse 1988. A critique of the remote procedure call mechanism. In R. Speth Ed., *Research into Networks and Distributed Applications*, Elsevier Science Publishers, Amsterdam, The Netherlands, 775–782.

151. ○ B. H. Tay and A. L. Ananda 1990. A survey of remote procedure calls. *Operating Systems Review 24*, 3 (July), 68–79.

152. ○ A. Trew and G. Wilson Eds. 1991. *Past, Present, Parallel: A Survey of Available Parallel Computing Systems.* Springer-Verlag, New York.

153. • J. Welsh and D. W. Bustard 1979. Pascal-Plus—another language for modular multiprogramming. *Software—Practice and Experience 9*, 11 (November), 947–957.

154. • R. L. Wexelblat Ed. 1981. *History of Programming Languages.* Academic Press, New York.

155. ○ J. E. White 1976. A high-level framework for network-based resource sharing. *National Computer Conference*, (June), 561–570.

156. ○ N. Wirth 1969. Letter to P. Brinch Hansen, (July 14).

157. • N. Wirth 1971. The programming language Pascal. *Acta Informatica 1*, 35–63.

158. • N. Wirth 1977a. Modula: a programming language for modular multiprogramming. *Software—Practice and Experience 7*, 1 (January–February), 3–35.

159. • N. Wirth 1977b. The use of Modula. *Software—Practice and Experience 7*, 1 (January–February), 37–65.

160. • N. Wirth 1977c. Design and implementation of Modula. *Software—Practice and Experience 7*, 1 (January–February), 67–84.

161. ○ W. A. Wulf, E. S. Cohen, W. M. Corwin, A. K. Jones, R. Levin, C. Pierson, and F. J. Pollack 1974. Hydra: the kernel of a multiprocessor operating system. *Communications of the ACM 17*, 6 (June), 337–345.

PART I

CONCEPTUAL INNOVATION

1

COOPERATING SEQUENTIAL PROCESSES

EDSGER W. DIJKSTRA

(1965)

INTRODUCTION

This chapter is intended for all those who expect that in their future activities they will become seriously involved in the problems that arise in either the design or the more advanced applications of digital information processing equipment; they are further intended for all those who are just interested in information processing.

The applications are those in which the activity of a computer must include the proper reaction to a possibly great variety of messages that can be sent to it at unpredictable moments, a situation which occurs in process control, traffic control, stock control, banking applications, automatization of information flow in large organizations, centralized computer service, and, finally, all information systems in which a number of computers are coupled to each other.

The desire to apply computers in the ways sketched above has often a strong economic motivation, but in this chapter the not unimportant question of efficiency will not be stressed too much. Logical problems which arise, for example, when speed ratios are unknown, communication possibilities restricted, etc., will be dealt with much more. This will be done in order to create a clearer insight into the origin of the difficulties one meets and into the nature of solutions. Deciding whether under given circumstances

E. W. Dijkstra, Cooperating sequential processes. Technological University, Eindhoven, The Netherlands, September 1965. Reprinted in *Programming Languages*, F. Genuys, Ed., Academic Press, New York, 1968, 43–112.

the application of our techniques is economically attractive falls outside the scope of this chapter.

There will not be a fully worked out theory, complete with Greek letter formulae, so to speak. The only thing that can be done under the present circumstances is to offer a variety of problems, together with solutions. And in discussing these we can only hope to bring as much system into it as we possibly can, to find which concepts are relevant, as we go along.

1 ON THE NATURE OF SEQUENTIAL PROCESSES

Our problem field proper is the co-operation between two or more sequential processes. Before we can enter this field, however, we have to know quite clearly what we call "a sequential process". To this preliminary question the present section is devoted.

To begin, here is a comparison of two machines to do the same example job, the one a non-sequential machine, the other a sequential one.

Let us assume that of each of four quantities, named `a[1]`, `a[2]`, `a[3]`, and `a[4]` respectively, the value is given. Our machine has to process these values in such a way that, as its reaction, it "tells" us which of the four quantities has the largest value. E.g. in the case:

```
a[1] = 7, a[2] = 12, a[3] = 2, a[4] = 9
```

the answer to be produced is `a[2]` (or only 2, giving the index value pointing to the maximum element).

Note that the desired answer would become incompletely defined if the set of values were—in order—`7, 12, 2, 12`, for then there is no unique largest element, and the answer `a[2]` would have been as good (or as bad) as `a[4]`. This is remedied by the further assumption that of the four values given, no two are equal.

Remark 1. If the required answer would have been the maximum value occurring among the given ones, the last restriction would have been superfluous, for the answer corresponding to the value set `7, 12, 2, 12` would then have been 12.

Remark 2. Our restriction "Of the four values no two are equal" is still somewhat loosely formulated, for what do we mean by "equal"? In the processes to be constructed pairs of values will be compared with one another, and what is really meant is that every two values will be sufficiently different, so that the comparator will unambiguously decide which of the two is the larger one. In other words, the difference between any two must be large compared with "the resolving power" of our comparators.

We shall first construct our non-sequential machine. When we assume our given values to be represented by currents we can imagine a comparator consisting of a two-way switch, the position of which is schematically controlled by the currents in the coils of electromagnets, as in Figs. 1 and 2.

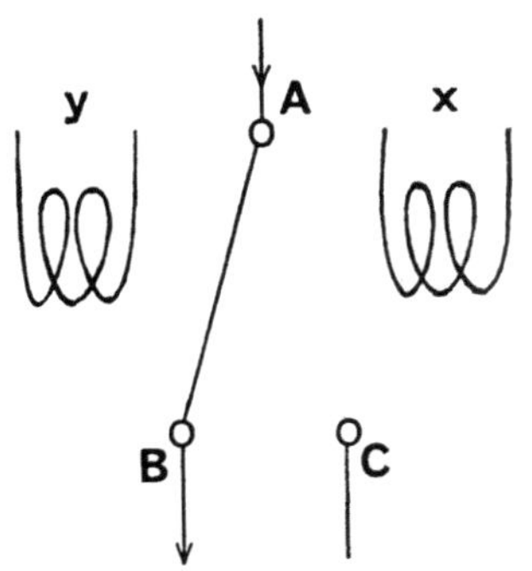

Fig. 1. $x<y$

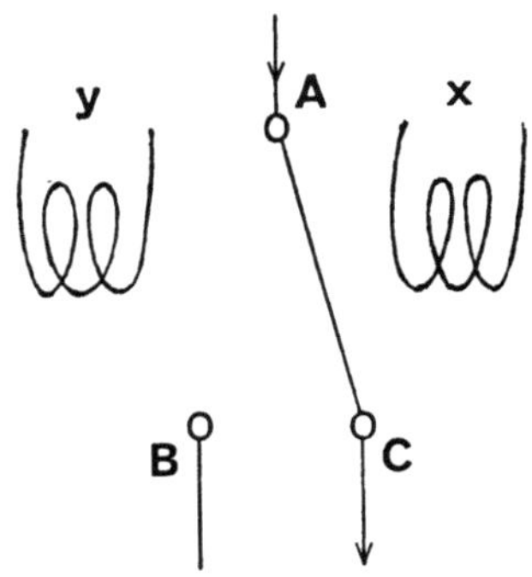

Fig. 2. $y<x$

When current y is larger than current x, the left electromagnet pulls harder than the right one and the switch switches to the left (Fig. 1) and the input A is connected to output B; if current x is the larger one we shall get the situation (Fig. 2), where the input A is connected to output C.

In our diagrams we shall omit the coils and shall represent such a comparator by a small box

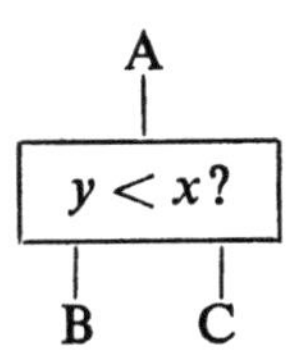

only representing at the top side the input and at the bottom side the two outputs. The currents to be led through the coils are identified in the question written inside the box, and the convention is that the input will be connected to the right-hand side output when the answer to the question is "Yes", to the left-hand side output when the answer is "No".

Now we can construct our machine as indicated in Fig. 3. At the output side we have drawn four indicator lamps, one, and only one, of which will light up to indicate the answer.

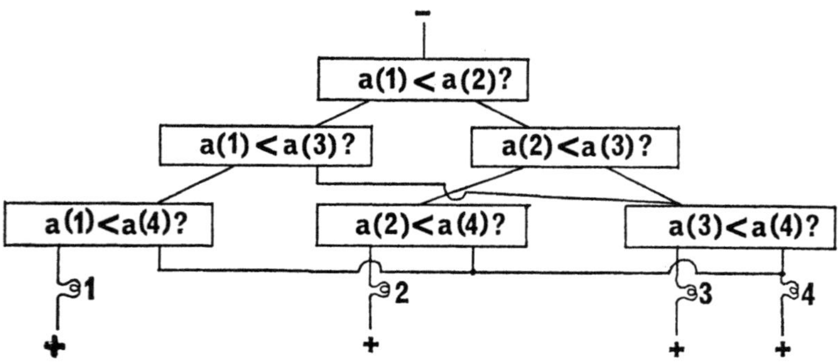

Fig. 3

In Fig. 4 we indicate the position of the switches when the value set 7, 12, 2, 9 is applied to it. In the boxes the positions of the switches are indicated, wires not connected to the input are drawn dotted.

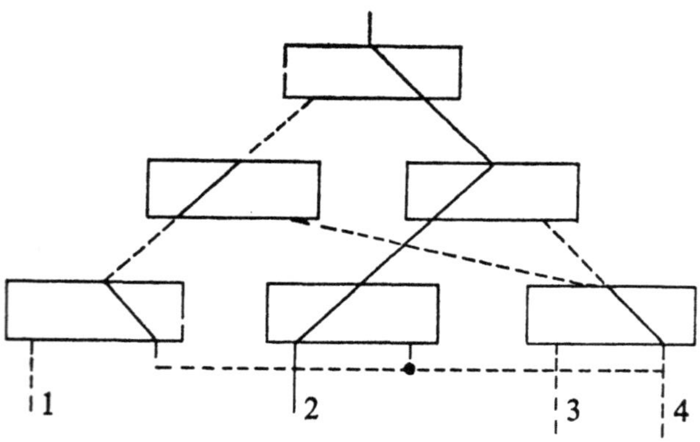

Fig. 4

We draw the reader's attention to the fact that now only the positions of the three switches that connect output 2 to the input matter; the reader is invited to convince himself that the position of the other three switches is indeed immaterial.

It is also worthwhile to give a moment's attention to see what happens in time when our machine of Fig. 3 is fed with four "value currents". Obviously it cannot be expected to give the correct answer before the four value currents start going through the coils. But one cannot even expect it to indicate the correct answer as soon as the currents are applied, for the switches must get into their correct position, and this may take some time. In other words, as soon as the currents are applied (simultaneously or the one after the other) we must wait a period of time —characteristic for the machine—and only after that the correct answer will be shown at the output side. What happens during this waiting time is immaterial, provided that the interval is long enough for all switches to find their final position. They may start switching simultaneously, the exact order in which they attain their final position is immaterial, and therefore we shall no longer pay any attention to it.

From the logical point of view the switching time can be regarded as a marker on the time axis: before it the input data have to be supplied, after it the answer is available.

In the use of our machine the progress of time is only reflected in the obvious "before-after" relation, which tells us that we cannot expect an answer before the question has been properly put. This sequence relation is so obvious (and fundamental) that it cannot be regarded as a characteristic property of our machine. And our machine is therefore called a "non-sequential machine" to distinguish it from the kind of equipment—or processes that can be performed by it—to be described now.

Up till now we have interpreted the diagram of Fig. 3 as the (schematic) picture of a machine to be built in space. But we can interpret this same diagram in a very different manner if we place ourselves in the mind of the electron entering at the top input and wondering where to go. First, it finds itself faced with the question whether `a[1] < a[2]` holds. Having found the answer to this question, it can proceed. Depending on the previous answer, it will enter one of the two boxes `a[1] < a[3]` or `a[2] < a[3]`, i.e. it will only know what to investigate next, after the first question has been answered. Having found the answer to the question selected from the second line, it will know which question to ask from the third line and, having found this last answer, it will now know which bulb should start to glow. Instead of regarding the diagram of Fig. 3 as that of a machine, the parts of which are spread out in space, we have regarded it as rules of behaviour, to be followed in time.

With respect to our earlier interpretation two differences are highly significant. In the first interpretation all six comparators started working simultaneously, although finally only three switch positions were relevant. In the second interpretation only three comparisons are actually evaluated—the wondering electron asks itself three questions—but the price of this gain is that they have to be performed the one after the other, as the outcome of the previous one decides what to ask next. In the second interpretation three questions have to be asked in *sequence*, the one after the other. The existence of such an order relation is the distinctive feature of the second interpretation, which in contrast to the first one is therefore called "a sequential process". We should like to make two remarks.

Remark 3. In actual fact, the three comparisons will each take a finite amount of time ("switching time", "decision time", or, in the jargon, "execution time"), and as a result the total time taken will at least be equal to the sum of these three execution times. We stress once more that for many investigations these executions can be regarded as ordered markers on a scaleless time axis and that it is only the relative ordering that matters from this (logical) point of view.

Remark 4. As a small side line we note that the two interpretations (call them "simultaneous comparisons" and "sequential comparisons") are only extremes. There is a way of, again, only performing three comparisons, in which two of them can be done independently from one another, i.e. simultaneously; the third one, however, can be done only after the other two have been completed. It can be represented with the aid of a box in which two questions are put and which, as a result, has four possible exits, as in Fig. 5.

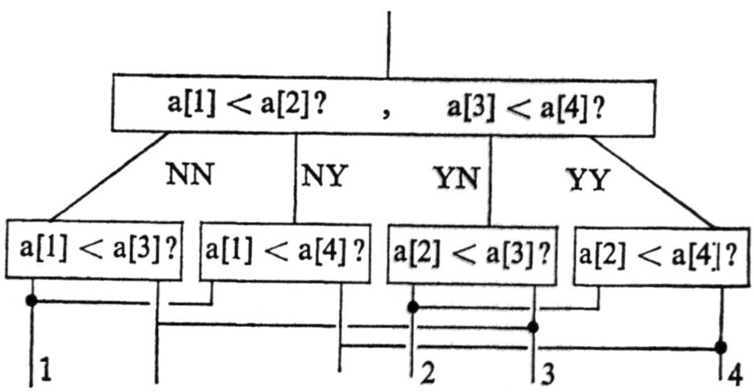

Fig. 5

The total time taken will be at least the sum of the comparison execution times. The process is of the first kind in the sense that the first two comparisons can be performed simultaneously, it is of sequential nature, as the third comparison can be selected from the second line only when the first two have both been completed.

We return to our purely sequential interpretation. Knowing that the diagram is meant for purely sequential interpretations, we can take advantage of this circumstance to make the description of the "rules of behaviour" more compact. The idea is that the two questions on the second line only one of which will be actually asked are highly similar: the questions on the same line differ only in the subscript value of the left operand of the comparison. And we may ask ourselves: "Can we map the questions on the same line of Fig. 3 on to a single question?"

This can be done, but it implies that the part that varies along a line—i.e. the subscript value in the left operand— must be regarded as a parameter, the task of which is to determine which of the questions mapped on each other is meant, when its turn to be executed has come. Obviously the value of this parameter must be defined by the past history of the process.

Such parameters, in which past history can be condensed for future use, are called "variables". To indicate that a new value has to be assigned to it we use the so-called assignment operator := (read: "becomes"), a kind of directed equality sign which defines the value of the left-hand side in terms of the value of the right-hand side.

We hope that the previous paragraph is sufficient for the reader to recognize also in the diagram of Fig. 6 a set of "rules of behaviour". Our variable is called `i`; and the reader may wonder why the first question, which is invariably `a[1] < a[2]` ? is not written that way, but with patience he will understand.

When we have followed the rules of Fig. 6 as intended from top till bottom, the final value of `i` will identify the maximum value, viz. `a[i]`.

The transition from the scheme of Fig. 3 to the one of Fig. 6 is a drastic change, for the latter's "rules of behaviour" can only be interpreted sequentially. And this is due to the introduction of the variable `i`: having only `a[1]`, `a[2]`, `a[3]`, and `a[4]` available as values to be compared, the question `a[i] < a[2]` ? is meaningless, unless it is known for which value of `i` this comparison has to be made.

Remark 5. It is somewhat unfortunate that the jargon of the trade calls the thing denoted by `i` a variable, because in normal mathematics the concept of a variable is a completely timeless concept. Time has nothing to do with the `x` in the relation

```
sin(2 * x) = 2 * sin(x) * cos(x)
```

if such a variable ever denotes a value it denotes "any value".

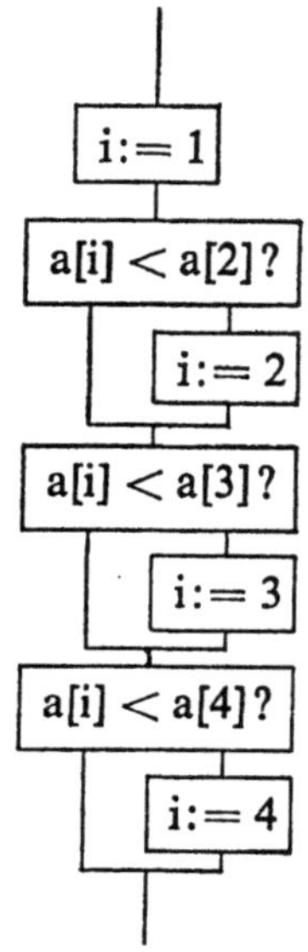

Fig. 6

Each time, however, that a variable in a sequential process is used—such as `i` in `a[i]`—it denotes a very specific value, viz. the last value assigned to it, and nothing else! As long as no new value is assigned to a variable, it denotes a constant value!

Remark 6. One may well ask what we are actually doing when we introduce a variable without specifying, for instance, a domain for it, i.e. a set of values which is guaranteed to comprise all its future actual values. We shall not pursue this question here.

Now we are going to subject our scheme to a next transformation. In Fig. 3 we have "wrapped up" the lines, now we are going to wrap up the scheme of Fig. 6 in the vertical direction, an operation to which we are invited by the repetitive nature of it and which can be performed at the price of a next variable, `j` say.

The change is a dramatic one, for the fact that the original problem was to identify the maximum value among *four* given values is no longer reflected in the "topology" of the rules of behaviour: in Fig. 7 we only find the number 4 mentioned once. By introducing another variable, say `n`, and replacing the 4 in Fig. 7 by `n` we have suddenly the rules of behaviour to identify the maximum occurring among the `n` elements `a[1]`, `a[2]`, ..., `a[n]`, and this practically only for the price that before application the variable `n` must be given its proper value.

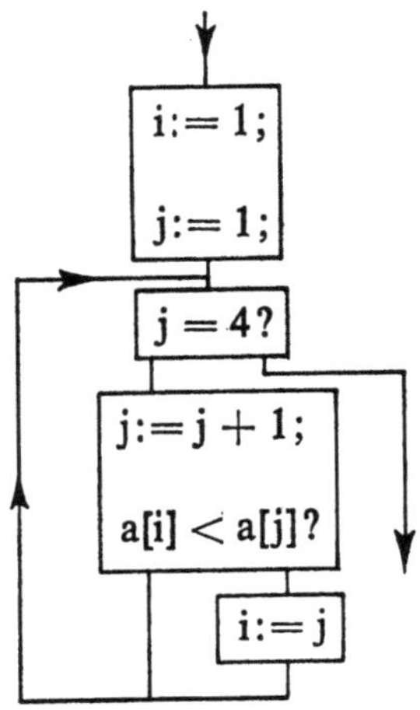

Fig. 7

The change is dramatic, for now we have not only given rules of behaviour which must be interpreted sequentially this was already the case with Fig. 6 but we have devised a single mechanism for identifying the maximum value among any number of given elements, whereas our original non-sequential machine could only be built for a previously well-defined number of elements. We have mapped our comparisons in time instead of in space, and if we wish to compare the two methods it is as if the sequential machine "extends itself" in terms of Fig. 3 as the need arises. It is our last transition which displays the sequential processes in their full glory.

The technical term for what we have called "rules of behaviour" is an algorithm or a program. (It is not customary to call it "a sequential program", although this name would be fully correct.) Equipment able to follow such rules, "to execute such a program" is called "a general-purpose sequential computer" or "computer" for short; what happens during such a program execution is called "a sequential process".

There is a commonly accepted technique of writing algorithms without the need of pictures such as we have used, viz. ALGOL 60 ("ALGOL" being short for Algorithmic Language). For a detailed discussion of ALGOL 60 I must refer the reader to the existing literature. We shall use it in future, whenever convenient for our purposes.

For the sake of illustration we shall describe the algorithm of Fig. 7 (but for n instead of 4) by a sequence of ALGOL statements:

```
        i:= 1; j:= 1;
back: if j <> n then
          begin j:= j + 1;
                if a[i] < a[j] then i:= j;
                goto back;
          end
```

The first two statements: `i:= 1; j:= 1` are—one hopes—self-explanatory. Then comes `back:`, a so-called label, used to identify this place in the program. Then comes `if j <> n then`, a so-called conditional clause. If the condition expressed by it is satisfied the following statement will be performed, otherwise it will be skipped. (Another example of it can be found two lines lower.) When the extent of the program which may have to be skipped presents itself primarily as a sequence of more than one statement, then one puts the so-called statement brackets `begin` and `end` around this sequence, thereby making it into a single statement as far as its surroundings are concerned. (This is entirely analogous to the effect of parentheses in algebraic formulae, such as `a * (b + c)` where the parenthesis pair indicates that the whole expression contained within it is to be taken as factor.) The last statement `goto back` means that the process should be continued at the point thus labelled; it does exactly the same thing for us as the upward-pointing line of Fig. 7.

2 LOOSELY CONNECTED PROCESSES

The subject matter of this chapter is the co-operation between loosely connected sequential processes, and this section will be devoted to a thorough discussion of a simple, but representative problem, in order to give the reader some feeling for the problems in this area.

In the previous section we have described the nature of a single sequential process, performing its sequence of actions autonomously, i.e. independent of its surroundings as soon as it has been started.

When two or more of such processes have to co-operate with each other they must be connected, i.e. they must be able to communicate with each other in order to exchange information. As we shall see below, the properties of these means of intercommunication play a vital role.

Furthermore, we have stipulated that the processes should be connected loosely; by this we mean that apart from the (rare) moments of explicit intercommunication, the individual processes themselves are to be regarded as completely independent of each other. In particular, we disallow any assumption about the relative speeds of the different processes. (Such an assumption—say, "processes geared to the same clock"—could be regarded as implicit intercommunication.) This independence of speed ratios is in strict accordance with our appreciation of the single sequential process: its only essential feature is that its elementary steps are performed in sequence If we prefer to observe the performance with a chronometer in our hand we may do so, but the process itself remains remarkably unaffected by this observation.

The consistent refusal to make any assumptions about the speed ratios will at first sight appear to the reader as a mean trick to make things more difficult than they already are. I feel, however, fully justified in my refusal. First, we may have to cope with situations in which, indeed, very little is known about the speeds. For instance, part of the system may be a manually operated input station, another part of the system might be such that it can be stopped externally for any period of time, thus reducing its speed temporarily to zero. Secondly—and this is much more important—when we think that we can rely upon certain speed ratios we shall discover that we have been "penny wise and pound foolish". It is true that certain mechanisms can be made simpler under the assumption of speed-ratio restrictions. The verification, however, that such an assumption is always justified is, in general, extremely tricky and the task to make, in a reliable manner, a well-behaved structure out of many interlinked components is seriously aggravated when such "analogue interferences" have to be taken into account as well. (For one thing: it will make the proper working a rather unstable equilibrium, sensitive to any change in the different speeds, as may easily arise by replacement of a component by another—say, replacement of a line printer by a faster model—or reprogramming of a certain portion.)

2.1 A Simple Example

In considering two sequential processes, `process 1` and `process 2`, they can for our purposes be regarded as cyclic. In each cycle a so-called "critical section" occurs, critical in the sense that at any moment at most one of the two processes is allowed to be engaged in its critical section. In order to effectuate this mutual exclusion, the two processes have access to a number of common variables. We postulate that inspecting the present value of such a common variable and assigning a new value to such a common variable are to be regarded as indivisible, non-interfering actions, i.e. when the two processes assign a new value to the same common variable "simultaneously", then the assignments are to be regarded as done the one after the other, the final value of the variable will be one of the two values assigned, but never a "mixture" of the two. Similarly, when one process inspects the value of a common variable "simultaneously" with the assignment to it by the other one, then the former process will find either the old or the new value, but never a mixture.

For our purposes ALGOL 60 as it stands is not suited, as ALGOL 60 has been designed to describe one single sequential process. We therefore propose the following extension to enable us to describe parallelism of execution. When a sequence of statements—separated by semicolons as usual in ALGOL 60—is surrounded by the special statement bracket pair **parbegin** and **parend** this is to be interpreted as parallel execution of the constituent statements. The whole construction—let us call it "a parallel compound"—can be regarded as a statement. Initiation of a parallel compound implies simultaneous initiation of all its constituent statements, its execution is completed after the completion of the execution of all its constituent statements. E.g.:

```
begin S1; parbegin S2; S3; S4 parend; S5 end
```

(in which S1, S2, S3, S4, and S5 are used to indicate statements) means that after the completion of S1, the statements S2, S3, and S4 will be executed in parallel, and only when they are all finished will the execution of statement S5 be initiated.

With the above conventions we can describe our first solution:

```
begin integer turn; turn:= 1;
      parbegin
      process 1: begin L1: if turn = 2 then goto L1;
                           critical section 1;
                           turn:= 2;
                           remainder of cycle 1, goto L1
                 end;
      process 2: begin L2: if turn = 1 then goto L2;
                           critical section 2;
                           turn:= 1;
                           remainder of cycle 2; goto L2
                 end;
      parend
end
```

(Note for the inexperienced ALGOL 60 reader. After begin in the first line we find the so-called declaration integer turn, thereby sticking to the rule of ALGOL 60 that program text is not allowed to refer to variables without having introduced them with the aid of a declaration. As this declaration occurs after the `begin` of the outermost statement bracket pair, it means that for the whole duration of the program a variable has been introduced that will only take on integer values and to which the program text can refer by means of the name `turn`.)

The two processes communicate with each other via the common integer `turn`, the value of which indicates which of the two processes is the first to perform (or rather: to finish) its critical section. From the program it is clear that after the first assignment the only possible values of the variable `turn` are 1 and 2. The condition for process 2 to enter its critical section is that it finds at some moment `turn <> 1`, i.e. `turn = 2`. But the only way in which the variable `turn` can get this value is by the assignment `turn:= 2` in process 1. As process 1 performs this assignment only at the completion of its critical section, process 2 can only initiate its critical section after the completion of critical section 1. And critical section 1 could indeed be initiated, because the initial condition `turn = 1` implied `turn <> 2`, so that the potential wait cycle, labelled `L1`, was initially inactive. After the assignment `turn:= 2` the roles of the two processes are interchanged. (N.B. It is assumed that the only references to the variable `turn` are the ones explicitly shown in the program.)

Our solution, though correct, is, however, unnecessarily restrictive: after the completion of critical section 1 the value of the variable `turn` becomes 2, and it must be = 1 again, before the next entrance into critical section 1.

As a result, the only admissible succession of critical sections is the strictly alternating one `1, 2, 1, 2, 1, 2, 1, ...`; in other words, the two processes are synchronized In order to stress explicitly that this is not the kind of solution we wanted, we impose the further condition: "If one of the processes is stopped well outside its critical section, this is not allowed to lead to potential blocking of the other process." This makes our previous solution unacceptable, and we have to look for another.

Our second effort works with two integers `c1` and `c2`, where `cl, c2 = 0/1` respectively will indicate that the corresponding process is inside/outside its critical section respectively. We may try the following construction:

```
begin integer c1, c2;
      c1:= 1; c2:= 1;
      parbegin
      process1: begin L1: if c2 = 0 then goto L1;
                          c1:= 0;
                          critical section 1;
                          c1:= 1;
                          remainder of cycle 1; goto L1
                end;
      process2: begin L2: if c1 = 0 then goto L2;
                          c2:= 0;
                          critical section 2;
                          c2:= 1;
                          remainder of cycle 2; goto L2
                end
      parend
end
```

The first assignments set both c's = 1, in accordance with the fact that the processes are started outside their critical sections. During the entire execution of critical section 1 the relation `c1 = 0` holds, and the first line of process 2 is effectively a wait: "Wait as long as process 1 is in its critical section." The trial solution gives indeed some protection against simultaneity of critical section execution, but is, alas, too simple, because it is wrong. Let first process 1 find that c2 = 1; let process 2 inspect c1 immediately afterwards, then it will (still) find c1 = 1. Both processes, each having found that the other is not in its critical section, will conclude that they can enter their own critical section safely!

We have been too optimistic, we must play a safer game. Let us invert, at the beginning of the parallel processes, the inspection of the `c` of the other and the setting of the own `c`. We then get the construction:

```
begin integer c1, c2;
      c1:= 1; c2:= 1;
      parbegin
      process 1: begin A1: c1:= 0;
                       L1: if c2 = 0 then goto L1;
                           critical section 1;
                           c1:= 1;
                           remainder of cycle 1; goto A1
                 end;
      process 2: begin A2: c2:= 0;
                       L2: if c1 = 0 then goto L2;
                           critical section 2;
                           c2:= 1;
                           remainder of cycle 2; goto A2
                 end
```

```
        parend
end
```

It is worthwhile to verify that this solution is at least completely safe.

Let us focus our attention on the moment that process 1 finds c2 = 1 and therefore decides to enter its critical section. At this moment we can conclude:

(1) that the relation `c1 = 0` already holds and will continue to hold until process 1 has completed the execution of its critical section;

(2) that, since `c2 = 1` holds, process 2 is well outside its critical section, which it cannot enter while `c1 = 0` holds, i.e. while process 1 is still engaged in its critical section.

Thus the mutual exclusion is indeed guaranteed.

But this solution, alas, must also be rejected: in its safety measures it has been too drastic, for it contains the danger of definite mutual blocking. When after the assignment `c1:= 0` but yet before the inspection of c2 (both by process 1) process 2 performs the assignment `c2:= 0`, then both processes have arrived at label L1 or L2 respectively and both relations `c1 = 0` and `c2 = 0` hold, with the result that both processes will wait for each other to eternity. Therefore this solution, too, must be rejected.

It was all right to set one's own `c` before inspecting the `c` of the other, but it was wrong to stick to one's own c-setting and just to wait. This is (somewhat) remedied in the following construction:

```
begin integer c1, c2;
        c1:= 1; c2: = 1;
        parbegin
        process 1: begin L1: c1:= 0;
                             if c2 = 0 then
                                    begin cl:= 1; goto L1 end;
                             critical section 1;
                             c1:= 1;
                             remainder of cycle 1; goto L1
                   end;
        process 2: begin L2: c2:= 0;
                             if c1 = 0 then
                                    begin c2:= 1; goto L2 end;
                             critical section 2;
                             c2:= 1;
                             remainder of cycle 2; goto L2
                   end
        parend
end
```

This construction is as safe as the previous one, and when the assignments `c1:= 0` and `c2:= 0` are performed "simultaneously" it will not necessarily lead to mutual blocking ad infinitum, because both processes will reset their own `c` back to 1 before restarting the entry rites, thereby enabling the other process to catch the opportunity. But our principles force us to reject this solution also, for the refusal to make any assumptions about the speed ratio implies that we have to cater for all speeds, and the last solution admits the speeds to be so carefully adjusted that the processes inspect the other's `c` only in those periods of time that its value is $= 0$. To make clear that we reject such solutions that only work with some luck, we state our next requirement: "If the two processes are about to enter their critical sections, it must be impossible to devise for them such finite speeds, that the decision which one of the two is the first to enter its critical section is postponed to eternity."

In passing we note that the solution just rejected is quite acceptable in everyday life, e.g. when two people are talking over the telephone and they are suddenly disconnected, as a rule both try to re-establish the connection. They both dial and if they get the signal "Number Engaged" they put down the receiver and, if not already called, they try "some" seconds later. Of course, this may coincide with the next effort of the other party, but as a rule the connection is re-established successfully after very few trials. In our mechanical circumstances, however, we cannot accept this pattern of behaviour: our parties might very well be identical!

Quite a collection of trial solutions have been shown to be incorrect, and at some moment people that had played with the problem started to doubt whether it could be solved at all. To the Dutch mathematician Th. J. Dekker the credit is due for the first correct solution. It is, in fact, mixture of our previous efforts: it uses the "safe sluice" of our last constructions, together with the integer **`turn`** of the first one, but only to resolve the indeterminacy when neither of the two immediately succeeds. The initial value of **`turn`** could have been 2 as well.

```
begin integer c1, c2, turn;
      c1:= 1; c2:= 1; turn:= 1;
      parbegin
      process 1: begin A1: c1:= 0;
                       L1: if c2 = 0 then
                              begin if turn = 1 then goto L1;
                                    c1:= 1;
                                B1: if turn = 2 then goto B1;
                                    goto A1
                              end;
                           critical section 1;
                           turn:= 2; c1:= 1;
                           remainder of cycle 1; goto A1
                 end;
      process 2: begin A2: c2:= 0;
                       L2: if c1 = 0 then
                              begin if turn = 2 then goto L2;
                                    c2:= 1;
                                B2: if turn = 1 then goto B2;
                                    goto A2
                              end;
                           critical section 2;
                           turn:= 1; c2:= 1;
                           remainder of cycle 2; goto A2
                 end
      parend
end
```

We shall now prove the correctness of this solution. Our first observation is that each process only operates on its own `c`. As a result, process 1 inspects `c2` only while `c1 = 0`, it will only enter its critical section provided it finds `c2 = 1`; for process 2 the analogous observation can be made.

In short, we recognize the safe sluice of our last constructions, and the solution is therefore safe in the sense that the two processes can never be in their critical sections simultaneously. The second part of the proof has to show that in case of doubt the decision which of the two will be the first to enter cannot be postponed until eternity. Now we should pay some attention to the integer `turn`: we note that assignment to this variable occurs only at the end or, if you wish, as part of critical sections, and therefore we can regard the variable `turn` as a constant during the decision process. Suppose that `turn = 1`. Then process 1 can only cycle via `L1`, that is with `c1 = 0` and only as long as it finds `c2 = 0`. But if `turn = 1`, then process 2 can only cycle via `B2`, but this state implies `c2 = 1`, so that process 1 cannot cycle and is bound to enter its critical section. For `turn 2` the mirrored reasoning applies. As third and final part of the proof we observe that stopping, say, process 1 in "remainder of cycle 1" will not restrict process 2: the relation `c1 = 1` will then hold, and process 2 can merrily enter its critical section, quite independently of the current value of **turn**. And this completes the proof of the correctness of Dekker's solution. Those readers that fail to appreciate its ingenuity are kindly asked to realize that for them I have prepared the ground by means of a carefully selected set of rejected constructions.

2.2 The Generalized Mutual Exclusion Problem

The problem of Section 2.1 has a natural generalization: given N cyclic processes, each with a critical section, can we construct them in such a way that at any moment at most one of them is engaged in its critical section? We assume the same means of intercommunication to be available, i.e. a set of commonly accessible variables. Furthermore, our solution has to satisfy the same requirements, viz. that stopping one process well outside its critical section may in no way restrict the freedom of the others, and that if more than one process is about to enter its critical section it must be impossible to devise for them such finite speeds that the decision which one of them is to be first to enter its critical section can be postponed to eternity.

In order to be able to describe the solution in ALGOL 60, we need the concept of the array. In Section 2.1 we had to introduce a c for each of the two processes and we did so by declaring

```
integer c1, c2
```

Instead of enumerating the quantities, we can declare—under the assumption that N has a well-defined positive value—

```
integer array c[1 : N]
```

which means, that at one stroke we have introduced N integers, accessible under the names

```
c[subscript]
```

where **subscript** might take the values 1, 2, ... N.

The next ALGOL 60 feature we introduce is the so-called "for clause", which we shall use in the following form:

```
for j:= 1 step 1 until N do statement S
```

and which enables us to express repetition of **statement S** quite conveniently. In principle, the for clause implies that **statement S** will be executed N times, with j in succession = 1, = 2,... = N. (We have added "in principle", for via a goto statement as constituent part of statement `S` and leading out of it, the repetition can be ended earlier.)

Finally, we need the logical operator that in this monograph is denoted by **and**. We have met the conditional clause in the form:

```
if condition then statement
```

We shall now meet:

```
if condition 1 and condition 2 then statement
```

meaning that statement `S` will be executed only if `condition 1` and `condition 2` are both satisfied. (Once more we should like to stress that this monograph is not an ALGOL 60 programming manual: the above—loose!—explanations of parts of ALGOL 60 have been introduced only to make this monograph as self-contained as possible.)

With the notational aids just sketched we can describe our solution for fixed N as follows.

The overall structure is:

```
begin integer array b, c[0 : N];
      integer turn;
      for turn:= 0 step 1 until N do
            begin b[turn]:= 1; c[turn]:= 1 end;
      turn:= 0;
      parbegin
      process 1: begin ... end;
      process 2: begin ... end;
           .
           .
           .
      process N: begin ... end;
      parend
end
```

The first declaration introduces two arrays with N + 1 elements each, the next declaration introduces a single integer `turn`. In the following for clause this variable `turn` is used to take on the successive values 1, 2, 3,... N, so that the two arrays are initialized with all elements 1. Then `turn` is set = 0 (i.e. none of the processes, numbered from 1 onwards, is privileged). After this the N processes are started simultaneously.

The N processes are all similar. The structure of the `i`th process is as follows ($1 \leq \mathtt{i} \leq \mathtt{N}$):

```
process i: begin integer j;
             Ai: b[i]:= 0;
             Li: if turn <> i then
                 begin c[i]:= 1;
                       if b[turn] = 1 then turn:= i;
                       goto Li
                 end;
                 c[i]:= 0;
                 for j:= 1 step 1 until N do
                    begin if j <> i and c[j] = 0 then goto Li
                    end;
                 critical section i;
                 turn:= 0; c[i]:= 1; b[i]:= 1;
                 remainder of cycle i; goto Ai
           end
```

Remark. The description of the N individual processes starts with a declaration `integer j`. According to the rules of ALGOL 60 this means that each process introduces its own, private, integer `j` (a so-called "local quantity").

We leave the proof to the reader. It has to show again:

(1) that at any moment at most one of the processes is engaged in its critical section;

(2) that the decision which of the processes is the first to enter its critical section cannot be postponed to eternity;

(3) that stopping a process in its "remainder of cycle" has no effect upon the others.

Of these parts, the second one is the more difficult one. (*Hint:* As soon as one of the processes has performed the assignment `turn:= i`, no new processes can decide to assign their number to turn before a critical section has been completed. Mind that two processes can decide "simultaneously" to assign their `i`-value to `turn`!)

(Remark that can be skipped at first reading)

The program just described inspects the value of `b[turn]` where both the array `b` and the integer `turn` are in common store. We have stated that inspecting a single variable is an indivisible action and inspecting `b[turn]` can therefore only mean: inspect the value of `turn`, and if this happens to be = 5, well, then inspect `b[5]`. Or, in more explicit ALGOL:

```
process i: begin integer j, k;
                      .
                      .
                      .
                      k:= turn; if b[k] = 1 then ...
```

implying that by the time that `b[k]` is inspected, `turn` may already have a value different from the current one of `k`.

Without the stated limitations in communicating with the common store, a possible interpretation of "the value of `b[turn]`" would have been "the value of the element of the array `b` as indicated by the current value of `turn`". In so-called uniprogramming i.e. a single sequential process operating on quantities local to it the two interpretations are equivalent. In multiprogramming, where other active processes may access and change the same common information, the two interpretations make a great difference! In particular, for the reader with extensive experience in uniprogramming this remark has been inserted as an indication of the subtleties of the games we are playing.

2.3 A Linguistic Interlude

In Section 2.2 we described the co-operation of N processes; in the overall structure we used a vertical sequence of dots between the brackets **parbegin** and **parend**. This is nothing but a loose formalism, suggesting to the human reader how to compose in our notation a set of N co-operating sequential processes, under the condition that the value of N has been fixed beforehand. It is a suggestion for the construction of 3, 4, or 5071 co-operating processes, it does not give a formal description of N such co-operating processes in which N occurs as a parameter, i.e. it is not a description valid for any value of N.

It is the purpose of this section to show that the concept of the so-called "recursive procedure" of ALGOL 60 caters for this. This concept will be sketched briefly.

We have seen how after **begin** declarations could occur in order to introduce and to name either single variables (by enumeration of their names) or whole ordered sets of variables (viz. in the array declaration). With the so-called "procedure declaration" we can define and name a certain action; such an action may then be invoked by using its name as a statement, thereby supplying the parameters to which the action should be applied.

As an illustration we consider the following ALGOL 60 program:

```
begin integer a, b;
      procedure square(u, v); integer u, v;
          begin u:= v * v end;
   L: square(a, 3); square(b, a); square(a, b)
end
```

In the first line the integers named a and b are declared. The next line declares the procedure named square" operating on two parameters, which are specified to be single integers (and not, say, complete arrays). This line is called "the procedure heading". The immediately following statement—the so-called "procedure body"—describes by definition the action named: in the third line—in which the bracket pair **begin** ... **end** is superfluous—it is told that the action of square is to assign to the first parameter the square of the value of the second one. Then, labelled L, comes the first statement. Before its execution the values of both a and b are undefined, after its execution a = 9. After the execution of the next statement the value of b is therefore = 81, after the execution of the last statement the value of a is = 6561, the value of b is still = 81.

In the previous example the procedure mechanism was essentially introduced as a means for abbreviation, a means for avoiding to have to write down the "body" three times, although we could have done so quite easily:

```
begin integer a, b;
   L: a:= 3 * 3; b:= a * a; a:= b * b
end
```

When the body is much more complicated than in this example a program along the latter lines tends to be much lengthier indeed.

This technique of "substituting for the call the appropriate version of the body" is, however, no longer possible as soon as the procedure is a so-called recursive one, i.e. may call itself. It is then that the procedure really extends the expressive power of the programming language.

A simple example might illustrate the recursive procedure. The greatest common divisor of two given natural numbers is:

(1) if they have the same value equal to this value;

(2) if they have different values equal to the greatest common divisor of the smaller of the two and their difference.

In other words, if the greatest common divisor is not trivial (first case) the problem is replaced by finding the greatest common divisor of two numbers with a smaller maximum value.

(In the following program the insertion `value v, w;` can be skipped by the reader as being irrelevant for our present purposes; it indicates that for the parameters listed the body is only interested in the numerical value of the actual parameter, as supplied by the call.)

```
begin integer a;
      procedure GCD(u, v, w); value v, w; integer u, v, w;
          if v = w then u:= v
                   else
              begin if v < w then GCD(u, v, w - v)
                                 else GCD(u, v - w, w)
              end;
      GCD(a, 12, 33)
end
```

(In this example the more elaborate form of the conditional statement is used, viz.:

```
if condition then statement 1 else statement 2,
```

meaning that if `condition` is satisfied, `statement 1` will be executed and `statement 2` will be skipped, and that if `condition` is not satisfied `statement 1` will be skipped and `statement 2` will be executed.)

The reader is invited to follow the pattern of calls of GCD and to see how the variable a becomes = 3; he is also invited to convince himself of the fact that the (dynamic) pattern of calls depends on the parameters supplied and that the substitution technique—replace call by body—as applied in the previous example would lead to difficulties here.

We shall now write a program to perform a matrix $*$ vector multiplication in which:

(1) the order in which the M scalar $*$ scalar products are to be calculated is indeed prescribed (the rows of the matrix will be scanned from left to right);

(2) the N rows of the matrix can be processed in parallel.

(Where we do not wish to impose the restriction of purely integer values, we have used the declarator `real` instead of the declarator `integer`; furthermore, we have introduced an array with two subscripts in what we hope is an obvious manner.)

It is assumed that, upon entry of this block of program, the integers `M` and `N` have positive values.

```
begin real array matrix[1 : N, 1 : M];
      real array vector[1 : M];
      real array product[1 : N];
      procedure rowmult(k); value k; integer k;
          begin if k > 0 then
                parbegin
                   begin real s; integer j;
                         s:= 0;
                         for j:= 1 step 1 until M do
                            s:= s + matrix[k, j] * vector[j];
                         product[k]:= s
                   end;
                   rowmult(k - 1)
                parend
           end
      .
      .
      .
      rowmult(N);
      .
      .
      .
end
```

3 THE MUTUAL EXCLUSION PROBLEM REVISITED

We return to the problem of mutual exclusion in time of critical sections, as introduced in Section 2.1 and generalized in Section 2.2. This section deals with a more efficient technique for solving this problem; only after having done so we have adequate means for the description of examples, with which I hope to convince the reader of the rather fundamental importance of the mutual exclusion problem, in other words, I must appeal to the patience of the wondering reader (suffering, as I am, from the sequential nature of human communication!).

3.1 The Need for a More Realistic Solution

The solution given in Section 2.2 is interesting in as far as it shows that the restricted means of communication provided are, from a theoretical point of view, sufficient to solve the problem. From other points of view, which are just as dear to my heart, it is hopelessly inadequate.

To start with, it gives rise to a rather cumbersome description of the individual processes, in which it is anything but transparent that the overall behaviour is in accordance with the (conceptually so simple) requirement of the mutual exclusion. In other words, in some way or another this solution is a tremendous mystification. Let us try to isolate in which respect this solution represents indeed a mystification, for this investigation could give the clue to improvement.

Let us consider the period of time during which one of the processes is in its critical section. We all know, that during that period no other processes can enter their critical section and that, if they want to do so, they have to wait until the current critical section execution has been completed. For the remainder of that period hardly any activity is required from them: they have to wait anyhow, and as far as we are concerned "they could go to sleep".

Our solution does not reflect this at all: we keep the processes busy setting and inspecting common variables all the time, as if no price has to be paid for this activity. But if our implementation—i.e. the ways in which or the means by which these processes are carried out—is such that "sleeping" is a less-expensive activity than this busy way of waiting, then we are fully justified (now also from an economic point of view) to call our solution misleading.

In present-day computers there are at least two ways in which this active way of waiting can be very expensive. Let me sketch them briefly. These computers have two distinct parts, usually called "the processor" and "the store". The processor is the active part, in which the arithmetic and logical operations are performed, it is "active and small"; in the store, which is "passive and large", there resides at any moment the information which is not being processed at that very moment but only kept there for future reference. In the total computational process information is transported from store to processor as soon as it has to play an active role, the information in store can be changed by transportation in the inverse direction.

Such a computer is a very flexible tool for the implementation of sequential processes. Even a computer with only one single processor can be used to implement a number of concurrent sequential processes. From a macroscopic point of view it will seem as though all these processes are being carried out simultaneously, a closer inspection will reveal, however, that at any "microscopic" moment the processor serves only one single program at a time, and the overall picture only results because at well-chosen moments the processor will switch from one process to another. In such an implementation the different processes share the same processor, and activity (i.e. a non-zero speed) of any single process will imply zero speed for the others; it is then undesirable that precious processor time is consumed by processes which cannot go on anyhow.

Apart from processor sharing, the store sharing could make the unnecessary activity of a waiting process undesirable. Let us assume that inspection of or assignment to a "common variable" implies the access to an information unit a so-called "word" in a ferrite-core store. Access to a word in a core store takes a non-zero time, and for technical reasons only one word can be accessed at a time. When more than one active process may wish access to words of the same core store the usual arrangement is that in the case of imminent coincidence the storage access requests from the different active processes are granted according to a built-in priority rule: the lower priority process is automatically held up. (The literature refers to this situation when it describes "a communication channel stealing a memory cycle from the processor".) The result is that frequent inspection of common variables may slow down any processes which share the same core storage for their local quantities.

3.2 The Synchronizing Primitices

The origin of the complications, which lead to such intricate solutions as the one described in Section 2.2, is the fact that the indivisible accesses to common variables are always "one-way information traffic": an individual process can either assign a new value or inspect a current value. Such an inspection itself, however, leaves no trace for the other processes, and the consequence is that, when a process wants to react to the current value of a common variable, that variable's value may have been changed by the other processes between the moment of its inspection and the following effectuation of the reaction to it. In other words: the previous set of communication facilities must be regarded as inadequate for the problem at hand, and we should look for more appropriate alternatives.

Such an alternative is provided by introducing:

(a) among the common variables special-purpose integers, which we shall call "semaphores";

(b) among the repertoire of actions, from which the individual processes have to be constructed, two new primitives, which we call the "P-operation" and the "V-operation" respectively.

The latter operations always operate on a semaphore and represent the only way in which the concurrent processes may access the semaphores.

The semaphores are essentially non-negative integers; when used only to solve the mutual exclusion problem the range of their values will even be restricted to 0 and 1. It is the merit of the Dutch physicist and computer designer C. S. Scholten to have shown a considerable field of applicability for semaphores that can also take on larger values. When there is a need for distinction we shall talk about "binary semaphores" and "general semaphores" respectively. The definition of the P- and V-operation that I shall give now holds regardless of this distinction.

Definition. The V-operation is an operation with one argument, which must be the identification of a semaphore. (If `S1` and `S2` denote semaphores we can write `V(S1)` and `V(S2)`.) Its function is to increase the value of its argument semaphore by 1; this increase is to be regarded as an indivisible operation.

Note that this last sentence makes `V(S1)` inequivalent to `S1:= S1 + 1`. For suppose that two processes A and B both contain the statement `V(S1)` and that both should like to perform this statement at a moment when, say, `S1 = 6`. Excluding interference with `S1` from other processes, A and B will perform their V-operations in an unspecified order—at least: outside our control—and after the completion of the second V-operation the final value of `S1` will be $= 8$. If `S1` had not been a semaphore but just an ordinary common integer, and if processes A and B had contained the statement `S1:= S1 +` instead of the V-operation on `S1`, then the following could happen. Process A evaluates `S1 + 1` and computes `7`; before effecting, however, the assignment of this new value, process B has reached the same stage and also evaluates `S1 + 1`, computing `7`. Thereafter both processes assign the value `7` to `S1`, and one of the desired incrementations has been lost. The requirement of the "indivisible operation" is meant to exclude this occurrence when the V-operation is used.

Definition. The P-operation is an operation with one argument, which must be the identification of a semaphore. (If `S1` and `S2` denote semaphores we can write `P(S1)` and `P(S2)`.) Its function is to decrease the value of its argument semaphore by 1 as soon as the resulting value would be non-negative. The completion of the P-operation—i.e. the decision that this is the appropriate moment to effectuate the decrease and the subsequent decrease itself—is to be regarded as an indivisible operation.

It is the P-operation which represents the potential delay, viz. when a process initiates a P-operation on a semaphore, that at that moment is $= 0$, in that case this P-operation cannot be completed until another process has performed a V-operation on the same semaphore and has given it the value 1. At that moment more than one process may have initiated a P-operation on that very same semaphore. The clause that completion of P-operation is an indivisible action means that when the semaphore has got the value 1 only one of the initiated P-operations on it is allowed to be completed. Which one, again, is left unspecified, i.e. at least outside our control.

At this stage we shall take the implementability of the P- and V-operations for granted.

3.3 The Synchronizing Primitives Applied to the Mutual Exclusion Problem

The construction of the N processes, each with a critical section, the executions of which must exclude one another in time (see Section 2.2) is now trivial. It can be done with the aid of a single binary semaphore, say `free`. The value of `free` equals the number of processes allowed to enter their critical section now, or;

`free = 1` means: none of the processes is engaged in its critical section
`free = 0` means: one of the processes is engaged in its critical section.

The overall structure of the solution becomes:

```
begin integer free; free:= 1;
  parbegin
  process 1: begin ... end;
  process 2: begin ... end;
     .
     .
     .
  process N: begin ... end;
  parend
end
```

with the `ith` process of the form:

```
process i: begin
             Li: P(free); critical section i; V(free);
                 remainder of cycle i; goto Li
           end
```

4 THE GENERAL SEMAPHORE

4.1 Typical Uses of the General Semaphore

We consider two processes, which are called the "producer" and the "consumer" respectively. The producer is a cyclic process, and each time it goes through its cycle it produces a certain portion of information that has to be processed by the consumer. The consumer is also a cyclic process, and each time it goes through its cycle it can process the next portion of information, as produced by the producer. A simple example is given by a computing process, producing as "portions of information" punched-card images to be punched out by a card punch, which plays the role of the consumer.

The producer-consumer relation implies a one-way communication channel between the two processes, along which the portions of information can be transmitted. We assume the two processes to be connected for this purpose via a buffer with unbounded capacity, i.e. the portions produced need not be consumed immediately, but they may queue in the buffer. The fact that no upper bound has been given for the capacity of the buffer makes this example slightly unrealistic, but this should not trouble us too much now.

(The reason for the name "buffer" becomes understandable when we investigate the consequences of its absence, viz. when the producer can only offer its next portion after the previous portion has been actually consumed. In the computer-card punch example, we may assume that the card punch can punch cards at a constant speed, say 4 cards per second. Let us assume that this output speed is well matched with the production speed, i.e. that the computer can perform the card image production process with the same average speed. If the connection between computing process and card punch is unbuffered, then the couple will only work continuously at full speed when the card-production process produces a card every quarter of a second. If, however, the nature of the computing process is such that after one or two seconds vigorous computing it produces 4 to 8 card images in a single burst, then unbuffered connection will result in a period of time during which the punch will be idle (for lack of information), followed by a period in which the computing process has to be idle, because it cannot get rid of the next card image before the preceding one has been actually punched. Such irregularities in production speed, however, can be smoothed out by a buffer of sufficient size and that is why such a queuing device is called "a buffer".)

In this section we shall not deal with the various techniques of implementing a buffer. It must be able to contain successive portions of information, it must therefore be a suitable storage medium, accessible to both processes. Furthermore, it must not only contain the portions themselves, it must also represent their linear ordering. (In the literature two well-known techniques are known as "cyclic buffering" and "chaining" respectively.) When the producer has prepared its next portion to be added to the buffer we shall denote this action simply by `add portion to buffer`, without going into further details; similarly, the `take portion from buffer` describes the consumer's behaviour, where the oldest portion still in the buffer is understood. (Another name of a buffer is a "First-In-First-Out-Memory".)

Omitting in the outermost block all declarations for the buffer, we can now construct the two processes with the aid of a single general semaphore, called `number of queuing portions`.

```
begin integer number of queuing portions;
      number of queuing portions:= 0;
      parbegin
      producer: begin
             again 1: produce the next portion;
                      add portion to buffer;
                      V(number of queuing portions);
                      goto again 1
                end;
      consumer: begin
             again 2: P(number of queuing portions);
                      take portion from buffer;
                      process portion taken;
                      goto again 2
                end
      parend
end
```

The first line of the producer represents the coding of the process which forms the next portion of information; it has a meaning quite independent of the buffer for which this portion is intended; when it has been executed the next portion has been successfully completed, the completion of its construction can no longer be dependent on other (unmentioned) conditions. The second line of coding represents the actions which define the finished portion as the next one in the buffer; after its execution the new portion has been added completely to the buffer, apart from the fact that the consumer does not know it yet. The V-operation finally confirms its presence, i.e. signals it to the consumer. Note that it is absolutely essential that the V-operation is preceded by the complete addition of the portion. About the structure of the consumer analogous remarks can be made.

Particularly in the case of buffer implementation by means of chaining the operations `add portion to buffer` and `take portion from buffer`—operating as they are on the same clerical status information of the buffer—may interfere with each other in a most undesirable fashion, unless we see to it, that they exclude each other in time. This can be catered for by a binary semaphore, called `buffer manipulation`, the values of which mean:

= 0: either adding to or taking from the buffer is taking place
= 1: neither adding to nor taking from the buffer is taking place.

The program is as follows:

```
begin integer number of queuing portions,
              buffer manipulation;
      number of queuing portions:= 0;
      buffer manipulation:= 1;
      parbegin
      producer: begin
             again 1: produce next portion;
                      P(buffer manipulation);
                      add portion to buffer;
                      V(buffer manipulation);
                      V(number of queuing portions);
                      goto again 1
                end;
      consumer: begin
             again 2: P(number of queuing portions);
                      P(buffer manipulation);
                      take portion from buffer;
                      V(buffer manipulation);
                      process portion taken;
                      goto again 2
                end
      parend
end
```

The reader is requested to convince himself that:

(a) the order of the two V-operations in the producer is immaterial;

(b) the order of the two P-operations in the consumer is essential.

Remark. The presence of the binary semaphore `buffer manipulation` has another consequence. We have given the program for one producer and one consumer, but now the extension to more producers and/or more consumers is straightforward: the same semaphore sees to it that two or more additions of new portions will never get mixed up, and the same applies to two or more takings of a portion by different consumers. The reader is requested to verify that the order of the two V-operations in the producer is still immaterial.

4.2 The Superfluity of the General Semaphore

In this section we shall show the superfluity of the general semaphore and we shall do so by rewriting the last program of the previous section, using binary semaphores only. (Intentionally I have written "we shall show" and not "we shall prove". We do not have at our disposal the mathematical apparatus that would be needed to give such a proof, and I do not feel inclined to develop such mathematical apparatus now. Nevertheless, I hope that my show will be convincing!) We shall first give a solution and postpone the discussion till afterwards.

```
begin integer numqueupor, buffer manipulation,
              consumer delay;
      numqueupor:= 0; buffer manipulation:= 1;
      consumer delay:= 0;
      parbegin
      producer: begin
             again 1: produce next portion;
                      P(buffer manipulation);
                      add portion to buffer;
                      numqueupor:= numqueupor + 1;
                      if numqueupor = 1 then
                            V(consumer delay);
                      V(buffer manipulation);
                      goto again 1
                end;
      consumer: begin integer oldnumqueupor;
                wait: P(consumer delay);
               go on: P(buffer manipulation);
                      take portion from buffer;
                      numqueupor:= numqueupor - 1;
                      oldnumqueupor:= numqueupor;
                      V(buffer manipulation);
                      process portion taken;
                      if oldnumqueupor = 0 then goto wait
                                           else goto go on
                end
      parend
end
```

Relevant in the dynamic behaviour of this program are the periods of time during which the buffer is empty. (As long as the buffer is not empty, the consumer can go on happily at its maximum speed.) Such a period can only be initiated by the consumer (by taking the last portion present from the buffer), it can only be terminated by the producer (by adding a portion to an empty buffer). These two events can be detected unambiguously, thanks to the binary semaphore `buffer manipulation`, that guarantees the mutual exclusion necessary for this detection. Each such period is accompanied by a P- and a V-operation on the new binary semaphore `consumer delay`. Finally, we draw attention to the local variable `oldnumqueupor` of the consumer: its value is set during the taking of the portion and fixes whether it was the last portion then present. (The more expert ALGOL readers will be aware that we only need to store a single bit of information, viz. whether the decrease of **numqueupor** resulted in a value = 0; we could have used a local variable of type Boolean for this purpose.) When the consumer decides to go to **wait**, i.e. finds **oldnumqueupor = 0**, at that moment **numqueupor** itself could already be greater than zero again!

In the previous program the relevant occurrence was the period with empty buffer. One can remark that emptiness is, in itself, rather irrelevant: it only matters, when the consumer should like to take a next portion, which is still absent. We shall program this version as well. In its dynamic behaviour we may expect less P- and V-operations on **consumer delay**: they will not occur when the buffer has been empty for a short while, but is filled again in time to make delay of the consumer unnecessary. Again we shall first give the program and then its discussion.

```
begin integer numqueupor, buffer manipulation,
      consumer delay;
      numqueupor:= 0; buffer manipulation:= 1;
      consumer delay:= 0;
      parbegin
      producer: begin
            again 1: produce next portion;
                     P(buffer manipulation);
                     add portion to buffer;
                     numqueupor:= numqueupor + 1;
                     if numqueupor = 0 then
                        begin V(buffer manipulation);
                              V(consumer delay) end
                                    else
                        V(buffer manipulation);
                     goto again 1
                end;
      consumer: begin
            again 2: P(buffer manipulation);
                     numqueupor:= numqueupor - 1;
                     if numqueupor = -1 then
                        begin V(buffer manipulation);
                              P(consumer delay);
                              P(buffer manipulation) end;
                     take portion from buffer;
                     V(buffer manipulation),
                     process portion taken;
                     goto again 2
                end
      parend
end
```

Again, the semaphore buffer manipulation caters for the mutual exclu- sion of critical sections. The last six lines of the producer could have been formulated as follows:

```
if numqueupor = 0 then V(consumer delay);
V(buffer manipulation); goto again 1
```

In not doing so I have followed a personal taste, viz. to avoid P- and V- operations within critical sections; a personal taste to which the reader should not pay too much attention.

The range of possible values of numqueupor has been extended with the value -1, meaning (outside critical section execution) "the buffer is not only empty, but its emptiness has already been detected by the consumer, which has decided to wait". This fact can be detected by the producer when, after the addition of one, numqueupor = 0 holds.

Note how, in the case of numqueupor = -1, the critical section of the consumer is dynamically broken into two parts: this is most essential, for otherwise the producer would never get the opportunity to add the portion that is already so much wanted by the consumer.

(The program just described is known as "The Sleeping Barber". There is a barbershop with a separate waiting room. The waiting room has an entry and next to it an exit to the room with the barber's chair, entry and exit sharing the same sliding door, which always closes one of them; furthermore, the entry is so small that only one customer can enter it at a time, thus fixing their order of entry. The mutual exclusions are thus guaranteed.

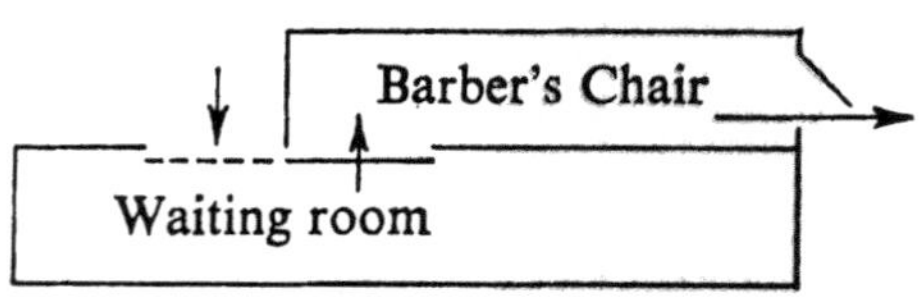

When the barber has finished a haircut he opens the door to the waiting room and inspects it. If the waiting room is not empty he invites the next customer, otherwise he goes to sleep in one of the chairs in the waiting room. The complementary behaviour of the customers is as follows: when they find zero or more customers in the waiting room they just wait their turn, when they find, however, the Sleeping Barber—numqueupor = -1—they wake him up.)

The two programs given present a strong indication that the general semaphore is, indeed, superfluous. Nevertheless, we shall not try to abolish the general semaphore: the one-sided synchronization restriction expressible by it is very common, and comparison of the solutions with and without the general semaphore shows convincingly that it should be regarded as an adequate tool.

4.3 The Bounded Buffer

I shall give a last simple example to illustrate the use of the general semaphore. In Section 4.1 we have studied a producer and a consumer coupled via a buffer with unbounded capacity. This is a typically one-sided restriction: the producer can be arbitrarily far ahead of the consumer; on the other hand, the consumer can never be ahead of the producer. The relation becomes symmetric when the two are coupled via a buffer of finite size, say of N portions. We give the program without discussion; we ask the reader to convince himself of the complete symmetry. ("The consumer produces and the producer consumes empty positions in the buffer.") The value N, as well as the buffer, is supposed to be defined in the surrounding universe into which the following program should be embedded.

```
begin integer number of queuing portions,
              number of empty positions,
              buffer manipulation;
      number of queuing portions:= 0;
      number of empty positions:= N;
      buffer manipulation:= 1;
      parbegin
      producer: begin
             again 1: produce next portion;
                      P(number of empty positions);
                      P(buffer manipulation);
                      add portion to buffer;
                      V(buffer manipulation);
                      V(number of queuing portions);
                      goto again 1
                end;
      consumer: begin
             again 2: P(number of queuing portions);
                      P(buffer manipulation);
                      take portion from buffer;
                      V(buffer manipulation);
                      V(number of empty positions);
                      process portion taken;
                      goto again 2
                end
      parend
end
```

5 CO-OPERATION VIA STATUS VARIABLES

In Sections 4.1 and 4.3 we have illustrated the use of the general semaphore. It proved an adequate tool, be it as implementation of a rather trivial form of interaction. The rules for the consumer are very simple: if there is something in the buffer, consume it. They are of the same simplicity as the behaviour of the wage-earner who spends all his money as soon as he has been paid and is broke until the next pay day.

In other words: when a group of co-operating sequential processes have to be constructed and the overall behaviour of these processes combined has to satisfy more elaborate requirements—the community, formed by them, has, as a whole, to be well behaved in some sense—we can only expect to be able to achieve this if the individual processes themselves and the ways in which they can interact will get more refined. We can no longer expect a ready-made solution, such as the general semaphore, to do the job. In general, we shall need such flexibility as can be expressed in a program for a general-purpose computer.

We now have the raw material, we can define the individual processes, they can communicate with each other via the common variables, and finally, we have the synchronizing primitives. How we can compose from it what we might want is, however, by no means obvious. We must now train ourselves to use the tools, we must develop a style of programming, a style of "parallel programming". Two points should be stressed.

We shall be faced with a great amount of freedom. Interaction may imply decisions bearing upon more than one process, and it is not always obvious which of the processes should then take the decisions. If we cannot find a guiding principle (e.g. efficiency considerations), then we must have the courage to impose some rule for the sake of clarity.

Secondly, if we are interested in systems that really work we should be able to convince ourselves (and anybody else who takes the trouble of doubting) of the correctness of our constructions. In uniprogramming one is already faced with the task of program verification a task the difficulty of which is often underestimated but there one can hope to debug by testing of the actual program. In our case the system will often have to work under irreproducible circumstances, and we can hardly expect any serious help from field tests. The duty of verification should concern us right from the start.

We shall attack a more complicated example in the hope that this will give us some of the experience which might be used as guiding principle.

5.1 An Example of a Priority Rule

In Section 4.3 we have used the general semaphore to couple a producer and a consumer via a bounded buffer. The solution given there is extendable to more producers and/or more consumers; it is applicable when the "portion" is at the same time a convenient unit of information, i.e. when we can regard the different portions as all being of the same size.

In the present problem we consider producers that offer portions of different sizes; we assume the size of these portions to be expressed in portions units. The consumers, again, will process the successive portions from the buffer, and will therefore have to be able to process portions the size of which is not given *a priori.* A maximum portion size will, however, be known.

The size of the portions is given in information units, we assume also that the maximum capacity of the buffer is given in information units: the question whether the buffer will be able to accommodate the next portion will therefore depend on the size of the portion offered. The requirement that "adding a portion to" and "taking a portion from the buffer" are still conceivable operations implies that the size of the buffer is not less than the maximum portion size.

We have a bounded buffer, and therefore a producer may have to wait before it can offer a portion. With fixed-size portions this would only occur when the buffer was full to the brim, now it can also happen because free space in the buffer, although present, is insucient for the portion concerned.

Furthermore, when we have more than one producer and one of them is waiting, then the other ones may go on and reach the state that they wish to offer a portion. Such a portion from a next producer may also be too large, or it may be smaller and it may fit in the available free space of the buffer.

Somewhat arbitrarily, we impose on our solution the requirement that the producer wishing to offer the larger portion gets priority over the producer wishing to offer the smaller portion to the buffer. (When two or more producers are offering portions that happen to be of the same size we just don't care.)

When a producer has to wait because the buffer cannot accommodate its portion, no other producers can therefore add their portions until further notice: they cannot do so if the new portion is larger (for then it will not fit either), they are not allowed to if the new portion is smaller, for then they have a lower priority and must leave the buffer for the earlier request.

Suppose a moment at which there is a completely filled buffer and three producers, waiting to offer portions of 1, 2, and 3 units respectively. When a consumer now comsumes a five-unit portion the priority rule implies that the producers with the 2-unit portion and the 3-unit portion will get the opportunity to go on and not the one offering the 1-unit portion. It is *not* meant to imply that in that case the 3-unit portion will actually be offered before the 2-unit portion!

We shall now try to introduce so-called "status variables" for the different components of the system, with the aid of which we can characterize the state of the system at any moment. Let us try.

For each producer we introduce a variable named `desire`; this variable will denote the number of buffer units needed for the portion it could not add to the buffer. As this number is always positive, we can attach to `desire = 0` the meaning that no request from this producer is pending. Furthermore, we shall introduce for each producer a private binary `producer semaphore`.

For the buffer we introduce the binary semaphore `bufman`, which takes care of the mutual exclusion of buffer manipulations in the widest sense (i.e. not only the adding to and taking from the buffer but also inspection and modification of the status variables concerned).

Next we need a mechanism to signal the presence of a next portion to the consumers. As soon as a next portion is in the buffer, it can be consumed and as we do not care which of the consumers takes it, we can hope that a general semaphore `number of queuing portions` will do the job. (Note that it counts portions queuing in the buffer and not number of filled information units in the buffer.)

Vacated buffer space must be signalled back to the producers, but the possible consequences of vacating buffer space are more intricate, and we cannot expect that a general semaphore will be adequate. Tentatively we introduce an integer status variable `number of free buffer units`. Note that this variable counts units, not portions.

Remark. The value of `number of free buffer units` will at most be equal to the size of the buffer diminished by the total size of the portions counted in `number of queuing portions`, but it may be less! I refer to the program given in section 4.3; there the sum

```
number of queuing portions + number of empty positions
```

is initially (and usually) = N, but it may be = N − 1, because the P-operation on one of the semaphores always precedes the V-operation on the other. (Verify that in the program of section 4.3 the sum can even be = N − 2 and that this value could even be lower had we had more producers and/or consumers.) Here we may expect the same phenomenon: the semaphore **number of queuing portions** will count the portions actually and completely filled and still unnoticed will count the completely free, unallocated units in the buffer. But the units which have been reserved for filling, which have been granted to a (waiting) producer, without already being filled, will not be counted in either of them.

Finally, we introduce the integer **buffer blocking**, the value of which equals the number of quantities **desire** that are positive. Obviously, this variable is superfluous; it has been introduced as a recognition of one of our earlier remarks, that as soon as one of the desires is positive, no further additions to the buffer can be made, until further notice. At the same time this variable may act as a warning to the consumers, that such a "further notice" is wanted.

We now propose the following program, written for N producers and M consumers. (N, M, **Buffer size**, and all that concerns the buffer is assumed to be declared in the surroundings of this program.)

```
begin integer array desire, producer semaphore[1 : N];
      integer number of queuing portions,
              number of free buffer units,
              buffer blocking, bufman, loop;
      for loop:= 1 step 1 until N do
          begin desire[loop]:= 0;
                producer semaphore[loop]:= 0
          end
      number of queuing portions:= 0 ;
      number of free buffer units:= Buffer size;
      buffer blocking:= 0; bufman:= 1;
      parbegin
      producer 1:
        begin ... end;
          .
          .
          .
      producer n:
         begin integer portion size;
         again n: produce next portion and set portion size;
               P(bufman);
               if buffer blocking = 0 and
                 number of free buffer units >= portion size
                                         then
               number of free buffer units:=
                 number of free buffer units - portion size
                                         else
               begin buffer blocking:= buffer blocking + 1;
                     desire[n]:= portion size; V(bufman);
                     P(producer semaphore[n]); P(bufman) end;
               add portion to buffer; V(bufman);
```

```
                V(number of queuing portions); goto again n
          end;
           .
           .
           .
        producer N:
          begin ... end;
        consumer 1:
          begin ... end;
           .
           .
           .
        consumer m:
         begin integer portion size, n, max, nmax;
         again m: P(number of queuing portions); P(bufman);
              take portion from buffer and set portion size;
              number of free buffer units:=
                number of free buffer units + portion size;
         test: if buffer blocking > 0 then
                  begin max:= 0,
                        for n:= 1 step 1 until N do
                        begin if max < desire[n] then
                          begin max:= desire[n]; nmax:= n
                          end end;
                        if max <=
                           number of free buffer units then
                        begin number of free buffer units:=
                                number of free buffer units
                                - max;
                              desire[nmax]:= 0;
                              buffer blocking:=
                                buffer blocking - 1;
                              V(producer semaphore[nmax]);
                              goto test
                        end
                  end;
                  V(bufman); process portion taken;
                  goto again m
         end;
          .
          .
          .
        consumer M:
         begin ... end
        parend
end
```

In the outermost block the common variables are declared and initialized. This part of the program hopefully presents no difficulties to the reader who has followed me until here.

Let us first try to understand the behaviour of the producer. When it wishes to add a new portion to the buffer there are essentially two cases: either it can do so immediately or not. It can add immediately under the combined condition:

```
buffer blocking = 0 and
  number of free buffer units >= portion size;
```

if so, it will decrease `number of free buffer units` and—dynamically speaking in the same critical section—it will add the portion to the buffer. The two following V-operations (the order of which is immaterial) close the critical section and signal the presence of the next portion to the combined consumers. If it cannot add immediately, i.e. if (either)

```
buffer blocking > 0 or
  number of free buffer units < portion size
```

(or both), then the producer decides to wait, "to go to sleep", and delegates to the combined consumers the task to wake it up again in due time. The fact that it is waiting is coded by `desire[n]` $>$ 0, `buffer blocking` is increased by 1 accordingly. After all clerical operations on the common variables have been carried out the critical section is left (by `V(bufman)`) and the producer initiates a P-operation on its private semaphore. When it has completed this P-operation it re-enters the critical section, merges dynamically with the first case and adds the portion to the buffer. (See also the consumer in the second program of section 4.2, where we have already met the cutting open of a critical section.) Note that in the waiting case the producer has skipped the decrease of `number of free buffer units`. Note also that the producer initiates the P-operation on its private semaphore at a moment that the latter may already be = 1, i.e. this P-operation, again, is only a potential delay.

Let us now inspect whether the combined consumers fulfil the tasks delegated to them. The presence of a next portion is correctly signalled to them via the general semaphore `number of queuing portions` and, as the P-operation on it occurs outside any critical section, there is no danger of consumers not initiating it. After this P-operation the consumer enters its critical section, takes a portion, and increases the number of free buffer units. If `buffer blocking = 0` holds, the following compound statement is skipped completely and the critical section is left immediately; this is correct, for `buffer blocking = 0` means that none of the quantities `desire` is positive, i.e. that none of the producers is waiting for the free space just created in the buffer. If, however, it finds `buffer blocking` $>$ 0 it knows that at least one of the producers has gone to sleep and it will inspect, whether one or more producers have to be woken up. It looks for the maximum value of `desire`. If this is not too large it decides that the corresponding producer has to go on. This decision has three effects:

(a) The `number of free buffer units` is decreased by the number of units desired. Thus we guarantee that the same free space in the buffer cannot be granted to more than one producer. Furthermore, this decrease is in accordance with the producer behaviour.

(b) `Desire` of the producer in question is set to zero; this is correct, for its request has now been granted; buffer blocking is decreased by 1 accordingly.

(c) A V-operation on the producer semaphore concerned wakes the sleeping producer.

After that, control of the consumer returns to `test` to inspect whether more sleeping producers should be woken up. The inspection process can end in one of two ways: either there are no sleeping producers left (`buffer blocking = 0`) or there are still sleeping processes, but the free space is insufficient to accommodate the maximum desire. The final value of `buffer blocking` is correct in both cases. After the waking up of the producers is done the critical section is left.

5.2 An Example of Conversations

In this section we shall discuss a more complicated example, in which one of the co-operating processes is not a machine but a human being, the "operator".

The operator is connected with the processes via a so-called "semi-duplex channel" (say "telex connection"). It is called a duplex channel because it conveys information in either direction: the operator can use a keyboard to type in a message for the processes, the processes can use the teleprinter to type out a message for the operator. It is called a semi-duplex channel, because it can only transmit information in one direction at a time.

Let us now consider the requirements of the total construction, admittedly somewhat simplified yet hopefully sufficiently complicated to pose to us a real problem, yet sufficiently simple so as not to drown the basic pattern of our solution in a host of inessential details.

We have N identical processes (numbered from 1 through N), and essentially they can each ask a single question, called `Q1`, meaning "How shall I go on ?", to which the operator may give one of two possible answers, called `A1` and `A2`. We assume that the operator must know which of the processes is asking the question since his answer might depend on this knowledge and we therefore specify that the `i`th process identifies itself when posing the question; we indicate this by saying that it transmits the question `Q1(i)`. In a sense this is a consequence of the fact that all N processes use the same communication channel.

A next consequence of this channel sharing between the different processes is that no two processes can ask their question simultaneously: behind the scenes some form of mutual exclusion must see to this. If only Q1-questions are mutually exclusive the operator may meet the following situation: a question—say `Q1(3)`—is posed, but before he has decided how to answer it a next question—say, `Q1(7)`—is put to him. Then the single answer `A1` is no longer sufficient, because now it is no longer clear whether this answer is intended for `process 7` or for `process 3`. This could be overcome by adding to the answers the identification of the process concerned, say, `A1(i)` and `A2(i)` with the appropriate value of `i`.

But this is only one way of doing it: an alternative solution is to make the question, followed by its answer, together a critical occurrence: it relieves the operator from the duty to identify the process, and we therefore select the latter arrangement. So we stick to the answers `A1` and `A2`. We have two kinds of conversations `Q1(i), A1` and `Q1(i), A2` with the rule that a next conversation can be initiated only when the previous one has been completed.

We shall now complicate the requirements in three respects.

First, the individual processes may wish to use the communication channel for single-shot messages `M(i)` say which do not require any answer from the operator.

Secondly, we wish to give the operator the possibility to postpone an answer. Of course, he can do so by just not answering, but this would have the undesirable effect that the communication channel remains blocked for the other N − 1 processes. We introduce a next answer `A3`, meaning: "The channel becomes free again, but the conversation with the process concerned remains unfinished." Obviously, the operator must have the opportunity to reopen the conversation again. He can do so via `A4(i)` or `A5(i)`, where `i` runs from 1 through N and identifies the process concerned, where `A4` indicates that the process should continue in the same way as after `A1`, while `A5` prescribes the reaction as to `A2`. Possible forms of conversation are now:

(a) `Q1(i), A1`

(b) `Q1(i), A2`

(c) `Q1(i), A3 - - - A4(i)`

(d) `Q1(i), A3 - - - A5(i)`

As far as process `i` is concerned (a) is equivalent with (c) and (b) is equivalent with (d).

The second-requirement has a profound influence: without it—i.e. only `A1` and `A2` permissible answers—the process of incoming message interpretation can always be subordinate to one of the N processes, viz. the one that has put the question, this can wait for an answer and can act accordingly. We do not know beforehand, however, when the message `A4(i)` or `A5(i)` will arrive, and we cannot delegate its interpretation to the `i`th process, because the discovery that this incoming message is concerned with the `i`th process is part of the message interpretation itself!

Thirdly, A4- and A5-messages must have priority over Q1- and M- messages, i.e. while the communication channel is occupied (in a Q1- or M-message), processes might reach the state that they want to use the channel, but the operator too might come to this conclusion at the same time. As soon as the channel becomes available, we wish that the operator can use it and that, if he so desires, it won't be snatched away by one of the processes. This implies that the operator has a means to express this desire a rudimentary form of input even if the channel itself is engaged in output.

We assume that the operator

(a) can give externally a

`V(incoming message)`

which he can use to announce a message (A1, A2, A3, A4, or A5);

(b) can detect by the machine's reaction, whether his intervention is accepted or ignored.

Remark. The situation is not unlike the school teacher shouting, "Now children, listen!" If this is regarded as a normal message it is nonsensical:

either the children are listening and it is therefore superfluous, or they are not listening and therefore they do not hear it. It is, in fact, a kind of "meta-message", which only tells that a normal message is coming and which should even penetrate if the children are not listening (talking, for instance).

This priority rule may cause the communication channel to be reserved for an announced A4—or A5 message. By the time the operator gets the opportunity to give it the situation or his mood may have changed, and therefore we extend the list of answers with `A6`—the dummy opening—which enables the operator to withhold, on second thoughts, the A4 or A5.

A final feature of the message interpreter is the applicability test. The operator is a human being, and we may be sure that he will make mistakes. The states of the message interpreter are such that at any moment not all incoming messages are applicable; when a message has been rejected as non-applicable the interpreter should return to such a state that the operator can then give the correct version.

Our attack will be along the following lines:

(1) Besides the N processes we introduce another process, called `message interpreter`; this is done because it is difficult to make the interpretation of the messages `A4`, `A5`, and `A6` subordinate to one of the N processes.

(2) Interpretation of a message always implies, besides the message itself, a state of the interpreter. (In the trivial case this is a constant state, viz. the willingness to understand the message.) We have seen that not all incoming messages are acceptable at all times, so our message interpreter will have to have different states. We shall code them via the (common) state variable `comvar`. The private semaphore, which can delay the action of the message interpreter, is the semaphore `incoming message`, already mentioned.

(3) For the N processes we shall introduce an array `procsem` of private semaphores and an array `procvar` of state variables, through which the different processes can communicate with each other, with the message interpreter, and vice versa.

(4) Finally, we introduce a single binary semaphore `mutex` which caters for the mutual exclusion during inspection and/or modification of the common variables.

(5) We shall use the binary semaphore `mutex` only for the purpose just described, and never, say, will `mutex = 0` be used to code that the channel is occupied. Such a convention would be a dead alley in the sense that the technique used would fall into pieces as soon as the N processes would have two channels (and two operators) at their disposal. We aim to make the critical sections, governed by `mutex`, rather short, and we won't shed a tear if some critical section is shorter than necessary.

The above five points are helpful, and in view of our previous experiences they seem a set of reasonable principles. One facet of this subject has been to present a solution along the lines just given and show that it is correct. I would do a better job if I could show as well how such a solution is found. Admittedly any such solution is found by trial and error, but even so, we could try to make the then prevailing guiding principle (in mathematics usually called "The feeling of the genius") somewhat more explicit. For we are still faced with problems:

(a) what structure should we give to the N + 1 processes?

(b) what states should we introduce (i.e. how many possible values should the state variables have and what should be their meanings)?

The problem (both in constructing and in presenting the solution) is that the two points just mentioned are interdependent. For the values of the state variables have only an unambiguous, interpretable meaning, when `mutex = 1` holds, i.e. when none of the processes is inside a critical section, in which these values are subject to change. In other words, the conditions under which the meaning of the state variable values should be applicable is only known when the programs have been constructed, but we can only construct the programs after we know what inspections of and operations on the state variables are to be performed. In my experience, one starts with a rough picture of both programs and state variables, then starts to enumerate the different states and finally tries to build the programs. Then two things may happen: either one finds that one has introduced too many states or one finds that—having overlooked a need for cutting a critical section into parts—one has not introduced enough of them. One modifies the states and then the program, and with luck and care the design process converges. Usually I found myself content with a working solution and did not bother to minimize the number of states introduced.

In my experience it is easier to conceive first the states (these being statically interpretable) and then the programs. In conceiving the states we have to bear three points in mind.

(a) State variables should have a meaning when `mutex` is = 1; on the other hand, a process must leave the critical section before it starts to wait for a private semaphore. We must be very keen on all those points where a process may have to wait for something more complicated than permission to complete `P(mutex)` .

(b) The combined state variables specify the total state of the system. Nevertheless, it helps a great deal if we can regard some state variables as "belonging to that and that process". If some aspect of the total state increases linearly with N it is easier to conceive that part as equally divided among the N processes.

(c) If a process decides to wait on account of a certain (partial) state each process that makes the system leave this partial state should inspect whether on account of this change some waiting process should go on. (This is only a generalization of the principle already illustrated in The Sleeping Barber.)

The first two points are mainly helpful in the conception of the different states, the last one is an aid to make the programs correct.

Let us now try to find a set of appropriate states. We start with the element **`procvar[i]`**, describing the state of process `i`.

```
procvar[i] = 0
```

This we call "the home position". It will indicate that none of the following situations applies, that process `i` does not require any special service from either the message interpreter or one of the other processes.

```
procvar[i] = 1
```

"On account of non-availability of the communication channel, process `i` has decided to wait on its private semaphore." This decision can be taken independently in each process, it is therefore reasonable to represent it in the state of the process. Up till now there is no obvious reason to distinguish between waiting upon availability for a M-message and for a Q1-question, so let us try to do without this distinction.

`procvar[i] = 2`

"Question `Q1(i)` has been answered by `A3`, viz. with respect to process `i` the operator has postponed his final decision." The fact of the postponement must be represented because it can hold for an indefinitely long period of time (observation *a*); it should be regarded as a state variable of the process in question, as it can hold in N-fold (observation *b*). Moreover, `procvar[i] = 2` will act as applicability criterion for the operator messages `A4[i]` and `A5[i]`.

`procvar[i] = 3`

"`Q1[i]` has been answered by `A1` or by `A3 - - - A4[i]`."

`procvar[i] = 4`

"`Q1[i]` has been answered by `A2` or by `A3 - - - A5[i]`."

First of all we remark that it is of no concern to the individual process whether the operator has postponed his final answer or not. The reader may wonder, however, that the answer given is coded in `procvar`, while only one answer is given at a time. The reason is that we do not know how long it will take the individual process to react to this answer: before it has done so, a next process may have received its final answer to the Q1-question.

Let us now try to list the possible states of the communication organisation. We introduce a single variable, called `comvar` to distinguish between these states. We have to bear in mind three different aspects:

(1) availability of the communication possibility for M-messages, Q1-questions, and the spontaneous message of the operator;

(2) acceptability—more general: interpretability—of the incoming messages.

(3) operator priority for incoming messages.

In order not to complicate matters too much at once, we shall start by ignoring the third point. Without operator priority we can see the following states.

`comvar = 0`

"The communication facility is idle", i.e. equally available for both processes and operator. For the processes `comvar = 0` means that the communication facility is available, for the message interpreter it means that an incoming message need not be ignored, but must be of type A4, A5, or A6.

`comvar = 1`

"The communication facility is used for a M-message or a Q1-question." In this period of time the value of `comvar` must be $\neq 0$, because the communication facility is not available for the processes; for the message interpreter it means that incoming messages have to be ignored.

`comvar = 2`

"The communication facility is reserved for an A1-, A2-, or A3-answer." When the M-message has been finished the communication facility becomes available again; after a Q1-question, however, it must remain reserved. During this period, characterized by `comvar = 2`, the message interpreter must know to which process the operator answer applies. At the end of the answer the communication facility becomes again available.

Let us now take the third requirement into consideration. This will lead to a duplication of (certain) states. When `comvar = 0` holds, an incoming message is accepted, when `comvar = 1`, an incoming message must be ignored. This occurrence must be noted down, because at the end of this occupation of the communication facility the operator must get his priority. We can introduce a new state:

`comvar = 3`

"As `comvar = 1` with operator priority requested."

When the transition to `comvar = 3` occurred during a M-message the operator could get his opportunity immediately at the end of it; if, however, the transition to `comvar = 3` took place during a Q1-question the priority can only be given to the operator after the answer to the Q1-question. Therefore, also state 2 is duplicated:

`comvar = 4`

"As `comvar = 2`, with operator priority requested."

Finally, we have the state:

`comvar = 5`

"The communication facility is reserved for, or used upon, instigation of the operator." For the processes this means non-availability, for the message interpreter the acceptability of the incoming messages of type A4, A5, and A6. Usually, these messages will be announced to the message interpreter while `comvar` is $= 0$. If we do not wish that the entire collection and interpretation of these messages is done within the same critical section the message interpreter can break it open. It is then necessary that `comvar` is $\neq 0$. We may try to use the same value 5 for this purpose: for the processes it just means non-availability, while the control of the message interpreter knows very well whether it is waiting for a spontaneous operator message (i.e. "reserved for ...") or interpreting such a message (i.e. "used upon instigation of ...").

Before starting to try to make the program we must bear in mind point *c*: remembering that availability of the communication facility is the great (and only) bottleneck, we must see to it that every process that ceases to occupy the communication facility decides upon its future usage. This occurs in the processes at the end of the M-message (and not so much at the end of the Q1-question, for then the communication facility remains reserved for the answer) and in the message interpreter at the end of each message interpretation.

The proof of the pudding is the eating: let us try whether we can make the program. (In the program the sequence of characters starting with `comment` and up to and including the first semicolon are inserted for explanatory purpose only. In ALGOL 60 such a comment is admitted only immediately after `begin`, but I do not promise to respect this (superfluous) restriction. The following program should be interpreted to be embedded in a universe in which the operator, the communication facility, and the semaphore `incoming message`—initially $= 0$—are defined.)

```
begin integer mutex, comvar, asknum, loop;
      comment The integer "asknum" is a state variable of the
      message interpreter, primarily during interpretation of
      the answers A1, A2, and A3. It is a common variable, as
      its value is set by the asking process;
      integer array procvar, procsem[1 : N];
      for loop:= 1 step 1 until N do
      begin procvar[loop]:= 0; procsem[loop]:= 0 end;
      comvar:= 0; mutex:= 1;
      parbegin
process 1: begin ... end;
                  .
                  .
```

```
process n: begin integer i; comment The integer "i" is a
                 local variable, very much like "loop";
                   .
                   .
                   .
      M message: P(mutex);
                 if comvar = 0 then
                 begin comment When the communication
                       facility is available, it is taken;
                       comvar:= 1; V(mutex) end
                               else
                 begin comment Otherwise the process records
                       itself as dormant and goes to sleep;
                       procvar[n]:= 1; V(mutex);
                       P(procsem[n])
                       comment At the completion of this
                       P-operation, "procsem[n]" will again
                       be = 0, but comvar - still untouched
                       by this process - will be = 1 or = 3;
                 end;
                 send M message;
                 comment Now the process has to analyse
                 whether the operator (first) or one of the
                 other processes should get the communication
                 facility; P(mutex);
                 if comvar = 3 then comvar:= 5
                               else
                 begin comment Otherwise "comvar = 1" will
                       hold and process n has to look whether
                       one of the other processes is waiting.
                       Note that "procvar[n] = 0" holds;
                       for i:= 1 step 1 until N do
                       begin if procvar[i] = 1 then
                             begin procvar[i]:= 0;
                                   V(procsem[i]); goto ready
                             end
                       end;
                       comvar:= 0
                 end
          ready: V(mutex);
                 .
                 .
                 .
    Q1 Question: P(mutex);
                 if comvar = 0 then
                 begin comvar:= 1; V(mutex) end
                               else
                 begin procvar[n]:= 1; V(mutex);
                       P(procsem[n])
                 end;
```

```
                  comment This entry is identical to that of
                  the M message. Note that we are out of the
                  critical section, nevertheless this process
                  will set "asknum". It can do so safely, for
                  neither another process nor the message
                  interpreter will access "asknum" as long as
                  "comvar = 1" holds;
                  asknum:= n, send question Q1(n);
                  P(mutex);
                  comment "comvar" will be = 1 or = 3;
                  if comvar = 1 then comvar:= 2
                                else comvar:= 4;
                  V(mutex); P(procsem[n]);
                  comment After completion of this
                  P-operation, procvar[n] will be = 3 or = 4.
                  This process can now inspect and reset its
                  procvar, although we are outside a critical
                  section;
                  if procvar[n] = 3 then Reaction 1
                                     else Reaction 2;
                  procvar[n]:= 0;
                  comment This last assignment is
                  superfluous;
                  .
                  .
                  .
              end;
              .
              .
              .
process N: begin ... end;
message interpreter:
              begin integer i;
              wait: P(incoming message);
                    P(mutex);
                    if comvar = 1 then comvar:= 3;
                    if comvar = 3 then
                    begin comment The message interpreter
                          ignores the incoming message, but in
                          due time the operator will get the
                          opportunity;
                          V(mutex); goto wait end;
                    if comvar = 2 or comvar = 4 then
                    begin comment Only A1, A2 and A3 are
                          admissible. The interpretation of the
                          message need not be done inside a
                          critical section;
                          V(mutex);
                          interpretation of the message coming
                          in;
                          if message = A1 then
```

```
                      begin procvar[asknum]:= 3;
                            V(procsem[asknum]);
                            goto after correct answer end;
                      if message = A2 then
                      begin procvar[asknum]:= 4;
                            V(procsem[asknum]);
                            goto after correct answer end;
                      if message = A3 then
                      begin procvar[asknum]: = 2;
                            goto after correct answer end;
                      comment The operator has given an
                      erroneous answer and should repeat the
                      message; goto wait;
  after correct answer: P(mutex);
                      if comvar = 4 then
                      begin comment The operator should now
                            get his opportunity;
                            comvar:= 5; V(mutex); goto wait
                      end;
perhaps comvar to zero:for i:= 1 step 1 until N do
                      begin if procvar[i] = 1 then
                            begin procvar[i]:= 0;
                                  comvar:= 1;
                                  V(procsem[i]); goto ready
                            end
                      end;
                      comvar:= 0;
               ready: V(mutex); goto wait
                end;
                comment The cases "comvar = 0" and
                "comvar = 5" remain.
                Messages A4, A5, and A6 are admissible;
                if comvar = 0 then comvar:= 5;
                comment See Remark 1 after the program;
                V(mutex);
                interpretation of the message coming in;
                P(mutex);
                if message = A4[process number] then
                begin i:= process number given in the
                          message;
                      if procvar[i] = 2 then
                      begin procvar[i]:= 3; V(procsem[i]);
                            goto perhaps comvar to zero end;
                      comment Otherwise process not waiting
                      for postponed answer;
                      goto wrong message
                end;
                if message = A5[process number] then
                begin i:= process number given in the
                          message;
                      if procvar[i] = 2 then
```

```
                                  begin procvar[i]:= 4; V(procsem[i]);
                                        goto perhaps comvar to zero end;
                                  comment Otherwise process not waiting
                                  for postponed answer;
                                  goto wrong message
                            end;
                            if message = A6 then
                            goto perhaps comvar to zero;
         wrong message:     comment "comvar = 5" holds, giving priority
                            to the operator to repeat his message;
                            V(mutex); goto wait
                    end
              parend
        end
```

Remark 1. If the operator, while comvar = 0 or comvar = 5 originally holds, gives an uninterpretable (or inappropriate) message the communication facility will remain reserved for his next trial.

Remark 2. The final interpretation of the A4 and A5 messages is done within the critical section, as their admissibility depends on the state of the process concerned. If we have only one communication channel and one operator this precaution is rather superfluous.

Remark 3. The for-loops in the program scan the processes in order, starting at process 1; by scanning them cyclically, starting at an arbitrary process (selected by means of a (pseudo) random number generator), we could have made the solution more symmetrical in the N processes.

Remark 4. In this section we have first presented a rather thorough exploration of the possible states and then the program. The reader might be interested to know that this is the true picture—"a live recording"— of the birth of this solution. When I started to write this section the problem posed was as new to me as it was to the reader: the program given is my first version, constructed on account of the considerations and explorations given. I hope that this section may thus give a hint as to how one may find such solutions.

5.2.1 Improvements of the Previous Program

In Section 5.2 we have given a first version of the program; this version has been included in the text, not because we are satisfied with it but because its inclusion completes the picture of the birth of a solution. Let us now try to embellish, in the name of greater conciseness, clarity, and, may be, efficiency. Let us try to discover in what respects we have made a mess of it.

Let us compare the information flows from a process to the message interpreter, and vice versa. In the one direction we have the common variable `asknum` to tell the message interpreter which process is asking the question. The setting and the inspection of `asknum` can safely take place outside the critical sections, governed by `mutex`, because at any moment at most one of the N + 1 processes will try to access `asknum`. In the inverse information flow, where the message interpreter has to signal back to the `i`th process the nature of the final operator answer, this answer is coded in `procvar`. This is mixing things up, as is shown:

(a) by the `procvar`-inspection (whether `procvar` is = 3 or = 4), which is suddenly allowed to take place outside a critical section;

(b) by the superfluity of its being reset to zero.

The suggestion is to introduce a new

```
integer array operanswer[1 : N]
```

the elements of which will be used in a similar fashion as `asknum`. (An attractive consequence is that the number of possible values of `procvar`— the more fundamental quantity (see below) will no longer increase with the number of possible answers to the question Q1.)

I should like to investigate whether we can achieve a greater clarity by separating the common variables into two (or perhaps more?) distinct groups, in order to reflect an observable hierarchy in the way in which they are used. Let us try to order them in terms of "basicness".

The semaphore `incoming message` seems at first sight a fairly basic one, being defined by the surrounding universe. This is, however, an illusion: within the parallel compound we should have programmed (as the N + 2nd process) the operator himself, and the semaphore `incoming message` is the private semaphore for the message interpreter just as `procsem[i]` is for the ith process.

Thus the most basic quantity is the semaphore `mutex` taking care of the mutual exclusion of the critical sections.

Then come the state variables `comvar` and `procvar`, which are inspected and can be modified within the critical sections.

The quantities just mentioned share the property that their values must be set before entering the parallel compound. This property is also shared by the semaphores `procsem` (and `incoming message`, see above) if we stick to the rules that parallel statements will access common semaphores via P- and V-operations exclusively.

(Without this restriction, request for the communication facility by `process n` could start with:

```
P(mutex);
if comvar = 0 then
begin comvar:= 1; V(mutex) end
              else
begin procvar[n]:= 1; procsem[n]:= 0;
      V(mutex); P(procsem[n]) end
```

We reject this solution on the further observation that the assignment `procsem[n]` is void, except for the first time that it is executed; the initialization of procsem's outside the parallel compound seems therefore appropriate.)

For the common variables listed thus far I should like to reserve the name "status variables", to distinguish them from the remaining ones, **asknum** and **operanswer**, which I should like to call "transmission variables".

The latter are called "transmission variables" because, whenever one of the processes assigns a value to such a variable, the information just stored is destinated for a well-known "receiving party". They are used to transmit information between well-known parties.

Let us now turn our attention from the common variables towards the programs. Within the programs we have learnt to distinguish the so-called "critical sections" for which the semaphores `mutex` caters for the mutual exclusion. Besides these, we can distinguish regions in which relevant actions occur, such as:

In the ith Process

Region 1:	sending an M-message
Region 2:	sending a Q1(i)-question
Region 3:	reacting to operanswer[i] (This region is somewhat openended).

In the Message Interpreter

Region 4:	ignoring incoming messages
Region 5:	expecting A1, A2, or A3
Region 6:	expecting A4(i), A5(i), or A6.

We come now to the following picture. In the programs we have critical sections, mutually excluded by the semaphore `mutex`. The purpose of the critical sections is to resolve any ambiguity in the inspection and modification of the remaining state variables, inspection and modification performed for the purpose of more intricate "sequencing patterns" of the regions. These sequencing patterns make the unambiguous use of the transmission variables possible. (If one process has to transmit information to another it can now do so via a transmission variable, provided that the execution of the assigning region is always followed by that of the inspecting region before that of the next assigning region.)

In the embellished version of the program we shall stick to the rule that the true state variables will only be accessed in critical sections (if they are not semaphores) or via P- and V-operations (if they are semaphores), while the transmission variables will only be accessed in the regions. (In more complicated examples this rule might prove too rigid, and duplication might be avoided by allowing transmission variables to be inspected at least within the critical section. In this example, however, we shall observe the rule.)

The remaining program improvements are less fundamental.

Coding will be smoothed if we represent the fact of requested operator priority not by additional values of `comvar` but by an additional two-valued state variable:

```
Boolean operator priority
```

(Quantities of type `Boolean` can take on the two values denoted by **`true`** and **`false`** respectively, viz. they have the same domain as "conditions" such as we have met in the if-clause.)

Furthermore we shall introduce two procedures; they are declared outside the compound and therefore at the disposal of the different constituents of the parallel compound.

We shall first give a short description of the new meanings of the values of the state variables `procvar` and `comvar`:

`procvar[i] = 0`	home position
`procvar[i] = 1`	waiting for availability of the communication facility for M or Q1(i)
`procvar[i] = 2`	waiting for the answer `A4(i)` or `A5(i)`.
`comvar = 0`	home position (communication facility free)
`comvar = 1`	communication facility for M or Q1
`comvar = 2`	communication facility for A1, A2, or A3
`comvar = 3`	communication facility for A4, A5, or A6.

We give the program without comments, and shall do so in two stages:

first the program outside the parallel compound and then the constituents of the parallel compound.

```
begin integer mutex, comvar, asknum, loop;
      Boolean operator priority;
      integer array procvar, procsem, operanswer[1: N];
      procedure M or Q entry(u); value u; integer u;
      begin P(mutex);
            if comvar = 0 then
            begin comvar:= 1; V(mutex) end
                          else
            begin procvar[u]:= 1; V(mutex); P(procsem[u]) end
      end;
      procedure select new comvar value;
      begin integer i;
            if operator priority then
            begin operator priority:= false; comvar:= 3 end
                                 else
            begin for i:= 1 step 1 until N do
                  begin if procvar[i] = 1 then
                        begin procvar[i]:= 0; comvar:= 1;
                              V(procsem[i]); goto ready end
                  end;
                  comvar:= 0;
    ready: end
      end;
      for loop:= 1 step 1 until N do
            begin procvar[loop]:= 0; procsem[loop]:= 0 end,
      comvar:= 0; mutex:= 1; operator priority:= false;
      parbegin
      process 1: begin ... end;
                  .
                  .
                  .
      process N: begin ... end;
      message interpreter:
                 begin ... end
      parend
end
```

Here the nth process will be of the form

```
process n:   begin
               .
               .
               .
M message:   M or Q entry(n);
Region 1:    send M message;
             P(mutex); select new comvar value; V(mutex);
               .
               .
```

```
Q1 question: M or Q entry(n);
Region 2:    asknum:= n;
             send Q1(n);
             P(mutex); comvar:= 2; V(mutex); P(procsem[n])
Region 3:    if operanswer[n] = 1 then Reaction 1
                                  else Reaction 2;

             end
```

When the message interpreter decides to enter Region 6 it copies, before doing so, the array `procvar`: if an answer A4(i) should be acceptable, then `procvar[i] = 2` should already hold at the moment of announcement of the answer.

Message Interpreter:

```
    begin integer i; integer array pvcopy[1: N];
wait:     P(incoming message); P(mutex);
          if comvar = 1 then
Region 4: begin operator priority:= true;
leave:          V(mutex); goto wait end;
          if comvar <> 2 then goto Region 6;
Region 5: V(mutex); collect message;
          if message <> A1 and message <> A2
          and message <> A3 then goto wait;
          i:= asknum;
          if message = A1 then operanswer[i]:= 1 else
          if message = A2 then operanswer[i]:= 2;
          P(mutex);
          if message = A3 then procvar[i]:= 2 else
signal to i: V(procsem[i]);
preleave: select new comvar value; goto leave;
Region 6: if comvar = 0 then comvar:= 3;
          for i:= 1 step 1 until N do pvcopy[i]:= procvar[i];
          V(mutex); collect message;
          if message = A6 then
          begin P(mutex); goto preleave end;
          if message <> A4(process number)
          and message <> A5(process number) then goto wait;
          i:= process number given in the message;
          if pvcopy[i] <> 2 then goto wait;
          operanswer[i]:= if message = A4 then 1 else 2;
          P(mutex); procvar[i]:= 0; goto signal to i
end
```

As an exercise we leave to the reader the version in which pending requests for Q1-questions have priority over those for M-messages. As a next extension we suggest a two-console configuration with the additional restriction that an A4- or A5-message is only acceptable via the console over which the conversation has been initiated. (Otherwise we have to exclude simultaneous, contradictory messages `A4(i)` and `A5(i)` via the two different consoles. The solution without this restriction is left to the really fascinated reader.)

5.2.2 Proving the Correctness

In this section title I have used the word "proving" in an informal way. I have not defined what formal conditions must be satisfied by a "legal proof", and I do not intend to do so. When I can find a way to discuss the program of Section 5.2.1, by which I can convince myself of—and hopefully anybody else that takes the trouble of doubting!—the correctness of the overall performance of this aggregate of processes I am satisfied.

In the following "state picture" we make a diagram of all the states in which a process may find itself "for any considerable length of time", i.e. outside sections critical to mutex. The arrows describe the transitions taking place within the critical sections; accompanying these arrows, we give the modifications of comvar or the conditions under which the transition from one state to another is made.

Calling the neutral region of a process before entry into a Region 1 or Region 2, `Region 0`, we can give the state picture

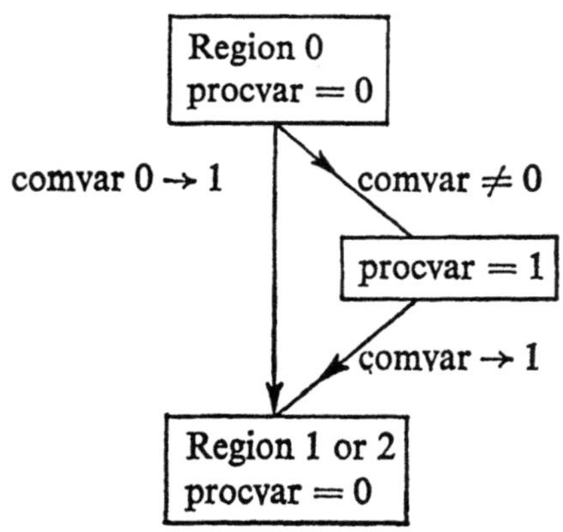

Leaving Region 1 can be pictured as:

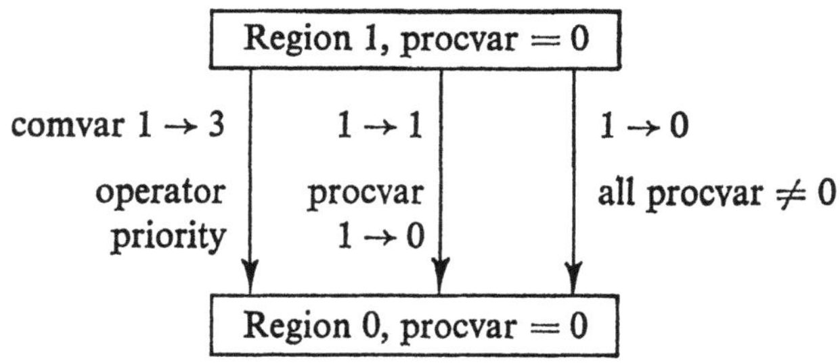

Leaving Region 2, with the possibility of a delayed answer, can be pictured as:

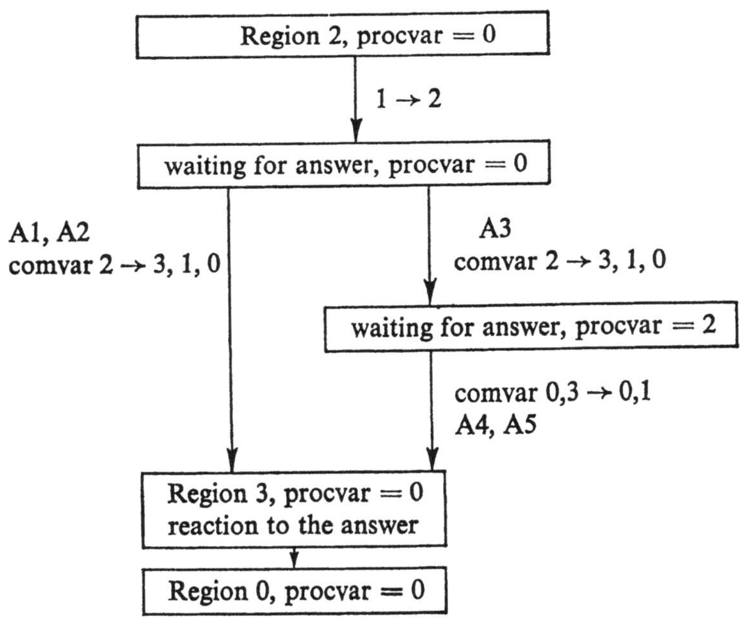

We can try to do the same for the message interpreter. Here we indicate along the arrows the relevant occurrences, such as changes of a procvar and the kind of message. We use `WIM` as abbreviation for "Waiting for Incoming Message".

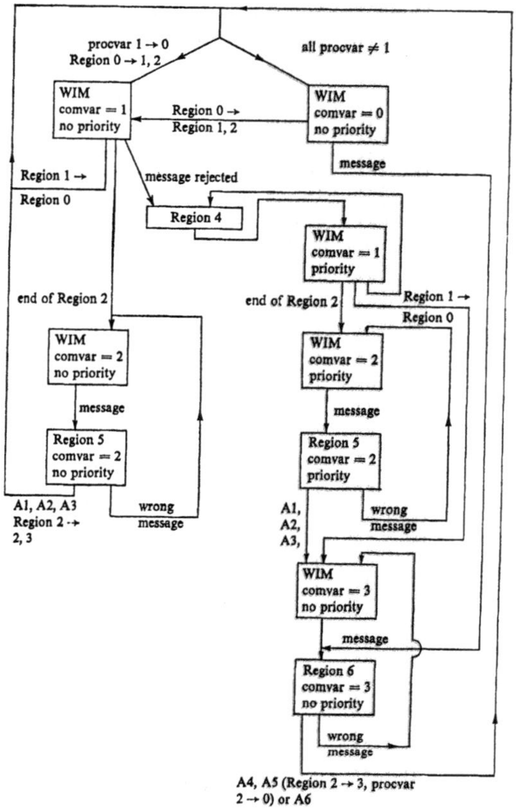

These diagrams, of course, tell us nothing new, but they may be a powerful aid to program inspection.

We verify first that `comvar = 0` represents indeed the home position of the communication facility, i.e. its availability either for entrance into Region 1 or Region 2 (by one of the processes) or for entrance into Region 6 (by the message interpreter, as result of an incoming message for which it is waiting).

If `comvar = 0` and one of the processes wants to enter Region 1 or Region 2, or a message comes from the operator, Region 1, 2, or 6 is entered; furthermore, this entrance is accompanied by either `comvar:= 1` or `comvar:= 3`, and in this way care is taken of the mutual exclusion of the Regions 1, 2, and 6.

The mutual exclusion implies that processes may fail to enter Region 1 or 2 immediately, or that an incoming message must be rejected when it comes at an inacceptable moment. In the first case the process sets `procvar:= 1`, in the second case (in Region 4) the message interpreter sets `operator priority:= true`.

These assignments are performed only under the condition `comvar <> 0`; furthermore, the assignment `comvar:= 0`—only occurring in the procedure `select new comvar value`—is only performed provided "non-operator priority and all procvar ≠ 1". From these two observations and the initial values we can conclude:

`comvar = 0` excludes `operator priority` as well as the occurrence of one or more `procvar = 1`.

Since all ways of ceasing to occupy the communication facility (i.e. the end of Region 1, 5, and 6) call `select new comvar value`, we have established:

(a) that entrance into the Region 1, 2, and 6 is only delayed if necessary;

(b) that such a delay is guaranteed to end at the earliest opportunity.

The structure of the message interpreter shows clearly that:

(a) it can execute Region 5 only if `comvar = 2`

(b) it can only execute Region 5 if `comvar = 2`

(c) execution of Region 5 is the only way to make `comvar` again ≠ 2.

The only assignment `comvar:= 2` occurs at the end of Region 2. As a result, each Region 2 can be followed only by a Region 5 and, conversely, each Region 5 must be preceded by a Region 2. This sequencing allows us to use the transmission variable `asknum`, which is set in Region 2 and inspected in Region 5.

For the uses of the transmission variables `operanswer` an analogous analysis can be made. Region 2 will be followed by Region 5 (see above); if here the final answer (Al or A2) is interpreted, `operanswer[i]` is set before `V(procsem[i])`, so that the transmission variable has been set properly before the process can (and will) enter Region 3, where its `operanswer` will be inspected. If in Region 5 the answer A3 is detected, the message interpreter sets `procvar[i]:= 2` for this process, thus allowing the answer A4 or A5 for this process exactly *once* in Region 6. Again `V(procsem[i])` is performed only after the assignment to `operanswer`. Thus we have verified that:

(a) `operanswer` is only set once by the message interpreter after a request in Region 2;

(b) this `operanswer` will only be inspected in the following Region 3 after the request to set it has been fulfilled (in Region 5 or Region 6).

This completes the analysis of the soundness of the use of the transmission variables `operanswer`.

Inspection of the message interpreter (particularly the scheme of its states) shows:

(a) that a rejected message (Region 4) sooner or later is bound to give rise to Region 6;

(b) that wrong messages are ignored, giving the operator the opportunity of correction.

By the above analysis we hope to have created sufficient confidence in the correctness of our construction. The analysis followed the steps already hinted at in section 5.2.1: after creation of the critical sections (with the aid of `mutex`) the latter are used to sequence Regions properly, thanks to which sequencing the transmission variables can be used unambiguously.

6 THE PROBLEM OF THE DEADLY EMBRACE

In the introductory part of this section I shall draw attention to a rather logical problem that arises in the co-operation between various processes when they have to share the same facilities. We have selected this problem for various reasons. First, it arises by a straightforward extension of the sound principle that no two persons should use a single compartment of a revolving door simultaneously. Secondly, its solution, which I regard as non-trivial and which will be given in Section 6.1, gives us a nice example of more subtle co-operation rules than we have met before. Thirdly, it gives us the opportunity to illustrate (in Section 6.2) a programming technique by which a further gain in clarity can be achieved.

Let me first give an example of the kind of facility-sharing I have in mind.

As "processes" we might take "programs", describing some computational process to be performed by a computer. Execution of such a computational process takes time, during which information must be stored in the computer. We restrict ourselves to those processes of which is known in advance:

(1) that their demand on storage space will not exceed a certain limit, and

(2) that each computational process will end, provided that storage space requested by the process will be put at its disposal. The ending of the computational process will imply that its demand on storage space will reduce to zero.

We assume that the available store has been subdivided into fixed-size "pages" which, from the point of view of the programs, can be regarded as equivalent.

The actual demand on storage space needed by a process may be a function varying in time as the process proceeds—subject, of course, to the *a priori* known upper bound. We assume that the individual processes request from and return to "available store" in single page units. By "equivalence" (see the last word of the previous paragraph) is meant that a process requiring a new page only asks for "a new page" but never for a special one nor one out of a special group.

We now request that a process, once initiated, will—sooner or later—get the opportunity to complete its action and reject any organization in which it may happen that a process may have to be killed half-way through its activity, thereby throwing away the computation time already invested in it.

If the computer has to perform the different processes one after the other the only condition that must be satisfied by a process is that its maximum demand does not exceed the total storage capacity.

If, however, the computer can serve more than one process simultaneously one can adhere to the rule that one only admits programs as long as the sum of their maximum demands does not exceed the total storage capacity. This rule, safe though it is, is unnecessarily restrictive, for it means that each process effectively occupies its maximum demand during the complete time of its execution. When we consider the following table (in which we regard the processes as "borrowing" pages from available store)

Process	Maximum demand	Present loan	Further claim
P1	80	40	40
P2	60	20 +	40
	Available store = 100 − 60 = 40		

(a total store of 100 pages is assumed), we have a situation in which is still nothing wrong. If, however, both processes request their next page, and if they should both get it, we should get the following situation:

Process	Maximum demand	Present loan	Further claim
P1	80	41	39
P2	60	21 +	39

Available store = 100 − 62 = 38

This is an unsafe situation, for both processes might want to realize their full further claim before returning a single page to available store. So each of them may first need a further 39 pages, while there are only 38 available.

This situation, when one process can continue only provided the other one is killed first, is called "The Deadly Embrace". The problem to be solved is: how can we avoid the danger of the Deadly Embrace without being unnecessarily restrictive.

6.1 The Banker's Algorithm

A banker has a finite capital expressed in florins. He is willing to accept customers, that may borrow florins from him on the following conditions:

1. The customer makes the loan for a transaction that will be completed in a finite period of time.
2. The customer must specify in advance his maximum "need" for florins for this transaction.
3. As long as the "loan" does not exceed the "need" stated in advance, the customer can increase or decrease his loan florin by florin.
4. A customer when asking for an increase in his current loan undertakes to accept without complaint the answer "If I gave you the florin you ask for you would not exceed your stated need, and therefore you are entitled to a next florin. At present, however, it is somewhat inconvenient for me to pay you, but I promise you the florin in due time."
5. His guarantee that this moment will indeed arrive is founded on the banker's cautiousness and the fact that his co-customers are subject to the same condition as he: that as soon as a customer has got the florin he asked for he will proceed with his transactions at a non-zero speed, i.e. within a finite period of time he will ask for a next florin or will return a florin or will finish the transaction, which implies that his complete loan has been returned (florin by florin).

The primary questions are:

(a) under which conditions can the banker enter into contract with a new customer?

(b) under which conditions can the banker pay a (next) florin to a requesting customer without running into the danger of the Deadly Embrace?

The answer to question (a) is simple: he can accept any customer, whose stated need does not exceed the banker's capital.

In order to answer question (b), we introduce the following terminology.

The banker has a fixed `capital` at his disposal; each new customer states in advance his maximum `need` and for each customer will hold

`need[i]` $\leq$ `capital` (for all `i`).

The current situation for each customer is characterized by his `loan`. Each loan is initially $= 0$ and shall satisfy at any instant

$0 \leq$ `loan[i]` $\leq$ `need[i]` (for all `i`).

A useful quantity to be derived from this is the maximum further `claim`, given by

`claim[i] = need[i] - loan[i]` (for all `i`).

Finally, the banker notes the amount in `cash`, given by

`cash = capital - sum of the loans`

Obviously

$0 \leq$ `cash` $\leq$ `capital`

has to hold.

In order to decide whether a requested florin can be paid to the customer, the banker essentially inspects the situation that would arise if he had paid it. If this situation is "safe", then he pays the florin, if the situation is not "safe" he has to say: "Sorry, but you have to wait."

Inspection whether a situation is safe amounts to inspecting whether all customer transactions can be guaranteed to be able to finish. The algorithm starts to investigate whether at least one customer has a claim not exceeding cash. If so, this customer can complete his transactions, and therefore the algorithm investigates the remaining customers as if the first one had finished and returned its complete loan. Safety of the situation means that all transactions can be finished, i.e. that the banker sees a way of getting all his money back.

If the customers are numbered from 1 through N the routine inspecting a situation can be written as follows:

```
integer free money; Boolean safe;
Boolean array finish doubtful[1 : N];
   free money:= cash;
   for i:= 1 step 1 until N do finish doubtful[i]:= true;
L: for i:= 1 step 1 until N do
   begin if finish doubtful[i] and claim[i] <= free money
            then
         begin finish doubtful[il:= false;
               free money:= free money + loan[i]; goto L
         end
   end;
   if free money = capital then safe:= true else safe:= false
```

The above routine inspects any situation. An improvement of the Algorithm has been given by L. Zwanenburg, who takes into account that the only situations to be investigated are those, where, starting from a safe situation, a florin has been tentatively given to `customer[i]`. As soon as `finish doubtful[i]:= false` can be executed the algorithm can decide directly on safety of the situation, for then clearly this attempted payment was reversible. This short cut will be implemented in the program in the next section.

6.2 The Banker's Algorithm Applied

In this example also the florins are processes. (Each florin, say, represents the use of a magnetic tape deck; the loan of a florin is then the permission to use one of the tape decks.)

We assume that the customers are numbered from 1 through N and that the florins are numbered from 1 through M. Each customer has a variable `florin number` in which, after each granting of a florin, it can find the number of the florin it has just borrowed; also each florin has a variable `customer number` in which it can find by which customer it has been borrowed.

Each customer has a state variable `cusvar`, where `cusvar = 1` means "I am anxious to borrow." (otherwise `cusvar = 0`); each florin has a state variable `flovar`, where `flovar = 1` means "I am anxious to get borrowed, i.e. I am in cash." (otherwise `flovar = 0`). Each customer has a binary semaphore **cussem**, each florin has a binary semaphore **flosem**, which will be used in the usual manner.

We assume that each florin is borrowed and returned upon customer indication, but that he cannot return a borrowed florin immediately. After the customer has indicated that he has no further use for this florin the florin may not be instantaneously available for subsequent use. It is as if the customer can say to a borrowed florin "run home to the banker". The actual loan will only be ended after the florin has indeed returned to cash: it will signal its return into the banker's cash to the customer from which it came via a customer semaphore **florin returned**. A P-operation on this semaphore should guard the customer against an inadvertent overdraft. Before each florin request the customer will perform a P-operation on its **florin returned**; the initial value of **florin returned** will be = **need**.

We assume that the constant integers N and M (= **capital**) and the constant integer array **need** are declared and defined in the universe in which the following program is embedded.

The procedure **try to give to** is made into a Boolean procedure, the value of which indicates whether a delayed request for a florin has been granted. In the florin program it is exploited that returning a florin may at most give rise to a single delayed request to be granted now. (If more than one type of facility is shared under control of the banker this will no longer hold. Jumping out of the for loop to the statement labelled **leave** at the end of the florin program is then not permissible.)

```
begin integer array loan, claim, cussem, cusvar,
                    florin number, florin returned[1 : N],
                    flosem, flovar, customer number[1 : M];
      integer mutex, cash, k;
      Boolean procedure try to give to (j); value j;
      integer j;
      begin if cusvar[j] = 1 then
            begin integer i, free money;
                  Boolean array finish doubtful[1 : N];
                  free money:= cash - 1;
                  claim[j]:= claim[j] - 1;
                  loan[j]:= loan[j] + 1;
                  for i:= 1 step 1 until N do
                    finish doubtful[i]:= true;
              L0: for i:= 1 step 1 until N do
                  begin if finish doubtful[i]
                        and claim[i] <= free money then
                        begin if i <> j then
                              begin
                                finish doubtful[i]:= false;
```

```
                                      free money:=
                                        free money + loan[i];
                                      goto L0
                                    end
                                              else
                                    begin comment Here more
                                          sophisticated ways for
                                          selecting a free florin
                                          may be implemented;
                                          i:= 0;
                                      L1: i:= i + 1;
                                          if flovar[i] = 0 then
                                          goto L1;
                                          florin number[j]:= i;
                                          customer number[i]:= j;
                                          cusvar[j]:= 0;
                                          flovar[i]:= 0;
                                          cash:= cash - 1;
                                          try to give to:= true;
                                          V(cussem[j]);
                                          V(flosem[i]);
                                          goto L2
                                    end
                               end
                          end;
                          claim[j]:= claim[j] + 1;
                          loan[j]:= loan[j] - 1
                     end;
                     try to give to:= false;
  L2: end,
      mutex:= 1; cash:= M;
      for k:= 1 step 1 until N do
      begin loan[k]:= 0; cussem[k]:= 0; cusvar[k]:= 0;
           claim[k]:= need[k]; florin returned[k]:= need[k]
      end;
      for k:= 1 step 1 until M do
      begin flosem[k]:= 0; flovar[k]:= 1 end;
      parbegin
customer 1: begin ... end;
                .
                .
                .
customer N: begin ... end;
florin 1:   begin ... end;
                .
                .
                .
florin M:   begin ... end
      parend
end
```

In customer n the request for a new florin consists of the following sequence of statements:

```
P(florin returned[n]);
P(mutex);
cusvar[n]:= 1; try to give to (n);
V(mutex);
P(cussem[n]);
```

after completion of the last statement `florin number[n]` gives the identity of the florin just borrowed, the customer has the opportunity to use it and the duty to return it in due time to the banker.

The structure of a florin is as follows:

```
florin m:
begin integer h;
start: P(flosem[m]);
       comment Now customer number[m] identifies the
       customer that has borrowed it. The florin can serve
       that customer until it has finished the task required
       from it during this loan. To return itself to the
       cash, the florin proceeds as follows;
       P(mutex);
       claim[customer number[m]]:=
            claim[customer number[m]] + 1;
       loan[customer number[m]]:=
            loan[customer number[m]] - 1;
       flovar[m]:= 1; cash:= cash + 1;
       V(florin returned[customer number[m]]);
       for h:= 1 step 1 until N do
            begin if try to give to(h) then goto leave end;
leave: V(mutex);
       goto start
end
```

Remark. Roughly speaking, a successful loan can take place only when two conditions are satisfied: the florin must be requested and the florin must be available. In this program the mechanism of `cusvar` and `cussem` is also used (by the customer) when the requested florin is immediately available, likewise the mechanism of `flovar` and `flosem` is also used (by the florin) if, after its return to `cash`, it can immediately be borrowed again by a waiting customer. This programming technique has been suggested by C. Ligtmans and P.A. Voorhoeve, and I mention it because in the case of more intricate rules of co-operation it has given rise to a simplification that proved to be indispensable. The underlying cause of this increase in simplicity is that the dynamic way through the topological structure of the program no longer distinguishes between an actual delay or not, just as in the case of the P-operation itself.

7 CONCLUDING REMARKS

In the literature one sometimes finds a sharp distinction between "concurrent programming"—more than one central processor operating on the same job—and "multi-programming"—a single processor dividing its time between different jobs. I have always felt that this distinction was rather artificial and therefore confusing. In both cases we have, macroscopically speaking, a number of sequential processes that have to co-operate with each other, and our discussions on this co-operation apply equally well to "concurrent programming" as to "multi-programming" or any mixture of the two. What in concurrent programming is spread out in space (e.q. equipment) is in multi-programming spread out in time: the two present themselves as different implementations of the same logical structure, and I regard the development of a tool to describe and form such structures themselves, i.e. independent of these implementational differences, as one of the major contributions of the work from which this monograph has been born. As a specific example of this unifying train of thought I should like to mention—for those that are only meekly interested in multi-processors, multi-programming, and the like—the complete symmetry between a normal sequential computer, on the one hand, and its peripheral gear, on the other (as displayed, for instance, in Section 4.3: "The Bounded Buffer").

Finally, I should like to express, once more, my concern about the correctness of programs, because I am not too sure whether all of it is duly reflected in what I have written.

If I suggest methods by which we could try to attain a greater security, then this is, of course, more psychology than, say, mathematics. I have the feeling that for the human mind it is just terribly hard to think in terms of processing evolving in time and that our greatest aid in controlling them is by attaching meanings to the values of identified quantities. For instance, in the program section

```
    i:= 10;
L0: x:= sqrt(x); i:= i - 1;
    if i > 0 then goto L0
```

we conclude that the operation `x:= sqrt(x)` is repeated ten times, but I have the impression that we can do so by attaching to `i` the meaning of "the number of times that the operation `x:= sqrt(x)` still has to be repeated". But we should be aware of the fact that such a timeless meaning (a statement of fact or relation) is not permanently correct: immediately after the execution of `x:= sqrt(x)` but before that of the subsequent `i:= i - 1` the value of `i` is "one more than the number of times that the operation `x:= sqrt(x)` still has to be repeated". In other words, we have to specify at what stages of the process such a meaning is applicable and, of course, it must be applicable in every situation where we rely on this meaning in the reasoning that convinces us of the desired overall performance of the program.

In purely sequential programming, as in the above example, the regions of applicability of such meanings are usually closely connected with places in the program text (if not, we have just a tricky and probably messy program). In multi-programming we have seen in particular in Section 5.2.1 that it is a worth-while effort to create such regions of applicability of meaning very consciously. The recognition of the hierarchical difference between the presence of a message and the message itself, here forced upon us, might give a clue even to clearer uniprogramming.

For example, if I am married to one out of ten wives, numbered from 1 through 10, this fact may be represented by the value of a variable `wife number` associated with me. If I may also be single it is a commonly used programmer's device to code the state of the bachelor as an eleventh value, say `wife number = 0`. The meaning of the value of this variable then becomes "If my wife number is = 0, then I am single, otherwise it gives the number of my wife". The moral is that the introduction of a separate Boolean variable `married` might have been more honest.

We know that the von Neumann-type machine derives its power and flexibility from the fact that it treats all words in store on the same footing. It is often insufficiently realized that, thereby, it gives the user the duty to impose structure wherever recognizable.

Sometimes it is. It has often been quoted as The Great Feature of the von Neumann-type machine that it can modify its own instructions, but most modern algorithmic translators, however, create an object program that remains in its entire execution phase just as constant as the original source text. Instead of chaotically modifying its own instructions just before or after their execution, creation of instructions and execution of these instructions now occur in different sequenced regions: the translation phase and the execution phase. And this for the benefit of us all.

It is my firm belief that in each process of any complexity the variables occurring in it admit analogous hierarchical orderings, and that when these hierarchies are clearly recognizable in the program text the gain in clarity of the program and in effiiciency of the implementation will be considerable. If this chapter gives any reader a clearer indication of what kind of hierarchical ordering can be expected to be relevant I have reached one of my goals. And may we not hope that a confrontation with the intricacies of Multiprogramming gives us a clearer understanding of what Uniprogramming is all about?

2

THE STRUCTURE OF THE "THE" MULTIPROGRAMMING SYSTEM

EDSGER W. DIJKSTRA

(1968)

A multiprogramming system is described in which all activities are divided over a number of sequential processes. These sequential processes are placed at various hierarchical levels, in each of which one or more independent abstractions have been implemented. The hierarchical structure proved to be vital for the verification of the logical soundness of the design and the correctness of its implementation.

Introduction

In response to a call explicitly asking for papers "on timely research and development efforts," I present a progress report on the multiprogramming effort at the Department of Mathematics at the Technological University in Eindhoven.

Having very limited resources (viz. a group of six people of, on the average, half-time availability) and wishing to contribute to the art of system design—including all the stages of conception, construction, and verification, we were faced with the problem of how to get the necessary experience. To solve this problem we adopted the following three guiding principles:

(1) Select a project as advanced as you can conceive, as ambitious as you can justify, in the hope that routine work can be kept to a minimum; hold out against all pressure to incorporate such system expansions that would

E. W. Dijkstra, The structure of the "THE" multiprogramming system. *Communications of the ACM 11*, 5 (May 1968), 341–346.

only result into a purely quantitative increase of the total amount of work to be done.

(2) Select a machine with sound basic characteristics (e.g. an interrupt system to fall in love with is certainly an inspiring feature); from then on try to keep the specific properties of the configuration for which you are preparing the system out of your considerations as long as possible.

(3) Be aware of the fact that experience does by no means automatically lead to wisdom and understanding; in other words, make a conscious effort to learn as much as possible from your previous experiences.

Accordingly, I shall try to go beyond just reporting what we have done and how, and I shall try to formulate as well what we have learned.

I should like to end the introduction with two short remarks on working conditions, which I make for the sake of completeness. I shall not stress these points any further.

One remark is that production speed is severely slowed down if one works with half-time people who have other obligations as well. This is at least a factor of four; probably it is worse. The people themselves lose time and energy in switching over; the group as a whole loses decision speed as discussions, when needed, have often to be postponed until all people concerned are available.

The other remark is that the members of the group (mostly mathematicians) have previously enjoyed as good students a university training of five to eight years and are of Master's or Ph.D. level. I mention this explicitly because at least in my country the intellectual level needed for system design is in general grossly underestimated. I am convinced more than ever that this type of work is very difficult, and that every effort to do it with other than the best people is doomed to either failure or moderate success at enormous expense.

The Tool and the Goal

The system has been designed for a Dutch machine, the EL X8 (N.V. Electrologica, Rijswijk (ZH)). Characteristics of our configuration are:

(1) core memory cycle time 2.5 μsec, 27 bits; at present 32K;

(2) drum of 512K words, 1024 words per track, rev. time 40 msec;

(3) an indirect addressing mechanism very well suited for stack implementation;

(4) a sound system for commanding peripherals and controlling of interrupts;

(5) a potentially great number of low capacity channels; ten of them are used (3 paper tape readers at 1000 char/sec; 3 paper tape punches at 150 char/sec; 2 teleprinters; a plotter; a line printer);

(6) absence of a number of not unusual, awkward features.

The primary goal of the system is to process smoothly a continuous flow of user programs as a service to the university. A multiprogramming system has been chosen with the following objectives in mind: (1) a reduction of turn-around time for programs of short duration, (2) economic use of peripheral devices, (3) automatic control of backing store to be combined with economic use of the central processor, and (4) the economic feasibility to use the machine for those applications for which only the flexibility of a general purpose computer is needed, but (as a rule) not the capacity nor the processing power.

The system is not intended as a multiaccess system. There is no common data base via which independent users can communicate with each other: they only share the configuration and a procedure library (that includes a translator for Algol 60 extended with complex numbers). The system does not cater for user programs written in machine language.

Compared with larger efforts one can state that quantitatively speaking the goals have been set as modest as the equipment and our other resources. Qualitatively speaking, I am afraid, we became more and more immodest as the work progressed.

A Progress Report

We have made some minor mistakes of the usual type (such as paying too much attention to eliminating what was not the real bottleneck) and two major ones.

Our first major mistake was that for too long a time we confined our attention to "a perfect installation"; by the time we considered how to make the best of it, one of the peripherals broke down, we were faced with nasty problems. Taking care of the "pathology" took more energy than we had expected, and some of our troubles were a direct consequence of our earlier ingenuity, i.e. the complexity of the situation into which the system could have maneuvered itself. Had we paid attention to the pathology at an earlier stage of the design, our management rules would certainly have been less refined.

The second major mistake has been that we conceived and programmed the major part of the system without giving more than scanty thought to the problem of debugging it. I must decline all credit for the fact that this mistake had no serious consequences—on the contrary! one might argue as an afterthought.

As captain of the crew I had had extensive experience (dating back to 1958) in making basic software dealing with real-time interrupts, and I knew by bitter experience that as a result of the irreproducibility of the interrupt moments a program error could present itself misleadingly like an occasional machine malfunctioning. As a result I was terribly afraid. Having fears regarding the possibility of debugging, we decided to be as careful as possible and, prevention being better than cure, to try to prevent nasty bugs from entering the construction.

This decision, inspired by fear, is at the bottom of what I regard as the group's main contribution to the art of system design. We have found that it is possible to design a refined multiprogramming system in such a way that its logical soundness can be proved a priori and its implementation can admit exhaustive testing. The only errors that showed up during testing were trivial coding error (occurring with a density of one error per 500 instructions) each of them located within 10 minutes (classical) inspection by the machine and each of them correspondingly easy to remedy. At the time this was written the testing had not yet been completed, but the resulting system is guaranteed to be flawless. When the system is delivered we shall not live in the perpetual fear that a system derailment may still occur in an unlikely situation, such as might result from an unhappy "coincidence" of two or more critical occurrences, for we shall have proved the correctness of the system with a rigor and explicitness that is unusual for the great majority of mathematical proofs.

A Survey of the System Structure

Storage Allocation. In the classical von Neumann machine, information is identified by the address of the memory location containing the information. When we started to think about the automatic control of secondary storage we were familiar with a system (viz. GIER ALGOL) in which all information was identified by its drum address (as in the classical von Neumann machine) and in which the function of the core memory was nothing more than to make the information "page-wise" accessible.

We have followed another approach and, as it turned out, to great advantage. In our terminology we made a strict distinction between memory units (we called them "pages" and had "core pages" and "drum pages") and corresponding information units (for lack of a better word we called them "segments"), a segment just fitting in a page. For segments we created a completely independent identification mechanism in which the number of possible segment identifiers is much larger than the total number of pages in primary and secondary store. The segment identifier gives fast access to a so-called "segment variable" in core whose value denotes whether the segment is still empty or not, and if not empty, in which page (or pages) it can be found.

As a consequence of this approach, if a segment of information, residing in a core page, has to be dumped onto the drum in order to make the core page available for other use, there is no need to return the segment to the same drum page from which it originally came. In fact, this freedom is exploited: among the free drum pages the one with minimum latency time is selected.

A next consequence is the total absence of a drum allocation problem: there is not the slightest reason why, say, a program should occupy consecutive drum pages. In a multiprogramming environment this is very convenient.

Processor Allocation. We have given full recognition to the fact that in a single sequential process (such as can be performed by a sequential automaton) only the time succession of the various states has a logical meaning, but not the actual speed with which the sequential process is performed. Therefore we have arranged the whole system as a society of sequential processes, progressing with undefined speed ratios. To each user program accepted by the system corresponds a sequential process, to each input peripheral corresponds a sequential process (buffering input streams in synchronism with the execution of the input commands), to each output peripheral corresponds a sequential process (unbuffering output streams in synchronism with the execution of the output commands); furthermore, we have the "segment controller" associated with the drum and the "message interpreter" associated with the console keyboard.

This enabled us to design the whole system in terms of these abstract "sequential processes." Their harmonious cooperation is regulated by means of explicit mutual synchronization statements. On the one hand, this explicit mutual synchronization is necessary, as we do not make any assumption about speed ratios; on the other hand, this mutual synchronization is possible because "delaying the progress of a process temporarily" can never be harmful to the interior logic of the process delayed. The fundamental consequence of this approach—viz. the explicit mutual synchronization—is that the harmonious cooperation of a set of such sequential processes can be established by discrete reasoning; as a further consequence the whole harmonious society of cooperating sequential processes is independent of the actual number of processors available to carry out these processes, provided the processors available can switch from process to process.

System Hierarchy. The total system admits a strict hierarchical structure.

At level 0 we find the responsibility for processor allocation to one of the processes whose dynamic progress is logically permissible (i.e. in view of the explicit mutual synchronization). At this level the interrupt of the real-time clock is processed and introduced to prevent any process to monopolize processing power. At this level a priority rule is incorporated to achieve quick response of the system where this is needed. Our first abstraction has been achieved; above level 0 the number of processors actually shared is no longer relevant. At higher levels we find the activity of the different sequential processes, the actual processor that had lost its identity having disappeared from the picture.

At level 1 we have the so-called "segment controller," a sequential process synchronized with respect to the drum interrupt and the sequential processes on higher levels. At level 1 we find the responsibility to cater to the bookkeeping resulting from the automatic backing store. At this level our next abstraction has been achieved; at all higher levels identification of information takes place in terms of segments, the actual storage pages that had lost their identity having disappeared from the picture.

At level 2 we find the "message interpreter" taking care of the allocation of the console keyboard via which conversations between the operator and any of the higher level processes can be carried out. The message interpreter works in close synchronism with the operator. When the operator presses a key, a character is sent to the machine together with an interrupt signal to announce the next keyboard character, whereas the actual printing is done through an output command generated by the machine under control of the message interpreter. (As far as the hardware is concerned the console teleprinter is regarded as two independent peripherals: an input keyboard and an output printer.) If one of the processes opens a conversation, it identifies itself in the opening sentence of the conversation for the benefit of the operator. If, however, the operator opens a conversation, he must identify the process he is addressing, in the opening sentence of the conversation, i.e.

this opening sentence must be interpreted before it is known to which of the processes the conversation is addressed! Here lies the logical reason for the introduction of a separate sequential process for the console teleprinter, a reason that is reflected in its name, "message interpreter."

Above level 2 it is as if each process had its private conversational console. The fact that they share the same physical console is translated into a resource restriction of the form "only one conversation at a time," a restriction that is satisfied via mutual synchronization. At this level the next abstraction has been implemented; at higher levels the actual console teleprinter loses its identity. (If the message interpreter had not been on a higher level than the segment controller, then the only way to implement it would have been to make a permanent reservation in core for it; as the conversational vocabulary might become large (as soon as our operators wish to be addressed in fancy messages), this would result in too heavy a permanent demand upon core storage. Therefore, the vocabulary in which the messages are expressed is stored on segments, i.e. as information units that can reside on the drum as well. For this reason the message interpreter is one level higher than the segment controller.)

At level 3 we find the sequential processes associated with buffering of input streams and unbuffering of output streams. At this level the next abstraction is effected, viz. the abstraction of the actual peripherals used that are allocated at this level to the "logical communication units" in terms of which are worked in the still higher levels. The sequential processes associated with the peripherals are of a level above the message interpreter, because they must be able to converse with the operator (e.g. in the case of detected malfunctioning). The limited number of peripherals again acts as a resource restriction for the processes at higher levels to be satisfied by mutual synchronization between them.

At level 4 we find the independent user programs and at level 5 the operator (not implemented by us).

The system structure has been described at length in order to make the next section intelligible.

Design Experience

The conception stage took a long time. During that period of time the concepts have been born in terms of which we sketched the system in the previous section. Furthermore, we learned the art of reasoning by which we could deduce from our requirements the way in which the processes should influence each other by their mutual synchronization so that these requirements would be met. (The requirements being that no information can be used before it has been produced, that no peripheral can be set to two tasks simultaneously, etc.). Finally we learned the art of reasoning by which ve could prove that the society composed of processes thus mutually synchronized by each other would indeed in its time behavior satisfy all requirements.

The construction stage has been rather traditional, perhaps even old-fashioned, that is, plain machine code. Reprogramming on account of a change of specifications has been rare, a circumstance that must have contributed greatly to the feasibility of the "steam method." That the first two stages took more time than planned was somewhat compensated by a delay in the delivery of the machine.

In the verification stage we had the machine, during short shots, completely at our disposal; these were shots during which we worked with a virgin machine without any software aids for debugging. Starting at level 0 the system was tested, each time adding (a portion of) the next level only after the previous level had been thoroughly tested. Each test shot itself contained, on top of the (partial) system to be tested, a number of testing processes with a double function. First, they had to force the system into all different relevant states; second, they had to verify that the system continued to react according to specification.

I shall not deny that the construction of these testing programs has been a major intellectual effort: to convince oneself that one has not overlooked "a relevant state" and to convince oneself that the testing programs generate them all is no simple matter. The encouraging thing is that (as far as we know) it could be done.

This fact was one of the happy consequences of the hierarchical structure.

Testing level 0 (the real-time clock and processor allocation) implied a number of testing sequential processes on top of it, inspecting together that under all circumstances processor time was divided among them according to the rules. This being established, sequential processes as such were implemented.

Testing the segment controller at level 1 meant that all "relevant states" could be formulated in terms of sequential processes making (in various combinations) demands on core pages, situations that could be provoked by explicit synchronization among the testing programs. At this stage the existence of the real-time clock—although interrupting all the time—was so immaterial that one of the testers indeed forgot its existence!

By that time we had implemented the correct reaction upon the (mutually unsynchronized) interrupts from the real-time clock and the drum. If we had not introduced the separate levels 0 and 1, and if we had not created a terminology (viz. that of the rather abstract sequential processes) in which the existence of the clock interrupt could be discarded, but had instead tried in a nonhierarchical construction, to make the central processor react directly upon any weird time succession of these two interrupts, the number of "relevant states" would have exploded to such a height that exhaustive testing would have been an illusion. (Apart from that it is doubtful whether we would have had the means to generate them all, drum and clock speed being outside our control.)

For the sake of completeness I must mention a further happy consequence. As stated before, above level 1, core and drum pages have lost their identity, and buffering of input and output streams (at level 3) therefore occurs in terms of segments. While testing at level 2 or 3 the drum channel hardware broke down for some time, but testing proceeded by restricting the number of segments to the number that could be held in core. If building up the line printer output streams had been implemented as "dumping onto the drum" and the actual printing as "printing from the drum," this advantage would have been denied to us.

Conclusion

As far as program verification is concerned I present nothing essentially new. In testing a general purpose object (be it a piece of hardware, a program, a machine, or a system), one cannot subject it to all possible cases: for a computer this would imply that one feeds it with all possible programs! Therefore one must test it with a set of relevant test cases. What is, or is not, relevant cannot be decided as long as one regards the mechanism as a black box; in other words, the decision has to be based upon the internal structure of the mechanism to be tested. It seems to be the designer's responsibility to construct his mechanism in such a way—i.e. so effectively structured—that at each stage of the testing procedure the number of relevant test cases will be so small that he can try them all and that what is being tested will be so perspicuous that he will not have overlooked any situation. I have presented a survey of our system because I think it a nice example of the form that such a structure might take.

In my experience, I am sorry to say, industrial software makers tend to react to the system with mixed feelings. On the one hand, they are inclined to think that we have done a kind of model job; on the other hand, they express doubts whether the techniques used are applicable outside the sheltered atmosphere of a University and express the opinion that we were successful only because of the modest scope of the whole project. It is not my intention to underestimate the organizing ability needed to handle a much bigger job, with a lot more people, but I should like to venture the opinion that the larger the project the more essential the structuring! A hierarchy of five logical levels might then very well turn out to be of modest depth. especially when one designs the system more consciously than we have done, with the aim that the software can be smoothly adapted to (perhaps drastic) configuration expansions.

Acknowledgments. I express my indebtedness to my five collaborators, C. Bron, A. N. Habermann, F. J. A. Hendriks, C. Ligtmans, and P. A. Voorhoeve. They have contributed to all stages of the design, and together we learned the art of reasoning needed. The construction and verification was entirely their effort; if my dreams have come true, it is due to their faith, their talents, and their persistent loyalty to the whole project.

Finally I should like to thank: the members of the program committee, who asked for more information on the synchronizing primitives and some justification of my claim to be able to prove logical soundness a priori. In answer to this request an appendix has been added, which I hope will give the desired information and justification.

APPENDIX

Synchronizing Primitives

Explicit mutual synchronization of parallel sequential processes is implemented via so-called "semaphores." They are special purpose integer variables allocated in the universe in which the processes are embedded; they are initialized (with the value 0 or 1) before the parallel processes themselves are started. After this initialization the parallel processes will access the semaphores only via two very specific operations, the so-called synchronizing primitives. For historical reasons they are called the P-operation and the V-operation.

A process, "Q" say, that performs the operation "P(sem)" decreases the value of the semaphore called "sem" by 1. If the resulting value of the semaphore concerned is nonnegative, process Q can continue with the execution of its next statement; if, however, the resulting value is negative, process Q is stopped and booked on a waiting list associated with the semaphore concerned. Until further notice (i.e. a V-operation on this very same semaphore), dynamic progress of process Q is not logically permissible and no processor will be allocated to it (see above "System Hierarchy," at level 0).

A process, "R" say, that performs the operation "V(sem)" increases the value of the semaphore called "sem" by 1. If the resulting value of the semaphore concerned is positive, the V-operation in question has no further effect; if, however, the resulting value of the semaphore concerned is nonpositive, one of the processes booked on its waiting list is removed from this waiting list, i.e. its dynamic progress is again logically permissible and in due time a processor will be allocated to it (again, see above "System Hierarchy," at level 0).

COROLLARY 1. *If a semaphore value is nonpositive its absolute value equals the number of processes booked on its waiting list.*

COROLLARY 2. *The P-operation represents the potential delay, the complementary V-operation represents the removal of a barrier.*

Note 1. P- and V-operations are "indivisible actions"; i.e. if they occur "simultaneously" in parallel processes they are noninterfering in the sense that they can be regarded as being performed one after the other.

Note 2. If the semaphore value resulting from a V-operation is negative, its waiting list originally contained more than one process. It is undefined—i.e. logically immaterial–which of the waiting processes is then removed from the waiting list.

Note 3. A consequence of the mechanisms described above is that a process whose dynamic progress is permissible can only loose this status by actually progressing, i.e. by performance of a P-operation on a semaphore with a value that is initially nonpositive.

During system conception it transpired that we used the semaphores in two completely different ways. The difference is so marked that, looking back, one wonders whether it was really fair to present the two ways as uses of the very same primitives. On the one hand, we have the semaphores used for mutual exclusion, on the other hand, the private semaphores.

Mutual Exclusion

In the following program we indicate two parallel, cyclic processes (between the brackets "parbegin" and "parend") that come into action after the surrounding universe has been introduced and initialized.

begin semaphore *mutex; mutex := 1;*
  parbegin
    begin *L1: P(mutex); critical section 1; V(mutex);*
      remainder of cycle 1; **go to** *L1*
    end;
    begin *L2: P(mutex); critical section 2; V(mutex);*
      remainder of cycle 2; **go to** *L2*
    end
  parend
end

As a result of the *P*- and *V*-operations on "mutex" the actions, marked as "critical sections" exclude each other mutually in time; the scheme given allows straightforward extension to more than two parallel processes, the maximum value of mutex equals 1, the minimum value equals $-(n-1)$ if we have n parallel processes.

Critical sections are used always, and only for the purpose of unambiguous inspection and modification of the state variables (allocated in the surrounding universe) that describe the current state of the system (as far as needed for the regulation of the harmonious cooperation between the various processes).

Private Semaphores

Each sequential process has associated with it a number of private semaphores and no other process will ever perform a *P*-operation on them. The universe initializes them with the value equal to 0, their maximum value equals 1, and their minimum value equals −1.

Whenever a process reaches a stage where the permission for dynamic progress depends on current values of state variables, it follows the pattern:

P(mutex);
"inspection and modification of state variables including
  a conditional V(private semaphore)";
V(mutex);
P(private semaphore)

If the inspection learns that the process in question should continue, it performs the operation "*V*(private semaphore)"—the semaphore value then changes from 0 to 1—otherwise, this *V*-operation is skipped, leaving to the other processes the obligation to perform this *V*-operation at a suitable moment. The absence or presence of this obligation is reflected in the final values of the state variables upon leaving the critical section.

Whenever a process reaches a stage where as a result of its progress possibly one (or more) blocked processes should now get permission to continue, it follows the pattern:

P(mutex);
"modification and inspection of state variables including
zero or more V-operations on private semaphores
of other processes";
V(mutex)

By the introduction of suitable state variables and appropriate programming of the critical sections any strategy assigning peripherals, buffer areas, etc. can be implemented.

The amount of coding and reasoning can be greatly reduced by the observation that in the two complementary critical sections sketched above the same inspection can be performed by the introduction of the notion of "an unstable situation," such as a free reader and a process needing a reader. Whenever an unstable situation emerges it is removed (including one or more V-operations on private semaphores) in the very same critical section in which it has been created.

Proving the Harmonious Cooperation

The sequential processes in the system can all be regarded as cyclic processes in which a certain neutral point can be marked, the so-called "homing position," in which all processes are when the system is at rest.

When a cyclic process leaves its homing position "it accepts a task"; when the task has been performed and not earlier, the process returns to its homing position. Each cyclic process has a specific task processing power (e.g. the execution of a user program or unbuffering a portion of printer output, etc.).

The harmonious cooperation is mainly proved in roughly three stages.

(1) It is proved that although a process performing a task may in so doing generate a finite number of tasks for other processes, a single initial task cannot give rise to an infinite number of task generations. The proof is simple as processes can only generate tasks for processes at lower levels of the hierarchy so that circularity is excluded. (If a process needing a segment from the drum has generated a task for the segment controller,

special precautions have been taken to ensure that the segment asked for remains in core at least until the requesting process has effectively accessed the segment concerned. Without this precaution finite tasks could be forced to generate an infinite number of tasks for the segment controller, and the system could get stuck in an unproductive page flutter.)

(2) It is proved that it is impossible that all processes have returned to their homing position while somewhere in the system there is still pending a generated but unaccepted task. (This is proved via instability of the situation just described.)

(3) It is proved that after the acceptance of an initial task all processes eventually will be (again) in their homing position. Each process blocked in the course of task execution relies on the other processes for removal of the barrier. Essentially, the proof in question is a demonstration of the absence of "circular waits": process P waiting for process Q waiting for process R waiting for process P. (Our usual term for the circular wait is "the Deadly Embrace.") In a more general society than our system this proof turned out to be a proof by induction (on the level of hierarchy, starting at the lowest level), as A. N. Habermann has shown in his doctoral thesis.

3

RC 4000 SOFTWARE: MULTIPROGRAMMING SYSTEM

PER BRINCH HANSEN

(1969)

The RC 4000 multiprogramming system consists of a monitor program that can be extended with a hierarchy of operating systems to suit diverse requirements of program scheduling and resource allocation. This manual defines the functions of the monitor and the basic operating system, which allows users to initiate and control parallel program execution from typewriter consoles. The excerpt reprinted here is the general description of the philosophy and structure of the system. This part will be of interest to anyone wishing an understanding of the system in order to evaluate its possibilities and limitations without going into details about exact conventions. The discussion treats the hardware structure of the RC 4000 only in passing.

1 SYSTEM OBJECTIVES

This chapter outlines the philosophy that guided the design of the RC 4000 multiprogramming system. It emphasizes the need for different operating systems to suit different applications.

The primary goal of *multiprogramming* is to share a central processor and its peripheral equipment among a number of programs loaded in the internal store. This is a meaningful objective if single programs only use a fraction of the system resources and if the speed of the machine is so fast, compared to that of peripherals, that idle time within one program can be utilized by other programs.

P. Brinch Hansen, *RC 4000 Software: Multiprogramming System*, Part I General Description. Regnecentralen, Copenhagen, Denmark, April 1969, 13–52.

The present system is implemented on the RC 4000 computer, a 24-bit, binary computer with typical instruction execution times of 4 microseconds. It permits practically unlimited expansion of the internal store and standardized connection of all kinds of peripherals. Multiprogramming is facilitated by concurrency of program execution and input/output, program interruption, and storage protection.

The aim has been to make multiprogramming feasible on a machine with a minimum internal store of 16 k words backed by a fast drum or disk. Programs can be written in any of the available programming languages and contain programming errors. The storage protection system guarantees noninterference among 8 parallel programs, but it is possible to start up to 23 programs provided some of them are error free.

The system uses standard multiprogramming techniques: the central processor is shared between loaded programs. Automatic swapping of programs in and out of the store is possible but not enforced by the system. Backing storage is organized as a *common data bank*, in which users can retain named files in a semi-permanent manner. The system allows a *conversational mode* of access from typewriter consoles.

An essential part of any multiprogramming system is an *operating system*, a program that coordinates all computational activities and input/output. An operating system must be in complete control of the strategy of program execution, and assist the users with such functions as operator communication, interpretation of job control statements, allocation of resources, and application of execution time limits.

For the designer of advanced information systems, a vital requirement of any operating system is that it allows him to change the mode of operation it controls; otherwise his freedom of design can be seriously limited. Unfortunately this is precisely what present operating systems do not allow. Most of them are based exclusively on a single mode of operation, such as batch processing, priority scheduling, real-time scheduling, or time-sharing.

When the need arises, the user often finds it hopeless to modify an operating system that has made rigid assumptions in its basic design about a specific mode of operation. The alternative—to replace the original operating system with a new one—is in most computers a serious, if not impossible, matter, the reason being that the rest of the software is intimately bound to the conventions required by the original system.

This unfortunate situation indicates that the main problem in the design of a multiprogramming system is not to define functions that satisfy specific operating needs, but rather to supply a system nucleus that can be extended with new operating systems in an orderly manner. This is the primary objective of the RC 4000 system.

The nucleus of the RC 4000 multiprogramming system is a *monitor* program with complete control of storage protection, input/output, and interrupts. Essentially the monitor is a software extension of the hardware structure, which makes the RC 4000 more attractive for multiprogramming. The following elementary functions are implemented in the monitor:

> scheduling of time slices among programs executed in parallel by means of a digital clock,
>
> initiation and control of program execution at the request of other running programs,
>
> transfer of messages among running programs,
>
> initiation of data transfers to or from peripherals.

The monitor has no built-in strategy of program execution and resource allocation; it allows any program to initiate other programs in a hierarchal manner and to execute them according to any strategy desired. In this *hierarchy of programs* an operating system is simply a program that controls the execution of other programs. Thus operating systems can be introduced in the system as other programs without modification of the monitor. Furthermore operating systems can be replaced dynamically, enabling each installation to switch among various modes of operation; several operating systems can, in fact, be active simultaneously.

In the following chapters we shall explain this dynamic operating system concept in detail. In accordance with our philosophy all questions about particular strategies of program scheduling will be postponed, and the discussion will concentrate on the fundamental aspects of the control of an environment of parallel processes.

2 ELEMENTARY MULTIPROGRAMMING PROBLEMS

This chapter introduces the elementary multiprogramming problems of mutual exclusion and synchronization of parallel processes. The discussion is restricted to the logical problems that arise when independent processes try to access common variables and shared resources. An understanding of these concepts is indispensable to the uninitiated reader, who wants to appreciate the difficulties of switching from uniprogramming to multiprogramming.

2.1 Multiprogramming

In multiprogramming the sharing of computing time among programs is controlled by a *clock*, which interrupts program execution frequently and activates a *monitor program*. The monitor saves the registers of the interrupted program and allocates the next slice of computing time to another program and so on. Switching from one program to another is also performed whenever a program must wait for the completion of input/output.

Thus although the computer is only able to execute one instruction at a time, multiprogramming creates the illusion that programs are being executed simultaneously, mainly because peripherals assigned to different programs indeed operate in parallel.

2.2 Parallel Processes

Most of the elementary problems in multiprogramming arise from the fact that one *process* (e.g. an executed program) cannot make any assumptions about the relative speed and progress of other processes. This is a potential source of conflict whenever two processes try to access a common variable or a shared resource.

It is evident that this problem will exist in a truly parallel system, in which programs are executed simultaneously on several central processors. It should be realized, however, that the problem will also appear in a quasi-parallel system based on the sharing of a single processor by means of interrupts; since a program cannot detect when it has been interrupted, it does not know how far other programs have progressed.

Another way of stating this is that if one considers the system as seen from within a program, it is irrelevant whether multiprogramming is implemented on one or more central processors—the logical problems are the same.

Consequently a multiprogramming system must in general be viewed as an environment with a number of truly *parallel processes*. Having reached this conclusion, a natural generalization is to treat not only program execution but input/output also as independent, parallel processes. This point will be illustrated abundantly in the following chapters.

2.3 Mutual Exclusion

The idea of multiprogramming is to share the computing equipment among a number of parallel programs. At any moment, however, a given resource must belong to one program only. In order to ensure this it is necessary to introduce global variables, which programs can inspect to decide whether a given resource is available or not.

As an example consider a typewriter used by all programs for messages to the operator. To control access to this device we might introduce a global boolean *typewriter available*. When a program p wishes to output a message, it must examine and set this boolean by means of the following instructions:

```
wait:  load      typewriter available
       skip if   true
       jump to   wait
       load      false
       store     typewriter available
```

While this is taking place the program may be interrupted after the loading of the boolean, but before inspection and assignment to it. The register containing the value of the boolean is then stored within the monitor, and program q is started. Q may load the same boolean and find that the typewriter is available. Q accordingly assigns the value false to the boolean and starts using the typewriter. After a while q is interrupted, and at some later time p is restarted with the original contents of the register reestablished by the monitor. Program p continues the inspection of the original value of the boolean and concludes erroneously that the typewriter is available.

This conflict arises because programs have no control over the interrupt system. Thus the only indivisible operations available to programs are single instructions such as load, compare, and store. This example shows that one cannot implement a multiprogramming system without ensuring a *mutual exclusion* of programs during the inspection of global variables. Evidently the entire reservation sequence must be executed as an *indivisible function*. One of the purposes of a monitor program is to execute indivisible functions in the disabled mode.

In the use of reservation primitives one must be aware of the problem of "the *deadly embrace*" between two processes, p and q, which attempt to share the resources r and s as follows:

```
process p: wait and reserve(r) ... wait and reserve(s) ...
process q: wait and reserve(s) ... wait and reserve(r) ...
```

This can cause both processes to wait forever, since neither is aware of that it wants what the other one has.

To avoid this problem we need a third process (an *operating system*) that controls the allocation of shared resources between p and q in a manner that guarantees that both will be able to proceed to completion (if necessary by delaying the other until resources become available).

2.4 Mutual Synchronization

In a multiprogramming system parallel processes must be able to *cooperate* in the sense that they can activate one another and exchange information. One example of a process activating another process is the initiation of input/output by a program. Another example is that of an operating system that schedules a number of programs. The exchange of information between two processes can also be regarded as a problem of mutual exclusion, in which the receiver must be prevented from inspecting the information until the sender has delivered it in a common storage area.

Since the two processes are independent with respect to speed, it is not certain that the receiver is ready to accept the information at the very moment the sender wishes to deliver it, or conversely the receiver can become idle at a time when there is no further information for it to process.

This problem of the *synchronization* of two processes during a transfer of information must be solved by indivisible monitor functions, which allow a process to be *delayed* on its own request and *activated* on request from another process.

For a more extensive analysis of multiprogramming fundamentals, the reader should consult E. W. Dijkstra's monograph: *Cooperating Sequential Processes.* Math. Dep. Technological University, Eindhoven, (Sep. 1965).

3 BASIC MONITOR CONCEPTS

This chapter opens a detailled description of the RC 4000 monitor. A multiprogramming system is viewed as an environment in which program execution and input/output are handled uniformly as cooperating, parallel processes. The need for an exact definition of the process concept is stressed. The purpose of the monitor is to bridge the gap between the actual hardware and the abstract concept of multiprogramming.

3.1 Introduction

The aim has been to implement a multiprogramming system that can be extended with new operating systems in a well-defined manner. In order to do this a sharp distinction must be made between the *control* and the *strategy* of program execution.

The mechanisms provided by the monitor solve the logical problems of the control of parallel processes. They also solve the safety problems that arise when erroneous or malicious processes try to interfere with other processes. They do, however, leave the choice of particular strategies of program scheduling to the processes themselves.

With this objective in mind we have implemented the following fundamental mechanisms within the monitor:

simulation of parallel processes,
communication among processes,
creation, control, and removal of processes.

3.2 Programs and Internal Processes

As a first step we shall assign a precise meaning to the process concept, i.e. introduce an unambiguous terminology for what a process is and how it is implemented on the RC 4000.

We distinguish between internal and external processes, roughly corresponding to program execution and input/output.

More precisely: an *internal process* is the execution of one or more interruptable programs in a given storage area. An internal process is identified by a unique *process name.* Thus other processes need not be aware of the actual location of an internal process in the store, but can refer to it by name.

The following figure illustrates a division of the internal store among the monitor and three internal processes, p, q, and r.

Later it will be explained how internal processes are created and how programs are loaded into them. At this point it should only be noted that an internal process occupies a fixed, contiguous storage area during its whole lifetime. The monitor has a *process description* of each internal process; this table defines the name, storage area, and current state of the process.

Computing time is shared cyclically among all active internal processes; as a standard the monitor allocates a maximum time slice of 25 milliseconds to each internal process in turn; after the elapse of this interval the process is interrupted and its registers are stored in the process description; following this the monitor allocates 25 milliseconds to the next internal process, and so on. The cyclic queue of active internal processes is called the *time slice queue.*

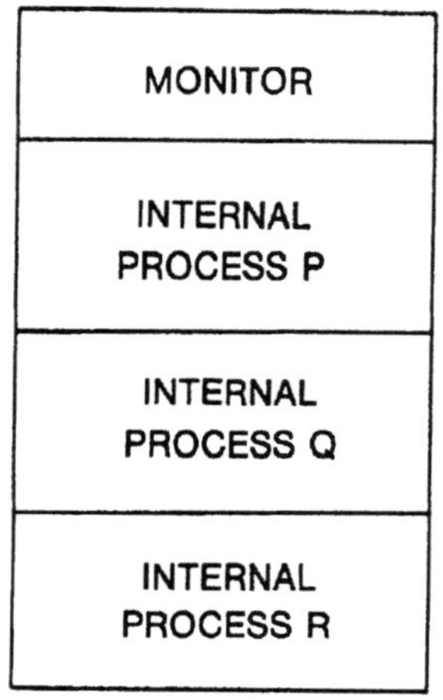

A sharp distinction is made between the concepts program and internal process. A *program* is a collection of instructions describing a computational process, whereas an internal process is the execution of these instructions in a given storage area.

An internal process like p can involve the execution of a sequence of programs, for example, editing followed by translation and execution of an object program. It is also possible that copies of the same program (e.g. the Algol compiler) can be executed simultaneously in two processes q and r. These examples illustrate the need for a distinction between programs and processes.

3.3 Documents and External Processes

In connection with input/output the monitor distinguishes between peripheral devices, documents, and external processes.

A *peripheral device* is an item of hardware connected to the data channel and identified by a device number.

A *document* is a collection of data stored on a physical medium. Examples of documents are:

a roll of paper tape,
a deck of punched cards,
a printer form,
a reel of magnetic tape,
a data area on the backing store.

By the expression *external process* we refer to the input/output of a given document identified by a unique process name. This concept implies that once a document has been mounted, internal processes can refer to it by name without knowing the actual device it uses.

For each external process the monitor keeps a process description defining its name, kind, device number, and current state. The *process kind* is an integer defining the kind of peripheral device on which the document is mounted.

For each kind of external process the monitor contains an interrupt procedure that can initiate and terminate input/output on request from internal processes.

3.4 Monitor

The monitor is a program activated by means of interrupts. It can execute privileged instructions in the disabled mode, meaning that (1) it is in complete control of input/output, storage protection, and the interrupt system, and that (2) it can execute a sequence of instructions as an indivisible entity.

After initial system loading the monitor resides permanently in the internal store. We do not regard the monitor as an independent process, but rather as a software extension of the hardware structure, which makes the computer more attractive for multiprogramming. Its function is to (1) keep descriptions of all processes; (2) share computing time among internal and external processes; and (3) implement procedures that processes can call in order to create and control other processes and communicate with them.

So far we have described the multiprogramming system as a set of independent, parallel processes identified by names. The emphasis has been on a clear understanding of relationships among resources (store and peripherals), data (programs and documents), and processes (internal and external).

4 PROCESS COMMUNICATION

This chapter deals with the monitor procedures for the exchange of information between two parallel processes. The mechanism of message buffering is defended on the grounds of safety and efficiency.

4.1 Message Buffers and Queues

Two parallel processes can cooperate by sending messages to each other. A *message* consists of eight words. Messages are transmitted from one process to another by means of *message buffers* selected from a common *pool* within the monitor.

The monitor administers a *message queue* for each process. Messages are linked to this queue when they arrive from other processes. The message queue is a part of the process description.

Normally a process serves its queue on a first-come, first-served basis. After the processing of a message, the receiving process returns an *answer* of eight words to the sending process in the same buffer.

As described in Section 2.4, communication between two independent processes requires a synchronization of the processes during a transfer of information. A process requests synchronization by executing a wait operation; this causes a delay of the process until another process executes a send operation.

The term *delay* means that the internal process is removed temporarily from the time slice queue; the process is said to be *activated* when it is again linked to the time slice queue.

4.2 Send and Wait Procedures

The following monitor procedures are available for communication among internal processes:

send message(receiver, message, buffer)
wait message(sender, message, buffer)
send answer(result, answer, buffer)
wait answer (result, answer, buffer)

Send message copies a message into the first available buffer within the pool and delivers it in the queue of a named receiver. The receiver is activated if it is waiting for a message. The sender continues after being informed of the address of the message buffer.

Wait message delays the calling process until a message arrives in its queue. When the process is allowed to proceed, it is supplied with the name of the sender, the contents of the message, and the address of the message buffer. The buffer is removed from the queue and is now ready to transmit an answer.

Send answer copies an answer into a buffer in which a message has been received and delivers it in the queue of the original sender. The sender of the message is activated if it is waiting for the answer. The answering process continues immediately.

Wait answer delays the calling process until an answer arrives in a given buffer. On arrival, the answer is copied into the process and the buffer is returned to the pool. The result specifies whether the answer is a response from another process, or a dummy answer generated by the monitor in response to a message addressed to a non-existing process.

The use of these procedures can be illustrated by the following example of a conversational process. The figure below shows one of several user processes, which deliver their output on the backing store. After completion of its output a user process sends a message to a converter process requesting it to print the output. The converter process receives and serves these requests one by one, thus ensuring that the line printer is shared by all user processes with a minimum delay.

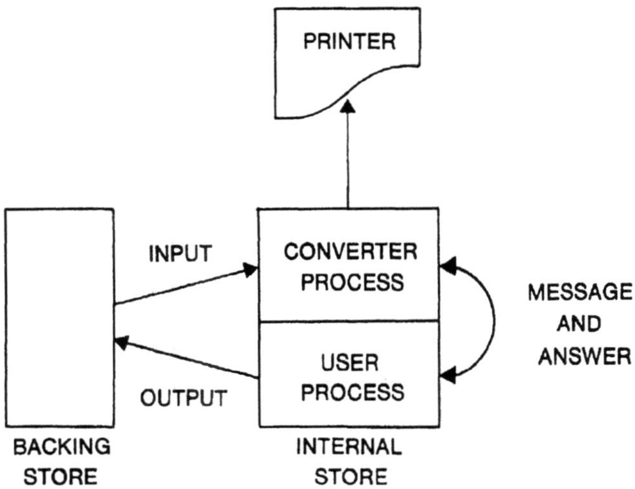

The algorithms of the converter and the user are as follows:

```
converter process:
   wait message(sender, message, buffer);
   print from backing store(message);
   send answer(result, answer, buffer);
   goto converter process;
```

```
user process:
  ...
  output on backing store;
  send message(converter, message, buffer);
  wait answer(result, answer, buffer);
```

4.3 General Event Procedures

The communication procedures enable a conversational process to receive messages simultaneously from several other processes. To avoid becoming a bottleneck in the system, however, a conversational process must be prepared to be actively engaged in more than one conversation at a time. As an example think of a conversational process that engages itself, on request from another process, in a conversation with one of several human operators in order to perform some manual operation (mounting of a tape etc.). If one restricts a conversational process to only accepting one request (i.e. a message) at a time, and to completing the requested action before receiving the next request, the unacceptable consequence of this is that other processes (including human operators at consoles) can have their requests for response delayed for a long or even undefined time.

As soon as a conversational process has started a lengthy action, by sending a message to some other process, it must receive further messages and initiate other actions. It will then be reminded later of the completion of earlier actions by means of normal answers. In general a conversational process is now engaged in several requests at one time. This introduces a scheduling and resource problem: when the process receives a request, some of its resources (storage or peripheral devices) can be tied up by already initiated actions; thus in some cases the process will not be able to honor new requests before old ones are completed. In this case the process wants to postpone the reception of some requests and leave them pending in the queue, while examining others.

The procedures *wait message* and *wait answer*, which force a process to serve its queue in a strict sequential order and delay itself while its own requests to other processes are completed, do not fulfill the above requirements.

Consequently we have introduced two more general communication procedures, which enable a process to wait for the arrival of the next message or answer and serve its queue in any order:

wait event(last buffer, next buffer, result)
get event(buffer)

The term *event* denotes a message or an answer. In accordance with this the queue of a process from now on will be called the *event queue.*

Wait event delays the calling process until either a message or an answer arrives in its queue after a given last buffer. The process is supplied with the address of the next buffer and a result indicating whether it contains a message or an answer. If the last buffer address is zero, the queue is examined from the start. The procedure does not remove the next buffer from the queue or in any other way change its status.

As an example, consider an event queue with two pending buffers A and B:

queue = buffer A, buffer B

The monitor calls: wait event(0, buffer) and wait event(A, buffer) will cause immediate return to the process with *buffer* equal to A and B, respectively; while the call: wait event(B, buffer) will delay the process until another message or answer arrives in the queue after buffer B.

Get event removes a given buffer from the queue of the calling process. If the buffer contains a message, it is made ready for the sending of an answer. If the buffer contains an answer, it is returned to the common pool. The copying of the message or answer from the buffer must be done by the process itself before *get event* is called.

The following algorithm illustrates the use of these procedures within a conversational process:

```
first event:     buffer:=0;
next event:      last buffer:=buffer;
                 wait event(last buffer, buffer, result);
                 if result = message then
                 begin
exam request:    if resources not available then go to next event;
init action:     get event(buffer);
                 reserve resources;
                 ...
                 send message to some other process;
                 save state of action;
                 end else
                 begin comment: result = answer;
term action:     restore state of action;
                 get event(buffer);
                 release resources,
                 send answer to original sender;
                 end;
                 go to first event;
```

The process starts by examining its queue; if empty, it awaits the arrival of the next event. If it finds a message, it checks whether it has the necessary resources to perform the requested action; if not, it leaves the message in the queue and examines the next event. Otherwise it accepts the message, reserves resources, and initiates an action. As soon as this involves the sending of a message to some other process, the conversational process saves information about the state of the incomplete action and proceeds to examine its queue from the start in order to engage itself in another action.

Whenever the process finds an answer in its queue, it immediately accepts it and completes the corresponding action. It can now release the resources used and send an answer to the original sender that made the request. After this it examines the entire queue again to see whether the release of resources has made it possible to accept pending messages.

One example of a process operating in accordance with this scheme is the basic operating system s, which creates internal processes on request from typewriter consoles. S can be engaged in conversations with several consoles at the same time. It will only postpone an operator request if its storage is occupied by other requests, or if it is already in the middle of an action requested from the same console.

4.4 Advantages of Message Buffering

In the design of the communication scheme we have given full recognition to the fact that the multiprogramming system is a dynamic environment, in which some of the processes may turn out to be black sheep.

The system is dynamic in the sense that processes can appear and disappear at any time. Therefore a process does not in general have a complete knowledge about the existence of other processes. This is reflected in the procedure *wait message*, which makes it possible for a process to be unaware of the existence of other processes until it receives messages from them.

On the other hand once a communication has been established between two processes (e.g. by means of a message), they need a common identification of it in order to agree on when it is terminated (e.g. by means of an answer). Thus we can properly regard the selection of a buffer as the creation of an identification of a conversation.

A happy consequence of this is that it enables two processes to exchange more than one message at a time. We must be prepared for the occurence of erroneous or malicious processes in the system (e.g. undebugged programs). This is tolerable only if the monitor ensures that no process can interfere with a conversation between two other processes. This is done by storing information about the sender and receiver in each buffer, and checking it whenever a process attempts to send or wait for an answer in a given buffer.

Efficiency is obtained by the queuing of buffers, which enables a sending process to continue immediately after delivery of a message or an answer regardless of whether the receiver is ready to process it or not.

In order to make the system dynamic it is vital that a process can be removed at any time, even if it is engaged in one or more conversations. In the previous example of user processes that deliver their output on the backing store and ask a converter process to print it, it would be sensible to remove a user process that has completed its task and is now only waiting for an answer from the converter process. In this case the monitor leaves all messages from the removed process undisturbed in the queues of other processes. When these processes terminate their actions by sending answers, the monitor simply returns the buffers to the common pool.

The reverse situation is also possible: during the removal of a process, the monitor finds unanswered messages sent to the process. These are returned as dummy answers to the senders. A special instance of this is the generation of a dummy answer to a message addressed to a process that does not exist.

The main drawback of message buffering is that it introduces yet another resource problem, since the common pool contains a finite number of buffers. If a process was allowed to empty the pool by sending messages to ignorant processes, which do not respond with answers, further communication within the system would be blocked. We have consequently set a limit to the number of messages a process can send simultaneously. By doing this, and by allowing a process to transmit an answer in a received buffer, we have placed the entire risk of a conversation on the process that opens it (see Section 7.4).

5 EXTERNAL PROCESSES

This chapter clarifies the meaning of the external process concept. It explains initiation of input/output by means of messages from internal processes, dynamic creation and removal of external processes, and exclusive access to documents by means of reservation. The similarity of internal and external processes is stressed.

5.1 Initiation of Input/Output

Consider the following situation, in which an internal process, p, inputs a block from an external process, q (say, a magnetic tape):

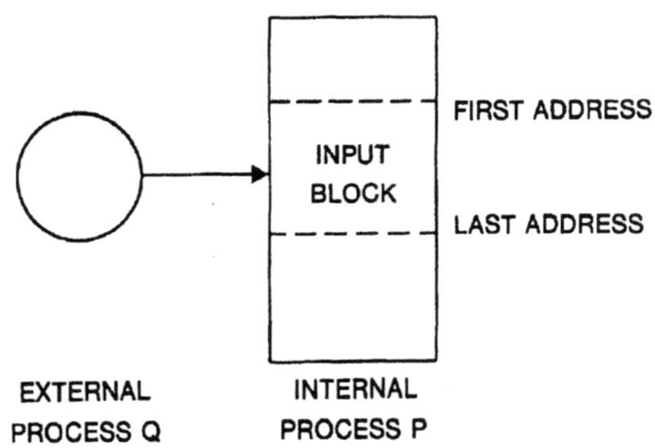

P initiates input by sending a message to q:

send message(q, message, buffer)

The message consists of eight words defining an input/output operation and the first and last addresses of a storage area within process p:

message: operation
first storage address
last storage address
(five irrelevant words)

The monitor copies the message into a buffer and delivers it in the queue of process q. Following this it uses the kind parameter in the process description of process q to switch to a piece of code common to all magnetic tapes. If the tape station is busy, the message is merely left in its queue; otherwise input is initiated to the given storage area. On return, program execution continues in process p.

When the tape station completes input by means of an interrupt, the monitor generates an answer and delivers it in the queue of p, which in turn receives it by calling *wait answer*:

wait answer(result, answer, buffer)

The answer contains status bits sensed from the device and the actual block length expressed as the number of bytes and characters input:

answer: status bits
number of bytes
number of characters
(five irrelevant words)

After delivery of the answer, the monitor examines the queue of the external process q and initiates its next operation (unless the queue is empty).

Essentially all external processes follow this scheme, which can be defined by the following algorithm:

```
external process: wait message;
                  analyse and check message;
                  initiate input/output;
                  wait interrupt;
                  generate answer;
                  send answer;
                  goto external process;
```

With low-speed, character-oriented devices, the monitor repeats input/output and the interrupt response for each character until a complete block has been transferred; (while this is taking place, the time between interrupts is of course shared among internal processes). Internal processes can therefore regard all input/output as block oriented.

5.2 Reservation and Release

The use of message buffering provides a direct way of sharing an external process among a number of internal processes: an external process can simply accept messages from any internal process and serve them in their order of arrival. An example of this is the use of a single typewriter for output of messages to a main operator. This method of sharing a device ensures that a block of data is input or output as an indivisible entity. When sequential media such as paper tape, punched cards, or magnetic tape are used, however, an internal process must have exclusive access to the entire document. This is obtained by calling the following monitor procedure:

reserve process(name, result)

The result indicates whether the reservation has been accepted or not. An external process that handles sequential documents of this kind rejects messages from all internal processes except the one that has reserved it. Rejection is indicated by the result of the procedure *wait answer.*

During the removal of an internal process, the monitor removes all reservations made by it. Internal processes can, however, also do this explicitly by means of the monitor procedure:

release process(name)

5.3 Creation and Removal

From the operator's point of view an external process is created when he mounts a document on a device and names it. The name must, however, be communicated to the monitor by means of an operating system, i.e. an internal process that controls the execution of programs. Thus it is more correct to say that external processes are created when internal processes assign names to peripheral devices. This is done by means of the monitor procedure:

create peripheral process(name, device number, result)

The monitor has, in fact, no way of ensuring whether a given document is mounted on a device. Furthermore, there are some devices which operate without documents, e.g. the real-time clock.

The name of an external process can be explicitly removed by a call of the monitor procedure:

remove process(name, result)

It is also possible to implement an automatic removal of the process name when the monitor detects operator intervention in a device. At present, this is done only in connection with magnetic tapes (see Section 10.1).

5.4 Replacement of External Processes

The decision to control input/output by means of interrupt procedures within the monitor, instead of using dedicated internal processes for each kind of peripheral device, was made to obtain immediate initiation of input/output after the sending of messages. In contrast the activation of an internal process merely implies that it is linked to the time slice queue; after activation several time slices can elapse before the internal process actually starts to execute instructions.

The price paid for the present implementation of external processes is a prolongation of the time spent in the disabled mode within the monitor. This limits the system's ability to cope with real-time events, i.e. data that are lost unless they are input and processed within a certain time.

An important consequence of the uniform handling of internal and external processes is that it allows us to replace any external process by an internal process of the same name; other processes that communicate with it are quite unaware of this replacement.

Thus it is possible to improve the response time of the system by replacing a time-consuming external process, such as the paper tape reader, by a somewhat slower internal process, which executes privileged instructions in the enabled mode.

This type of replacement also makes it possible to enforce more complex rules of access to a document. In the interests of security, for example, one might want to limit the access of an internal process to one of several files recorded on a particular magnetic tape. This can be ensured by an internal process that traps all messages to the tape and decides whether they should be passed on to it.

As a final example let us consider the problem of debugging a process control system before it is connected to an industrial plant. A convenient way of doing this is to replace analog inputs with an internal process that simulates relevant values of actual measuring instruments.

We conclude that the ability to replace any process in the system with another process is a very useful tool. This can now be seen as a practical result of the general, but somewhat vague idea (expressed in Section 2.2) that internal and external processes are independent processes, which differ only in their processing capability.

6 INTERNAL PROCESSES

This chapter explains the creation and control of internal processes. The emphasis is on the hierarchal structuring of internal processes, which makes it possible to extend the system with new operating systems. The dynamic behaviour of the system is explained in terms of process states and the transition between these.

6.1 Creation, Control, and Removal

Internal processes are *created* on request from other internal processes by means of the monitor procedure:

create internal process(name, parameters, result)

The monitor initializes the process description of the new internal process with its name and storage area selected by the *parent process*. The storage area must be within the parent's own area. Also specified by the parent is a protection key, which must be set in all storage words of the *child process* before it is started.

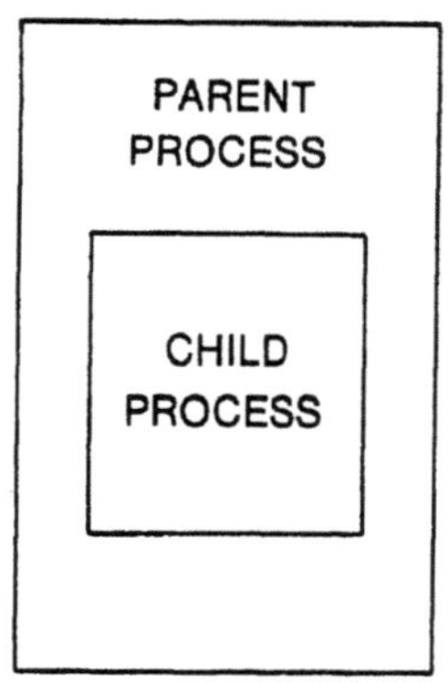

After creation the child process is simply a named storage area, which is described within the monitor. It has not yet been linked to the time slice queue.

The parent process can now *load* a program into the child process by means of an input operation. Following this the parent can *initialize* the *registers* of its child using the monitor procedure:

modify internal process(name, registers, result)

The register values are stored in the process description until the child process is started. As a standard convention adopted by parent processes (but not enforced by the monitor), the registers inform the child about the process descriptions of itself, its parent, and the typewriter console it can use for operator communication.

Finally the parent can *start* program execution within the child by calling:

start internal process(name, result)

which sets the protection keys within the child and links it to the time slice queue. The child now shares time slices with other active processes including the parent.

On request from a parent process, the monitor waits for the completion of all input/output initiated by a child process and *stops* it, i.e. removes it from the time slice queue:

stop internal process(name, buffer, result)

The meaning of the message buffer will be made clear in Section 6.3.

In the stopped state a child process can be modified and started again, or it can be completely *removed* by the parent process:

remove process(name, result)

During removal, the monitor generates dummy answers to all messages sent to the child and releases all external processes used by it. Finally the protection keys are reset to the value used within the parent process. The parent can now use the storage area to create other child processes.

6.2 Process Hierarchy

The idea of the *monitor* has been described as the simulation of an environment in which program execution and input/output are handled uniformly as parallel, cooperating processes. A fundamental set of procedures allows the dynamic creation and control of processes as well as communication among them.

For a given installation we still need, as part of the system, programs that control strategies for operator communication, program scheduling, and resource allocation. But it is essential for the orderly growth of the systems that these *operating systems* be implemented as other programs. Since the difference between operating systems and production programs is one of jurisdiction only, this problem is solved by arranging the internal processes in a *hierarchy* in which parent processes have complete control over child processes.

After initial loading the internal store contains the monitor and an internal process, s, which is the *basic operating system*. S can create parallel processes, a, b, c, etc., on request from consoles. These processes can in turn create other processes, d, e, f, etc. Thus while s acts as a primitive operating system for a, b, and c, these in turn act as operating systems for their children, d, e, f, etc. This is illustrated by the following figure, which shows a *family tree* of processes on the left and the corresponding storage allocation on the right:

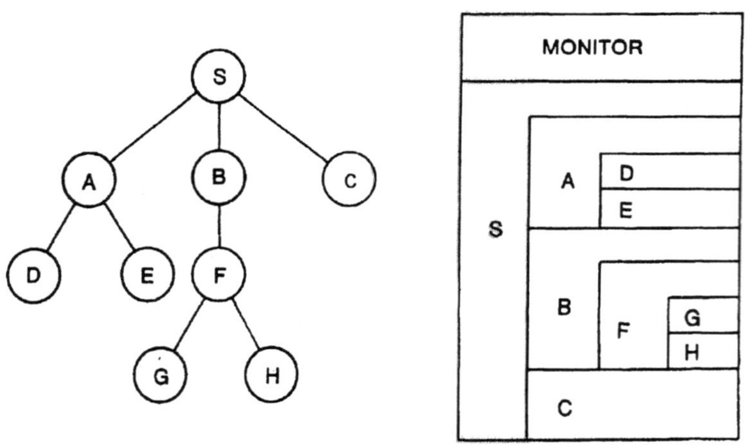

This family tree of processes can be extended to any level, subject only to a limitation of the total number or processes. At present the maximum number of internal processes is 23 including the basic operating system s. It must, however, be remembered that the storage protection system only provides mutual protection of 8 independent processes. When this number is exceeded, one must rely on some of the processes being error free.

In this multiprogramming system all privileged functions are implemented in the monitor, which has no built-in strategy. Strategies can be introduced at the various higher levels, where each process has the power to control the scheduling and resource allocation of its own children. The only rules enforced by the monitor are the following: a process can only allocate a subset of its own resources (including storage) to its children; a process can only modify, start, stop, and remove its own children.

The structure of the family tree is defined in the process descriptions within the monitor. We emphasize that the only function of the tree is to define the basic rules of process control and resource allocation. Time slices are shared evenly among active processes regardless of their position in the hierarchy, and each process can communicate with all other processes.

As regards the future development of operating systems, the most important characteristics can now be seen as the following:

1. *New operating systems can be implemented as other programs* without modification of the monitor. In this connection we should mention that the Algol and Fortran languages for the RC 4000 contain facilities for calling the monitor and initiating parallel processes. Thus it is possible to write operating systems in high-level languages.

2. *Operating systems can be replaced dynamically*, thus enabling an installation to switch among various modes of operation; several operating systems can, in fact, be active simultaneously,

3. *Standard programs and user programs can be executed under different operating systems* without modification; this is ensured by a standardization of communication between parents and children.

6.3 Process States

We are now in a position to define the possible states of an internal process as described within the monitor. An understanding of the transition from one state to the other is vital as a key to the dynamic behaviour of the system.

An internal process is either *running* (executing instructions or ready to do so) or *waiting* (for an event outside the process). In the running state the process is linked to the time slice queue; in the waiting state it is temporarily removed from this queue.

A process can either be *waiting* for a *message*, an *answer*, or an *event*, as explained in Chapter 4.

Of a more complex nature are the situations in which a process is *waiting* to be *stopped* or *started* by another process. In order to explain this we shall once more refer to the family tree shown in the previous section.

Let us say that process b wants to stop its child f. The purpose of doing this is to ensure that all program execution and input/output within the storage area of process f is stopped. Since a part of the storage area has been allocated to children of f, it is obviously necessary to stop not only the *child* f but also all *descendants* of f. This is complicated by the fact that some of these descendants may already have been stopped by their own parents. In the present example process g may still be running, while process h may have been stopped by its parent f. Consequently the monitor should only stop processes f and g.

Consider now the reverse situation, in which process b starts its child f again. Now the purpose is to reestablish the situation exactly as it was before process f was stopped. Thus the monitor must be very careful only to start those descendants of f that were stopped along with f. In our example the monitor must start processes f and g but not h. Otherwise we confuse f, which still relies on its child h being stopped.

Obviously, then, the monitor must distinguish between processes that are stopped by their *parents* and by their *ancestors.*

The possible *states* of an internal process are the following:

running
running after error
waiting for message
waiting for answer
waiting for event
waiting for start by parent
waiting for stop by parent
waiting for start by ancestor
waiting for stop by ancestor
waiting for process function

A process is created in the state *waiting for start by parent.* When it is started, its state becomes *running.* The meaning of the state *running after error* is explained in Section 8.1.

When a parent wants to stop a child, the state of the child is changed to *waiting for stop by parent*, and all running descendants of the child are described as *waiting for stop by ancestor.* At the same time these processes are removed from the time slice queue.

What remains to be done is to ensure that all input/output initiated by these processes is terminated. In order to control this each internal process description contains an integer called the *stop count.* The stop count is increased by one each time the internal process initiates input/output from an external process. On arrival of an answer from an external process, the monitor decreases the stop count by one and examines the state of the internal process. If the stop count becomes zero and the process is *waiting for stop by parent* (or *ancestor*), its state is changed to *waiting for start by parent* (or *ancestor*).

Only when all involved processes are waiting for start is the stop operation finished. This can last some time, and it may not be acceptable to the parent (being an operating system with many other duties) to be inactive for so long. For this reason the stop operation is split into two parts. The stop procedure:

stop internal process(name, buffer, result)

only initializes the stopping of a child and selects a message buffer for the parent. When the child and its running descendants are completely stopped, the monitor delivers an answer to the parent in this buffer. Thus the parent can use the procedures *wait answer* or *wait event* to wait for the completion of the stop.

A process can be in any state when a stop is initiated. If it is waiting for a message, answer, or an event, its state will be changed to waiting for stop, as explained above, but at the same time its instruction counter is decreased by two in order that it can, repeat the call of *wait message*, *wait answer*, or *wait event* when it is started again.

It should be noted that a process can receive messages and answers in its queue in any state. This ensures that a process does not loose contact with its surroundings while stopped.

The meaning of the state *waiting for process function* is explained in Section 9.1.

7 RESOURCE CONTROL

This chapter describes a set of monitor rules that enables a parent process to control the allocation of resources to its children.

7.1 Introduction

In the multiprogramming system the internal processes compete for the following limited resources:

computing time
storage and protection keys
message buffers
process descriptions
peripheral devices
backing storage

Initially all resources are owned by the basic operating system s. As a basic principle enforced by the monitor a process can only allocate a subset of its own resources to a child process. These are returned to the parent process when the child is removed.

7.2 Time Slice Scheduling

All running processes are allocated *time slices* in a cyclical manner. Depending on the interrupt frequency of the hardware interval timer, the length of a time slice can vary between 1.6 and 1638.4 milliseconds. A reasonable time slice is 25.6 milliseconds; with shorter intervals the percentage of computing time consumed by timer interrupts grows drastically; with longer intervals the delay between activation and execution of an internal process increases.

In practice internal processes often initiate input/output and wait for it in the middle of a time slice. This creates a scheduling problem when internal processes are activated by answers: Should the monitor link processes to the beginning or to the end of the time slice queue? The first possibility ensures that processes can use peripherals with maximum speed, but there is the danger that a process can monopolize computing time by communicating frequently with fast devices. The second choice prevents this, but introduces a delay in the time slice queue, which slows down peripherals.

We have introduced a modified form of round-robin scheduling to solve this dilemma. As soon as a process is removed from the time slice queue, the monitor stores the actual value of the *time quantum* used by it. When the process is activated again, the monitor compares this quantum with the maximum time slice. As long as this limit is not exceeded, the process is linked to the beginning of the queue; otherwise it is linked to the end of the queue and its time quantum is reset to zero. The same test is applied when the interval timer interrups an internal process.

This scheduling attempts to share computing time evenly among active internal processes regardless of their position in the hierarchy. It permits a process to be activated immediately until it threatens to monopolize the central processor, only then is it pushed into the background to give other processes a chance. This is admittedly a built-in strategy at the microlevel. Parent processes can in fact only control the allocation of computing time to their children in larger portions (on the order of seconds) by means of the procedures *start* and *stop internal process.*

For accounting purposes the monitor retains the following information for each internal process: the time at which the process was created and the sum of time quantums used by it; these quantities are denoted *start time* and *run time.*

7.3 Storage Allocation and Protection

An internal process can only create child processes within its own storage area. The monitor does not check whether storage areas of child processes overlap each other. This freedom can be used to implement time-sharing of a common storage area among several processes as described in Sections 10.2 and 10.4.

During creation of an internal process the parent must specify the values of the *protection register* and the *protection key* used by the child. In the protection register each bit corresponds to one of the eight possible protection keys; if a bit is zero the process can change or execute storage words with the corresponding key.

The protection key is the key that is set in all storage words of the child process itself. A parent process can only allocate a subset of its own protection keys to a child. It has complete freedom to allocate identical or different keys to its children. The keys remain accessible to the parent after creation of a child.

7.4 Message Buffers and Process Descriptions

The monitor only has room for a finite number of message buffers and tables describing internal processes and the so-called area processes (files on the backing store used as external processes). A message buffer is selected when a message is sent to another process; it is released when the sending process receives an answer. A process description is selected when an internal process creates another internal process or an area process, and released when the process is removed.

Thus it is clear that message buffers and process descriptions only assume an identity when they are actually used. As long as they are unused, they can be regarded as anonymous pools of resources. Consequently it is sufficient to specify the maximum number of each resource an internal process can use. These so-called *buffer claim*, *internal claim*, and *area claim* are defined by the parent when a child process is created. The claims must be a subset of the parent's own claims, which are diminished accordingly, they are returned to the parent when the child is removed.

The buffer claim defines the maximum number of messages an internal process can exchange simultaneously with other internal and external processes. The internal claim limits the number of children an internal process can have at the same time. The area claim defines how many backing store areas an internal process can access simultaneously.

The monitor decreases a claim by one each time a process actually uses one of its resources, and increases it by one when the resource is released again. Thus at any moment the claims define the number of resources that can still be used by the process.

7.5 Peripheral Devices

A distinction has been made between peripheral devices and external processes. An external process is created when a name is assigned to a device.

Thus it is also true of peripheral devices that they only assume an identity when they are actually used for input/output. Indeed the whole idea of identification by name is to give the operator complete freedom in allocation of devices. It would therefore seem natural to control the allocation of devices to internal processes by a complete set of claims—one for each kind of device.

In a system with remote peripherals, however, it is unrealistic to treat all devices of a given kind as a single, anonymous pool. An operating system must be able to force its children and their human operators to remain within a certain geographical *configuration* of devices. It should be noted that the concept of configuration must be defined in terms of physical devices and not in terms of external processes, since a parent generally speaking does not know in advance which documents its children are going to use.

Configuration control is exercised as follows. From the point of view of other processes an internal process is identified by a name. Within the monitor, however, an internal process can also be identified by a single bit in a machine word. The process descriptions of peripheral devices include a word in which each bit indicates whether the corresponding internal process is a *potential user* of the device. Another word indicates the *current user* that has reserved the device in order to obtain exclusive access to a document.

Initially the basic operating system s is a potential user of all peripherals. A parent process can *include* or *exclude* a child as a user of any device, provided the parent is also a user of it:

include user(child, device number, result)
exclude user(child, device number, result)

During removal of a child, the monitor excludes it as a user of all devices.

All in all three conditions must be fulfilled before an internal process can initiate input/output:

The device must be an external process with a unique name.

The internal process must be a user of the device.

The internal process must reserve the external process if it controls a sequential document.

7.6 Privileged Functions

Files on the backing store are described in a catalog, which is also kept on the backing store. Clearly there is a need to be able to prevent an internal process from reserving an excessive amount of space in the catalog or on the backing store as such. It seems difficult, however, to specify a reasonable rule in the form of a claim that is defined once and for all when a child process is created. The main difficulty is that catalog entries and data areas can survive the removal of the process that created them; in other words backing storage is a resource a parent process can loose permanently by allocating it to its children.

As a half-hearted solution we have introduced the concept of *privileged monitor procedures*. A parent process must supply each of its children with a *function mask*, in which each bit specifies whether the child is allowed to perform a certain monitor function. The mask must be a subset of the parent's own mask.

At present the privileged functions include all monitor procedures that:

change the catalog on the backing store,
create and remove names of peripheral devices,
change the real-time clock.

8 MONITOR FEATURES

This chapter is a survey of specific monitor features such as internal interruption, the real-time clock, conversational access from consoles, and permanent storage of files on the backing store. Although these are not essential primitive concepts, they are indispensable features of practical multiprogramming systems.

8.1 Internal Interruption

The monitor can assist internal processes with the detection of infrequent events such as violation of storage protection or arithmetic overflow. This causes an interruption of the internal process followed by a jump to an *interrupt procedure* within the process.

The interrupt procedure is defined by calling the monitor procedure:

set interrupt(interrupt address, interrupt mask)

When an internal interrupt occurs, the monitor stores the values of registers at the head of the interrupt procedure and continues execution of the internal process in the body of the procedure:

interrupt address: working registers
instruction counter
interrupt cause
(execution continues here)

The system distinguishes between the following *causes* of internal interruption:

protection violation
integer overflow
floating-point overflow or underflow
parameter error in monitor call
breakpoint forced by parent

The *interrupt mask* specifies whether arithmetic overflow should cause internal interruption. Other kinds of internal interrupts cannot be masked off.

If an internal process provokes an interrupt without having defined an interrupt procedure after its creation, the monitor removes the process from the time slice queue and changes its state to *running after error*. The process does not receive any more computing time in this state, but from the point of view of other processes it is still an existing process. The parent of the erroneous process can, however, reactivate it by means of stop and start.

A parent can force a *breakpoint* in a child process as follows: first, stop the child; second, fetch the registers and interrupt address from the process description of the child and store the registers in the interrupt area together with the cause; third, modify the registers of the child to ensure that program execution continues in the interrupt procedure; fourth, start the child again.

8.2 Real-Time Clock

Real time is measured by means of a hardware interval timer, which counts modulo 16384 in units of 0.1 msec and interrupts the computer regularly (normally every 25.6 msec).

The monitor uses this timer to update a programmed *real-time clock* of 48 bits. This clock can be initialized and sensed by means of the procedures:

set clock(clock)
get clock(clock)

The setting of the clock is a privileged function. A standard convention adopted by operating systems (but not enforced by the monitor) is to let the clock express the time interval elapsed since midnight 31 December 1967 in units of 0.1 msec.

The interval timer is also used to implement an external process that permits the synchronization of internal processes with real time. All internal processes can send messages to this *clock process*. After the elapse of a time interval specified in the message, the clock process returns an answer to the sender. In order to avoid a heavy overhead time of clock administration, the clock process only examines its queue every second.

8.3 Console Communication

A multiprogramming system encourages a conversational mode of operation, in which users interact directly with internal processes from typewriter consoles. The external processes for consoles clearly reflect this objective.

Initially all program execution is ordered by human operators who communicate with the basic operating system. It would be very wasteful if the operating system had to examine all consoles regularly for possible operator requests. Therefore our first requirement is that consoles be able to activate internal processes by sending messages to them. Note that other external processes are only able to receive messages.

Second, it must of course be possible for an internal process to open a conversation with any console.

Third, a console should accept messages simultaneously from several internal processes. This will enable us to control more than one internal process from the same console, which is valuable in a small installation.

In short, consoles should be independent processes that can open conversations with any internal process and vice versa. The console should assist the operator with the identification of the internal processes using it.

An operator opens a conversation by depressing an interrupt key on the console. This causes the monitor to select a line buffer and connect it to the console. The operator must now identify the internal process to which his message is addressed. Following this he can input a message of one line, which is delivered in the queue of the receiving process.

A message to the basic operating system s can, for example, look like this (the word in italics is output by the console process in response to the key interrupt):

to s
new pbh run

An internal process opens a conversation with a console by sending a message to it. Before the input/output operation is initiated, the console identifies the internal process to the operator. This identification is suppressed after the first of a series of messages from the same process.

In the following example internal processes a and b share the same console for input/output. Process identifications are in italics:

> *to a*
> first input line to a
> second input line to a
> *from b*
> first output line from b
> second output line from b
> *from a*
> first output line from a
> etc.

Note that these processes are unaware of their sharing the same console. From the point of view of internal processes the identification of user processes makes it irrelevant whether the system contains one or more consoles. (Of course one cannot expect operators to feel the same way about it).

8.4 Files on Backing Store

8.4.1 Introduction

The monitor permits semi-permanent storage of files on a backing store consisting of one or more drums and disks. The monitor makes these appear as a single backing store with a number of segments of 256 words each. This *logical backing store* is organized as a collection of named *data areas.* Each area occupies a consecutive number of segments on a single backing store device. A fixed part of the backing store is reserved for a *catalog* describing the names and locations of data areas.

Data areas are treated as external processes by the internal processes; input/output is initiated by sending messages to the areas specifying input/output operations, storage areas, and relative segment numbers within the areas. The identification of a data area requires a catalog search. In order to reduce the number of searches, input/output must be preceded by an explicit creation of an *area process* description within the monitor.

8.4.2 Catalog Entries

The catalog is a fixed area on the backing store divided into a number of *entries* identified by unique *names.* Each entry is of fixed length and consists of a *head,* which identifies the entry, and a *tail,* which contains the rest of the information. The monitor distinguishes between entries describing data areas on the backing store and entries describing other things.

An entry is *created* by calling the monitor procedure:

create entry(name, tail, result)

The first word of the *tail* defines the *size* of an area to be reserved and described in the entry; if the size is negative or zero, no area is reserved. The rest of the tail contains nine *optional parameters*, which can be selected freely by the internal process.

Internal processes can *look up*, *change*, *rename*, or *remove* existing entries by means of the procedures:

look up entry(name, tail, result)
change entry(name, tail, result)
rename entry(name, new name, result)
remove entry(name, result)

The catalog describes itself in an entry named *catalog*.

The search for catalog entries is minimized by using a hashed value of names to define the first segment to be examined. Each segment contains 15 entries; thus most catalog searches only require the input of a single segment unless the catalog is filled to the brim. The allocation of data areas is speeded up by keeping a bit table of available segments within the monitor. In practice the creation or modification of an entry therefore requires only the input and output of a single catalog segment.

8.4.3 Catalog Protection

Since many users share the backing store as a common data base, it is vital that they have a means of protecting their files gainst unintentional modification or complete removal. The protection system used is similar to the storage protection system: each catalog entry is supplied with a *catalog key* in its head; the rules of access within an internal process are defined by a *catalog mask* set by the parent of the internal process. Each bit in this mask corresponds to one of 24 possible catalog keys; if a bit is one, the internal process can modify or remove entries with the corresponding key; otherwise it can only look up these entries. A parent can only allocate a subset of its own catalog keys to a child process. Initially the basic operating system owns all keys.

In order to prevent the catalog and the rest of the backing store from being filled with irrelevant data, the concept of *temporary entry* is introduced.

This is an entry that can be removed by another internal process as soon as the internal process that created the entry has been removed. Typical examples are working areas used during program compilation and data areas created, but not removed, by faulty programs.

This concept is implemented as follows. After creation of an internal process, the monitor increases an integer *creation number* by one and stores it within the new process description. Each time an internal process creates a catalog entry, the monitor includes its creation number in the entry head indicating that it is temporary. Internal processes can at any time scan the catalog and remove all temporary entries provided the corresponding creators no longer exist within the monitor. Thus in accordance with our basic philosophy the monitor only provides the necessary mechanism for the handling of temporary entries, but leaves the actual strategy of removal to the hierarchy of processes.

In order to ensure the survival of a catalog entry, an internal process must call the privileged monitor function:

permanent entry(name, catalog key, result)

to replace the creation number with a catalog key. A process can of course only set one of its own keys in the catalog; otherwise it might fill the catalog with highly protected entries, which could be difficult to detect and remove.

8.4.3 Area Processes

In order to be used for input/output a data area must be looked up in the catalog and described as an external process within the monitor:

create area process(name, result)

The area process is created with the same name as the catalog entry.

Following this internal processes can send messages with the following format to the area process:

message: input/output operation
first storage address
last storage address
first relative segment

The reader is reminded that the tables used to describe area processes within the monitor are a limited resource, which is controlled by means of area claims defined by parent processes (Section 7.4).

The backing store is a random access medium that serves as a common data base. ln order to utilize this property fully internal processes should be able to input simultaneously from the same area (e.g. when several copies of the Algol compiler are executed in parallel). On the other hand access to an area should be exclusive during output, because its content is undefined from the point of view of other processes.

Consequently we distinguish between internal processes that are *potential users* of an area process and the single process that may have *reserved* the area exclusively. This distinction was also made for peripheral devices (Section 5.2), but the rules of access are different here: An internal process is a user of an area after the creation of it. This enables the internal process to perform input as long as no other process reserves it. An internal process can reserve an area process if its catalog mask permits modification of the corresponding catalog entry. After reservation the internal process can perform both input and output.

Finally we should mention that the catalog is described permanently as an area process within the monitor. This enables internal processes to input and scan the catalog sequentially, for instance, during the detection and removal of temporary entries. Only the monitor itself, however, can perform output to the catalog.

9 SYSTEM IMPLEMENTATION

This chapter gives important details about the implementation as well as figures about the size and performance of the system.

9.1 Interruptable Monitor Functions

Some of the monitor functions are too long to be executed entirely in the disabled mode, e.g. updating of the catalog on the backing store and creation, start, stop, and removal of processes. These so-called *process functions* are called as other monitor procedures, but behind the scenes they are executed by an anonymous internal process, which only operates in disabled mode for short intervals while updating monitor tables, otherwise the anonymous process shares computing time with other internal processes.

When an internal process calls a process function, the following takes place: the calling process is removed from the time slice queue and its state is changed to *waiting for process function.* At the same time the process description is linked to the event queue of the anonymous process that is activated. The anonymous process serves the calling processes one by one and returns them to the time slice queue after completion of each function.

Process functions are interruptable like other internal processes. From the point of view of calling processes, however, process functions are indivisible, since (1) they are executed only by the anonymous process one at a time in their order of request, and (2) calling processes are delayed until the functions are completed.

The following monitor procedures are implemented as interruptable functions:

create entry
look up entry
change entry
rename entry
remove entry
permanent entry
create area process
create peripheral process
create internal process
start internal process
stop internal process
modify internal process
remove process

9.2 Stopping Processes

According to theory an internal process cannot be stopped while input/output is in progress within its storage area (Section 6.3). This requirement is inevitable in the case of high-speed devices such as a drum or a magnetic tape station, which are beyond program control during input/output. On the other hand it is not strictly necessary to enforce this for low-speed devices controlled by the monitor on a character-by-character basis.

In practice the monitor handles the stop situation as follows:

Before an external process initiates *high-speed input/output*, it examines the state of the sending process. If the sender is stopped (or waiting to be stopped), input/output is not initiated, but the external process immediately returns an answer with block length zero; the sender must then repeat input/output after restart. If the sender is not stopped, its stop count is increased and input/output is initiated. Note that if the stop count was increased immediately after the sending of a message, the sending process could only be stopped after completion of all previous operations pending in the external queue. By increasing the stop count as late as possible, we ensure that high-speed peripherals at most prevent the stopping of internal processes during a single block transfer.

Low-speed devices never increase the stop count. During output an external process fetches one word at a time from the sending process and outputs it character by character regardless of whether the sender is stopped meanwhile. Before fetching a word the external process examines the state of the sender. If it is stopped (or waiting to be stopped), output is terminated by an answer defining the actual number of characters output; otherwise output continues. During input an external process examines the state of the sender after each character. If the sender is stopped (or waiting to be stopped), input is terminated by an answer; otherwise the character is stored and input continues. Some devices, such as the typewriter, lose the last input character when stopped; others, such as the paper tape reader, do not. It can be seen that low-speed devices never delay the stopping of a process.

9.3 System Size

After initial system loading the monitor and the basic operating system s occupy a fixed part of the internal store. The size of a typical system is as follows:

		words:
monitor procedures:		2400
code for external processes:		1150
clock	50	
backing store	100	
typewriters	300	
paper tape readers	250	
paper tape punches	150	
line printers	100	
magnetic tape stations	200	
process descriptions and buffers:		1250
15 peripheral devices	350	
20 area processes	200	
6 internal processes	200	
25 message buffers	300	
6 console buffers	200	
basic operating system s		1400
total system		6200

It should be noted that the 6 internal processes include the anonymous process and the basic operating system, thus leaving room for 4 user processes. As a minimum the standard programs (editor, assembler, and compilers) require an internal process of 5–6000 words for their execution. This means that a 16 k store can only hold the system plus 1–2 standard programs, while a 32 k store enables parallel execution of 4 such programs. A small store can of course hold more programs, if these are written in machine code and executed without the assistance of standard programs.

9.4 System Performance

The following execution times of monitor procedures are conservative estimates based on a manual count of instructions. The reader should keep in mind that the basic instruction execution time of the RC 4000 computer is 4 μsec. A complete conversation between two internal processes takes about 2 milliseconds distributed as follows:

	msec
send message	0.6
wait answer	0.4
wait message	0.4
send answer	0.6

It can be seen that one internal process can activate another internal process in 0.6 msec, this is also approximately the time required to activate an external process. An analysis shows that the 2 msec required by an internal communication are used as follows:

	percent
validity checking	25
process activation	45
message buffering	30

This distribution is so even that one cannot hope to speed up the system by introducing additional, *ad hoc* machine instructions. The only realistic solution is to make the hardware faster.

The maximum time spent in the disabled mode within the monitor limits the system's response to real-time events. The monitor procedures themselves are only disabled for 0.2–1 msec. The situation is worse in the case of interrupt procedures that handle low-speed devices with hardware buffers, because the monitor empties or fills such buffers in the disabled mode after each interrupt. For the paper tape reader (flexowriter input) and the line printer, the worst-case figures are:

empty reader buffer (256 characters)	20 msec
fill printer buffer (170 characters)	7 msec

It should be noted, however, that these buffers normally only contain 64–70 characters corresponding to 4–5 msec. The worst-case situations can be remedied either by using smaller input/output areas within internal processes, or by replacing these external processes with dedicated internal processes (Section 5.4).

Finally we shall look at the interruptable monitor functions. An internal process of 5000 words can be created and controlled by a parent process with the following speed:

	msec
create internal process	3
modify internal process	2
start internal process	26
stop internal process	4
remove internal process	30

Most of the time required to start and remove an internal process is used to set storage protections keys.

Assuming that the backing store is a drum with a transfer time of 15 msec per segment, the catalog can be accessed with the following speed:

	msec
create entry	38
look up entry	20
change entry	38
rename entry	85
remove entry	38
permanent entry	38

The execution time of process functions should be taken with some reservations. First it must be remembered that process functions, like other internal processes, can be delayed for some time before they receive a time slice. In practice process functions will be activated immediately as long as they have not used a complete time slice (Section 7.2). Second one must take into consideration the fact that process function calls are queued within the monitor. Thus when a process wants to stop another process, the worst thing that can happen is that the anonymous process is engaged in updating the catalog. In this situation the stop is not initiated before the catalog has been updated. One also has to keep in mind that process functions share the drum or disk with other processes, and must wait for the completion of all input/output operations that preceed their own in the drum or disk queue. The execution times given here assume that process functions and catalog input/output are initiated instantly.

9.5 System Tape

The first version of the multiprogramming system consists of the monitor, the basic operating system s, and a program for initializing the catalog. It is programmed in the Slang 3 language. Before assembly the system is edited to include process descriptions of the peripheral devices connected to a particular installation and to define the following *options*:

number of storage bytes
number of internal processes
number of area processes
number of message buffers
number of console buffers
maximum time slice
inclusion of code for external processes
backing store configuration
size of catalog

The system is delivered in the form of a binary paper tape, which can autoload and initialize itself. After loading the system starts the basic operating system. Initially the operating system executes a program that can initialize the backing store with catalog entries and binary Slang programs input from paper tape. When this has been done, the operating system is ready to accept operator commands from consoles.

10 SYSTEM POSSIBILITIES

The strength of the monitor is the generality of its basic concepts, its weakness that it must be supported by operating systems to obtain realistic multiprogramming. We believe that the ultimate limits to the use of the system will depend on the imagination of designers of future operating systems. The purpose of this chapter is to stimulate creative thinking by pointing out a few of the possibilities inherent in the system.

10.1 Identification of Documents

In tape-oriented installations, operating systems should assist the operator with automatic identification of magnetic tapes. At present the external process concept gives the operator complete freedom to mount a magnetic tape on any station and identify it by name. When a tape station is set in the *local* mode, the monitor immediately removes its name to indicate that the operator has interfered with it. The station gives an interrupt when the operator returns it to the *remote* mode. Thus the monitor distinguishes between three states of a tape station:

document removed (after intervention)
unidentified document mounted (after remote interruption)
identified document mounted (after process creation)

It is a simple matter to introduce a *watch-dog process* in the monitor, to which internal processes can send messages in order to receive answers each time an unidentified tape is mounted somewhere. After reception of an answer, an internal process can give the actual station a temporary name, identify the tape by reading its label, and rename it accordingly.

Automatic identification requires general aggreement on the format of tape labels, at least to the extent of assigning a standard position to the names of tapes.

10.2 Temporary Removal of Programs

We have not imposed any restrictions on individual programs with respect to their demand for storage, run time, and peripherals. It is taken for granted that some programs will need most of the system resources for several hours. Such large programs must not, however, prevent other users from obtaining immediate access to the machine in order to execute more urgent programs of short duration. Thus the system must permit temporary removal of a program in order to make its storage area and peripherals available for other programs. One example, where this is absolutely necessary, is the periodic supervision of a real-time process combined with the execution of large background programs in idle intervals.

A program can be removed temporarily by stopping the corresponding internal process and dumping its storage area on the backing store by an output operation. Note that this dump automatically includes all children and descendants created within the area. The monitor is only aware of the process being stopped; it is still described within the monitor and can receive messages from other processes.

It is now possible to create and start other processes in the same storage area, since the monitor does not check whether internal processes overlap each other as long as they remain within their parent processes. Peripherals can also be taken from the dumped process and assigned to others simply by mounting new documents and renaming the peripherals.

Temporary removal makes sense only if it is possible to restart a program at a later stage. This requires reloading the program into its original storage area as well as mounting and repositioning of its documents. After restart the internal process can detect interference with its documents in one of two ways: either it finds that a document does not exist any more, whereupon it must ask the operator to mount and name it; or it discovers that an existing document no longer is reserved by it, meaning that the operator has mounted it, but that it needs to be repositioned. These cases are indicated by the result parameter after a call of *wait answer.*

The need for repositioning can also arise during normal program execution, if the operator interferes with a peripheral device (by mistake or in order to move a document to a more reliable device). Consequently all major programs should consider each input/output operation as a potential restart situation.

10.3 Batch Processing

In the design of a batch processing system the distinction between parent and child processes prevents the batch of programs from destroying the operating system. Note that in general an operating system must remove a child process (and not merely stop it) to ensure that all its resources are released again (Section 7.4). Even then, it must be remembered that messages sent by a child to other processes remain in their queues until these processes either answer them or are removed (Section 4.4).

The multiprogramming capabilities can be utilized to accept job requests in a conversational mode during execution of the batch. Thus a *batch processing* system can include facilities for *remote job entry* combined with *priority scheduling* of programs.

10.4 Time-Sharing

The basic requirement of a *time-sharing* system, in which a large number of users have conversational access to the system from consoles, is the ability to swap programs between the internal store and the backing store. A time-sharing operating system must create an internal process for each user, and make these processes share the same storage area by frequent removal and restart of programs (say, every few seconds). The problem is that stopping a process temporarily also means stopping its communication with peripherals. Thus in order to keep typewriter input/output alive while a user process is dumped, the system must include an internal process that buffers all data between programs and consoles.

10.5 Real-Time Scheduling

We conclude these hints with an example of a *real-time* system. The application we have in mind is a process control system, in which a number of programs must perform data logging, alarm scanning, trend logging, and so forth periodically under the real-time control of an operating system.

This can be organized as follows: initially all task programs send messages to the operating system and wait for answers. The operating system communicates with the clock process and is activated every second in order to scan a time table of programs. If the real time exceeds the start time of a task program, the operating system activates the program by an answer. After completion of its task, the program again sends a message to the operating system and waits for the answer. In response the operating system increases the start time of the program by the period between two successive executions of the task.

Acknowledgements

The design of the system is based on the ideas of Jørn Jensen, Søren Lauesen, and the author; Leif Svalgaard participated in its implementation.

4

HIERARCHICAL ORDERING OF SEQUENTIAL PROCESSES

EDSGER W. DIJKSTRA

(1971)

One of the primary functions of an operating system is to rebuild a machine that must be regarded as non-deterministic (on account of cycle stealing and interrupts) into a more or less deterministic automaton. Taming the degree of indeterminacy in steps will lead to a layered operating system. A bottom layer will be discussed and so will the adequacy of the interface it presents. An analysis of the requirements of the correctness proofs will give us an insight into the logical issues at hand. A "director-secretary" relationship will be introduced to reflect a possible discipline in the use of sequencing primitives.

The processing unit of a working computer performs in a short period of time a sequence of millions of instructions and as far as the processing unit is concerned this sequence is extremely monotonous: it just performs instructions one after the other. And if we dare to interpret the output, if we dare to regard the whole happening as "meaningful", we do so because we have mentally grouped sequences of instructions in such a way that we can distinguish a structure in the whole happening. Similar considerations apply to the store: high speed stores contain typically millions of bits stored in a monotonous sequence of consecutively numbered but otherwise equivalent storage locations. And again, if we dare to attach a meaning to such a vast amount of bits, we can only do so by grouping them in such a way that we can distinguish some sort of structure in the vast amount of information.

E. W. Dijkstra, Hierarchical ordering of sequential processes. *Acta Informatica 1*, 2 (October 1971), 115–138.

In both cases the structure is *our* invention and *not* an inherent property of the equipment: with respect to the structure mentioned the equipment itself is absolutely neutral. It might even be argued that this "neutrality" is vital for its flexibility. On the other hand, it then follows that it is the programmer's obligation to structure "what is happening where" in a useful way. It is with this obligation that we shall concern ourselves. And it is in view of this obligation that we intend to start with a rather machine-bound, historical introduction: this gives us the unordered environment in which we have to create order, to invent structure adequate for our purposes.

In the very old days, machines were strictly sequential, they were controlled by what was called "a program" but could be called very adequately "a sequential program". Characteristic for such machines is that when the same program is executed twice—with the same input data, if any—both times the same sequence of actions will be evoked. In particular: transport of information to or from peripherals was performed as a program-controlled activity of the central processor.

With the advent of higher electronic speeds the discrepancy in speed between the central processor on the one hand and the peripheral devices on the other became more pronounced. As a result there came for instance a strong economic pressure to arrange matters in such a way that two or more peripherals could be running simultaneously.

In the old arrangement one could write a program reading information from a paper tape, say at a maximum speed of 50 char/sec. In that case the progress through that piece of program would be synchronized with the actual movement of the paper tape through the reader. Similarly one could write a program punching a paper tape, say at a maximum speed of 30 char/sec. To have *both* peripherals running simultaneously and also closely to their maximum speed would require a tricky piece of program specifically designed for this mixture of activities. This was clearly too unattractive and other technical solutions have been found. Channels were invented; a channel is a piece of hardware dedicated to the task of regulating the information traffic between the store and the peripheral to which it is attached, and doing this synchronized to the natural speed of the peripheral device, thus doing away with the implicit mutual synchronization of the peripheral devices that would be caused if both were controlled by the same sequential program execution.

The introduction of channels created two problems, a microscopic and a macroscopic one. The microscopic problem has to do with access to the store. In the old arrangement only the central processor required access to the store and when the central processor required access to the store it could get it. In the new arrangement, with the channels added—channels that can be regarded as "special purpose processors"—a number of processors can be competing with each other as regards access to the store because such accesses from different processors very often exclude each other in time (for technical or local reasons). This microscopic problem has been solved by the invention of the "switch", granting the competing processors access to the store according to some priority rule. Usually the channels have a lower traffic density and a higher priority than the central processor: the processor works at full speed until a channel requests access to the store, an arrangement which is called "cycle stealing". We draw attention to the fact that the unit of information in which this interleaving takes place—usually "a word"—is somewhat arbitrary; in a few moments we shall encounter a similar arbitrariness.

The macroscopic problem has to do with the coordination of central processor activity and channel activity. The central processor issues a command to a channel and from that moment onwards, two activities are going on simultaneously and—macroscopically speaking—independent of each other: the central processor goes on computing and the channel transports information. How does the central processor discover, when the execution of the channel command has been completed? The answer to this has been the "interrupt". Upon completion of a channel command the channel sets an interrupt flip-flop; at the earliest convenient moment (but never sooner than after completion of the current instruction) the central processor interrupts the execution of the current program (in such a neat way that the interrupted computation can be resumed at a later moment as if nothing had happened) and starts executing an interrupt program instead, under control of which all now appropriate actions will be taken. From the point of view of the central processor it interleaves the various program executions, the unit of interleaving being—similarly arbitrarily—"the instruction".

The above scheme can be recognized in all larger, modern computers that I have studied. It has been embellished in many directions but we don't need to consider those embellishments now. We go immediately to the next questions: given a piece of equipment constructed along the lines just sketched, what are the problems when we try to use it and in what direction should we look for their solution?

What are the problems? Well the main point is that from the point of view of program control such a piece of equipment must be regarded as a non-deterministic machine. Measured in a grain of time appropriate for the description of the activity of the central processing unit—clockpulse or instruction execution time—the time taken by a peripheral transport must be regarded as undefined. If completion of such a peripheral is signalled to the central processor by means of an interrupt, this means that we must regard the moment when the interrupt will take place (or more precisely: the point of progress where the computation will be interrupted) as unpredictable. The problem is that in spite of this indeterminacy of the basic hardware, we must make a more or less deterministic automaton out of this equipment: from the outside world the machine will be confronted with a well-defined computational task and it has to produce a well-defined result in a microscopically unpredictable way!

Let me give a simple example to explain what I mean by "a more or less deterministic automaton". Suppose that offering a program to the machine consists of loading a pack of cards into a card reader (and pushing some button on the reader in order to signal that it has been loaded). Suppose now that we have a machine with two readers and that we want to load it with two programs, A and B, and that we can do this by loading both card readers and pressing both buttons. We assume that the two card readers are not mutually synchronized, i.e. we regard both speeds as unpredictable. To what extent will the total configuration be a deterministic automaton? It will be fully deterministic in the sense that eventually it will produce both output A and output B. If these outputs are to be produced by the same printer, they will be produced in some order and the system may be such that the order in which the respective outputs appear on the printer *does* depend on the relative speeds of the two readers. As far as the operator is concerned, who has to take the output from the printer and to dispatch it to the customers, the installation is non-deterministic; what *he* has to do depends on the unpredictable speed ratio of the two readers, which may cause output A to precede or to follow output B. For both cases the operator has his instructions such that in both cases all output is dispatched to the proper customer. The "computation centre"—i.e. installation and operator together—are deterministic. We can regard the operator's activity as an outer layer, "wrapping up the installation", shielding from the outside world a level of interior indeterminacy.

Now, even if the operator is aware of not having a fully deterministic machine, we should recognize that he has only to deal with two cases—

output A before output B or the other way round—while the number of possible sequences of occurrences at cycle time level is quite fantastic. In other words, by far the major part of the "shielding of indeterminacy" is done by the installation itself. We call the resulting installation "more or less deterministic" because as the case may be, a few degrees of limited freedom—here one Boolean degree of freedom—may be left unpredictable.

We have called the operator's activity "an outer layer", shielding a level of indeterminacy, and of course we did so on purpose. At the other end we may distinguish an inner layer, viz. in the channel signalling (via an interrupt signal) that the next card has been read: it tells the central processor that the next card image is available in core, regardless which storage cycles have been stolen to get it there. The terms "inner layer" and "outer layer" have been chosen in order to suggest that in the total organization we shall be able to distinguish many layers in between. But an important remark is immediately appropriate: I assume that with the card read command an area in core has been designated to receive this card image: the remark that the interrupt signalled the completed transfer of the card image irrespective of which cycles had been stolen to transport its constituents is only true, provided that no other access to the designated core area took place in the period of time ranging from the moment the command was given up to the moment that the completion was signalled! Obvious but vital.

It draws our attention to an element of structure that must be displayed by the remaining programs if we wish to make the total organization insensitive to the exact identity of the cycles stolen by the channel. And from the above it is clear that this insensitivity must be one of our dearest goals. And on next levels (of software) we shall have to invent similar elements of structure, making the total organization insensitive (or "as insensitive as possible") to the exact moment when interrupts are honoured. Again it is clear that this must be one of our dearest goals. And on a next level we must make our organization insensitive (or "as insensitive as possible") to the exact number of cards put into the readers for program A and B, and so on .... This "layered insensitivity" is, in two words, our grand plan.

I have used the term "layer" on purpose, because it has seemed to provide an attractive terminology in terms of which to talk about operating systems and their total task. We can regard an operating system as the basic software that "rebuilds" a given piece of hardware into a (hopefully) more attractive machine. An operating system can then be regarded as a sequence of layers, built on top of each other and each of them implementing a given "improvement". Before going on, let me digress for a moment and try to explain why I consider such an approach of ordered layers a fruitful one.

There is an alternative approach, which I would like to call the approach via unordered modules. There one makes a long list of all the functions of the operating system to be performed, for each function a module is programmed and finally all these modules are glued together in the fervent hope that they will cooperate correctly and will not interfere disastrously with each other's activity. It is such an approach which has given rise to the assumed law of nature, that complexity grows as the square of the number of program components, i.e. of the number of "functions".

In the layered approach we start at the bottom side with a given hardware machine A_0, we add our bottom layer of software rebuilding A_0 into the slightly more attractive machine A_1, for which the next layer of software is programmed rebuilding it into the still more attractive machine A_2 etc. As the machines in the sequence A_0, A_1, A_2,... get more and more attractive, adding a further layer gets easier and easier. This is in sharp contrast to the approach via unordered modules, where adding new functions seems to get progressively worse!

1. So much in favour of a layered approach in general. When one wishes to design an operating system, however, one is immediately faced with the burning question, which "improvement" is the most suitable candidate to be implemented in the bottom layer.

For the purpose of this discussion I will choose a very modest bottom layer. I do so for two reasons. Firstly, it is a choice with which for historical reasons I myself am most familiar. Secondly, as a bottom layer it is very modest and neutral, so neutral in fact that it provides us with a mental platform from where we can discuss various alternatives for the structure of what is going to be built on top of it. As a bottom layer it seems close to the choice of minimal commitment. The fact that this bottom layer is chosen as a starting point for our discussion is by no means to be interpreted as the suggestion that this is the best possible choice: on the contrary, one of the later purposes of this discussion is the consideration of alternatives.

With the hardware taking care of the cycle stealing we felt that the software's first responsibility was to take care of the interrupts, or, to put it a little more strongly, to do away with the interrupt, to abstract from its existence. (Besides all rational arguments this decision was also inspired by fear based on the earlier experience that, due to the irreproducibility of the interrupt moments, a program bug could present itself misleadingly like an incidental machine malfunctioning.) What does it mean "to do away with the interrupt"? Well, without the interrupt the central processor continues the execution of the current sequential process while it is the function of the interrupt to make the central processor available for the continuation of another sequential process. We would not need interrupt signals if each sequential process had its own dedicated processor. And here the function of the bottom layer emerged: to create a virtual machine, able to execute a number of sequential programs in parallel as if each sequential program had its own private processor. The bottom layer has to abstract of the existence of the interrupt or, what amounts to the same thing, it has to abstract from the identity of the single hardware processor. If this abstraction is carried out rigorously it implies that everything built on top of this bottom layer will be equally applicable to a multiprocessor installation, provided that all processors are logically equivalent (i.e. have the same access to main memory etc.). The remaining part of the operating system and user programs together then emerges as a set of harmoniously cooperating sequential processes.

The fact that these sequential processes out of the family have to cooperate harmoniously implies that they must have the means of doing so; in particular, they must be able to communicate with each other and they must be able to synchronize their activities with respect to each other. For reasons which, in retrospect, are not very convincing, we have separated these two obligations. The argument was that we wished to keep the bottom layer as modest as possible, giving it only the duty of processor allocation; in particular it would leave the "neutral, monotonous memory" as it stood; it would not rebuild that part of the machine, and immediately above the bottom layer the processes could communicate with each other via the still available, commonly accessible memory.

The mutual synchronization, however, is a point of concern. Closely related to this is the question: given the bottom layer, what will be known about the speed ratios with which the different sequential processes progress? Again we have made the most modest assumption we could think of, viz. that they would proceed with speed ratios, unknown but for the fact that the speed ratios would differ from zero; i.e. each process (when logically allowed to proceed, see below) is guaranteed to proceed with some unknown, but finite speed. In actual fact we can say more about the way in which the bottom layer grants processor time to the various candidates: it does it "fairly" in the sense that in the long run a number of identical processes will proceed at the same macroscopic speed. But we don't tell, how "long" this run is and the said fairness has hardly a logical function.

This assumption about the relative speeds is a very "thin" one, but as such it has great advantages. From the point of view of the bottom layer, we remark that it is easy to implement: to prevent a running program from monopolizing the processor an interrupting clock is all that is necessary. From the point of view of the structure built on top of it is also extremely attractive: the absence of any knowledge about speed ratios forces the designer to code all synchronization measures explicitly. When he has done so he has made a system that is very robust in more than one sense.

Firstly he has made a system that will continue to operate correctly when an actual change in speed ratios is caused, and this may happen in a variety of ways. The actual strategy for processor allocation as implemented by the bottom layer, may be changed. In a multiprocessor installation the number of active processors may change. A peripheral may temporarily work with speed zero, e.g. when it requires operator attention. In our case the original line printer was actually replaced by a faster model. But under all those changes the system will continue to operate correctly (although perhaps not optimally, but that is quite another matter).

Secondly—and we shall return to this in greater detail—the system is robust thanks to the relative simplicity of the arguments that can convince us of its proper operation. Nothing being guaranteed about speed ratios means that in our understanding of the structure built on top of the bottom layer we have to rely on discrete reasoning and there will be no place for analog arguments, for other purposes than overall justification of chosen strategies. I trust that the strength of this remark will become apparent as we proceed.

2. Let us now focus our attention upon the synchronization. Here a key problem is the so-called "mutual exclusion problem". Given a number of cyclic processes of the form

```
cycle begin entry;
            critical section;
            exit;
            remainder of cycle
      end
```

program `entry` and `exit` in such a way that at any moment at most one of the processes is engaged in its critical section. The solution must satisfy the following requirements:

(a) The solution must be symmetrical between the processes; as a result we are not allowed to introduce a static priority.

(b) Nothing may be assumed about the ratio of the finite speeds of the processes; we may not even assume their speeds to be constant in time.

(c) If any of the processes is stopped somewhere in `remainder of cycle`, this is not allowed to lead to potential blocking of any of the others.

(d) If more than one process is about to enter its critical section, it must be impossible to devise for them such finite speeds, that the decision to determine which of them will enter its critical section first is postponed until eternity. In other words, constructions in which "After you"—"After you"—blocking, although improbable, is still possible, are not to be regarded as valid solutions.

I called the mutual exclusion problem "a key problem". We have met something similar in the situation of programs A and B producing their output in one of the two possible orders via the same printer: obviously those two printing processes have to exclude each other mutually in time. But this is a mutual exclusion on a rather macroscopic scale and in all probability it is not acceptable that the decision to grant the printer to either one of the two activities will be taken on decount of the requirement of mutual exclusion alone: in all probability considerations of efficiency or of smoothness of service require a more sophisticated printer granting strategy. The explanation why mutual exclusion must be regarded as a key problem must be found at the microscopic end of the scale. The switch granting access to store on word basis provides a built in mutual exclusion, but only on a small, fixed and rather arbitrary scale. The same applies to the single processor installation which can honour interrupts in between single instructions: this is a rather arbitrary grain of activity. The problem arises when more complicated operations on common data have to take place. Suppose that we want to count the number of times something has happened in a family of parallel processes. Each time such an occurrence has taken place, the program could try to count it via

```
n:= n+1
```

If in actual fact such a statement is coded by three instructions

```
R:= n;
R:= R+1;
n:= R
```

then one of the increases may get lost when two such sequences are executed, interleaved on single instruction basis. The desire to compound such (and more complicated) operators on common variables is equivalent to the desire to have more explicit control over the degree of interleaving than provided by the neutral, standard hardware. This more explicit control is provided by a solution to the mutual exclusion problem.

We still have to solve it. Our solution depends critically on the communication facilities available between the individual processes and the common store. We can assume that the only mutual exclusion provided by the hardware is to exclude a write instruction or a read instruction, writing or reading a single word. Under that assumption the problem has been solved for two processes by T. J. Dekker in the early sixties. It has been solved by me for N processes in 1965 (CACM 8, 9 (1965), p.569). The solution for two processes was complicated, the solution for N processes was terribly complicated. (The program pieces for **enter** and **exit** are quite small, but they are by far the most difficult pieces of program I ever made. The solution is only of historical interest.)

It has been suggested that the problem could be solved when the individual processes had at their disposal an indivisible "add to store" which would leave the value thus created in one of the private process registers as well, so that this value is available for inspection if so desired. Indicating this indivisible operation with braces the suggested form of the parallel programs was:

```
cycle begin while {x:= x+1} <> 1 do {x:= x-1};
            critical section;
            {x:= x-1};
            remainder of cycle
      end
```

Where the "add to store" operation is performed on the common variable x which is initialized with the value zero before the parallel programs are started.

As far as a single process is concerned the cumulative Δx as affected by this process since its start is = 0 or = 1; in particular, when a process is in its critical section its cumulative Δx = 1. As a result we conclude that at any moment when N processes are in their critical section simultaneously, `x` ≥ `N` will hold.

A necessary and sufficient condition for entering a critical section is that this process effectuates for `x` the transition from 0 to 1. As long as one process is engaged in its critical section (N = 1), `x` ≥ `1` will hold. This excludes the possibility of the transition from 0 to 1 taking place and therefore no other process can enter its critical section. We conclude that mutual exclusion is indeed guaranteed. Yet the solution must be rejected: it is not difficult to see that even with two processes (after at least one successful execution of a critical section) "After you"—"After you"—blocking may occur (with the value of `x` oscillating between 1 and 2).

A correct solution exists when we assume the existence of an indivisible operation, **`swap`** which causes a common variable (`x`) and a private variable (`loc`) to exchange their values. With initially `x` = 0 the structure of the parallel programs is:

```
begin integer loc; loc:= 1;
      cycle begin repeat swap(x, loc) until loc = 0;
                  critical section;
                  swap(x, loc);
                  remainder of cycle
            end
      end
```

The invariant relation is that of the N+1 variables (i.e. the N `loc`'s and the single `x`) always exactly one will be = 0, the others being = 1. A process is in its critical section if and only if its own `loc` = 0, as a result at most one process can be engaged in its critical section. When none of the processes is in its critical section, `x` = 0 and "After you"—"After you"—blocking is impossible. So this is a correct solution.

In a multiprogramming environment, however, the correct solutions referred to or shown have a great drawback: the program section called **`enter`** contains a loop in which the process will cycle when it cannot enter its critical section. This so-called "busy form of waiting" is expensive in terms of processing power, because in a multiprogramming environment (with more parallel processes than processing units) there is a fair chance that there will be a more productive way of spending processing power than giving it to a process that, to all intents and purposes, could go to sleep for the time being.

If we want to do away with the busy form of waiting we need some sort of synchronizing primitives by means of which we can indicate those program points where—depending on the circumstances—a process may be put to sleep. Similarly we must be able to indicate that potential sleepers may have to be woken up. What form of primitives?

Suppose that process 1 is in its critical section and that process 2 will be the next one to enter it. Now there are two possible cases.

(a) process 1 will have done `exit` before process 2 has tried to `enter`; in that case no sleeping occurs

(b) process 2 tries to `enter` before process 1 has done `exit`; in that case process 2 has to go to sleep temporarily until it is woken up as a side-effect of the `exit` done by process 1.

When both occurrences have taken place, i.e. when process 2 has successfully entered its critical section it is no longer material whether we had case (a) or case (b). In that sense we are looking for primitives (for `enter` and `exit`) that are commutative. What are the simplest commutative operations on common variables that we can think of? The simplest operation is inversion of a common Boolean, but that is too simple for our purpose: then we have only one operation at our disposal and lack the possibility of distinguishing between `enter` and `exit`. The next simplest commutative operations are addition to (and subtraction from) a common integer. Furthermore we observe that `enter` and `exit` have to compensate each other: if only the first process passes its critical section the common state before its `enter` equals the common state after its `exit` as far as the mutual exclusion is concerned. The simplest set of operations we can think of are increasing and decreasing a common variable by 1 and we introduce the special synchronizing primitives

```
P(s): s:=s-1
```

and

```
V(s): s:=s+1
```

special in the sense that they are "indivisible" operations: if a number of P and V-operations on the same common variable are performed "simultaneously" the net effect of them is as if the increases and decreases are done "in some order".

Now we are very close to a solution: we have still to decide how we wish to characterize that a process may go to sleep. We can do this by making the P- and V-operations operate not on just a common variable, but on a special purpose integer variable, a so-called *semaphore*, whose value is by definition non-negative, i.e. $\mathtt{s} \geq 0$.

With that restriction, the V-operation can always be performed: unsynchronized execution of the P-operation, however, could violate it.

We therefore postulate that whenever a process initiates a P-operation on a semaphore whose current value equals zero, the process in question will go to sleep until (another) process has performed a V-operation on that very same semaphore. A little bit more precise: if a semaphore value equals zero, one or more processes may be blocked by it, eager to perform a P-operation on it. If a V-operation is performed on a semaphore blocking a number of processes, one of them is woken up, i.e. will perform its now admissible P-operation and proceed. The choice of this latter process is such that no process wlll be blocked indefnitely long. A way to implement this is to decide that no two processes will initiate the blocking P-operation simultaneously and that they will be treated on the basis "first come, first served" (but it need not be done that way, see below).

With the aid of these two primitives the mutual exclusion problem is solved very easily. We introduce a semaphore **mutex** say, with the initial value

```
mutex = 1
```

after which the parallel processes controlled by the program

```
cycle begin P(mutex);
            critical section;
            V(mutex);
            remainder of cycle
      end
```

are started.

Before proceeding vith the discussion I would like to insert a remark. In languages specifically designed for process control I have met two other primitives, called "wait" and "cause", operating on an "event variable", which is a (possibly empty) queue of waiting processes. Whenever a process executes a "wait" it attaches itself to the queue until the next "cause" for the same event, which empties the queue and signals to all processes in the queue that they should proceed. Experience has shown that such primitives are very hard to use. The reason for this is quite simple: a "wait" in one process and a "cause" in another are non-commutative operations, their net effect depends on the order in which they take place and at the level where we need the synchronizing primitives we must assume that we have not yet effective control over this ordering. The limited usefulness of such "wait", and "cause" primitives could have been deduced a priori.

3. As a next interlude I am going to prove the correctness of our solution. One may ask "Why bother about such a proof, for the solution is obviously correct". Well, in due time we shall have to prove the correctness of the implementation of more sophisticated rules of synchronization and the proof structure of this simple case may then act as a source of inspiration.

With each process j we introduce a state variable C_j, characterizing the progress of the process.

$C_j = 0$ process$_j$ is in the `remainder of cycle`
$C_j = 1$ process$_j$ is in its `critical section`.

While process$_j$ performs (i.e. "completes") the operation $P(\text{mutex})_j$ the translation $C_j{=}0 \rightarrow C_j{=}1$ takes place, when it performs the operation $V(\text{mutex})_j$ the transition $C_j{=}1 \rightarrow C_j{=}0$ takes place. (Note that the C_j are not variables occurring in the program, they are more like functions defined on the current value of the order counters.) In terms of the C_j the number of processes engaged in its critical section equals

$$\sum_{j=1}^{N} C_j$$

In order to prove that this number will be at most = 1, we follow the life history of the quantity

$$K = \text{mutex} + \sum_{j=1}^{N} C_j$$

The quantity K will remain constant as long as its constituents are constant: the only operations changing its constituents are the 2N mutually exclusive primitive actions $P(\text{mutex})_i$ and $V(\text{mutex})_i$ (for $1 \leq i \leq N$).

We have as a result of

$$\begin{aligned} P(\text{mutex})_i : \Delta K &= \Delta\text{mutex} + \Delta\left(\sum_{j=1}^{N} C_j\right) \\ &= \Delta\text{mutex} + \Delta C_i \\ &= -1 + 1 = 0 \end{aligned}$$

and similarly, as a result of

$$\begin{aligned} V(\text{mutex})_i : \Delta K &= \Delta\text{mutex} + \Delta C_i \\ &= +1 - 1 = 0 \end{aligned}$$

As these 2N operations are the only ones affecting K's constituents, we conclude that K is constant, in particular, that it is constantly equal to its initial value,

$$K = 1 + \sum_{j=1}^{N} 0 = 1$$

As a result

$$\sum_{j=1}^{N} C_j = 1 - \text{mutex}$$

Because mutex is a semaphore, we have

$$0 \leq \text{mutex}$$

and from the last two relations we conclude

$$\sum_{j=1}^{N} C_j \leq 1$$

Because this sum is the sum of non-negative terms we know

$$0 \leq \sum_{j=1}^{N} C_j$$

Combining this with

$$\text{mutex} = 1 - \sum_{j=1}^{N} C_j$$

We conclude

$$\text{mutex} \leq 1$$

i.e. mutex is a so-called "binary semaphore", only taking on the values 0 and 1.

Finally we observe that no process will be kept out of its critical section without justification: if all processes are outside their critical sections, all C_j's are = 0 and therefore mutex is = 1, thereby allowing the first process that wants to enter its critical section to do so.

For later reference we summarize the structure of this proof. A central role is played by an invariant relation among common variables (here only the semaphore) and "progress variables" (here the C_j's). Its invariance is proved by observing the net effect of the (mutually exclusive) operators operating on its constituents, without any further assumptions about their mutual synchronization, about which we can then make assertions on account of the established invariance. In the sequel we shall see that this pattern of proof is very generally applicable.

4. Before proceeding with more complicated examples of synchronization we must make a little detour and make a connection with earlier observations. When a process is engaged in its critical section, a great number of other processes may go to sleep. When the first one leaves its critical section, it is undefined which of the sleepers is woken up, the only requirement being that no single process is kept sleeping indefinitely long. (This latter assumption we have to make when, later, we wish to prove assertions about the finite progress of individual processes.) In this sense our "family of sequential processes" is still a mechanism of an undeterministic nature, but the degree of undeterminacy is a mild one compared with the original hardware, in which an interrupt could occur between any pair of instructions: the only indeterminacy left is the relative order of much larger units of action, viz. the critical sections. In this respect the bottom layer of our operating system achieves a step towards our goal of "layered insensitivity".

It is in this connection that I should like to make another remark of quantitative nature. The choice of the process to be woken up is left undefined because it is assumed that it does not matter, i.e. we assume the system load to be such that the total period of time that any of the processes will be engaged in its critical section will be a negligible fraction of real time, in other words, nearly always mutex = 1 will hold. It is for that reason that such a neutral policy for waking up a sleeper is permissible. This is no longer true for our macroscopic concerns regarding so-called "resource allocation". In the case of a number of programs producing their output via the same printer, these printing actions have to exclude each other mutually in time, but it is no longer true that the total time spent in printing will be a negligible fraction of real time! On the contrary: in a well-balanced system the printer will be used with a duty cycle close to 100 per cent! In order to achieve this—and to satisfy other, perhaps conflicting design requirements—such a neutral policy which is adequate for granting entrance into critical sections will certainly be inadequate for granting a scarce resource like a printer. For the implementation of a less neutral granting policy we shall use the critical sections, entrance to which is granted on a neutral basis. (For an example of a more elaborate synchronization implemented with the aid of critical sections we refer to the Problem of the Dining Philosophers to be treated later.) This is the counterpart of the "layered insensitivity": going upwards in levels we gain more and more control over the microscopic indeterminacy, but simultaneously macroscopic strategic concerns begin to enter the picture: it seems vital that the bottom layer with its microscopic concerns does not bother itself with such macroscopic considerations. This observation seems to apply to all well-designed systems: I would call it a principle if I had a better formulation for it.

5. We now turn to a slightly more complicated example, viz. a bunch of producers and a bunch of consumers, coupled to each other via an unbounded buffer. In this example all producers are regarded as equivalent to each other and all consumers are regarded as equivalent to each other. Under these assumptions—which are not very realistic—the semaphores provide us with a ready-made solution.

In the commonly accessible universe we have

(a) a buffer, initialized empty

(b) a semaphore `mutex`, initialized = 1; this semaphore caters for the mutual exclusion of operations changing buffer contents

(c) a semaphore `numqueuepor`; this gives (a lower bound of) the number of portions queueing in the buffer.

Then a producer may have the form

```
cycle begin produce next portion;
            P(mutex);
            add portion produced to buffer;
            V(numqueuepor);
            V(mutex)
      end
```

with consumers of the following structure

```
cycle begin P(numqueuepor);
            P(mutex);
            take portion from buffer;
            V(mutex);
            consume portion taken
      end
```

Notes:

1. The order of the V-operations in the producer is immaterial, the order of the P-operations in the consumer is absolutely essential.

2. The assumption is that the operations `produce next portion` and `consume portion taken` are the slow, time-consuming operations—possible in synchronism with other equipment—for which parallelism is of interest, while the actions `add portion produced to buffer` and `take portion from buffer` are very fast "clerical" operations.

In the above program the semaphore `numqueuepor` is a so-called "general semaphore", i.e. a semaphore whose possible values are not restricted to 0 and 1. We shall now give an alternative program, using only binary semaphores.

In the commonly accessible universe we have

(a) a buffer and an integer `n`, counting the number of portions in the buffer. The buffer is initialized empty (incl. `n:=0`)

(b) a semaphore `mutex` initialized = 1; this semaphore caters for the mutual exclusion of the operations changing the buffer contents, the value of `n` and the inspection of `n`.

(c) a semaphore `consal`, initialized = 0; if this semaphore is = 1, a next consumption is allowed.

Then a producer may have the form

```
cycle begin produce next portion;
            P(mutex);
            add portion to buffer (incl. n:=n+1);
            if n=1 do V(consal);
            V(mutex)
      end
```

with consumers of the following structure

```
cycle begin P(consal);
            P(mutex);
            take portion from the buffer (incl. n:=n-1);
            if n > 0 do V(consal);
            V(mutex);
            consume portion taken
      end
```

Although it is not too hard to convince ourselves "by inspection"—whatever that may mean—that the above bunch of programs work properly, it is illuminating to give a somewhat more formal treatment of their cooperation. (I am now used to calling such a more formal treatment of their cooperation "a correctness proof", although I did not formalize the requirements that such a piece of reasoning should satisfy in order to be a "valid proof".)

The proof consists of two steps. The first step uses our earlier result, viz. that the `P(mutex)` and `V(mutex)` establish mutual exclusion of the critical sections. (Inside these critical sections we find no P-operations, as a result they cannot give rise to deadlock situations.) This observation allows us to regard the critical sections as indivisible operations and to confine our attention to the state of the system at the discrete moments with `mutex` $= 1$ (i.e. no one engaged in its critical section).

In the second step we define three mutually exclusive states for the whole system and shall show that whenever the system is started in one of these states, it will remain within these states. For the purpose of state description we introduce a function defined on the progress of the consumers, viz.

K = the number of consumers that have performed `P(consal)` but have not yet entered the following critical section.

Now we can introduce our three states

S1: `n=0 and K=0 and consal=0`
S2: `n>0 and K=0 and consal=1`
S3: `n>0 and K=1 and consal=0`

Three operations; (viz. `P(consal)` and the two critical sections) operate on the constituents of these Boolean expressions; for each state we investigate all three.

S1: (initial state)
`P(consal)`: impossible (on account of `consal`=0)
critical producer section: transition to S2
critical consumer section: impossible (on account of `K`=0)

S2:
`P(consal)`: transition to S3
critical producer section: transition to S2
critical consumer section: impossible (on account of `K`=0)

S3:
`P(consal)`: impossible (on account of `consal`=0)
critical producer section: transition to S3
critical consumer section: transition to S1 or S2

This concludes the second step, showing the invariance of

S1 or S2 or S3

(from which we conclude $\mathtt{N}\geq 0$ and $\mathtt{consal}\leq 1$.

A few remarks, however, are in order, for we have cheated slightly. Let us repair our cheating first and then give our further comments. In our second step we have investigated the *isolated* effect of either `P(consal)` or the critical producer section or the critical consumer section. For the critical sections this is all right for they exclude each other mutually in time; the operation `P(consal)`, however, can take place *during* a critical section, and we did not pay any attention to such coincidence. We can save the situation by observing that in the case of coincidence the net effect is equal to the execution of the critical section immediately followed by `P(consal)`. This is really a messy patching up of a piece of reasoning that was intended to be clean. Now our further comments.

1. The proof shows why the mutual exclusion problem is worthy, of the name "a key problem". Thanks to the mutual exclusion of critical sections we only need to consider the net effect of each single, isolated section. If these sections were not critical, i.e. could take place in arbitrary interleaving, we would have to consider the net effect of one section, the net effect of two sections together, of three sections together, of four etc.! With N cooperating processes the number of cases to be investigated would grow like 2^N (i.e. the powerset!). This is one of the strongest examples showing how the amount of intellectual effort needed for a correctness proof may depend critically on structural aspects of the program, here the aspect of mutual exclusion. It is

this observation that is meant to justify the inclusion of the above proof in this text.

2. The proof is complicated considerably by the fact that `P(consal)` is an operation sequentially separate from the following critical section: this caused the messy patching up of our piece of reasoning, it called for the introduction of the function `K`. If the conditional entrance of critical sections is going to be a standard feature of the system, a more direct way of expressing this would be essential. A minimal departure of the current formation would be the introduction of the parallel P-operation, allowing us to combine the two P-operations of the consumer into

```
P(consal, mutex)
```

3. For the sake of completeness we mention that in the T.H.E. multiprogramming system, where we used general semaphores to control synchronization along information streams, each information stream had at any moment in time at most one consumer attached to it. As a result a general semaphore could block at most one process and when a V-operation was performed on it there was never the problem which process should be woken up. The absence of the possibility that more than one process is blocked by a general semaphore is not surprising: it is the semaphore `consal` that may be equal to zero for a long period of time; as a result it is not to be expected that it is irrelevant which of the processes will be woken up when a V-operation is performed on it. In the design phase of the T.H.E. multiprogramming system the parallel P-operation has been considered but finally it has not been implemented because we felt that it contained the built-in solution to an irrealistic problem. But it would have simplified proof procedures.

6. We now turn to the problem of the Five Dining Philosophers. The life of a philosopher consists of an alternation of thinking and eating:

```
cycle begin think;
            eat
      end
```

Five philosophers, numbered from 0 through 4 are living in a house where the table is laid for them, each philosopher having his own place at the table:

Their only problem—besides those of philosophy—is that the dish served is a very difficult kind of spaghetti, that has to be eaten with two forks. There are two forks next to each plate, so that presents no difficulty: as a consequence, however, no two neighbours may be eating simultaneously.

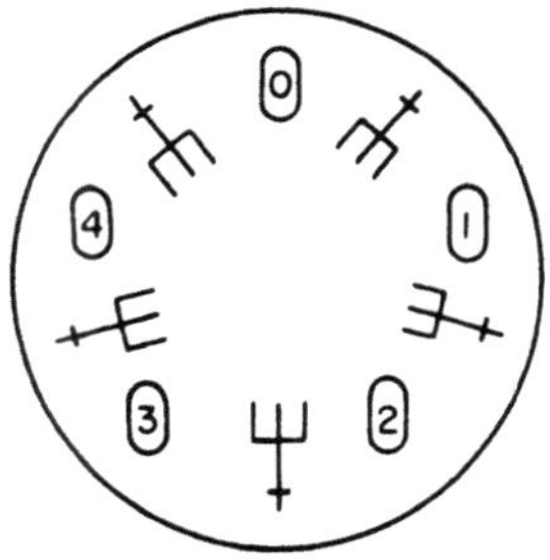

A very naive solution associates with each fork a binary semaphore with the initial value=1 (indicating that the fork is free) and, naming in each philosopher these semaphores in a local terminology, we could think the following solution for the philosopher's life adequate

```
cycle begin think;
            P(left-hand fork); P(right-hand fork);
            eat;
            V(left-hand fork); V(right-hand fork)
      end
```

But this solution—although it guarantees that no two neighbours are eating simultaneously—must be rejected because it contains the danger of the deadly embrace. When all five philosophers get hungry simultaneously, each will grab his left-hand fork and from that moment onwards the group is stuck. This could be overcome by the introduction of the parallel P-operation, combining the two P-operations into the single

```
P(left-hand fork, right-hand fork)
```

For the time being we assume the parallel P-operation denied to us—later we shall reject the solution using it on other grounds—and we shall show how (using only single P-operations and binary semaphores) we can derive our solution in a reasonably controlled manner.

In order to be able to give a formal description of our restriction, we associate with each philosopher a state variable, `C` say, where

`C[i] = 0`	means:	philosopher `i` is thinking
`C[i] = 2`	means:	philosopher `i` is eating.

In accordance with their first act, all `C`'s will be initialized = 0. In terms of the `C`'s we can state that it is disallowed

$$\exists_{\mathtt{i}}(\mathtt{C[i]} \ = \ 2 \ \mathtt{and} \ \mathtt{C[(i+1)} \ \mathtt{mod} \ 5] \ = \ 2) \qquad (1)$$

in words: no philosopher may be eating while his left hand neighbour is eating as well. From this formula it *follows* that for a C the transition from 2 to 0 can never cause violation of the restriction (1), while the transition from 0 to 2 can. Therefore we introduce for the last transition an intermediate state

C[i] = 1 means: philosopher i is hungry

Now each philosopher will go cyclically through the states 0, 1, 2, 0.... The next question to ask is: when has the (dangerous) transition from 1 to 2 to take place for philosopher K? Well, three conditions have to be satisfied

(1) C[K] = 1, i.e. he himself must be hungry

(2) C[(K+1) mod 5] $\neq$ 2, because otherwise
C[K]:=2 would cause violation of (1) for i=K

(3) C[(K-1) mod 5] $\neq$ 2, because otherwise
C[K]:=2 would cause violation of (1) for i=(K-1) mod 5.

As a result we have to see to it that the state

$$\exists_{\mathtt{K}}(\mathtt{C[(K-1)} \ \mathtt{mod} \ 5] \neq 2 \ \mathtt{and} \ \mathtt{C[K]} \ = \ 1 \ \mathtt{and} \ \mathtt{C[(K+1)} \ \mathtt{mod} \ 5] \neq 2) \qquad (2)$$

is unstable: whenever it occurs, it has to be resolved by assigning C[K]:=2 and sending philosopher K to the table.

In a similar analysis we ask: which transitions in the life of philosopher w can cause the unstable situation and for which values of K?

(1) when C[w]:=1 is executed, instability may be created for K = w

(2) when C[w]:= 0—i.e. when C[w] loses the value 2—instability may be created for K=(w+1) mod 5 and for K=(w-1) mod 5.

In words: when philosopher w gets hungry, the test whether he himself should be sent to the table is appropriate, when he leaves the table the test should be done for both his neighbours.

In the universe we assume declared

(1) the **semaphore** mutex, initially = 1

(2) the **integer array** C[0:4], with initially all elements = 0

(3) the **semaphore array** prisem[0:4] with initially all elements = 0

(4)
```
procedure test(integer value K);
  if C[(K-1) mod 5] ≠ 2 and C[K] = 1
    and C[(K+1) mod 5] ≠ 2 do
      begin C[K]:=2; V(prisem[K]) end;
```

(This procedure, which resolves unstability for K when present, will only be called from within a critical section.)

In this universe the life of philosopher w can now be coded

```
cycle begin think;
            P(mutex);
              C[w]:= 1; test(w);
            V(mutex);
            P(prisem[w]); eat
            P(mutex);
              C[w]:= 0;
              test[(w+1) mod 5];
              test[(w-1) mod 5];
            V(mutex)
      end
```

And this concludes the solution I was aiming at. I have shown it, together with the way in which it was derived, for the following reasons.

(1) The arrangement with the private semaphore for each process and the common semaphore for mutual exclusion in order to allow for unambiguous inspection and modification of common state variables is typical for the way in which in the T.H.E. multiprogramming system all synchronization restrictions have been implemented that were more complicated than straightforward mutual exclusion or synchronization along an information stream (the latter synchronization has been implemented directly with the aid of a general semaphore).

(2) The solution (including the need for the introduction of the intermediate state called "hungry") has been derived by means of a formal analysis of the synchronization restriction. It is exemplar for the way in which the flows of mutual obligations for waking up have been derived in the design phase of the T.H.E. multiprogramming system. It is this analysis that I have called "A constructive approach to the problem of program correctness".

With respect to this particular solution I would like to make some further remarks.

Firstly the solution as presented is free from the danger of deadlock, as it should be. Yet it is highly improbable that a solution like this can be accepted because it contains the possibility of a particular philosopher being starved to death by a conspiration of his two neighbours. This can be overcome by more sophisticated rules (introducing besides the state "hungry" also the state "very hungry"); this requires a more complicated analysis but by and large it follows the same pattern as the derivation shown. This was another reason not to introduce the parallel P-operation: for the solution with the parallel P-operation we did not see an automatic way of avoiding the danger of individual starvation.

Secondly we could have made a more crude solution: the procedure `test` has a parameter indicating for which philosopher the test has to be done; also in the critical sections we call the procedure `test` precisely for those philosophers for whom there is a chance that they should be woken up and for no others. This is very refined: we could have made a test procedure without parameter that would simply test for any `K` if there was an unstability to be removed. But the problem could have been posed for 9 or 25 philosophers and the larger the number of philosophers, the more prohibitive the overhead of the crude solution would get.

Thirdly, I have stated that we "derived our solution in a reasonably controlled manner": although the formal analysis has been carried out almost mechanically, I would not like to suggest that it should be done automatically, because in real life, whether we like it or not, the situation can be more complicated.

We consider two classes of processes, class A and class B, sharing the same resource from a large pool. (The situation occurred in the T.H.E. multiprogramming system with the total pool of pages in the system.) Suppose now that processes from class A ask and return items from this pool at high frequency, while those from class B do so at low frequency only. In that case it is highly unattractive to pose upon the highly frequent item releases of class A the (possibly) considerable overhead involved in the analysis of whether it is necessary to wake up one or more blocked processes. This high-frequency overhead was avoided by delegating the waking-up obligation to (some) processes of class B and by guaranteeing that at least one of these processes would be active when the boundary of the resource restriction was in danger of being approached. In other words, in order to reduce system overhead we removed the highly frequent inspection whether processes had to be woken up at the price of increasing the "reaction time" there where an ultra short "response" was not required. The taking of such decisions seems a basic responsibility of the system designer and I don't see how they could be taken automatically.

The above concludes my discussion of the chosen bottom layer. In the final part of this paper I would like to discuss briefly an alternative solution.

7. The chosen bottom layer implements a family of sequential processes plus a few synchronizing primitives, the remaining part of the system, to be composed on top of it, will exist of a set of harmoniously cooperating sequential processes. The interface is characterized by a number of features

(a) the bottom layer treats all sequential processes on the same footing

(b) the sequential processes communicate with each other via commonly accessible variables

(c) critical sections ensure the unambiguous interpretation and modification of these common variables.

One or two objections can be raised to this organization; they center around the observation that each sequential process can be in one of two mutually exclusive radically different states: either the process is inside its critical section or it is not. Inside its critical section it is allowed to access the common variables, outside it is not. In actual fact this difference does not only pertain to accessibility of information it has also a bearing on processor allocation as implemented in the bottom layer. Given a process without hurry it is permissible to take the processor away from it for longer periods of time, but it is unattractive to do so in the middle of a critical section: if a process is stopped within a critical section it blocks for the other processes the mechanism needed for their cooperation and the remaining processes are bound to come to a grinding halt. In the T.H.E. multiprogramming system this has been overcome by giving processes two colours—red or white—by making each process red while it is in a critical section and by never granting the processor to a white process if a red one is logically allowed to proceed.

Furthermore there is the aspect of reproducibility. To an individual user, offering a strictly sequential program to the system, we should like to present a strictly deterministic automation. In the system a number of sequential processes are dedicated to the processing of user programs, they act as slots into which a user program can be inserted; whenever the user program refers to a shared resource the translator effectively inserts—via a subroutine call—the critical section required for this cooperation. As a result, what happens in this slot is perfectly reproducible as long as the sequential process remains outside critical sections. But if we wish to charge our user and also insist that the charge be reproducible, we can only charge him for the activity of the slot outside critical sections! What happens inside the critical sections is situation dependent system overhead: it does not really "belong" to the activity of the process in which the critical section occurs.

Finally, we know how to interpret the evolution of a sequential process as a path through "its" state space as is spanned by "its" variables. But for this interpretation to be valid it is necessary that all variables "belong" uniquely to one sequential process.

It is this collection of observations that was an incentive to redo some of our thinking about sequential processes and to reorder the total activity taking place in the system. Instead of N sequential processes cooperating in critical sections via common variables, we take out the critical sections and combine them into a N+1st process, called a "secretary"; the remaining N processes are called "directors". Instead of N equivalent processes, we now have N directors served by a common secretary. (We have used the metaphor of directors and a common secretary because in the director-secretary relation in real-life organization it's also unclear who is the master and who is the slave!)

What used to be critical sections in the N processes are in the directors "calls upon the secretary".

The relation between a set of directors and their common secretary shows great resemblance to the relation between a set of mutually independent programs and a common library. What is regarded as a single, unanalysed action on the level of a director, is a finite sequential process on the level of the secretary, similar to the relation between main program and subroutines.

But there is also a difference. In the case of a common library of re-entrant procedures, the library does not need to have a private state space; whenever a library procedure is called its local state space can be embedded (for the duration of the call) in the (extendable) state space of the calling program.

A secretary, however, has her own private state space, comprising all "common variables". One of the main reasons to introduce the concept of "a secretary" is that now we have identified a process to which the "common variables" belong: they belong to the common secretary.

To stress the specific nature of a secretary, I call her "a semi-sequential process". A fully sequential process consists of a number of actions to be performed one after the other in an order determined by the evolution of this process. A secretary is a bunch of actions—"operators in her state space"—to be performed one after the other, but in undefined order, i.e. depending on the calls of her directors.

A secretary presents itself primarily as a bunch of non-reentrant routines with common state space. But as far as the activity of the main program is concerned there is a difference between the routine of a secretary and a normal subroutine. During a normal subroutine call we can regard the main program "asleep", while the return from the subroutine "wakes" the main program again. When a director calls a secretary—for instance when a philosopher wishes to notity the secretary that now he is hungry—the secretary may decide to keep him asleep, a decision that implies that she should wake him up in one of her later activities. As a result the identity of the calling program cannot remain anonymous as in the case of the normal subroutine. The secretary must have variables of type "process identity" whenever she is called the identity of the calling process is handed over in an implicit input parameter, when she signals a release—analogous to the return of the normal subroutine—she will supply the identity of the process to be woken up.

In real time a director can be in three possible states with respect to his secretaries.

(a) "active", i.e. his progress is allowed

(b) "calling", i.e. he has tried to initiate a call on a secretary, but the call could not be honoured, e.g. because the secretary was busy with another call.

(c) "sleeping", i.e. a call has been honoured but the secretary's activity in which he will be released has not ended.

The state "calling" has hardly any logical significance: it would not occur if the director was stopped just before the call that could not be honoured.

With respect to her directors a secretary can be

(a) "busy", i.e. engaged in one of her (finite) algorithms

(b) "idle", i.e. ready to honour a next call from one of her directors.

Note that a secretary may be simultaneously busy with respect to her directors and calling or sleeping with respect to one of her subsecretaries.

In two respects, the above scheme asks for embellishments. Firstly, a secretary may be in such a state that certain calls on her service are inconvenient. With each call we can associate a masking bit, stating whether with respect to that call she is "responding" or "deaf". A secretary managing an unbounded buffer could be deaf for the consumer's call when her buffer is empty. Here we have another reason why a director may be in the state "calling": besides being busy the secretary could be deaf for the call concerned. For the reasons stated I have my doubts as to whether this embellishment is very useful, but I mention it because it seems more useful than similar embellishments that have been suggested, e.g. making a secretary responding to an enumerated list of directors. The secretary has to see to it that certain constraints will not be violated i.e. she may be in such a state that she can not allow certain of her possible *actions* to take place. This has nothing to do with the identity of the director calling for such an action.

A more vital embellishment is parameter passing: in general a director will like to send a message to his secretary when calling her—a producing director will wish to hand over the portion to be buffered; in general a director will require an answer back from his secretary when she has released his call—a consuming director will wish to receive the portion to be unbuffered.

Note that this message passing system is much more modest than various mail box systems that have been suggested in which processes can send messages (and proceed!) to other processes. In such systems elaborate message queues can be built up. Such systems suffer from two possible drawbacks. Firstly, implementation reasons are apt to impose upper limits to lengths of message queues: "message queue full" may be another reason to delay a process and to show the absence of the danger of deadly embraces may prove to be very diffcult. Secondly, and that seems worse, with the queueing messages we have reintroduced state information that cannot be associated with an individual process.

From an aesthetic point of view the relation director-secretary is very pleasing because it allows secretaries to act as directors with respect to subsecretaries. This places our processes in a hierarchy which avoids deadly embraces as far as mutual exclusion is concerned in exactly the same way in which mutual exclusion semaphore would need to be ordered in the case of nested critical sections. Whether, however, actual systems can be built up with a meaningful hierarchy of secretaries of reasonable depth—say larger than two—remains to be seen. That is why I called this point of view "aesthetically pleasing".

Finally: I can only view a well-structured system as a hierarchy of layers and in the design process the interface between these layers has to be designed and decided upon each time. I am not so much bothered by designer's willingness and ability to propose such interfaces, I am seriously bothered by the lack of commonly accepted yardsticks along which to compare and evaluate such proposals. My "playing" with a bottom layer should therefore not be regarded as a definite proposal for yet another interface, it was meant to illustrate a way of thinking.

Acknowledgement is due to my former students J. Bomhoff and W. H. J. Feyen and to Professor C. A. R. Hoare from the Queen's University of Belfast.

References

Koestler, A., The act of creation. Macmillan, New York, 1970.
Simon, H.A., The sciences of the artificial. MIT Press, Cambridge, 1969.

PART II

PROGRAMMING LANGUAGE CONCEPTS

5

TOWARDS A THEORY OF PARALLEL PROGRAMMING

C. A. R. HOARE

(1971)

OBJECTIVES

The objectives in the construction of a theory of parallel programming as a basis for a high-level programming language feature are:

1. Security from error. In many of the applications of parallel programming the cost of programming error is very high, often inhibiting the use of computers in environments for which they would otherwise be highly suitable. Parallel programs are particularly prone to time-dependent errors, which either cannot be detected by program testing nor by run-time checks. It is therefore very important that a high-level language designed for this purpose should provide complete security against time-dependent errors by means of a *compile-time check.*
2. Efficiency. The spread of real-time computer applications is severely limited by computing costs; and in particular by the cost of main store. If a feature to assist in parallel programming is to be added to a language used for this purpose, it must not entail any noticeable extra run-time overhead in space or speed, neither on programs which use the feature heavily, nor on programs which do not; efficient implementation should be possible on a variety of hardware designs, both simple and complex; and there should be no need for bulky or slow compilers.

C. A. R. Hoare, Towards a theory of parallel programming. In *Operating Systems Techniques*, Proceedings of a Seminar at Queen's University, Belfast, Northern Ireland, August–September 1971. C. A. R. Hoare and R. H. Perrott, Eds. Academic Press, New York (1972), 61–71.

3. Conceptual simplicity. A good high-level language feature should provide a simple conceptual framework within which the programmer can formulate his problems and proceed in an orderly fashion to their solution. In particular, it should give guidance on how to structure a program in a perspicuous fashion, and verify that each component of the structure contributes reliably to a clearly defined overall goal.
4. Breadth of application. The purposes for which parallel programming have been found useful are:

(a) To take advantage of genuine multi-processing hardware.

(b) To achieve overlap of lengthy input or output operations with computing.

(c) Operating system implementation.

(d) Real-time applications.

(e) Simulation studies.

(f) Combinatorial or Heuristic Programming.

Ideally, a language feature for parallel programming suitable for inclusion in a general-purpose programming language should cater adequately for all these highly disparate purposes.

The design of high-level programming languages which simultaneously satisfy these four objectives is one of the major challenges to the invention, imagination and intellect of Computer Scientists of the present day. The solutions proposed in this paper cannot claim to be final, but it is believed that they form a sound basis for further advance.

PARALLEL PROCESSES

The concept of two or more processes occurring simultaneously in the real world is a familiar one; however, it has proved exceptionally difficult to apply the concept to programs acting in parallel in a computer. The usual definition of the effect of parallel actions is in terms of "an arbitrary interleaving of units of action from each program". This presents three difficulties:

1. That of defining a "unit of action".
2. That of implementing the interleaving on genuinely parallel hardware.

3. That of designing programs to control the fantastic number of combinations involved in arbitrary interleaving.

Our approach to the solution of these problems is based on the observation that in the real world simultaneous processes generally occur in different parts of physical space (it is difficult to give any explanation of what it would mean for two processes to be occurring in the same place). Thus our normal concept of simultaneity is closely bound up with that of spatial separation. The concept of spatial separation has an analogue in computer programs that are operating on entirely disjoint sets of variables, and interacting with their environment through entirely disjoint sets of peripheral equipment. Obvious examples are programs being run on separate computers, or on the same computer under the control of a conventional multiprogramming system.

In such cases, where there is no possibility of communication or interaction between the programs, the question whether a given action of one program preceded, followed, or was simultaneous with a given action of the other program is wholly without significance. On a "Newtonian" view, the question must have a definite answer, even if we can neither know nor care what it is. For practical purposes, it is equally acceptable to take an "Einsteinian" view that there is no relative ordering between events occurring in disjoint programs being executed in parallel; and that each action of one program is simultaneous with all the actions of the other programs.

We introduce the notation

$$\{Q_1//Q_2//\ldots//Q_n\}$$

to indicate that the program statements Q_1, Q_2, ..., Q_n are disjoint processes to be executed in parallel. It is expected that the compiler will check the disjointness of the processes by ensuring that no variable subject to change in any of the Q_j is referred to at all in any Q_i for $i \neq j$. Thus it can be guaranteed by a compile-time check that no time-dependent errors could ever occur at run time. It is is assumed that the high-level language in use has the decent property that it is possible to tell by inspection which variables and array names appear to the left of an assignment which might be executed in any given statement or program.

The desired effect of the parallel statement described above is to initiate execution of each of the Q_i in parallel; and when they are all terminated, execution of the parallel statement is also complete. Each Q_i may contain any of the normal program features—assignments, conditionals, iterations, blocks, declarations, subroutine calls—of the base language; but if recursion or dynamic storage allocation is used, this will involve replacing the simple stack by a "cactus" stack. It would be wise to ban the use of jumps out of a parallel statement, since these would be not only difficult to define and to use correctly, but can also cause considerable implementation problems. In a language designed for parallel programming there is an even stronger case for the abolition of jumps than in more conventional high-level languages.

Some languages (e.g. PL/I) give the programmer the ability to specify and even to change the priorities of the parallel processes. For most applications this appears to be an unnecessary complexity, whose effective use will depend on many detailed machine and implementation oriented considerations. In practice it has been found that the general-purpose scheduling method of giving control to the process which has used least computer time in the recent past achieves acceptably high efficiency in most circumstances. The programmer can therefore safely be encouraged to "abstract from" the relative speeds and priorities of his processes, and allow the implementor of his programming language to decide on his behalf.

The way in which parallel programs can be proved to achieve some desired objective is simple. Suppose each Q_i is designed to ensure that R_i is true when it finishes, on the assumption that P_i is true before it starts. Then on completion of

$$\{Q_1//Q_2//\ldots//Q_n\}$$

all the R_i will be true, provided that all the P_i were true beforehand. Thus each Q_i makes its contribution to the common goal. But one caution is necessary: none of the P_i or R_i may mention any variable which is subject to change in any of the Q_j for $j \neq i$. A formal statement of this and following program proving principles will be found in the Appendix.

The facility for specifying parallelism of disjoint programs appears to be adequate for use of genuine multiprocessing hardware, and for the overlap of input and output operations with computing. But of course the more interesting problems require some form of interaction between the parallel programs; and this will be the topic of the following sections.

Example: input/output overlap.

A simple program inputs an array, processes it, and outputs it. In order to achieve overlap of input, output and processing, it adopts a simple buffering scheme.

```
input(lastone);
{process(lastone)//input(thisone)};
while some remain do
begin {input(nextone)//process(thisone)//output(lastone)}
      lastone := thisone; thisone := nextone
end;
{process(thisone)//output (lastone)};
output(thisone).
```

RESOURCE CONSTRAINTS

One of the reasons why parallel programs need to interact with each other is because they need to share some limited resource. For example, several parallel programs may need to communicate with a single operator through a single console; or to present a series of lines for output on a single line printer. In such cases it is usually important that no other process be permitted to access the resource while a given process is using it; for example, one process must be permitted to complete its conversation with the operator without interruption from other processes; and an "arbitrary interleaving" of lines from files output by different parallel processes would be wholly unacceptable.

We may thus envisage the action of each parallel process as follows: for part of the time it operates freely in parallel with all the other processes, but occasionally it enters a so-called *critical region* `C`; and while it is executing `C`, it must have exclusive use of some resource `r`. On completion of `C`, the resource is freed, and may be allocated to any other process (or the same one again) which wishes to enter a critical region with respect to the same resource. Thus the effect of a critical region is to re-establish the necessary degree of serialism into the parallel execution, so that only one of the processes may enter its critical region at any time. Thus critical regions from different processes are executed strictly serially, in an arbitrarily interleaved order.

This reintroduction of "arbitrary interleaving" does not suffer from the disadvantages mentioned earlier since:

1. The unit of action (= critical region) is defined by the programmer.
2. The necessary synchronization will be relatively infrequent, so that software-assisted implementation is acceptable.
3. The user has no desire or need to control the "interleaving" involved in the use of common resources, since these make no difference whatsoever to the results of his program.

If a parallel statement is to include critical regions with respect to a resource constraint, I suggest the following notation

```
{resource r; Q1//Q2//...//Qn}
```

where r is the name of the non-local quantity (e.g. lineprinter, console, etc.) which constitutes the resource.

Then inside the processes Q_1, Q_2, ..., Q_n, a critical region C is signalled by the notation

```
with r do C
```

The compiler is expected to check that no resource is used or referred to outside its critical regions.

The run-time implementation of this feature will depend on the nature of the basic synchronization facility provided by the hardware of the computer. If we assume that a Boolean semaphore mechanism is "built-in", the implementation is trivial. A resource declaration causes a Boolean Semaphore to be created; each critical region in the object code is preceded by seizing this semaphore (the P-operation), and followed by releasing it (the V-operation).

This method of dealing with resource constraints encourages the programmer to ignore the question of which of several outstanding requests for a resource should be granted. In general, the density of utilization of a resource should be sufficiently low that the chance of two requests arriving during the critical period of a third process should be relatively infrequent; for if the resource is a serious bottleneck, it is hardly worth setting up parallelism at all. Thus the relatively simple strategy of granting the resource to the one that has waited longest would seem to be perfectly adequate. Where it is not adequate, the facilities described on in the next section can be used to program a more subtle strategy.

Another problem which arises from resource constraints is that of the deadly embrace. Fortunately, a simple compile-time check can guarantee against this danger, if the programmer is willing to observe a simple discipline; when one critical region is nested inside another, the resource involved in the outer region should always have been declared as such *before* that declared in the inner region. This will mean that sometimes resources are acquired rather *before* they are actually needed, just as the nested nature of critical regions may mean that resources are kept longer than needed. Even when this occurs, it may be preferable to the alternatives, which include run-time checks and the generalized banker's algorithm.

The proof of programs which share resources will be virtually identical to that of non-sharing processes. However, the non-local variables which constitute the resource must be regarded for proof purposes as though they were local to each of their regions; since their initial values must be regarded as arbitrary, and their final values are "lost" to the program on exit from the critical region. This shows that from an abstract point of view, the seizure of a common resource could have been replaced simply by a local declaration of the variable required; and the only reason for introducing the constraint is because limitations of hardware availability make it unwise or impossible to provide enough "local" quantities to enable two processes to enter their critical regions together.

COOPERATING PROCESSES

In order for processes to cooperate on a common task, it is necessary that they communicate or interact through some common item of data. Within each process, any updating of this item must be regarded as a critical region, not interruptable by similar updatings in other processes. However, on exit from a critical region, this data item *retains* its value, which can then be examined and updated by other processes. Thus with the understanding of the retention of the value of the "resource", it appears that no new language feature is required to permit the construction of programs involving cooperating processes.

In order to see how such a facility might be used, it is helpful to draw an analogy. The resource `r` may be a potentially large structure (building) which starts off in some null condition (empty site), and which is built up to some desired state by performance of a number of operations of different types; $C_1//C_2//\ldots//C_m$ (laying a brick, fitting a window). It does not matter much in what order these operations are performed, so their execution may be delegated to a set of parallel processes (builders), each of which will on occasion invoke one of the permissible operations. Since an operation will update the common resource `r`, it must be invoked as a critical region. When each process detects that it has fulfilled its task, it terminates. When the tasks of all processes are complete, the structure `r` will also be complete.

In many cases it will not be permissible to perform the updating operations on `r` in a wholly random order; for example, the windows cannot be inserted in a building until the frames are installed. In general, a process must be allowed to test the state of `r` before entering a critical region, to see whether the corresponding operation is permissible or not; and if not, to wait until other processes have brought `r` into a state in which the operation can be carried out. Let `B` be a Boolean expression which tests the permissibility of an operation carried out by a critical region `C`. Then I suggest the notation:

```
with r when B do C
```

to specify that `C` is not to be carried out until `B` is true.

Some care must be exercised in the implementation of this new feature. The first action (as before) is to seize the semaphore associated with `r`. Then the condition `B` is tested. If it is *false*, the given process will hang itself up on a queue of processes waiting for `r`, and must then release the semaphore. If `B` is true, the critical region `C` is executed normally; and on completion the queue of waiting processes (if any) will be inspected, in the order of longest wait.

Then the waiting condition `B` for each waiting process is re-evaluated. If it is still *false*, the process remains on the queue. If *true*, it executes its critical region `C`, and then repeats the scan of the queue. Thus it is guaranteed that `B` will be true on entry to a critical region prefixed by `when B`; it is also guaranteed at all times (outside critical regions) that no process is waiting when its `B` is *true*; for `B` can only *become* true as a result of some critical operation by another process, and it is retested after each such operation. The programmer must be encouraged to ensure that this retesting is not too time-consuming.

In order to verify the correctness of a system of cooperating processes, it is necessary to define what is meant by a permissible operation on the resource `r`. This may usually be accomplished by giving some propositional formula `I`, specifying some property of `r`, which must remain true at all times (outside critical regions); such a proposition is known as an *invariant* for the resource. Obviously `I` must not mention any variable subject to change in any of the parallel processes. Now the condition for harmonious cooperation of the processes is that each process after updating the resource in a critical region must leave the resource in a state which satisfies `I`; and in return the process may assume that `I` is true before each entry to one of its own critical regions. Also, each process may assume that its condition `B` for entry of a critical region will be true before execution of the critical region starts. If all processes of a parallel program cooperate harmoniously, and if `I` is true before entering the program, then it is known that on completion of the program `I` will still be true.

Example: Bounded Buffer.

A process Q_1 produces a stream of values which are consumed by a parallel process Q_2. Since the production and consumption of values proceeds at a variable but roughly equal pace, it is profitable to interpose a buffer between the two processes; but since storage is limited the buffer can only contain N values. Our program takes the form (using Pascal notations):

```
B: record inpointer, outpointer, count: Integer;
         buffer:array 0..N-1 of T end;
{resource B; Q1//Q2}
```

We maintain the following variables:

count:	the number of values in the buffer.
inpointer:	if count < N, this is first empty place in the buffer; otherwise it equals outpointer.
outpointer:	if count > 0 this is the place where the next consumed value will be taken from; otherwise it equals inpointer.

The initial values of these variables are all zero.

The critical region inside the producer is as follows:

```
with B when count < N do
     begin buffer[inpointer]:= next value;
           inpointer:= (inpointer + 1) mod N;
           count:= count + 1
     end
```

The critical region inside the consumer is

```
with B when count > 0 do
     begin this value:= buffer[outpointer];
           outpointer:= (outpointer + 1) mod N;
           count:=count - 1
     end
```

Example: Spaghetti Eaters

Five Benthamite philosophers spend their lives between eating and thinking. To provide them sustenance, a wealthy benefactor has given each of them his own place at a round table, and in the middle is a large and continually replenished bowl of spaghetti, from which they can help themselves when they are seated. The spaghetti is so long and tangled that it requires *two* forks to be conveyed to the mouth; but unfortunately the wealthy benefactor has provided only five forks in all, one between each philosopher's

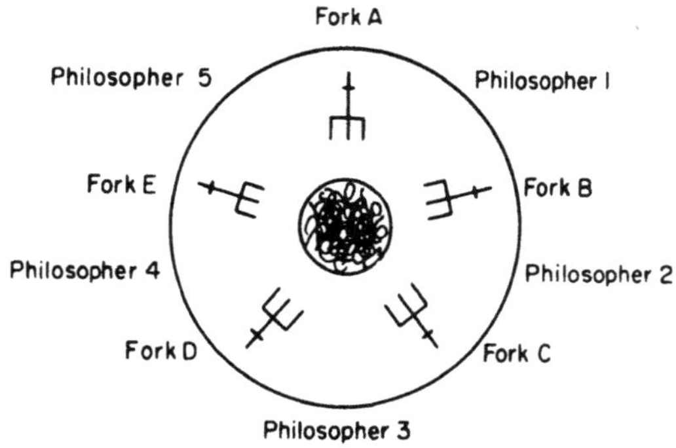

place. The only forks that a philosopher can pick up are those on his immediate right and his immediate left.

It can be seen that no two neighbours can be eating at a time. The problem is to write a program for each philosopher which will ensure that he contributes at all times to the greatest good of the greatest number.

When a philosopher is hungry, he must go to his own place and pick up two forks. Supposing each philosopher adopts the practice of picking up his left fork first. Then there is a grave danger that all philosophers will get hungry simultaneously, and all pick up their left forks; then they would slowly but inexorably starve to death. If the philosophers all put their left forks down on finding the right fork unobtainable, there is still a danger that they will continue to starve while repeatedly picking up and putting down their left forks in perfect unison.

One solution to this vicious circle is to arrange that one of the philosophers always picks up his *right* fork first. Then either he or the philosopher on his left must always have the opportunity of eating. This is basically the solution suggested earlier, of establishing a linear sequence of resources, and ensuring that all claims of more than one resource observe the standard sequence. The period of eating for each philosopher may be regarded as critical a region with respect to his right fork, nested immediately within the critical region for his left fork, for example:

```
with fork A do with fork B do eat spaghetti;
```

but for the last philosopher the nesting is reversed:

```
with fork A do with fork E do eat spaghetti
```

This solution is a great improvement, and certainly prevents universal starvation; but it still does not ensure optimum utilization of resources, since it is possible for three adjacent philosophers to remain holding one fork each while one of their colleagues is eating; and one would hope that a slightly more intelligent strategy could be devised in such a case to enable the middle one to eat.

The correct solution requires the use of synchronization facilities to guarantee that each philosopher either picks up *no* forks or he picks up *both* his forks. Picking up a single fork must be avoided. Thus we introduce an array:

```
integer array possforks[0:4];
```

`possforks[i]` takes values 0, 1 or 2 (with initial value 2), and indicates the number of forks available to philosopher `i`. This array itself is a resource, which can be inspected or updated by any philosopher. Each philosopher on feeling hungry first waits until two forks are available to him, and then reduces the number of forks available to his immediate neighbours, seizes the forks, and eats. On completion, he increases the number of forks available to his neighbours. Thus three successive critical regions are required in philosopher `i`:

```
with possforks when possforks[i] = 2 do
     begin possforks[(i-1)mod 5]:= possforks[(i-1)mod 5]-1;
           possforks[(i+1)mod 5]:= possforks[(i+1)mod 5]-1
     end;
with fork A do with fork B do eat spaghetti;
with possforks do
     begin possforks[(i-1)mod 5]:= possforks[(i-1)mod 5]+1;
           possforks[(i+1)mod 5]:= possforks[(i+1)mod 5]+1
     end
```

ADDITIONAL POINTS

It is hoped that the basic concepts and facilities introduced in the previous sections will be found adequate for most purposes. However, it seems that a few additional simple notations and features may increase their convenience and range of application.

Array remapping

This paper proposes that the introduction of parallelism is meaningful only when no process refers to variables changed by another process (excluding critical regions). However, a compile time check on the observance of this discipline is sometimes too restrictive, since it would prevent two processes operating in parallel on different elements of the same array. A proposal to mitigate this problem is to permit the programmer to declare a local *remapping* of an array, within a block; this splits the array down into disjoint parts, each with its own name; and these separate names can now be updated in separate processes. A notation for expressing the remapping might be:

```
begin map a[1:12], b, c[0:i] on X; ... end
```

which declares a as a local name for an array consisting of the first 12 elements of X, b as the thirteenth element, and the next i + 1 elements are renamed c. C itself should not be referred to within the block.

Example: Quicksort.

Using this facility it is possible, if sufficient parallel hardware is available, to sort an array of size N in time proportional to N.

```
procedure Quicksort(A, m, n);
    begin integer i, j;
          partition(A, i, j, m, n);
          begin map B[m:j] X[j+1:i-1], C[i:n] on A;
                {Quicksort(B, m, j)//Quicksort(C, i, n)}
          end
    end Quicksort
```

Resource arrays

The facility for remapping storage gives a simple method by which parallel processes can operate simultaneously on different parts of a data structure. However, it can be used only when it is known in advance which parts are going to be used by each process. Sometimes, the choice of which element or elements of an array are to be seized for a particular critical region can only be made on entry to that region; this means that each element of the array must be regarded as a separate resource, which can be allocated and deallocated independently of its neighbours. Such an array may be declared

```
resource array R
```

and the critical regions may take the form:

```
with r = R[i] do Q
```

where r is used within Q as a local name for R[i]; and R itself must not be mentioned in Q.

One obvious application of resource arrays is in the real time maintenance of a table of information; and if a random access file is regarded as a form of sparse array, this gives the facility of the PL/I EXCLUSIVE attribute. Another application is in dealing with a set of homogeneous resources, such as disc handlers, where the programmer does not care *which* handler(s) he is allocated in a particular critical region. As an example of the use of the feature, we suppose that the number of handlers required in each critical region is different, and that as before we wish to avoid the possibility that more than one process should have a partially fulfilled request.

To achieve this, we use a resource **request**, which is allocated to a process during the time that its request is being fulfilled. There is also a set resource **free** which contains the numbers of all free handlers; **mine** is a local set variable, containing the numbers of the handlers allocated to me. A critical region requiring two handlers would be surrounded by small critical regions which carry out the administration, thus:

```
with request do {with free when size(free) ≥ 2 do
                    {mine:=first two of (free); free:= free & ¬ mine}}
with a = handler[first(mine)] do {with b = handler[second(mine)] do
                    use a and b};
with free do free := free ∨ mine;
```

ACKNOWLEDGEMENTS

It will be obvious to all how much this paper owes to the thought and writings of Professor E. W. Dijkstra, to whom I owe the concepts of the critical region, the semaphore, the deadly embrace and the simple method of its avoidance; and the examples of the bounded buffer and the spaghetti eaters. Less obvious but equally invaluable has been his constant encouragement in the search for a concept to "replace" the semaphore in a high-level programming language, and my ambition of meeting his high standards of rigour and programming style.

I am also deeply indebted to many friends and colleagues who have kindly followed me in many a wild goose chase, and in particular to Maurice Clint, whose advice and experience have been especially valuable.

APPENDIX

Formal definition

It has been suggested that a specification of proof procedures for proving correctness of programs would be a useful method of defining languages with a certain desired degree of indeterminacy. This appendix applies the formal language definition technique to parallel programming.

Let V_i be the set of variables subject to change in Q_i. Then it is assured,

1. no variable of $V_i - \{r\}$ occurs free in I or in P_j, Q_j, or R_j for $j \neq i$
2. r is not free in P, R, P_i, Q_i, R_i, except in a critical region with respect to r.

Then letting r inv I state that I is the invariant for r, we can formulate the following two rules:

Criticality:

$$\frac{\texttt{r inv I, B \& I \& P \{C\} R \& I}}{\texttt{P \{with r when B do C\} R}}$$

Simultaneity:

$$\frac{\texttt{r inv I, } P_1\{Q_1\}R_1\texttt{, } P_2\{Q_2\}R_2\texttt{, } \ldots\texttt{, } P_n\{Q_n\}R_n}{\texttt{I \& } P_1 \texttt{ \& } P_2 \texttt{ \& } \ldots \texttt{ \& } P_n \texttt{ \{resource r; } Q_1//Q_2//\ldots//Q_n\texttt{\} I \& } R_1 \texttt{ \& } R_2 \texttt{ \& } \ldots \texttt{ \& } R_n}$$

These two rules cover all cases if we adopt the conventions:

1. **when true** can be omitted.
2. If there are no critical regions with respect to r, **resource** r can be omitted; and I may then be taken as **true**.

6

AN OUTLINE OF A COURSE ON OPERATING SYSTEM PRINCIPLES

PER BRINCH HANSEN

(1971)

In 1970 the author began writing a comprehensive textbook on operating system principles. This is a description of its structure and how far it had progressed a year later.

COMPUTER SCIENCE AND OPERATING SYSTEMS

In November 1970 I began writing a textbook on operating system principles at Carnegie-Mellon University. This is a description of its structure and how far it has progressed.

The goal is to give students of computer science and professional programmers a general understanding of operating systems. The only background required is an understanding of the basic structure of computers and programming languages and some practical experience in writing and testing non-trivial programs. In a few cases a knowledge of elementary calculus and probability theory is also needed. The components of the course are well-known to a small group of designers, but most operating systems reveal an inadequate understanding of them.

The first and most obvious problem is to delimit the subject and consider its place in computer science education. I define an *operating system* as a set of manual and automatic procedures which enable a group of users to share a computer system efficiently. The keyword in this definition is *sharing*: it means competetion for the use of physical resources but also cooperation

P. Brinch Hansen, An outline of a course on operating system principles. In *Operating Systems Techniques*, Proceedings of a Seminar at Queen's University, Belfast, Northern Ireland, August–September 1971. C. A. R. Hoare and R. H. Perrott, Eds. Academic Press, New York (1972), 29–36.

among users exchanging programs and data on the same computer system. All shared computer systems must *schedule* user computations in some order, *protect* them against one each other, and give them means of *long-term storage* of programs and data. They must also perform *accounting* of the cost of computing and *measure* the actual performance of the system.

In early computer systems, operators carried out most of these functions, but during the last fifteen years the programs that we call operating systems have gradually taken over these aspects of sharing.

Although most components of present computers are sequential in nature, they can work simultaneously to some extent. This influences the design of operating systems so much that the subject can best be described as the *management of shared multiprogramming systems.*

Operating systems are large programs developed and used by a changing group of people. They are often modified considerably during their lifetime. Operating systems must necessarily impose certain restrictions on all users. But this should not lead us to regard them as being radically different from other programs. They are just examples of large programs based on fundamental principles of computer science. The proper aim of education is to identify these fundamentals.

The student should realize that principles and methods of resource sharing have a general utility that goes beyond operating systems. Any large programming effort will be heavily influenced by the presence of several levels of storage, by the possibility of executing smaller tasks independently, and by the need for sharing a common set of data among such tasks. We find it convenient to distinguish between operating systems and user computations because the former can *enforce* certain rules of behavior on the latter. It is important, however, to realize that each level of programming solves some aspect of resource allocation.

I argue therefore that the study of operating systems leads to the recognition of general principles which should be taught as part of a core of computer science. Assuming that the student has an elementary background in *programming languages*, *data structures* and *computer organization*, the course concentrates on the following areas of computer science: *concurrent computations*, *resource sharing* and *program construction.*

Let us look at the course in some detail. It consists of eight parts which are summarized in the Appendix. The following is a more informal presentation of its basic attitude.

TECHNOLOGICAL BACKGROUND

The necessity of controlling access to shared computer systems automatically is made clear by simple arguments about the poor utilization of equipment in an *open shop* operated by the users themselves, one at a time. As a first step in this direction, I describe the classical *batch processing system* which carries out computations on a main computer while a smaller computer prepares and prints magnetic tapes. The strict sequential nature of the processors and their backing storage in this early scheme made it necessary to prevent human interaction with computations and schedule them in their order of arrival inside a batch.

These restrictions on scheduling disappear to some extent with the introduction of multiprogramming techniques and large backing stores with random access. This is illustrated by two simple operating systems: the first one is a *spooling system* which handles a continuous stream of input, computation and output on a multiprogrammed computer with drum storage; the other is an *interactive system* in which main storage is shared cyclically among several computations requested from remote terminals.

Through a chain of simple arguments the student gradually learns to appreciate the influence of *technological constraints* on the service offered by operating systems.

THE SIMILARITY OF OPERATING SYSTEMS

The main theme of the course is the similarity of problems faced by all operating systems. To mention one example: all shared computer systems must handle concurrent activities at some level. Even if a system only schedules one computation at a time, users can still make their requests simultaneously. This problem can, of course, be solved by the users themselves (forming a waiting line) and by the operators (writing down requests on paper). But the observation is important, since our goal is to handle the problems of sharing automatically.

It is also instructive to compare a batch processing and a spooling system. Both achieve high efficiency by means of concurrent activities: in a batch processing system independent processors work together; in a spooling system a single processor switches among independent programs. Both systems use backing storage (tape and drum) as a buffer to compensate for speed variations between the producers and consumers of data.

As another example, consider real-time systems for process control or conversational interaction. In these systems, concurrent processes must be able to exchange data in order to cooperate on common tasks. But again, this problem exists in all shared computer systems: in a spooling system user computations exchange data with concurrent input/output processes; and in a batch processing system we have another set of concurrent processes which exchange data by means of tapes mounted by operators.

So I find that all operating systems face a common set of problems. To recognize these we must reject the established classification of operating systems into batch processing, time sharing, and real time systems which stresses the dissimilarities of various forms of technology and user service. This does not mean that the problems of adjusting an operating system to the constraints of a certain environment are irrelevant. But the students will solve them much better when they have grasped the underlying common principles.

You will also look in vain for chapters on input/output and filing systems. For a particular operating system considerations about how these problems are handled are highly relevant; but again I have concentrated on the more elementary problems involved in these complicated tasks, namely, process synchronization, storage management and resource protection.

SEQUENTIAL AND CONCURRENT COMPUTATIONS

After this introduction, the nature of computations is described. A *computation* is a set of operations applied to a set of data in order to solve a problem. The operations must be carried out in a certain order to ensure that the results of some of them can be used by others. In a *sequential process* operations are carried out strictly one at a time. But most of our computational problems only require a partial ordering of operations in time: some operations must be carried out before others, but many of them can be carried out concurrently.

The main obstacles to the utilization of concurrency in computer systems are economy and human imagination. Sequential processes can be carried out cheaply by repeated use of simple equipment; concurrent computations require duplicated equipment and time-consuming synchronization of operations. Human beings find it extremely difficult to comprehend the combined effect of a large number of activities which evolve simultaneously with independent rates. In contrast, our understanding of a sequential process is independent of its actual speed of execution. All that matters is that operations are carried out one at a time with finite speed, and that certain relations hold between the data before and after each operation.

So sequential processes closely mirror our thinking habits, but a computer system is utilized better when its various parts operate concurrently. As a compromise, we try to partition our problems into a moderate number of sequential activities which can be programmed separately and then combined for concurrent execution. These processes are *loosely connected* in the sense that they can proceed simultaneously with arbitrary rates except for short intervals when they exchange data.

After a brief review of methods of structuring data and sequential programs, I consider the synchronizing requirements of *concurrent processes.* It is shown that the results of concurrent processes which share data cannot be predicted unless some operations exclude each other in time. Operations which have this property are called *critical regions.* Mutual exclusion can be controlled by a data structure, called a *semaphore*, consisting of a boolean, defining whether any process is inside its critical region, and a queue, containing the set of processes waiting to enter their regions.

A critical region is one example of a timing constraint or *synchronization* imposed on concurrent processes. Synchronization is also needed when some processes produce data which are consumed by other processes. The simplest *input/output relationship* is the exchange of *timing signals* between processes. The constraint here is that signals cannot be received faster than they are sent. This relationship can be represented by an integer semaphore accessed by *signal* and *wait* operations only.

Realistic *communication* between processes requires the exchange of data structures. This problem can be solved by synchronizing primitives operating on semaphores and data structures which are accessible to all the processes involved. It is tempting to conclude that critical regions, common data, and wait and signal operations are the proper concepts to include in a programming language. Experience shows that the slightest mistake in the use of these tools can result in erroneous programs which are practically impossible to correct because their behavior is influenced by external factors in a time-dependent, irreproducible manner.

A more adequate solution is to include *message buffers* as primitive data structures in the programming language and make them accessible only through well-defined *send* and *receive* operations. The crucial point of this language feature is that storage containing shared data (messages) is accessible to at most one process at a time. It has been proved that when a set of smaller systems with time-independent behavior are connected by means of message buffers only, the resulting system can also be made time-independent in behavior.

The most general form of process interaction is one in which a process must be delayed until another process has ensured that certain relationships hold between the components of a shared data structure. This form of synchronization can be expressed directly by means of *conditional critical regions.*

The conceptual simplicity of simple and conditional critical regions is achieved by ignoring the sequence in which waiting processes enter these regions. This abstraction is unrealistic for heavily used resources. In such cases, the operating system must be able to identify competing processes and control the scheduling of resources among them. This can be done by means of a *monitor*—a set of shared procedures which can delay and activate individual processes and perform operations on shared data.

Finally, I consider the problems of *deadlocks* and their prevention by hierarchical ordering of process interactions.

RESOURCE MANAGEMENT

Most of the previous concepts are now widely used. Far more controversial are the problems of how abstract computations are represented and managed on physical systems with limited resources. At first sight, problems caused by the physical constraints of computers seem to be of secondary importance to the computational problems we are trying to solve. But in practice most programming efforts are dominated by technological problems and will continue to be so. It will always be economically attractive to share resources among competing computations, use several levels of storage, and accept occasional hardware malfunction.

It seems unrealistic to look for a unifying view of how different kinds of technology are used efficiently. The student should realize that these issues can only be understood in economic terms. What we can hope to do is to describe the circumstances under which certain techniques will work well.

The implementation of the process concept is considered in two chapters on *processor multiplexing* and *storage organization.* The first of these describes the representation of processes and scheduling queues at the lowest level of programming and the implementation of synchronizing primitives. Hardware registers, clocks and interrupts are treated as technological tools which in many cases can be replaced by more appropriate concepts at higher levels of programming. The second of these chapters discusses the compromises between associative and location-dependent addressing, and the dynamic allocation of fixed and variable-length data structures in storage with one or more levels.

Following this, I discuss the influence of various *scheduling algorithms*: first-come first-served, shortest job next, highest response ratio next, round robin, and so on, on the behavior of the system in terms of average response times to user requests.

A CASE STUDY

At the end of the course, the conceptual framework is used to describe an existing operating system in depth using a consistent terminology.

I have selected the RC 4000 multiprogramming system (Brinch Hansen 1970) as a case study, because it is the only one I know in detail, and is a small, consistent design which illustrates essential ideas of concurrent processes, message communication, scheduling and resource protection.

THE CHOICE OF A DESCRIPTION LANGUAGE

So far nearly all operating systems have been written partly or completely in machine language. This makes them unnecessarily difficult to understand, test and modify. I believe it is desirable and possible to write efficient operating systems almost entirely in a *high-level language.* This language must permit *hierarchal structuring* of data and program, extensive *error checking* at compile time, and production of *efficient machine code.*

To support this belief, I have used the programming language *Pascal* (Wirth 1971) throughout the text to define operating system concepts concisely by algorithms. Pascal combines the clarity needed for teaching with the efficiency required for design. It is easily understood by programmers familiar with Algol 60 or Fortran, but is a far more natural tool than these for the description of operating systems because of the presence of data structures of type record, class and pointer.

At the moment, Pascal is designed for sequential programming only, but I extend it with a suitable notation for multiprogramming and resource sharing. I have illustrated the description of operating systems in Pascal elsewhere (Brinch Hansen 1971a, 1971b).

STATUS OF THE COURSE

I conceived the plan for the course in March 1970 and started to work on it in November 1970. Now, in November 1971, drafts have been written of parts 1–4, and 6 (see the Appendix). Most of the work on parts 5, and 7–8 remains to be done. It is unlikely that the structure of the course will change significantly, although the details certainly will.

APPENDIX: THE CONTENTS OF THE COURSE

1. An overview of operating systems

The purpose of an operating system. Technological background: manual scheduling, non-interactive scheduling with sequential and random access backing storage, interactive scheduling. The similarity of operating systems. Special versus general-purpose systems.

2. Sequential processes

Abstraction and structure. Data and operations. Sequential and concurrent computations. Methods of structuring data and sequential programs. Hierarchal program construction. Programming levels viewed as virtual machines. Our understanding and verification of programs.

3. Concurrent processes

Time-dependent programming errors in concurrent computations. Definition of functional behavior in terms of input/output histories. The construction of functional systems from smaller functional components. Concurrent systems with inherent time-dependent behavior: priority scheduling and shared processes.

Disjoint and interacting processes. Mutual exclusion of operations on shared data. Simple and conditional critical regions. Process communication by semaphores and message buffers. Explicit control of process scheduling by monitors.

The deadlock problem. Prevention of deadlocks by hierarchal ordering of process interactions.

4. Processor multiplexing

Short-term and medium-term scheduling. A computer system with identical processors connected to a single store. Peripheral versus central processors.

Process descriptions, states and queues. Processor execution cycle. Scheduling of critical regions by means of a storage arbiter. Implementation of the scheduling primitives wait, signal, initiate and terminate process. Influence of critical regions on preemption. Processor multiplexing with static and dynamic priorities. Implementation details: hardware registers, clock, interrupts. Timing constraints.

5. Storage organization

Properties of abstract and physical storage. Methods of address mapping: searching, key transformation and base registers.

Single-level storage: fixed partitioning, dynamic allocation of fixed and variable-length data structures. Compacting and fragmentation.

Hierarchal storage: swapping, demand paging and extended storage. Locality principle. Prevention of thrashing. Placement and replacement strategies. Hardware support.

Influence of input/output, process communication, and scheduling on storage allocation.

6. Scheduling algorithms

Objectives of scheduling policies. Queueing models of user requests and computations. Performance measures. A conservation law for a class of priority scheduling algorithms.

Non-preemptive scheduling: fixed priorities, first-come first-served, shortest job next, and highest response ratio next.

Preemptive scheduling: round robin with swapping. Methods of reducing transfers between storage levels. Scheduling with performance feedback.

7. Resource protection

The concept of a process environment of shared objects. Requirements of naming and protection. Existing protection mechanisms: privileged execution state, storage protection, file systems with private and public data, user password identification, protection levels and process hierarchies.

8. A case study

A detailed analysis of the structure, size and performance of the RC 4000 multiprogramming system.

Acknowledgements

Without the encouragement of Alan Perlis this work would not have been undertaken. I am indebted to Nico Habermann, Anita Jones and Bill Wulf who read and criticized all or part of the manuscript. I learned much from discussions with Tony Hoare. It should also be mentioned that without the foundation of laid by Edsger Dijkstra (1965) we would still be unable to separate principles from their applications in operating systems. The idea of looking upon the management of shared computer systems as a general data processing problem was inspired by a similar attitude of Peter Naur (1966) towards program translation.

References

Brinch Hansen, P. 1970. The nucleus of a multiprogramming system. *Communications of the ACM 13*, 4 (April), 238–250.

Brinch Hansen, P. 1971a. Short-term scheduling in multiprogramming systems. *3rd ACM Symposium on Operating System Principles*, Stanford University, Stanford, CA, (October), 101–105.

Brinch Hansen, P. 1971b. A comparison of two synchronizing concepts. (November). In *Acta Informatica 1*, 3 (1972), 190–199.

Dijkstra, E.W. 1965. Cooperating sequential processes. Technological University, Eindhoven, The Netherlands, (September).

Naur, P. 1966. Program translation viewed as a general data processing problem. *Communications of the ACM 9*, 3 (March), 176–179.

Wirth, N. 1971. The programming language Pascal. *Acta Informatica 1*, 1, 35–63.

7

STRUCTURED MULTIPROGRAMMING

PER BRINCH HANSEN

(1972)

This paper presents a proposal for structured representation of multiprogramming in a high level language. The notation used explicitly associates a data structure shared by concurrent processes with operations defined on it. This clarifies the meaning of programs and permits a large class of time-dependent errors to be caught at compile time. A combination of critical regions and event variables enables the programmer to control scheduling of resources among competing processes to any degree desired. These concepts are sufficiently safe to use not only within operating systems but also within user programs.

1 Introduction

The failure of operating systems to provide reliable long-term service can often be explained by excessive emphasis on functional capabilities at the expense of efficient resource utilization, and by inadequate methods of program construction.

In this paper, I examine the latter cause of failure and propose a language notation for structured multiprogramming. The basic idea is to associate data shared by concurrent processes explicitly with operations defined on them. This clarifies the meaning of programs and permits a large class of time-dependent errors to be caught at compile time.

The notation is presented as an extension to the sequential programming language Pascal (Wirth 1971). It will be used in a forthcoming textbook to

P. Brinch Hansen, Structured multiprogramming. *Communications of the ACM 15*, 7 (July 1972), 574–578.

explain operating system principles concisely by algorithms (Brinch Hansen 1971). Similar ideas have been explored independently by Hoare. The conditional critical regions proposed in (Hoare 1971) are a special case of the ones introduced here.

2 Disjoint Processes

Our starting point is the *concurrent statement*

$$\textbf{cobegin } S_1;\ S_2;\ \ldots;\ S_n \textbf{ coend}$$

introduced by Dijkstra (1965). This notation indicates that statements S_1, S_2, ..., S_n can be executed concurrently; when all of them are terminated, the following statement in the program (not shown here) is executed.

This restricted form of concurrency simplifies the understanding and verification of programs considerably, compared to unstructured *fork* and *join* primitives (Conway 1963).

Algorithm 1 illustrates the use of the concurrent statement to copy records from one sequential file to another.

```
var f, g: file of T;
  s, t: T; eof: Boolean;
begin
  input(f, s, eof);
  while not eof do
    begin t := s;
      cobegin
        output(g, t);
        input(f, s, eof);
      coend
    end
end
```

Algorithm 1 Copying of a sequential file.

The variables here are two sequential files, *f* and *g*, with records of type *T*; two buffers, *s* and *t*, holding one record each; and a Boolean, *eof*, indicating whether or not the end of the input file has been reached.

Input and output of single records are handled by two standard procedures. The algorithm inputs a record, copies it from one buffer to another, outputs it, and at the same time, inputs the next record. The copying, output, and input are repeated until the input file is empty.

Now suppose the programmer by mistake expresses the repetition as follows:

```
while not eof do
  cobegin
    t := s;
    output(g, t);
    input(f, s, eof);
  coend
```

The copying, output, and input of a record can now be executed concurrently. To simplify the argument, we will only consider cases in which these processes are arbitrarily *interleaved* but *not overlapped* in time. The erroneous concurrent statement can then be executed in six different ways with three possible results: (1) if copying is completed before input and output are initiated, the *correct* record will be output; (2) if output is completed before copying is initiated, the *previous* record will be output again; and (3) if input is completed before copying is initiated, and this in turn completed before output is initiated, the *next* record will be output instead.

This is just for a single record of the output file. If we copy a file of 10,000 records, the program can give of the order of $3^{10,000}$ different results!

The actual sequence of operations in time will depend on the presence of other (unrelated) computations and the (possibly time-dependent) scheduling policy of the installation. It is therefore very unlikely that the programmer will ever observe the same result twice. The only hope of locating the error is to study the program text. This can be very frustrating (if not impossible) when it consists of thousands of lines and one has no clues about where to look.

Multiprogramming is an order of magnitude more hazardous than sequential programming unless we ensure that the results of our computations are *reproducible in spite of errors.* In the previous example, this can easily be checked at compile time.

In the correct version of Algorithm 1, the output and input processes operate on disjoint sets of variables (g, t) and $(f,\ s,\ eof)$. They are called *disjoint* or *noninteracting processes.*

In the erroneous version of the algorithm, the processes are not disjoint: the output process refers to a variable t changed by the copying process; and the latter refers to a variable s changed by the input process.

This can be detected at compile time if the following rule is adopted: a concurrent statement defines disjoint processes $S_1, S_2, \ldots, S_n$ which can be executed concurrently. This means that a variable v_i changed by statement S_i cannot be referenced by another statement S_j (where $j \neq i$). In other words, we insist that a variable subject to change by a process must be strictly *private* to that process; but disjoint processes can refer to *shared* variables not changed by any of them.

Throughout this paper, I tacitly assume that sequential statements and assertions made about them only refer to variables which are *accessible* to the statements according to the rules of disjointness and mutual exclusion. The latter rule will be defined in Section 3.

Violations of these rules must be detected at compile time and prevent execution. To enable a compiler to check the disjointness of processes the language must have the following property: it must be possible by simple inspection of a statement to distinguish between its constant and variable parameters. I will not discuss the influence of this requirement on language design beyond mentioning that it makes unrestricted use of *pointers* and *side-effects* unacceptable.

The rule of disjointness is due to Hoare (1971). It makes the *axiomatic property* of a concurrent statement S very simple: if each component statement S_i terminates with a result R_i provided a predicate P_i holds before its execution then the combined effect of S is the following:

$$\text{“}P\text{”}\ S\ \text{“}R\text{”}$$

where

$$P \equiv P_1 \ \&\ P_2 \ \&\ \cdots \ \&\ P_n$$
$$R \equiv R_1 \ \&\ R_2 \ \&\ \cdots \ \&\ R_n$$

As Hoare puts it: “Each S_i makes its contribution to the common goal.”

3 Mutual Exclusion

The usefulness of disjoint processes has its limits. We will now consider *interacting processes*—concurrent processes which access shared variables.

A *shared variable* v of type T is declared as follows:

var v: **shared** T

Concurrent processes can only refer to and change a shared variable inside a structured statement called a *critical region*

region v **do** S

This notation associates a statement S with a shared variable v.

Critical regions referring to the same variable exclude each other in time. They can be arbitrarily interleaved in time. The idea of progressing towards a final result (as in a concurrent statement) is therefore meaningless. All one can expect is that each critical region leaves certain relationships among the components of a shared variable v unchanged. These relationships can be defined by an assertion I about v which must be true after initialization of v and before and after each subsequent critical region associated with v. Such an assertion is called an *invariant.*

When a process enters a critical region to execute a statement S, a predicate P holds for the variables accessible to the process outside the critical region and an invariant I holds for the shared variable v accessible inside the critical region. After the completion of S, a result R holds for the former variables and invariant I has been maintained. So a critical region has the following axiomatic property:

"P"
region v **do** "$P\&I$" S "$R\&I$";
"R"

4 Process Communication

Mutual exclusion of operations on shared variables makes it possible to make meaningful statements about the effect of concurrent computations. But when processes cooperate on a common task they must also be able to wait until certain conditions have been satisfied by other processes.

For this purpose I introduce a synchronizing primitive, **await**, which delays a process until the components of a shared variable v satisfy a condition B:

region v **do**
begin ... **await** B; ... **end**

The await primitive must be textually enclosed by a critical region. If critical regions are nested, the synchronizing condition B is associated with the innermost enclosing region.

The await primitive can be used to define *conditional critical regions* of the type proposed in (Hoare 1971):

"Consumer"	"Producer"
region v **do**	**region** v **do** S_2
begin await B; S_1 **end**	

The implementation of critical regions and await primitives is illustrated in Fig. 1. When a process, such as the consumer above, wishes to enter a critical region, it enters a *main queue* Q_v associated with a shared variable v. After entering its critical region, the consumer inspects the shared variable to determine whether it satisfies a condition B. In that case, the consumer completes its critical region by executing a statement S_1; otherwise, the process leaves its critical region *temporarily* and joins an *event queue* Q_e associated with the shared variable.

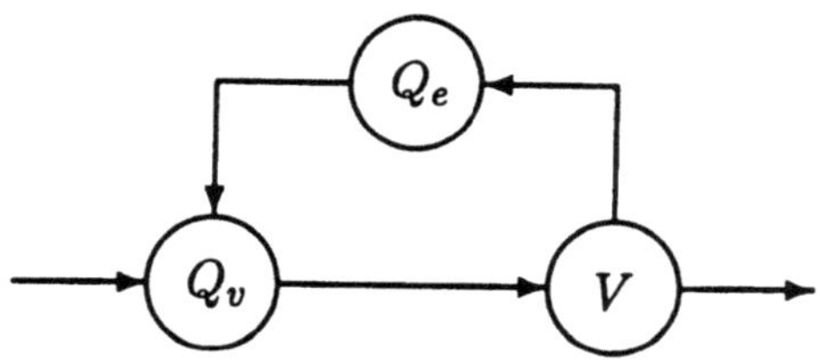

Figure 1 Scheduling of conditional critical regions V by means of process queues Q_v and Q_e.

All processes waiting for one condition or another on variable v enter the same event queue. When another process (here called the producer) changes v by a statement S_2 inside a critical region, it is possible that one or more of the conditions expected by processes in the event queue will be satisfied. So, after completion of a critical region, all processes in the event queue Q_e are transferred to the main queue Q_v to enable them to reenter their critical regions and inspect the shared variable v again.

It is possible that a *consumer* will be transferred in vain between Q_v and Q_e several times before its condition B holds. But this can only occur as frequently as *producers* change the shared variable. This controlled amount of *busy waiting* is the price we pay for the conceptual simplicity achieved by using arbitrary Boolean expressions as synchronizing conditions.

The desired *invariant* I for the shared variable v must be satisfied before an *await* primitive is executed. When the waiting cycle terminates, the assertion B & I holds.

As an example, consider the following resource allocation problem: two kinds of concurrent processes, called readers and writers, share a single resource. The readers can use the resource simultaneously, but the writers must have exclusive access to it. When a writer is ready to use the resource, it should be enabled to do so as soon as possible.

This problem is solved by Algorithm 2. Here variable v is a record consisting of two integer components defining the number of *readers* currently using the resource and the number of *writers* currently waiting for or using the resource. Both *readers* and *writers* are initialized to zero.

```
var v: shared record readers, writers: integer end
    w: shared Boolean;

"Reader"
region v do
begin
  await writers = 0;
  readers := readers + 1;
end
read;
region v do
readers := readers - 1;

"Writer"
region v do
begin
  writers := writers + 1;
  await readers = 0;
end
region w do write;
region v do
writers := writers - 1;
```

Algorithm 2 Resource sharing by readers and writers.

Mutual exclusion of readers and writers is achieved by letting readers wait until the number of writers is zero, and vice versa. Mutual exclusion of individual writers is ensured by the critical region on the Boolean w.

The priority rule is obeyed by increasing the number of writers as soon as one of them wishes to use the resource. This will delay subsequent reader requests until all pending writer requests are satisfied.

A correctness proof of Algorithm 2 is outlined in (Brinch Hansen 1972). In this paper I also point out the superiority of conditional critical regions over *semaphores* (Dijkstra 1965). Compared to the original solution to the problem (Courtois 1971) Algorithm 2 demonstrates the conceptual advantage of a structured notation.[1]

The conceptual simplicity of critical regions is achieved by ignoring details of scheduling: the programmer is unaware of the sequence in which waiting processes enter critical regions and access shared resources. This assumption is justified for processes which are so *loosely connected* that simultaneous requests for the same resource rarely occur.

But in most computer installations *resources* are *heavily used* by a large group of users. In this situation, an operating system must be able to *control the scheduling of resources explicitly* among competing processes.

To do this a programmer must be able to associate an arbitrary number of event queues with a shared variable and control the transfers of processes to and from them. In general, I would therefore replace the previous proposal for conditional delays with the following one:

The declaration

var e: **event** v;

associates an event queue e with a shared variable v.

A process can leave a critical region associated with v and join the event queue e by executing the standard procedure

await(e)

Another process can enable all processes in the event queue e to reenter their critical regions by executing the standard procedure

cause(e)

A consumer/producer relationship must now be expressed as follows:

"Consumer"	"Producer"
region v **do**	**region** v **do**
begin	**begin**
while not B **do** await(e);	S_2;
S_1;	cause(e);
end	**end**

[1]The original solution includes the following refinement: when a writer decides to make a request at most one more reader can complete a request ahead of it. This can be ensured by surrounding the reader request in Algorithm 2 with an additional critical region associated with a shared Boolean r.

```
var v: shared record
                available: set of R;
                requests: set of P;
                grant: array P of event v;
              end

procedure reserve(process: P; var resource: R);
region v do
begin
  while empty(available) do
  begin enter(process, requests);
    await(grant[process]);
  end
  remove(resource, available);
end

procedure release(resource: R);
var process: P;
region v do
begin enter(resource, available);
  if not empty(requests) then
  begin remove(process, requests);
    cause(grant[process]);
  end
end
```

Algorithm 3 Scheduling of heavily used resources.

Although less elegant than the previous notation, the present one still clearly shows that the consumer is waiting for condition B to hold. And we can now control process scheduling to any degree desired.

To simplify explicit scheduling, I suggest that processes reentering their critical regions from event queues take priority over processes entering critical regions directly through a main queue (see Fig. 1). If the scheduling rule is completely unknown to the programmer as before, additional variables are required to ensure that resources granted to waiting processes remain available to them until they reenter their critical regions.

Algorithm 3 is a simple example of completely controlled resource allocation. A number of processes share a pool of equivalent resources. Processes and resources are identified by indices of type P and R respectively. When resources are *available*, a process can *acquire* one immediately; otherwise, it must enter a request in a data structure of type *set of P* and wait until a resource is *granted* to it. It is assumed that the program controls the entry and removal of set elements completely.

5 Conclusion

I have presented structured multiprogramming concepts which have simple axiomatic properties and permit extensive compile time checking and generation of efficient machine code.

The essential properties of these concepts are:

1. A distinction between disjoint and interacting processes;
2. An association of shared data with operations defined on them;
3. Mutual exclusion of these operations in time;
4. Synchronizing primitives which permit partial or complete control of process scheduling.

These are precisely the concepts needed to implement *monitor procedures* such as the ones described in (Brinch Hansen 1970). They appear to be sufficiently safe to use not only within operating systems but also within user programs to control local resources.

References

Brinch Hansen, P. 1970. The nucleus of a multiprogramming system. *Communications of the ACM 13*, 4 (April), 238–250.

Brinch Hansen, P. 1971. An outline of a course on operating system principles. *International Seminar on Operating System Techniques*, Belfast, Northern Ireland, (August–September).

Brinch Hansen, P. 1972. A comparison of two synchronizing concepts. *Acta Informatica 1*, 190–199.

Conway, M.E. 1963. A multiprocessor system design. *Proc. AFIPS FJCC 24*, Spartan Books, New York, 139–146.

Courtois, P.J, Heymans, F., and Parnas, D.L. 1971. Concurrent control with "readers" and "writers." *Communications of the ACM 14*, 10 (October), 667–668.

Dijkstra, E.W. 1965. Cooperating sequential processes. Technological University, Eindhoven. Also in *Programming Languages*, F. Genyus, Ed. Academic Press, New York, 1968.

Hoare, C.A.R. 1971. Towards a theory of parallel programming. *International Seminar on Operating System Techniques*, Belfast, Northern Ireland, (August–September).

Wirth, N. 1971. The programming language Pascal. *Acta Informatica 1*, 35–63.

8

SHARED CLASSES

PER BRINCH HANSEN

(1973)

The author discusses the close relationship between data and operations and suggests that a compiler should be able to check that data structures are accessed by meaningful procedures only. This idea leads to the introduction of shared classes—a programming notation for the monitor concept. The notation is illustrated by a message buffer for concurrent processes.

We will discuss the close relationship between data and operations and use it to define a very important form of resource protection.

If we consider variables of *primitive types* such as *integer* and *boolean*, it is quite possible that values of different types will be represented by identical bit strings at the machine level. For example both the *boolean* value *true* and the *integer* value 1 might be represented by the bit string

000...001

in single machine words.

So data of different types are distinguished not only by the representation of their values, but also by the operations associated with the types. An *integer*, for example, is a datum subject only to arithmetic operations, comparisons, and assignments involving other data subject to the same restrictions.

Now consider *structured types*. Take for example a variable that represents a message buffer which contains a sequences of messages sent, but not

P. Brinch Hansen, *Operating System Principles*, Section 7.2 Class Concept, Prentice Hall, Englewood Cliffs, NJ, (July 1973), 226–232.

yet received. A *static* picture of process communication can be defined by assertions about the relationships of the components of the message buffer. But to understand how and when messages are exchanged *dynamically*, one must also study the *send* and *receive* procedures defined for a message buffer. These operations in turn are only meaningful for the particular representation of the message buffer chosen and can only be understood precisely by studying its type definition.

These examples illustrate the point made by Dahl (1972): "Data and operations on data seem to be so closely connected in our minds, that it takes elements of both kinds to make any concept useful for understanding computing processes."

Simon (1962) has pointed out that the search for state and process descriptions of the same phenomenon is characteristic of problem solving: "These two modes of apprehending structure are the warp and weft of our experience. Pictures, blueprints, most diagrams, chemical structural formulae are state descriptions. Recipes, differential equations, equations for chemical reactions are process descriptions. The former characterize the world as sensed; they provide the criteria for identifying objects, often by modeling the objects themselves. The latter characterize the world as acted upon; they provide the means for producing or generating objects having the desired characteristics."

"The distinction between the world as sensed and the world as acted upon defines the basic condition for the survival of adaptive organisms. The organism must develop correlations between goals in the sensed world and actions in the world of process."

In Section 2.6 on program construction, I have illustrated this alternation between a refinement of data (representing states) and program (representing processes). The essence of this form of problem solving is the following:

When a programmer needs a concept such as process communication, he first postulates a set of operations (in this case, *send* and *receive*) that have the desired effect at his present level of thinking. Later, he chooses a specific representation of a data structure (a message buffer), that enables him to implement the operations efficiently on the available machine.

When the programmer is trying to convince himself of the correctness of a program (by formal proof or testing), he will tacitly assume that these operations (*send* and *receive*) are the only ones carried out on data structures of this type (*message buffers*).

If other statements in his program are able to operate on message buffers, he cannot make this assumption. The most extreme case is unstructured machine language, which potentially permits each statement to influence any other statement, intentionally or by mistake. This makes program verification an endless task since one can never be sure, when a new component is added to a large program, how this will influence previously tested components.

If, on the other hand, the previous assumption is justified, the programmer can convince himself of the correctness of process communication by studying only the type definition of a message buffer and the procedures *send* and *receive*. Once this program component has been shown to be correct, the designer can be confident that subsequent addition of other components will not invalidate this proof. This makes the task of verification grow linearly with the number and size of components—an essential requirement for the design of large, reliable programs.

According to the previous definition, it is an obvious protection problem to check that data are accessed by operations consistent with their type. To what extent do the structures of present high-level languages enable a compiler to do this?

A decent compiler for an algorithmic language such as *Fortran*, *Algol 60*, or *Pascal* will check the compatibility of data and operations on them for *primitive types* (Naur 1963). The compiler can do this because the permissible operations on primitive types are part of the language definition.

But in the case of *structured types*, only the most rudimentary kind of checking is possible with these languages. All the compiler can check is that data in assignment statements and comparisons for equality are of the same type. But, since the languages mentioned do not enable the programmer to associate a set of procedures with a type definition, the compiler cannot check whether the operations on a message buffer are restricted to *send* and *receive* procedures as intended by the programmer. This is a serious deficiency of most programming languages available today.

An exception is the *Simula 67* language (Dahl 1968), an extension of Algol 60 originally designed for simulation. In Simula 67, the definition of a structured data type and the meaningful operations on it form a single, syntactical unit called a class.[1]

I will briefly describe a simplified, restricted form of the Simula 67 class concept in a Pascal-inspired notation.

[1]Readers of the Pascal report by Wirth (1971) should notice that the Simula class concept is completely unrelated to the Pascal class concept.

The notation

$$\textbf{class } T = v_1\text{: } T_1\text{; } v_2\text{: } T_2\text{; } \ldots\text{; } v_m\text{: } T_m\text{;}$$

$$\textbf{procedure } P_1(\ldots) \textbf{ begin } S_1 \textbf{ end}$$

$$\ldots$$

$$\textbf{procedure } P_n(\ldots) \textbf{ begin } S_n \textbf{ end}$$

$$\textbf{begin } S_0 \textbf{ end}$$

defines: (1) a data structure of type T consisting of the components v_1, v_2, ..., v_m of types T_1, T_2, ..., T_m; (2) a set of procedures (or functions), P_1, P_2, ..., P_n that operate on the data structure; and (3) a statement S_0 that can define its initial value.

A variable v of type T is declared as usual:

$$\textbf{var } v\text{: } T$$

Upon entry to the context in which the variable v is declared, storage is allocated for its components v_1, v_2, ..., v_m, and the initial statement S_0 is carried out for this variable.

A call of a procedure P_i on the variable v is denoted:

$$v.P_i(\ldots)$$

Procedure P_i can refer to the components v_1, v_2, ..., v_m of v, to its own local variables, and to the parameters of the given call. The operations P_1, P_2, ..., P_n are the only ones permitted on the variable v.

An obvious idea is to represent critical regions by the concept *shared class*, implying that the operations P_1, P_2, ..., P_n on a given variable v of type T exclude one another in time.

The concept *message buffering* is defined as a shared class in Algorithm 1. A buffer variable b and a message variable t are declared and accessed as follows:

```
var b: B; t: T;

b.send(t)    b.receive(t)
```

Strictly speaking, assignment to a message parameter m can only be made within the class B if its type T is primitive. But it seems reasonable to retain the simple type definition

```
shared class B =
  buffer: array 0..max−1 of T;
  p, c: 0..max−1;
  full: 0..max;

procedure send(m: T);
begin
  await full < max;
  buffer[p] := m;
  p := (p + 1) mod max;
  full := full + 1;
end

procedure receive(var m: T);
begin
  await full > 0;
  m := buffer[c];
  c := (c + 1) mod max;
  full := full − 1;
end

begin p := 0; c := 0; full := 0 end
```

Algorithm 1 Representation of a message buffer by a shared class.

type T = <type>

to indicate that variables of this type can be accessed directly.

The class concept in Simula 67 has several other aspects, among them a mechanism for defining a hierarchy of classes (Dahl 1972). My main purpose here is to show a notation which explicitly restricts operations on data and enables a compiler to check that these restrictions are obeyed. Although such restrictions are not enforced by Simula 67, this would seem to be essential for effective protection.

Many computers support a restricted form of shared class at the machine level of programming. I am referring to the *basic monitor* procedures and data structures which control the sharing of processors, storage, and peripherals at the lowest level of programming. This class concept enforced at run time is implemented as follows: The address mapping performed by a central processor prevents computations from referring directly to data structures belonging to the basic monitor, but permits them to call a well-defined set of monitor procedures. Mutual exclusion in time of such calls is achieved by means of an arbiter and by delaying interrupt response. To prevent computations from bypassing the monitor and referring directly to physical resources, the central processor recognizes two states of execution: the *privileged state*, in which all machine instructions can be executed; and the *user state*, in which certain instructions cannot be executed (those that control program interruption, input/output, and address mapping). The privileged state is entered after a monitor call; the user state is entered after a monitor return.

In Chapter 1 I said "It is now recognized that it is desirable to be able to distinguish in a more flexible manner between many levels of protection (and not just two)." We have seen that it is indeed desirable to be able to enforce a separate set of access rules for each data type used. The class concept is a general structuring tool applicable at all levels of programming, sequential as well as concurrent.

The class concept was introduced here to protect *local* data structures within a program against inconsistent operations. But the concept is applicable also to data structures which are *retained* within the computer after the termination of computations.

One example of retained data structures are those used within an *operating system* to control resource sharing among unrelated computations. These data structures must be accessed only through well-defined procedures; otherwise, the operating system might crash. So an operating system defines a set of standard procedures which can be called by computations. Since these procedures remain unchanged over reasonable periods of time, a compiler should be able to use a description of them to perform type checking of calls of them within user programs in advance of their execution.

We are thus lead to the idea of maintaining *data structures defining environments of compilation and execution.* An environment defines a set of retained data structures and procedures accessible to a given computation.

Another example of retained data structures are files stored semipermanently on backing stores. In most present *file systems*, a computation can either be denied access to a given file or be permitted to *read*, *write*, or *execute* it. This seems a rather crude distinction. In most cases, a data file is intended to be used only in a particular manner; for example, a source text of a program is intended to be edited or compiled by a particular compiler; most other operations on it may be entirely meaningless from the user's point of view. To maintain the integrity of a file, its creator should therefore be able to associate it with a set of procedures through which it can be accessed in a meaningful manner. This is possible, for example, in the file system for the *B5500* computer (McKeag 1971).

Assuming that this set of procedures remains unchanged over reasonable periods of time, it would again be possible to check the consistency of references to files within user programs at compile time. The basic requirement is that the access rules remain fixed between compilation and execution of programs.

Such a system differs from the present ones in two aspects: (1) a program is compiled to be executed in a particular environment; and (2) a compiled program may become invalid if its environment changes. This is acceptable only if most programs are compiled shortly before execution or if they operate in a fairly constant environment. The benefits of this approach would be an early detection of program errors and a more efficient execution because fewer protection rules would have to be checked dynamically.

References

Dahl, O.-J., Myhrhaug, B., and Nygaard, K. 1968. Simula 67—common base language. Norsk Regnesentral, Oslo, Norway, (May).

Dahl, O.-J., and Hoare, C.A.R. 1972. Hierarchical program structures. In *Structured Programming*, O.-J. Dahl, E.W. Dijkstra, and C.A.R. Hoare, Eds., Academic Press, New York, 175–220.

McKeag, R.M. 1971. Burroughs B5500 master control program. In *Studies in Operating Systems*, R.M. McKeag and R. Wilson, Academic Press, New York, (1976), 1–66.

Naur, P. 1963. The design of the GIER Algol compiler. *BIT 3*, 2–3, 124–140 and 145–166.

Simon, H.A. 1962. The architecture of complexity. *Proceedings of the American Philosophical Society 106*, 6, 468–482.

Wirth, N. 1971. The programming language Pascal. *Acta Informatica 1*, 1, 35–63.

9

MONITORS: AN OPERATING SYSTEM STRUCTURING CONCEPT

C. A. R. HOARE

(1974)

This paper develops Brinch Hansen's concept of a monitor as a method of structuring an operating system. It introduces a form of synchronization, describes a possible method of implementation in terms of semaphores and gives a suitable proof rule. Illustrative examples include a single resource scheduler, a bounded buffer, an alarm clock, a buffer pool, a disk head optimizer, and a version of the problem of readers and writers.

1 Introduction

A primary aim of an operating system is to share a computer installation among many programs making unpredictable demands upon its resources. A primary task of its designer is therefore to construct resource allocation (or scheduling) algorithms for resources of various kinds (main store, drum store, magnetic tape handlers, consoles, etc.). In order to simplify his task, he should try to construct separate schedulers for each class of resource. Each scheduler will consist of a certain amount of local administrative data, together with some procedures and functions which are called by programs wishing to acquire and release resources. Such a collection of associated data and procedures is known as a *monitor*; and a suitable notation can be based on the *class* notation of Simula 67 (Dahl 1972).

C. A. R. Hoare, Monitors: an operating system structuring concept, *Communications of the ACM 17*, 10 (October 1974), 549–557.

```
monitorname: monitor
  begin ... declarations of data local to the monitor;
    procedure procname (... formal parameters ...);
      begin ... procedure body ... end;
    ... declarations of other procedures local to the monitor;
    ... initialization of local data of the monitor ...
  end;
```

Note that the procedure bodies may have local data, in the normal way.

In order to call a procedure of a monitor, it is necessary to give the name of the monitor as well as the name of the desired procedure, separating them by a dot:

monitorname.procname(...actual parameters...);

In an operating system it is sometimes desirable to declare several monitors with identical structure and behaviour, for example to schedule two similar resources. In such cases, the declaration shown above will be preceded by the word *class*, and the separate monitors will be declared to belong to this class:

monitor 1, *monitor 2*: *classname*;

Thus the structure of a class of monitors is identical to that described for a data representation in Hoare (1972b), except for addition of the basic word *monitor*. Brinch Hansen (1973) used the word *shared* for the same purpose.

The procedures of a monitor are common to all running programs, in the sense that any program may at any time attempt to call such a procedure. However, it is essential that only one program at a time actually succeed in entering a monitor procedure, and any subsequent call must be held up until the previous call has been completed. Otherwise, if two procedure bodies were in simultaneous execution, the effects on the local variables of the monitor could be chaotic. The procedures local to a monitor should not access any nonlocal variables other than those local to the same monitor, and these variables of the monitor should be inaccessible from outside the monitor. If these restrictions are imposed, it is possible to guarantee against certain of the more obscure forms of time-dependent coding error; and this guarantee could be underwritten by a visual scan of the text of the program, which could readily be automated in a compiler.

Any dynamic resource allocator will sometimes need to delay a program wishing to acquire a resource which is not currently available, and to resume that program after some other program has released the resource required. We therefore need: a "wait" operation, issued from inside a procedure of the monitor, which causes the calling program to be delayed; and a "signal" operation, also issued from inside a procedure of the same monitor, which causes exactly one of the waiting programs to be resumed immediately. If there are no waiting programs, the signal has no effect. In order to enable other programs to release resources during a wait, a wait operation must relinquish the exclusion which would otherwise prevent entry to the releasing procedure. However, we decree that a signal operation be followed immediately by resumption of a waiting program, without possibility of an intervening procedure call from yet a third program. It is only in this way that a waiting program has an absolute guarantee that it can acquire the resource just released by the signalling program without any danger that a third program will interpose a monitor entry and seize the resource instead.

In many cases, there may be more than one reason for waiting, and these need to be distinguished by both the waiting and the signalling operation. We therefore introduce a new type of "variable" known as a "condition"; and the writer of a monitor should declare a variable of type condition for each reason why a program might have to wait. Then the wait and signal operations should be preceded by the name of the relevant condition variable, separated from it by a dot:

condvariable.wait;
condvariable.signal;

Note that a condition "variable" is neither true nor false; indeed, it does not have any stored value accessible to the program. In practice, a condition variable will be represented by an (initially empty) queue of processes which are currently waiting on the condition; but this queue is invisible both to waiters and signallers. This design of the condition variable has been deliberately kept as primitive and rudimentary as possible, so that it may be implemented efficiently and used flexibly to achieve a wide variety of effects. There is a great temptation to introduce a more complex synchronization primitive, which may be easier to use for many purposes. We shall resist this temptation for a while.

As the simplest example of a monitor, we will design a scheduling algorithm for a single resource, which is dynamically acquired and released by an unknown number of customer processes by calls on procedures:

procedure acquire;
procedure release;

A variable[1]

busy: Boolean

determines whether or not the resource is in use. If an attempt is made to acquire the resource when it is busy, the attempting program must be delayed by waiting on a variable,

nonbusy: condition

which is signalled by the next subsequent release. The initial value of busy is false. These design decisions lead to the following code for the monitor:

```
single resource: monitor
begin busy: Boolean;
    nonbusy: condition;
  procedure acquire;
    begin if busy then nonbusy.wait;
          busy := true
    end;
  procedure release;
    begin busy := false;
          nonbusy.signal
    end;
    busy := false; comment initial value;
end single resource
```

Notes

1. In designing a monitor, it seems natural to design the procedure headings, the data, the conditions, and the procedure bodies, in that order. All subsequent examples will be designed in this way.
2. The acquire procedure does not have to retest that busy has gone false when it resumes after its wait, since the release procedure has guaranteed that this is so; and as mentioned before, no other program can intervene between the signal and the continuation of exactly one waiting program.
3. If more than one program is waiting on a condition, we postulate that the signal operation will reactivate the longest waiting program. This gives a simple neutral queuing discipline which ensures that every waiting program will eventually get its turn.

---

[1] As in Pascal (Wirth 1971), a variable declaration is of the form:
<variable identifier>: *<type>*;

4. The single resource monitor simulates a Boolean semaphore (Dijkstra 1968a) with *acquire* and *release* used for *P* and *V* respectively. This is a simple proof that the monitor/condition concepts are not in principle less powerful than semaphores, and that they can be used for all the same purposes.

2 Interpretation

Having proved that semaphores can be implemented by a monitor, the next task is to prove that monitors can be implemented by semaphores.

Obviously, we shall require for each monitor a Boolean semaphore "mutex" to ensure that the bodies of the local procedures exclude each other. The semaphore is initialized to 1; a *P(mutex)* must be executed on entry to each local procedure, and a *V(mutex)* must usually be executed on exit from it.

When a process signals a condition on which another process is waiting, the signalling process must wait until the resumed process permits it to proceed. We therefore introduce for each monitor a second semaphore "urgent" (initialized to 0), on which signalling processes suspend themselves by the operation *P(urgent)*. Before releasing exclusion, each process must test whether any other process is waiting on urgent, and if so, must release it instead by a *V(urgent)* instruction. We therefore need to count the number of processes waiting on *urgent*, in an integer "urgentcount" (initially zero). Thus each exit from a procedure of a monitor should be coded:

if urgentcount > 0 **then** V(urgent) **else** V(mutex)

Finally, for each condition local to the monitor, we introduce a semaphore "condsem" (initialized to 0), on which a process desiring to wait suspends itself by a *P(condsem)* operation. Since a process signalling this condition needs to know whether anybody is waiting, we also need a count of the number of waiting processes held in an integer variable "condcount" (initially 0). The operation *cond.wait* may now be implemented as follows (recall that a waiting program must release exclusion before suspending itself):

condcount := condcount + 1;
if urgentcount > 0 **then** V(urgent) **else** V(mutex);
P(condsem); **comment** This will always wait;
condcount := condcount − 1

The signal operation may be coded:

```
urgentcount := urgentcount + 1;
if condcount > 0 then {V(condsem); P(urgent)};
urgentcount := urgentcount − 1
```

In this implementation, possession of the monitor is regarded as a privilege which is explicitly passed from one process to another. Only when no one further wants the privilege is *mutex* finally released.

This solution is not intended to correspond to recommended "style" in the use of semaphores. The concept of a condition-variable is intended as a substitute for semaphores, and has its own style of usage, in the same way that while-loops or coroutines are intended as a substitute for jumps.

In many cases, the generality of this solution is unnecessary, and a significant improvement in efficiency is possible.

1. When a procedure body in a monitor contains no *wait* or *signal*, exit from the body can be coded by a simple *V(mutex)*, since *urgentcount* cannot have changed during the execution of the body.
2. If a *cond.signal* is the last operation of a procedure body, it can be combined with monitor exit as follows:

```
     if condcount > 0 then V(condsem)
else if urgentcount > 0 then V(urgent)
                        else V(mutex)
```

3. If there is no other wait or signal in the procedure body, the second line shown above can also be omitted.
4. If *every* signal occurs as the last operation of its procedure body, the variables *urgentcount* and *urgent* can be omitted, together with all operations upon them. This is such a simplifcation that O.-J. Dahl suggests that signals should always be the last operation of a monitor procedure; in fact, this restriction is a very natural one, which has been unwittingly observed in all examples of this paper.

Significant improvements in efficiency may also be obtained by avoiding the use of semaphores, and by implementing conditions directly in hardware, or at the lowest and most uninterruptible level of software (e.g. supervisor mode). In this case, the following optimizations are possible.

1. *urgentcount* and *condcount* can be abolished, since the fact that someone is waiting can be established by examining the representation of the semaphore, which cannot change surreptitiously within noninterruptible mode.
2. Many monitors are very short and contain no calls to other monitors. Such monitors can be executed wholly in non-interruptible mode, using, as

it were, the common exclusion mechanism provided by hardware. This will often involve *less* time in non-interruptible mode than the establishment of separate exclusion for each monitor.

I am grateful to J. Bezivin, J. Horning, and R. M. McKeag for assisting in the discovery of this algorithm.

3 Proof rules

The analogy between a monitor and a data representation has been noted in the introduction. The mutual exclusion on the code of a monitor ensures that procedure calls follow each other in time, just as they do in sequential programming; and the same restrictions are placed on access to nonlocal data. These are the reasons why the same proof rules can be applied to monitors as to data representations.

As with a data representation, the programmer may associate an invariant $\mathcal{J}$ with the local data of a monitor, to describe some condition which will be true of this data before and after every procedure call. $\mathcal{J}$ must also be made true after initialization of the data, and before *every* wait instruction; otherwise the next following procedure call will not find the local data in a state which it expects.

With each condition variable b the programmer may associate an assertion B which describes the condition under which a program waiting on b wishes to be resumed. Since other programs may invoke a monitor procedure during a wait, a waiting program must ensure that the invariant $\mathcal{J}$ for the monitor is true beforehand. This gives the proof rule for waits:

$$\mathcal{J}\ \{\text{b.wait}\}\ \mathcal{J}\&\text{B}$$

Since a signal can cause immediate resumption of a waiting program, the conditions $\mathcal{J}\&B$ which are expected by that program must be made true before the signal; and since B may be made false again by the resumed program, only $\mathcal{J}$ may be assumed true afterwards. Thus the proof rule for a signal is:

$$\mathcal{J}\&\text{B}\ \{\text{b.signal}\}\ \mathcal{J}$$

This exhibits a pleasing symmetry with the rule for waiting.

The introduction of condition variables makes it possible to write monitors subject to the risk of deadly embrace (Dijkstra 1968a). It is the responsibility of the programmer to avoid this risk, together with other scheduling disasters (thrashing, indefinitely repeated overtaking, etc. (Dijkstra 1972c)). Assertion-oriented proof methods cannot prove absence of such risk; perhaps it is better to use less formal methods for such proofs.

Finally, in many cases an operating system monitor constructs some "virtual" resource which is used in place of actual resources by its "customer" programs. This virtual resource is an abstraction from the set of local variables of the monitor. The program prover should therefore define this abstraction in terms of its concrete representation, and then express the intended effect of each of the procedure bodies in terms of the abstraction. This proof method is described in detail in Hoare (1972b)

4 Example: bounded buffer

A bounded buffer is a concrete representation of the abstract idea of a sequence of portions. The sequence is accessible to two programs running in parallel: the first of these (the producer) updates the sequence by appending a new portion x at the end; and the second (the consumer) updates it by removing the first portion. The initial value of the sequence is empty. We thus require two operations:

(1) *append(x: portion);*

which should be equivalent to the abstract operation

$$\text{sequence} := \text{sequence} \cap \langle \text{x} \rangle;$$

where $\langle x \rangle$ is the sequence whose only item is x and $\cap$ denotes concatenation of two sequences.

(2) *remove(***result** *x: portion);*

which should be equivalent to the abstract operations

$$\text{x} := \text{first(sequence)}; \ \text{sequence} := \text{rest(sequence)};$$

where *first* selects the first item of a sequencc and *rest* denotes the sequence with its first item removed. Obviously, if the sequence is empty, *first* is undefined; and in this case we want to ensure that the consumer waits until the producer has made the sequence nonempty.

We shall assume that the amount of time taken to produce a portion or consume it is large in comparison with the time taken to append or remove it from the sequence. We may therefore be justifed in making a design in which producer and consumer can both update the sequence, but not simultaneously.

The sequence is represented by an array:

buffer: **array** 0..N−1 **of** portion;

and two variables:

(1) lastpointer: 0..N−1;

which points to the buffer position into which the next append operation will put a new item, and

(2) count: 0..N;

which always holds the length of the sequence (initially 0).

We define the function

$$\text{seq}(b,l,c) =_{df} \textbf{if } c = 0 \textbf{ then } \text{empty} \\ \textbf{else } \text{seq}(b,l\ominus 1,c-1) \cap \langle b[l\ominus 1]\rangle$$

where the circled operations are taken modulo N. Note that if $c \neq O$,

$$\text{first}(\text{seq}(b,l,c)) = b[l\ominus c]$$

and

$$\text{rest}(\text{seq}(b,l,c)) = \text{seq}(b,l,c-1)$$

The definition of the abstract sequence in terms of its concrete representation may now be given:

$$\text{sequence} =_{df} \text{seq}(\text{buffer, lastpointer, count})$$

Less formally, this may be written

$$\text{sequence} =_{df} \langle \text{buffer}[\text{lastpointer}\ominus\text{count}], \\ \text{buffer}[\text{lastpointer}\ominus\text{count}\oplus 1], \\ \ldots, \\ \text{buffer}[\text{lastpointer}\ominus 1]\rangle$$

Another way of conveying this information would be by an example and a picture, which would be even less formal. The invariant for the monitor is:

$$0 \leq \text{count} \leq \text{N} \ \& \ 0 \leq \text{lastpointer} \leq \text{N} - 1$$

There are two reasons for waiting, which must be represented by condition variables:

nonempty: condition;

means that the count is greater than 0, and

nonfull: condition;

means that the count is less than N.

With this constructive approach to the design (Dijkstra 1968b), it is relatively easy to code the monitor without error.

```
bounded buffer: monitor
  begin buffer: array 0..N−1 of portion;
        lastpointer: 0..N−1;
        count: 0..N;
        nonempty, nonfull: condition;
    procedure append(x: portion);
      begin if count = N then nonfull.wait;
            note 0 ≤ count < N;
            buffer[lastpointer] := x;
            lastpointer := lastpointer ⊕ 1;
            count := count + 1;
            nonempty.signal
      end append;
    procedure remove(result x: portion);
      begin if count = 0 then nonempty.wait;
            note 0 < count ≤ N;
            x := buffer[lastpointer ⊖ count];
            count := count − 1;
            nonfull.signal
      end remove;
    count := 0; lastpointer := 0
  end bounded buffer;
```

A formal proof of the correctness of this monitor with respect to the stated abstraction and invariant can be given if desired by techniques described in Hoare (1972b). However, these techniques seem not capable of dealing with subsequent examples of this paper.

Single-buffered input and output may be regarded as a special case of the bounded buffer with $N = 1$. In this case, the array can be replaced by a single variable, the *lastpointer* is redundant, and we get:

```
iostream: monitor
begin buffer: portion;
        count: 0..1;
        nonempty,nonfull: condition;
  procedure append(x: portion);
    begin if count = 1 then nonfull.wait;
      buffer := x;
      count := 1;
      nonempty.signal
    end append;
  procedure remove(result x: portion);
    begin if count = 0 then nonempty.wait;
      x:= buffer;
      count := 0;
      nonfull.signal
    end remove;
  count := 0;
end iostream;
```

If physical output is carried out by a separate special-purpose channel, then the interrupt from the channel should simulate a call of *iostream.remove(x);* and similarly for physical input, simulating a call of *iostream.append(x)*.

5 Scheduled waits

Up to this point, we have assumed that when more than one program is waiting for the same condition, a signal will cause the longest waiting program to be resumed. This is a good simple scheduling strategy, which precludes indefinite overtaking of a waiting process.

However, in the design of an operating system, there are many cases when such simple scheduling on the basis of first-come-first-served is not adequate. In order to give a closer control over scheduling strategy, we introduce a further feature of a conditional wait, which makes it possible to specify as a parameter of the wait some indication of the priority of the waiting program, e.g.:

```
busy.wait(p);
```

When the condition is signalled, it is the program that specified the lowest value of p that is resumed. In using this facility, the designer of a monitor must take care to avoid the risk of indefinite overtaking; and often it is advisable to make priority a nondecreasing function of the time at which the wait commences.

This introduction of a "scheduled wait" concedes to the temptation to make the condition concept more elaborate. The main justifications are:
1. It has no effect whatsoever on the *logic* of a program, or on the formal proof rules. Any program which works without a scheduled wait will work with it, but possibly with better timing characteristics.
2. The automatic ordering of the queue of waiting processes is a simple fast-scheduling technique, except when the queue is exceptionally long—and when it is, central processor time is not the major bottleneck.
3. The maximum amount of storage required is one word per process. Without such a built-in scheduling method, each monitor may have to allocate storage proportional to the number of its customers; the alternative of dynamic storage allocation in small chunks is unattractive at the low level of an operating system where monitors are found.

I shall yield to one further temptation, to introduce a Boolean function of conditions:

```
condname.queue
```

which yields the value true if anyone is waiting on *condname* and false otherwise. This can obviously be easily implemented by a couple of instructions, and affords valuable information which could otherwise be obtained only at the expense of extra storage, time, and trouble.

A trivially simple example is an *alarmclock* monitor, which enables a calling program to delay itself for a stated number n of time units, or "ticks". There are two entries:

```
procedure wakeme(n: integer);
procedure tick;
```

The second of these is invoked by hardware (e.g. an interrupt) at regular intervals, say ten times per second. Local variables are

```
now: integer;
```

which records the current time (initially zero) and

```
wakeup: condition;
```

on which sleeping programs wait. But the *alarmsetting* at which these programs will be aroused is known at the time when they start the wait; and this can be used to determine the correct sequence of waking up.

```
alarmclock: monitor
begin now: integer;
    wakeup: condition;
  procedure wakeme(n: integer);
    begin alarmsetting: integer;
      alarmsetting := now + n;
      while now < alarmsetting do wakeup.wait(alarmsetting);
      wakeup.signal;
      comment In case the next process is due to wake up at the
      same time;
    end;
  procedure tick;
    begin now:= now + 1;
      wakeup.signal
    end;
  now:= 0
end alarmclock
```

In the program given above, the next candidate for wakening is actually woken at every tick of the clock. This will not matter if the frequency of ticking is low enough, and the overhead of an accepted signal is not too high.

I am grateful to A. Ballard and J. Horning for posing this problem.

6 Further examples

In proposing a new feature for a high-level language it is very diffcult to make a convincing case that the feature will be both easy to use efficiently and easy to implement efficiently. Quality of implementation can be proved by a single good example, but ease and efficiency of use require a great number of realistic examples; otherwise it can appear that the new feature has been specially designed to suit the examples, or vice versa. This section contains a number of additional examples of solutions of familiar problems. Further examples may be found in Hoare (1973).

6.1 Buffer allocation

The bounded buffer described in Section 4 was designed to be suitable only for sequences, with small portions, for example, message queues. If the buffers contain high-volume information (for example, files for pseudo off-line input and output), the bounded buffer may still be used to store the *addresses* of the buffers which are being used to hold the information. In this way, the producer can be filling one buffer while the consumer is emptying another buffer of the same sequence. But this requires an allocator for dynamic acquisition and relinquishment of *buffer addresses*. These may be declared as a type

type bufferaddress= 1..B;

where B is the number of buffers available for allocation.

The buffer allocator has two entries:

procedure acquire(**result** b: bufferaddress);

which delivers a free *buffer address b*; and

procedure release(b: bufferaddress);

which returns a *buffer address* when it is no longer required. In order to keep a record of free buffer addresses the monitor will need:

freepool: **powerset** bufferaddress;

which uses the Pascal powerset facility to define a variable whose values range over all sets of *buffer addresses*, from the empty set to the set containing all buffer addresses. It should be implemented as a bitmap of B consecutive bits, where the ith bit is 1 if and only if i is in the set. There is only one condition variable needed:

nonempty: condition

which means that $freepool \neq empty$. The code for the allocator is:

```
bufferallocator: monitor
begin freepool: powerset bufferaddress;
   nonempty: condition;
  procedure acquire(result b: bufferaddress);
   begin if freepool = empty then nonempty.wait;
     b := first(freepool);
     comment Any one would do;
     freepool := freepool − {b};
     comment Set subtraction;
   end acquire;
  procedure release(b: bufferaddress);
   begin freepool:= freepool + {b};
     nonempty.signal
   end release;
  freepool := all buffer addresses
end buffer allocator
```

The action of a producer and consumer may be summarized:

```
producer: begin b: bufferaddress;...
            while not finished do
            begin bufferallocator.acquire(b);
               ...fill buffer b...;
               bounded buffer.append(b)
            end;...
          end producer;

consumer: begin b: bufferaddress;...
            while not finished do
            begin bounded buffer.remove(b);
               ...empty buffer b...;
               buffer allocator.release(b)
            end;...
          end consumer;
```

This buffer allocator would appear to be usable to share the buffers among several streams, each with its own producer and its own consumer, and its own instance of a bounded buffer monitor. Unfortunately, when the streams operate at widely varying speeds, and when the freepool is empty, the scheduling algorithm can exhibit persistent undesirable behaviour. If two producers are competing for each buffer as it becomes free, a first-come-first-served discipline of allocation will ensure (apparently fairly) that each gets alternate buffers; and they will consequently begin to produce at equal speeds. But if one consumer is a 1000 lines/min printer and the other is a 10 lines/min teletype, the faster consumer will be eventually reduced to the speed of the slower, since it cannot forever go faster than its producer. At this stage nearly all buffers will belong to the slower stream, so the situation could take a long time to clear.

A solution to this is to use a scheduled wait, to ensure that in heavy load conditions the available buffers will be shared reasonably fairly between the streams that are competing for them. Of course, inactive streams need not be considered, and streams for which the consumer is currently faster than the producer will never ask for more than two buffers anyway. In order to achieve fairness in allocation, it is sufficient to allocate a newly freed buffer to that one among the competing producers whose stream currently owns fewest buffers. Thus the system will seek a point as far away from the undesirable extreme as possible.

For this reason, the entries to the allocator should indicate for what stream the buffer is to be (or has been) used, and the allocator must keep a count of the current allocation to each stream in an array:

```
count: array stream of integer;
```

The new version of the allocator is:

```
bufferallocator: monitor
  begin freepool: powerset bufferaddress;
    nonempty: condition
    count: array stream of integer;
  procedure acquire(result b: bufferaddress; s: stream);
    begin if freepool = empty then nonempty.wait(count[s]);
      count[s] := count[s] + 1;
      b:= first(freepool);
      freepool := freepool − {b}
     end acquire;
  procedure release(b: bufferaddress; s: stream)
    begin count[s] := count[s] − 1;
      freepool := freepool + {b};
      nonempty.signal
    end
  freepool := all buffer addresses;
  for s: stream do count[s] := 0
end bufferallocator
```

Of course, if a consumer stops altogether, perhaps owing to mechanical failure, the producer must also be halted before it has acquired too many buffers, even if no one else currently wants them. This can perhaps be most easily accomplished by appropriate fixing of the size of the bounded buffer for that stream and/or by ensuring that at least two buffers are reserved for each stream, even when inactive. It is an interesting comment on dynamic resource allocation that, as soon as resources are heavily loaded, the system must be designed to fall back toward a more static regime.

I am grateful to E. W. Dijkstra (1972b) for pointing out this problem and its solution.

6.2 Disk head scheduler

On a moving-head disk, the time taken to move the heads increases monotonically with the distance travelled. If several programs wish to move the heads, the average waiting time can be reduced by selecting, first, the program which wishes to move them the shortest distance. But unfortunately this policy is subject to an instability, since a program wishing to access a cylinder at one edge of the disk can be indefinitely overtaken by programs operating at the other edge or the middle.

A solution to this is to minimize the frequency of change of direction of movement of the heads. At any time, the heads are kept moving in a given direction, and they service the program requesting the nearest cylinder in that direction. If there is no such request, the direction changes, and the heads make another sweep across the surface of the disk. This may be called the "elevator" algorithm, since it simulates the behaviour of a lift in a multi-storey building.

There are two entries to a disk head scheduler:

(1) request(dest: cylinder);

where

type cylinder = 0..cylmax;

which is entered by a program just *before* issuing the instruction to move the heads to cylinder *dest*.

(2) release;

which is entered by a program when it has made all the transfers it needs on the current cylinder.

The local data of the monitor must include a record of the current head position, *headpos*, the current direction of *sweep*, and whether the disk is *busy*:

```
headpos: cylinder;
direction: (up, down);
busy: Boolean
```

We need two conditions, one for requests waiting for an *upsweep* and the other for requests waiting for a *downsweep*:

```
upsweep, downsweep: condition
```

```
diskhead: monitor
begin headpos: cylinder;
    direction: (up, down);
    busy: Boolean;
    upsweep, downsweep: condition;
  procedure request(dest: cylinder);
    begin if busy then
      {if headpos < dest ∨ headpos = dest & direction = up
        then upsweep.wait(dest)
        else downsweep.wait(cylmax − dest)};
      busy := true; headpos := dest
    end request;
  procedure release;
    begin busy := false;
      if direction = up then
        {if upsweep.queue then upsweep.signal
                          else {direction := down;
                                downsweep.signal}}
      else if downsweep.queue then downsweep.signal
                              else {direction := up;
                                    upsweep.signal}
    end release;
    headpos := 0; direction := up; busy := false
end diskhead;
```

6.3 Readers and writers

As a more significant example, we take a problem which arises in on-line real-time applications such as airspace control. Suppose that each aircraft is represented by a record, and that this record is kept up to date by a number of "writer" processes and accessed by a number of "reader" processes. Any number of "reader" processes may simultaneously access the same record, but obviously any process which is updating (writing) the individual components of the record must have exclusive access to it, or chaos will ensue.

Thus we need a class of monitors; an instance of this class local to *each* individual aircraft record will enforce the required discipline for that record. If there are many aircraft, there is a strong motivation for minimizing local data of the monitor; and if each read or write operation is brief, we should also minimize the time taken by each monitor entry.

When many readers are interested in a single aircraft record, there is a danger that a writer will be indefinitely prevented from keeping that record up to date. We therefore decide that a new reader should not be permitted to start if there is a writer waiting. Similarly, to avoid the danger of indefinite exclusion of readers, all readers waiting at the end of a write should have priority over the next writer. Note that this is a very different scheduling rule from that propounded in Courtois (1971a), and does not seem to require such subtlety in implementation. Nevertheless, it may be more suited to this kind of application, where it is better to read stale information than to wait indefinitely!

The monitor obviously requires four local procedures:

startread	entered by reader who wishes to read.
endread	entered by reader who has finished reading.
startwrite	entered by writer who wishes to write.
endwrite	entered by writer who has finished writing.

We need to keep a count of the number of users who are reading, so that the last reader to finish will known this fact:

readercount: integer

We also need a *Boolean* to indicate that someone is actually writing:

busy: Boolean;

We introduce separate conditions for readers and writers to wait on:

OKtoread, OKtowrite: condition;

The following annotation is relevant:

OKtoread $\equiv \neg$ busy
OKtowrite $\equiv \neg$ busy & readercount $= 0$
invariant: busy $\Rightarrow$ readercount $= 0$

2. Do not seek to present the user with a virtual machine which is better than the actual hardware; merely seek to pass on the speed, size, and flat unopiniated structure of a simple hardware design.
3. Use preemptive techniques in preference to nonpreemptive ones where possible.
4. Use "grain of time" (Dijkstra 1972a) methods to secure independence of scheduling strategies.
5. Keep a low variance (as well as a low mean) on waiting times.
6. Avoid fixed priorities; instead, try to ensure that every program in the system makes reasonably steady progress. In particular, avoid indefinite overtaking.
7. Ensure that when demand for resources outstrips the supply (i.e. in overload conditions), the behaviour of the scheduler is satisfactory (i.e. thrashing is avoided).
8. Make rules for the correct and sensible use of monitor calls, and assume that user programs will obey them. Any checking which is necessary should be done not by a central shared monitor, but rather by an algorithm (called "user envelope") which is local to each process executing a user program. This algorithm should be implemented at least partially in the hardware (e.g. base and range registers, address translation mechanisms, capabilities, etc.).

It is the possibility of constructing separate monitors for different purposes, and of separating the scheduling decisions embodied in monitors from the checking embodied in user envelopes, that may justify a hope that monitors are an appropriate concept for the structuring of an operating system.

Acknowledgements

The development of the monitor concept is due to frequent discussions and communications with E. W. Dijkstra and P. Brinch Hansen. A monitor corresponds to the "secretary" described in Dijkstra (1972a), and is also described in Brinch Hansen (1972a, 1973).

Acknowledgement is also due to the support of IFIP WG.2.3, which provides a meeting place at which these and many other ideas have been germinated, fostered, and tested.

References

Brinch Hansen, P. 1972a. Structured multiprogramming. *Communications of the ACM* *15*, 7 (July), 574–578.

Brinch Hansen. P. 1972b. A comparison of two synchronizing concepts. *Acta Informatica 1*, 190–199,

Brinch Hansen, P. 1973. *Operating System Principles.* Prentice-Hall, Englewood Cliffs, NJ, (July).

Courtois, P.J., Heymans, F. and Parnas, D.L. 1971a. Concurrent control with readers and writers. *Communications of the ACM 14*, 10 (October), 667–668.

Courtois, P.J., Heymans, F. and Parnas, D.L. 1971b. Comments on "A comparison of two synchronizing concepts." *Acta Informatica 1*, 375–376.

Dahl, O.-J. 1972. Hierarchical program structures. In *Structured Programming*, O.-J. Dahl, E.W. Dijkstra and C.A.R. Hoare, Eds., Academic Press, New York, 175–220.

Dijkstra, E.W. 1968a. Cooperating sequential processes. In *Programming Languages*, F. Genuys, Ed., Academic Press, New York, 43–112.

Dijkstra, E.W. 1968b. A constructive approach to the problem of program correctness. *BIT 8*, 174–186.

Dijkstra, E.W. 1972a. Hierarchical ordering of sequential processes. In *Operating Systems Techniques*, C.A.R. Hoare and R.H. Perrott, Eds., Academic Press, New York, 72–93.

Dijkstra, E.W. 1972b. Information streams sharing a finite buffer. *Information Processing Letters 1*, 5 (October), 179–180.

Dijkstra, E.W. 1972c. A class of allocation strategies inducing bounded delays only. *AFIPS Spring Joint Computer Conference 40*, AFIPS Press, Montvale, NJ, 933–936.

Hoare, C.A.R. 1972a. Towards a theory of parallel programming. In *Operating Systems Techniques*, C.A.R. Hoare and R.H. Perrott, Eds., Academic Press, New York, 61–71.

Hoare, C.A.R. 1972b. Proof of correctness of data representations. *Acta Informatica 1*, 271–281.

Hoare, C.A.R. 1973. A structured paging system. *Computer Journal 16*, 3 (August), 209–215.

Wirth, N. 1971. The programming language Pascal. *Acta Informatica 1*, 35–63.

PART III

CONCURRENT PROGRAMMING LANGUAGES

10

THE PROGRAMMING LANGUAGE CONCURRENT PASCAL

PER BRINCH HANSEN

(1975)

The paper describes a new programming language for structured programming of computer operating systems. It extends the sequential programming language Pascal with concurrent programming tools called processes and monitors. Part I explains these concepts informally by means of pictures illustrating a hierarchical design of a simple spooling system. Part II uses the same example to introduce the language notation. The main contribution of Concurrent Pascal is to extend the monitor concept with an explicit hierarchy of access rights to shared data structures that can be stated in the program text and checked by a compiler.

I THE PURPOSE OF CONCURRENT PASCAL

A Background

Since 1972 I have been working on a new programming language for structured programming of computer operating systems. This language is called Concurrent Pascal. It extends the sequential programming language Pascal with concurrent programming tools called processes and monitors (Wirth 1971; Brinch Hansen 1973; Hoare 1974).

This is an informal description of Concurrent Pascal. It uses examples, pictures, and words to bring out the creative aspects of new programming concepts without getting into their finer details. I plan to define these concepts precisely and introduce a notation for them in later papers. This form

P. Brinch Hansen, The programming language Concurrent Pascal, *IEEE Transactions on Software Engineering 1*, 2 (June 1975), 199–207.

of presentation may be imprecise from a formal point of view, but is perhaps more effective from a human point of view.

B Processes

We will study concurrent processes inside an operating system and look at one small problem only: How can large amounts of data be transmitted from one process to another by means of buffers stored on a disk?

Figure 1 shows this little system and its three components: A process that produces data, a process that consumes data, and a disk buffer that connects them.

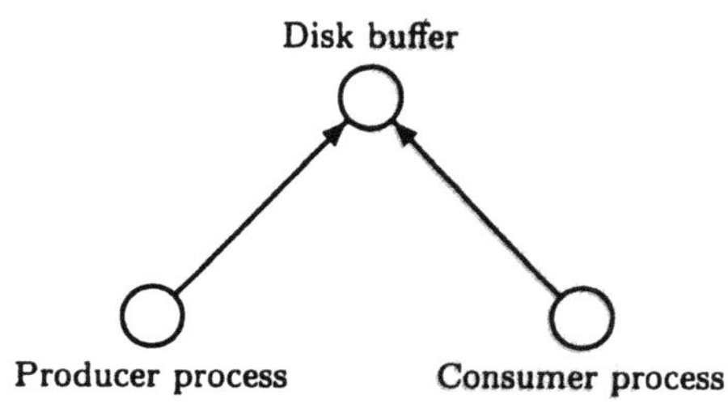

Figure 1 Process communication

The circles are *system components* and the arrows are the *access rights* of these components. They show that both processes can use the buffer (but they do not show that data flows from the producer to the consumer). This kind of picture is an *access graph.*

The next picture shows a process component in more detail (Fig. 2).

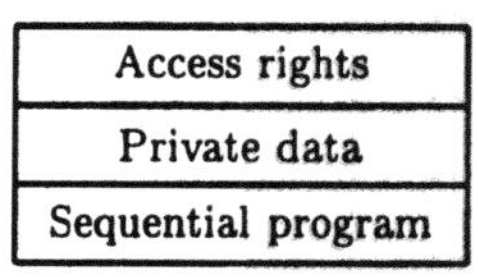

Figure 2 Process.

A *process* consists of a *private data* structure and a *sequential program* that can operate on the data. One process cannot operate on the private data of another process. But concurrent processes can share certain data structures (such as a disk buffer). The *access rights* of a process mention the shared data it can operate on.

C Monitors

A disk buffer is a data structure shared by two concurrent processes. The details of how such a buffer is constructed are irrelevant to its users. All the processes need to know is that they can *send* and *receive* data through it. If they try to operate on the buffer in any other way it is probably either a programming mistake or an example of tricky programming. In both cases, one would like a compiler to detect such misuse of a shared data structure.

To make this possible, we must introduce a language construct that will enable a programmer to tell a compiler how a shared data structure can be used by processes. This kind of system component is called a monitor. A monitor can synchronize concurrent processes and transmit data between them. It can also control the order in which competing processes use shared, physical resources. Figure 3 shows a monitor in detail.

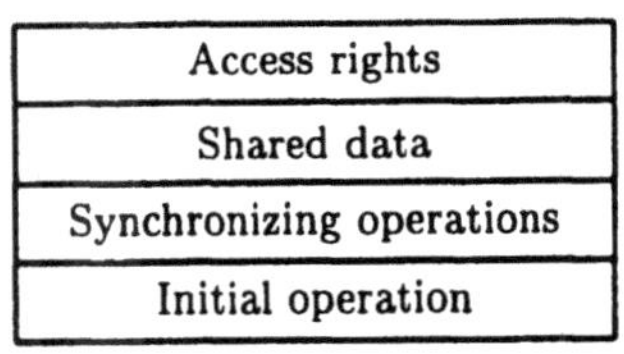

Figure 3 Monitor.

A *monitor* defines a *shared data* structure and all the operations processes can perform on it. These synchronizing operations are called *monitor procedures*. A monitor also defines an *initial operation* that will be executed when its data structure is created.

We can define a *disk buffer* as a monitor. Within this monitor there will be shared variables that define the location and length of the buffer on the disk. There will also be two monitor procedures, *send* and *receive*. The initial operation will make sure that the buffer starts as an empty one.

Processes cannot operate directly on shared data. They can only call monitor procedures that have access to shared data. A monitor procedure is executed as part of a calling process (just like any other procedure).

If concurrent processes simultaneously call monitor procedures that operate on the same shared data these procedures will be executed strictly one at a time. Otherwise, the results of monitor calls would be unpredictable. This means that the machine must be able to delay processes for short periods of time until it is their turn to execute monitor procedures. We will not be concerned with how this is done, but will just notice that a monitor procedure has *exclusive access* to shared data while it is being executed.

So the (virtual) machine on which concurrent programs run will handle *short-term scheduling* of simultaneous monitor calls. But the programmer must also be able to delay processes for longer periods of time if their requests for data and other resources cannot be satisfied immediately. If, for example, a process tries to receive data from an empty disk buffer it must be delayed until another process sends more data.

Concurrent Pascal includes a simple data type, called a *queue*, that can be used by monitor procedures to control *medium-term scheduling* of processes. A monitor can either *delay* a calling process in a queue or *continue* another process that is waiting in a queue. It is not important here to understand how these queues work except for the following essential rule: A process only has exclusive access to shared data as long as it continues to execute statements within a monitor procedure. As soon as a process is delayed in a queue it loses its exclusive access until another process calls the same monitor and wakes it up again. (Without this rule, it would be impossible to enter a monitor and let waiting processes continue their execution.)

Although the disk buffer example does not show this yet, monitor procedures should also be able to call procedures defined within other monitors. Otherwise, the language will not be very useful for hierarchical design. In the case of the disk buffer, one of these other monitors could perhaps define simple input/output operations on the disk. So a monitor can also have *access rights* to other system components (see Fig. 3).

D System Design

A process executes a sequential program—it is an active component. A monitor is just a collection of procedures that do nothing until they are called by processes—it is a passive component. But there are strong similarities between a process and a monitor: both define a data structure (private or shared) and the meaningful operations on it. The main difference between processes and monitors is the way they are scheduled for execution.

It seems natural therefore to regard processes and monitors as *abstract data types* defined in terms of the operations one can perform on them. If a compiler can check that these operations are the only ones carried out on data structures, then we may be able to build very reliable, concurrent programs in which *controlled access* to data and physical resources is guaranteed before these programs are put into operation. We have then to some extent solved the *resource protection* problem in the cheapest possible manner (without hardware mechanisms and run time overhead).

So we will define processes and monitors as data types and make it possible to use several instances of the same component type in a system. We can, for example, use two disk buffers to build a *spooling system* with an input process, a job process, and an output process (Fig. 4).

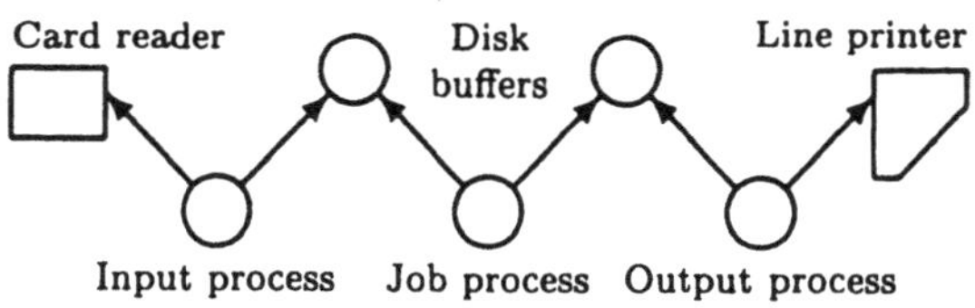

Figure 4 Spooling system.

I will distinguish between definitions and instances of components by calling them *system types* and *system components.* Access graphs (such as Fig. 4) will always show system components (not system types).

Peripheral devices are considered to be monitors implemented in hardware. They can only be accessed by a single procedure *io* that delays the calling process until an input/output operation is completed. Interrupts are handled by the virtual machine on which processes run.

To make the programming language useful for stepwise system design it should permit the division of a system type, such as a disk buffer, into smaller system types. One of these other system types should give a disk buffer access to the disk. We will call this system type a *virtual disk.* It gives a disk buffer the illusion that it has its own private disk. A virtual disk hides the details of disk input/output from the rest of the system and makes the disk look like a data structure (an array of disk pages). The only operations on this data structure are *read* and *write* a page.

Each virtual disk is only used by a single disk buffer (Fig. 5). A system component that cannot be called simultaneously by several other compo-

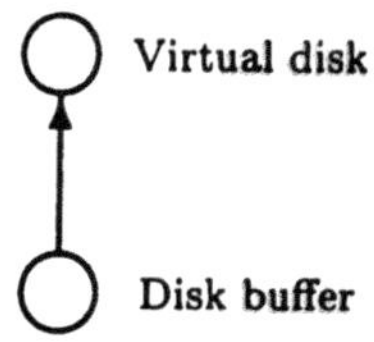

Figure 5 Buffer refinement.

nents will be called a *class.* A class defines a data structure and the possible operations on it (just like a monitor). The exclusive access of class procedures to class variables can be guaranteed completely at compile time. The virtual machine does not have to schedule simultaneous calls of class procedures at run time, because such calls cannot occur. This makes class calls considerably faster than monitor calls.

The spooling system includes two virtual disks but only one real disk. So we need a single *disk resource* monitor to control the order in which competing processes use the disk (Fig. 6). This monitor defines two procedures, *request* and *release* access, to be called by a virtual disk before and after each disk transfer.

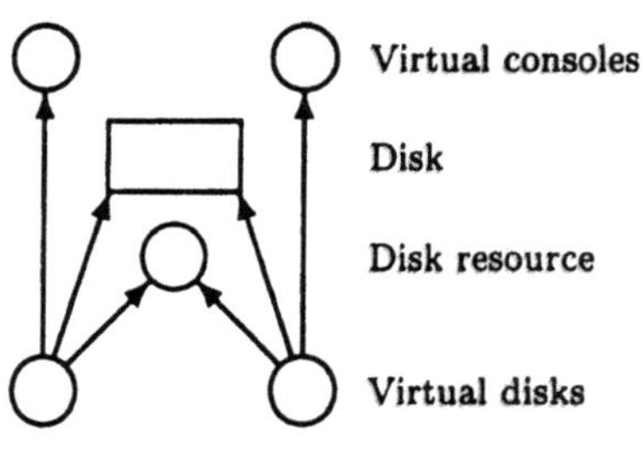

Figure 6 Decomposition of virtual disks.

It would seem simpler to replace the virtual disks and the disk resource by a single monitor that has exclusive access to the disk and does the input/output. This would certainly guarantee that processes use the disk one at a time. But this would be done according to the built-in short-term scheduling policy of monitor calls.

Now to make a virtual machine efficient, one must use a very simple short-term scheduling rule, such as first-come, first-served (Brinch Hansen 1973). If the disk has a moving access head this is about the worst possible algorithm one can use for disk transfers. It is vital that the language make it possible for the programmer to write a medium-term scheduling algorithm that will minimize disk head movement (Hoare 1974). The data type *queue* mentioned earlier makes it possible to implement arbitrary scheduling rules within a monitor.

The difficulty is that while a monitor is performing an input/output operation it is impossible for other processes to enter the same monitor and join the disk queue. They will automatically be delayed by the short-term scheduler and only allowed to enter the monitor one at a time after each disk transfer. This will, of course, make the attempt to control disk scheduling within the monitor illusory. To give the programmer complete control of disk scheduling, processes should be able to enter the disk queue during disk transfers. Since *arrival* and *service* in the disk queueing system potentially are simultaneous operations they must be handled by different system components, as shown in Fig. 6.

If the disk fails persistently during input/output this should be reported on an operator's console. Figure 6 shows two instances of a class type, called a *virtual console.* They give the virtual disks the illusion that they have their own private consoles.

The virtual consoles get exclusive access to a single, real console by calling a *console resource* monitor (Fig. 7). Notice that we now have a standard technique for dealing with virtual devices.

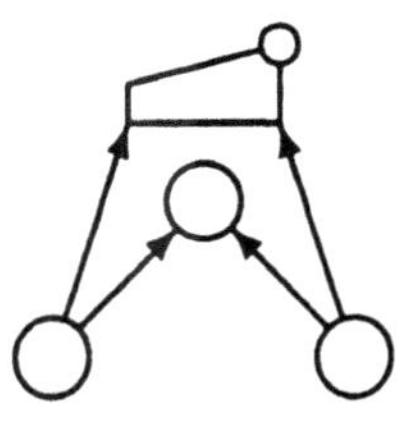

Figure 7 Decomposition of virtual consoles.

If we put all these system components together, we get a complete picture of a simple spooling system (Fig. 8). Classes, monitors, and processes are marked C, M, and P.

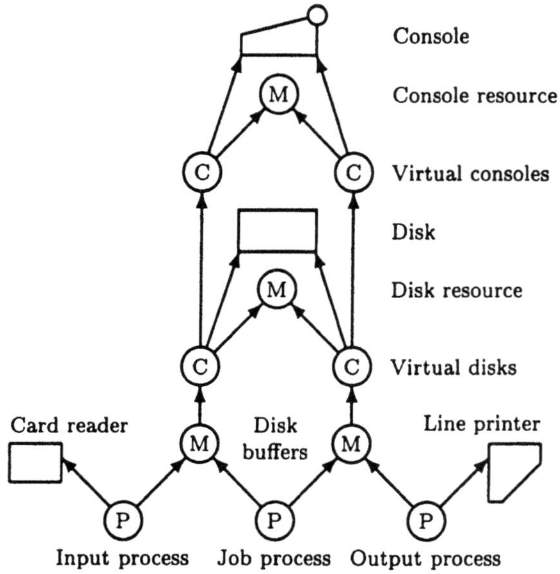

Figure 8 Hierarchical system structure.

E Scope Rules

Some years ago I was part of a team that built a multiprogramming system in which processes can appear and disappear dynamically (Brinch Hansen 1970). In practice, this system was used mostly to set up a fixed configuration of processes. Dynamic process deletion will certainly complicate the semantics and implementation of a programming language considerably. And since it appears to be unnecessary for a large class of real-time applications, it seems wise to exclude it altogether. So an operating system written in Concurrent Pascal will consist of a fixed number of processes, monitors, and classes. These components and their data structures will exist forever after system initialization. An operating system can, however, be extended by recompilation. It remains to be seen whether this restriction will simplify or complicate operating system design. But the poor quality of most existing operating systems clearly demonstrates an urgent need for simpler approaches.

In existing programming languages the data structures of processes, monitors, and classes would be called "global data." This term would be misleading in Concurrent Pascal where each data structure can be accessed by a single component only. It seems more appropriate to call them *permanent data structures.*

I have argued elsewhere that the most dangerous aspect of concurrent programming is the possibility of *time-dependent programming errors* that are impossible to locate by testing ("lurking bugs") (Brinch Hansen 1972, 1973, 1974b). If we are going to depend on real-time programming systems in our daily lives, we must be able to find such obscure errors before the systems are put into operation.

Fortunately, a compiler can detect many of these errors if processes and monitors are represented by a structured notation in a high-level programming language. In addition, we must exclude low-level machine features (registers, addresses, and interrupts) from the language and let a virtual machine control them. If we want real-time systems to be highly reliable, we must stop programming them in assembly language. (The use of hardware protection mechanisms is merely an expensive, inadequate way of making arbitrary machine language programs behave almost as predictably as compiled programs.)

A Concurrent Pascal compiler will check that the private data of a process only are accessed by that process. It will also check that the data structure of a class or monitor only is accessed by its procedures.

Figure 8 shows that *access rights* within an operating system normally are not tree structured. Instead they form a directed graph. This partly explains why the traditional scope rules of block-structured languages are inconvenient for concurrent programming (and for sequential programming as well). In Concurrent Pascal one can state the access rights of components in the program text and have them checked by a compiler.

Since the execution of a monitor procedure will delay the execution of further calls of the same monitor, we must prevent a monitor from calling itself recursively. Otherwise, processes can become *deadlocked.* So the compiler will check that the access rights of system components are hierarchically ordered (or, if you like, that there are no cycles in the access graph).

The *hierarchical ordering* of system components has vital consequences for system design and testing (Brinch Hansen 1974a).

A hierarchical operating system will be tested component by component, bottom up (but could, of course, be conceived top down or by iteration). When an incomplete operating system has been shown to work correctly (by proof or testing), a compiler can ensure that this part of the system will continue to work correctly when new untested program components are added on top of it. Programming errors within new components cannot cause old components to fail because old components do not call new components, and new components only call old components through well-defined procedures that have already been tested.

(Strictly speaking, a compiler can only check that single monitor calls are made correctly; it cannot check sequences of monitor calls, for example whether a resource is always reserved before it is released. So one can only hope for compile time assurance of *partial correctness.*)

Several other reasons besides program correctness make a hierarchical structure attractive:

1. A hierarchical operating system can be studied in a step-wise manner as a sequence of *abstract machines* simulated by programs (Dijkstra 1971).

2. A partial ordering of process interactions permits one to use *mathematical induction* to prove certain overall properties of the system, such as the absence of deadlocks (Brinch Hansen 1973).

3. *Efficient resource utilization* can be achieved by ordering the program components according to the speed of the physical resources they control, with the fastest resources being controlled at the bottom of the system (Dijkstra 1971).

4. A hierarchical system designed according to the previous criteria is often *nearly decomposable* from an analytical point of view. This means that one can develop stochastic models of its dynamic behavior in a stepwise manner (Simon 1962).

F Final Remarks

It seems most natural to represent a hierarchical system structure, such as Fig. 8, by a two-dimensional picture. But when we write a concurrent program we must somehow represent these access rules by linear text. This limitation of written language tends to obscure the simplicity of the original structure. That is why I have tried to explain the purpose of Concurrent Pascal by means of pictures instead of language notation.

The class concept is a restricted form of the class concept of Simula 67 (Dahl 1972). Dijkstra (1971) suggested the idea of monitors. The first structured language notation for monitors was proposed in Brinch Hansen (1973), and illustrated by examples in Hoare (1974). The queue variables needed by monitors for process scheduling were suggested in Brinch Hansen (1972) and modified in Hoare (1974).

The main contribution of Concurrent Pascal is to extend monitors with explicit access rights that can be checked at compile time. Concurrent Pascal has been implemented at Caltech for the PDP 11/45 computer. Our system uses sequential Pascal as a job control and user programming language.

II THE USE OF CONCURRENT PASCAL

A Introduction

In Part I the concepts of Concurrent Pascal were explained informally by means of pictures of a hierarchical spooling system. I will now use the same example to introduce the language notation of Concurrent Pascal. The presentation is still informal. I am neither trying to define the language precisely nor to develop a working system. This will be done in other papers. I am just trying to show the flavor of the language.

B Processes

We will now program the system components in Fig. 8 one at a time from top to bottom (but we could just as well do it bottom up).

Although we only need one *input process*, we may as well define it as a general system type of which several copies may exist:

```
type inputprocess =
process(buffer: diskbuffer);
var block: page;
cycle
  readcards(block);
  buffer.send(block);
end
```

An input process has access to a *buffer* of type diskbuffer (to be defined later). The process has a private variable *block* of type page. The data type page is declared elsewhere as an array of characters:

```
type page = array [1..512] of char
```

A process type defines a *sequential program*—in this case, an endless cycle that inputs a block from a card reader and sends it through the buffer to another process. We will ignore the details of card reader input.

The *send* operation on the buffer is called as follows (using the block as a parameter):

```
buffer.send(block)
```

The next component type we will define is a *job process*:

```
type jobprocess =
process(input, output: diskbuffer);
var block: page;
cycle
  input.receive(block);
  update(block);
  output.send(block);
end
```

A job process has access to two disk buffers called *input* and *output*. It receives blocks from one buffer, updates them, and sends them through the other buffer. The details of updating can be ignored here.

Finally, we need an *output process* that can receive data from a disk buffer and output them on a line printer:

```
type outputprocess =
process(buffer: diskbuffer);
var block: page;
cycle
  buffer.receive(block);
  printlines(block);
end
```

The following shows a declaration of the main system components:

```
var buffer1, buffer2: diskbuffer;
  reader: inputprocess;
  master: jobprocess;
  writer: outputprocess;
```

There is an input process, called the *reader*, a job process, called the *master*, and an output process, called the *writer*. Then there are two disk buffers, *buffer1* and *buffer2*, that connect them.

Later I will explain how a disk buffer is defined and initialized. If we assume that the disk buffers already have been initialized, we can initialize the input process as follows:

init reader(buffer1)

The *init* statement allocates space for the *private variables* of the reader process and starts its execution as a sequential process with access to buffer1.

The *access rights* of a process to other system components, such as buffer1, are also called its *parameters*. A process can only be initialized once. After initalization, the parameters and private variables of a process exist forever. They are called *permanent variables*.

The init statement can be used to start concurrent execution of several processes and define their access rights. As an example, the statement

init reader(buffer1), master(buffer1, buffer2), writer(buffer2)

starts concurrent execution of the reader process (with access to buffer1), the master process (with access to both buffers), and the writer process (with access to buffer2).

A process can only access its own parameters and private variables. The latter are not accessible to other system components. Compare this with the more liberal scope rules of block-structured languages in which a program block can access not only its own parameters and local variables, but also those declared in outer blocks. In Concurrent Pascal, all variables accessible to a system component are declared within its type definition. This access rule and the init statement make it possible for a programmer to state access rights explicitly and have them checked by a compiler. They also make it possible to study a system type as a self-contained program unit.

Although the programming examples do not show this, one can also define constants, data types, and procedures within a process. These objects can only be used within the process type.

C Monitors

The *disk buffer* is a monitor type:

```
type diskbuffer =
monitor(consoleaccess, diskaccess: resource;
  base, limit: integer);

var disk: virtualdisk; sender, receiver: queue;
  head, tail, length: integer;

procedure entry send(block: page);
begin
  if length = limit then delay(sender);
  disk.write(base + tail, block);
  tail := (tail + 1) mod limit;
  length := length + 1;
  continue(receiver);
end;

procedure entry receive(var block: page);
begin
  if length = 0 then delay(receiver);
  disk.read(base + head, block);
  head := (head + 1) mod limit;
  length := length - 1;
  continue(sender);
end;

begin "initial statement"
  init disk(consoleaccess, diskaccess);
  head := 0; tail := 0; length := 0;
end
```

A disk buffer has access to two other components, *consoleaccess* and *diskaccess*, of type resource (to be defined later). It also has access to two integer constants defining the *base* address and *limit* of the buffer on the disk.

The monitor declares a set of *shared variables*: The *disk* is declared as a variable of type virtualdisk. Two variables of type queue are used to delay the *sender* and *receiver* processes until the buffer becomes nonfull and nonempty. Three integers define the relative addresses of the *head* and *tail* elements of the buffer and its current *length.*

The monitor defines two *monitor procedures*, send and receive. They are marked with the word *entry* to distinguish them from local procedures used within the monitor (there are none of these in this example).

Receive returns a page to the calling process. If the buffer is empty, the calling process is *delayed* in the receiver queue until another process sends a page through the buffer. The receive procedure will then read and remove a page from the head of the disk buffer by calling a *read* operation defined within the virtualdisk type:

```
disk.read(base + head, block)
```

Finally, the receive procedure will *continue* the execution of a sending process (if the latter is waiting in the sender queue).

Send is similar to receive.

The queueing mechanism will be explained in detail in the next section.

The *initial statement* of a disk buffer initializes its virtual disk with access to the console and disk resources. It also sets the buffer length to zero. (Notice, that a disk buffer does not use its access rights to the console and disk, but only passes them on to a virtual disk declared within it.)

The following shows a declaration of two system components of type resource and two integers defining the base and limit of a disk buffer:

```
var consoleaccess, diskaccess: resource;
  base, limit: integer;
  buffer: diskbuffer;
```

If we assume that these variables already have been initialized, we can initialize a disk buffer as follows:

```
init buffer(consoleaccess, diskaccess, base, limit)
```

The *init* statement allocates storage for the parameters and shared variables of the disk buffer and executes its initial statement.

A monitor can only be initialized once. After initialization, the parameters and shared variables of a monitor exist forever. They are called *permanent variables.* The parameters and local variables of a monitor procedure, however, exist only while it is being executed. They are called *temporary variables.*

A monitor procedure can only access its own temporary and permanent variables. These variables are not accessible to other system components. Other components can, however, call procedure entries within a monitor. While a monitor procedure is being executed, it has *exclusive access* to the permanent variables of the monitor. If concurrent processes try to call procedures within the same monitor simultaneously, these procedures will be executed strictly one at a time.

Only monitors and constants can be permanent parameters of processes and monitors. This rule ensures that processes only communicate by means of monitors.

It is possible to define constants, data types, and local procedures within monitors (and processes). The local procedures of a system type can only be called within the system type. To prevent *deadlock* of monitor calls and ensure that access rights are hierarchical the following rules are enforced: A procedure must be declared before it can be called; procedure definitions cannot be nested and cannot call themselves; a system type cannot call its own procedure entries.

The absence of recursion makes it possible for a compiler to determine the store requirements of all system components. This and the use of permanent components make it possible to use *fixed store allocation* on a computer that does not support paging.

Since system components are permanent they must be declared as permanent variables of other components.

D Queues

A monitor procedure can delay a calling process for any length of time by executing a *delay* operation on a queue variable. Only one process at a time can wait in a queue. When a calling process is delayed by a monitor procedure it loses its exclusive access to the monitor variables until another process calls the same monitor and executes a continue operation on the queue in which the process is waiting.

The *continue* operation makes the calling process return from its monitor call. If any process is waiting in the selected queue, it will immediately resume the execution of the monitor procedure that delayed it. After being resumed, the process again has exclusive access to the permanent variables of the monitor.

Other variants of process queues (called "events" and "conditions") are proposed in Brinch Hansen (1972) and Hoare (1974). They are multiprocess queues that use different (but fixed) scheduling rules. We do not yet know from experience which kind of queue will be the most convenient one for operating system design. A single-process queue is the simplest tool that gives the programmer complete control of the scheduling of individual processes.

Later, I will show how multiprocess queues can be built from single-process queues.

A queue must be declared as a permanent variable within a monitor type.

E Classes

Every disk buffer has its own virtual disk. A *virtual disk* is defined as a class type:

```
type virtualdisk =
class(consoleaccess, diskaccess: resource);

var terminal: virtualconsole; peripheral: disk;

procedure entry read(pageno: integer; var block: page);
var error: boolean;
begin
  repeat
    diskaccess.request;
    peripheral.read(pageno, block, error);
    diskaccess.release;
    if error then terminal.write('disk failure');
  until not error;
end;

procedure entry write(pageno: integer; block: page);
begin "similar to read" end;

begin "initial statement"
  init terminal(consoleaccess), peripheral;
end
```

A virtual disk has access to a console resource and a disk resource. Its permanent variables define a virtual console and a disk. A process can access its virtual disk by means of *read* and *write* procedures. These procedure entries *request* and *release* exclusive access to the real disk before and after each block transfer. If the real disk fails, the virtual disk calls its virtual console to report the error.

The *initial statement* of a virtual disk initializes its virtual console and the real disk.

Section II-C shows an example of how a virtual disk is declared and initialized (within a disk buffer).

A class can only be initialized once. After initialization, its parameters and private variables exist forever. A class procedure can only access its own temporary and permanent variables. These cannot be accessed by other components.

A class is a system component that cannot be called simultaneously by several other components. This is guaranteed by the following rule: A class must be declared as a permanent variable within a system type; a class can be passed as a permanent parameter to another class (but not to a process or monitor). So a chain of nested class calls can only be started by a single process or monitor. Consequently, it is not necessary to schedule simultaneous class calls at run time—they cannot occur.

F Input/Output

The real *disk* is controlled by a class

```
type disk = class
```

with two procedure entries

```
read(pageno, block, error)
write(pageno, block, error)
```

The class uses a standard procedure

```
io(block, param, device)
```

to transfer a block to or from the disk device. The io parameter is a record

```
var param:
  record
    operation: iooperation;
    result: ioresult;
    pageno: integer
  end
```

that defines an input/output operation, its result, and a page number on the disk. The calling process is delayed until an io operation has been completed.

A *virtual console* is also defined as a class

```
type virtualconsole =
class(access: resource);
var terminal: console;
```

It can be accessed by read and write operations that are similar to each other:

```
procedure entry read(var text: line);
begin
  access.request;
  terminal.read(text);
  access.release;
end
```

The real *console* is controlled by a class that is similar to the disk class.

G Multiprocess Scheduling

Access to the console and disk is controlled by two monitors of type *resource*. To simplify the presentation, I will assume that competing processes are served in first-come, first-served order. (A much better disk scheduling algorithm is defined in Hoare (1974). It can be programmed in Concurrent Pascal as well, but involves more details than the present one.)

We will define a multiprocess queue as an array of single-process queues

```
type multiqueue = array [0..qlength-1] of queue
```

where qlength is an upper bound on the number of concurrent processes in the system.

A first-come, first-served scheduler is now straightforward to program:

```
type resource =
monitor

var free: boolean; q: multiqueue;
  head, tail, length: integer;

procedure entry request;
var arrival: integer;
begin
  if free then free := false
  else
    begin
      arrival := tail;
      tail := (tail + 1) mod qlength;
      length := length + 1;
      delay(q[arrival]);
    end;
end;

procedure entry release;
var departure: integer;
begin
  if length = 0 then free := true
  else
    begin
      departure := head;
      head := (head + 1) mod qlength;
      length := length - 1;
      continue(q[departure]);
    end;
end;

begin "initial statement"
  free := true; length := 0;
  head := 0; tail := 0;
end
```

H Initial Process

Finally, we will put all these components together into a concurrent program. A Concurrent Pascal program consists of nested definitions of system types. The outermost system type is an anonymous process, called the *initial process.* An instance of this process is created during system loading. It initializes the other system components.

The initial process defines system types and instances of them. It executes statements that initializes these system components. In our example, the initial process can be sketched as follows (ignoring the problem of how base addresses and limits of disk buffers are defined):

```
type
  resource = monitor ... end;
  console = class ... end;
  virtualconsole = class(access: resource); ... end;
  disk = class ... end;
  virtualdisk = class(consoleaccess, diskaccess: resource); ... end;
  diskbuffer =
    monitor(consoleaccess, diskaccess: resource; base, limit: integer); ...
    end;
  inputprocess = process(buffer: diskbuffer); ... end;
  jobprocess = process(input, output: diskbuffer); ... end;
  outputprocess = process(buffer: diskbuffer); ... end;
var
  consoleaccess, diskaccess: resource;
  buffer1, buffer2: diskbuffer;
  reader: inputprocess;
  master: jobprocess;
  writer: outputprocess;
begin
  init consoleaccess, diskaccess,
    buffer1(consoleaccess, diskaccess, base1, limit1),
    buffer2(consoleaccess, diskaccess, base2, limit2),
    reader(buffer1),
    master(buffer1, buffer2),
    writer(buffer2);
end.
```

When the execution of a process (such as the initial process) terminates, its private variables continue to exist. This is necessary because these variables may have been passed as permanent parameters to other system components.

Acknowledgements

It is a pleasure to acknowledge the immense value of a continuous exchange of ideas with C.A.R. Hoare on structured multiprogramming. I also thank my students L. Medina and R. Varela for their helpful comments on this paper.

References

Brinch Hansen, P. 1970. The nucleus of a multiprogramming system. *Communications of the ACM 13*, 4 (April), 238–250.

Brinch Hansen, P. 1972. Structured multiprogramming. *Communications of the ACM 15*, 7 (July), 574–578.

Brinch Hansen, P. 1973. *Operating System Principles.* Prentice-Hall, Englewood Cliffs, NJ, (July).

Brinch Hansen, P. 1974a. A programming methodology for operating system design. *Proceedings of the IFIP Congress 74*, Stockholm, Sweden, (August). North-Holland, Amsterdam, The Netherlands, 394–397.

Brinch Hansen, P. 1974b. Concurrent programming concepts. *ACM Computing Surveys 5*, 4 (December), 223–245.

Dahl, O.-J., and Hoare, C.A.R. 1972. Hierarchical program structures. In *Structured Programming*, O.-J. Dahl, E.W. Dijkstra, and C.A.R. Hoare, Eds. Academic Press, New York.

Dijkstra, E.W. 1971. Hierarchical ordering of sequential processes. *Acta Informatica 1*, 2, 115–138.

Hoare, C.A.R. 1974. Monitors: An operating system structuring concept. *Communications of the ACM 17*, 10 (October), 549–557.

Simon, H.A. 1962. The architecture of complexity. *Proceedings of the American Philosophical Society 106*, 6, 468–482.

Wirth, N. 1971. The programming language Pascal. *Acta Informatica 1*, 1, 35–63.

PART IV

MODEL OPERATING SYSTEMS

11

THE SOLO OPERATING SYSTEM: A CONCURRENT PASCAL PROGRAM

PER BRINCH HANSEN

(1976)

This is a description of the single-user operating system Solo written in the programming language Concurrent Pascal. It supports the development of Sequential and Concurrent Pascal programs for the PDP 11/45 computer. Input/output are handled by concurrent processes. Pascal programs can call one another recursively and pass arbitrary parameters among themselves. This makes it possible to use Pascal as a job control language. Solo is the first major example of a hierarchical concurrent program implemented in terms of abstract data types (classes, monitors and processes) with compile-time control of most access rights. It is described here from the user's point of view as an introduction to another paper describing its internal structure.

INTRODUCTION

This is a description of the first operating system *Solo* written in the programming language Concurrent Pascal (Brinch Hansen 1975). It is a simple, but useful single-user operating system for the development and distribution of Pascal programs for the PDP 11/45 computer. It has been in use since May 1975.

From the user's point of view there is nothing unusual about the system. It supports editing, compilation and storage of Sequential and Concurrent Pascal programs. These programs can access either console, cards, printer,

P. Brinch Hansen, The Solo operating system: a Concurrent Pascal program. *Software—Practice and Experience 6*, 2 (April–June 1976), 141–149.

tape or disk at several levels (character by character, page by page, file by file, or by direct device access). Input, processing, and output of files are handled by concurrent processes. Pascal programs can call one another recursively and pass arbitrary parameters among themselves. This makes it possible to use Pascal as a job control language (Brinch Hansen 1976a).

To the system programmer, however, Solo is quite different from many other operating systems:

1. Less than 4 per cent of it is written in machine language. The rest is written in Sequential and Concurrent Pascal.

2. In contrast to machine-oriented languages, Pascal does not contain low-level programming features, such as registers, addresses and interrupts. These are all handled by the virtual machine on which compiled programs run.

3. System protection is achieved largely by means of compile-time checking of access rights. Run-time checking is minimal and is not supported by hardware mechanisms.

4. Solo is the first major example of a hierarchical concurrent program implemented by means of abstract data types (classes, monitors, and processes).

5. The complete system consisting of more than 100,000 machine words of code (including two compilers) was developed by a student and myself in less than a year.

To appreciate the usefulness of Concurrent Pascal one needs a good understanding of at least one operating system written in the language. The purpose of this description is to look at the Solo system from a user's point of view before studying its internal structure (Brinch Hansen 1976b). It tells how the user operates the system, how data flow inside it, how programs call one another and communicate, how files are stored on disk, and how well the system performs in typical tasks.

JOB CONTROL

The user controls program execution from a display (or a teletype). He calls a program by writing its name and its parameters, for example:

```
move(5)
read(maketemp, seqcode, true)
```

The first command positions a magnetic tape at file number 5. The second one inputs the file to disk and stores it as sequential code named maketemp. The boolean true protects the file against accidental deletion in the future.

Programs try to be helpful to the user when he needs it. If the user forgets which programs are available, he may for example type:

```
help
```

(or anything else). The system responds by writing:

```
not executable, try
    list(catalog, seqcode, console)
```

The suggested command lists the names of all sequential programs on the console.

If the user knows that the disk contains a certain program, but is uncertain about its parameter conventions, he can simply call it as a program without parameters, for example:

```
read
```

The program then gives the necessary information:

```
try again
    read(file: identifier; kind: filekind; protect: boolean)
using
    filekind = (scratch, ascii, seqcode, concode)
```

Still more information can be gained about a program by reading its manual:

```
copy(readman, console)
```

A user session may begin with the input of a new Pascal program from cards to disk:

```
copy(cards, sorttext)
```

followed by a compilation:

pascal(sorttext, printer, sort)

If the compiler reports errors on the program listing:

pascal:
compilation errors

the next step is usually to edit the program text:

edit(sorttext)
...

and compile it again. After a successful compilation, the user program can now be called directly:

sort(...)

The system can also read job control commands from other media, for example:

do(tape)

A task is preempted by pushing the bell key on the console. This causes the system to reload and initialize itself. The command *start* can be used to replace the Solo system with any other concurrent program stored on disk.

DATA FLOW

Figure 1 shows the data flow inside the system when the user is processing a single text file sequentially by copying, editing, or compiling it.

The input, processing, and output of text take place simultaneously. Processing is done by a *job process* that starts input by sending an argument through a buffer to an input process. The argument is the name of the input device or disk file.

The *input process* sends the data through another buffer to the job process. At the end of the file the input process sends an argument through yet another buffer to the job process indicating whether transmission errors occurred during the input.

Output is handled similarly by means of an *output process* and another set of buffers.

In a single-user operating system it is desirable to be able to process a file continuously at the highest possible speed. So the data are buffered in core instead of on disk. The capacity of each buffer is 512 characters.

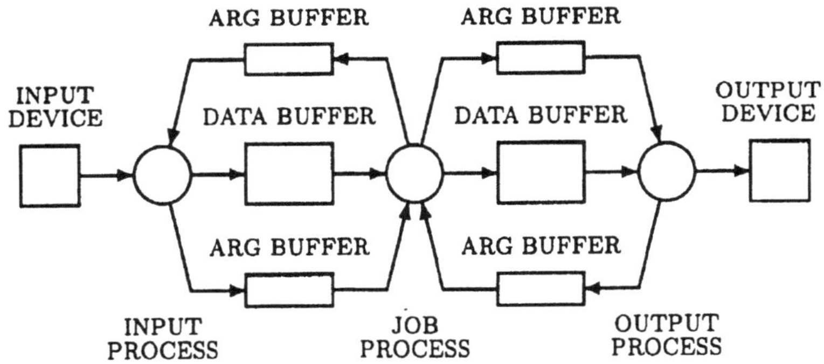

Figure 1 Processes and buffers.

CONTROL FLOW

Figure 2 shows what happens when the user types a command such as:

edit(cards, tape)

After system loading the machine executes a Concurrent Pascal program (Solo) consisting of three processes. Initially the input and output processes both load and call a sequential program *io* while the job process calls another sequential program *do*. The do program reads the user command from the console and calls the *edit* program with two parameters, *cards* and *tape*.

The editor starts its input by sending the first parameter to the io program executed by the input process. This causes the io program to call another program *cards* which then begins to read cards and send them to the job process.

The editor starts its output by sending the second parameter to the io program executed by the output process. The latter then calls a program *tape* which reads data from the job process and puts them on tape.

At the end of the file the cards and tape programs return to the io programs which then await further instructions from the job process. The editor returns to the do program which then reads and interprets the next command from the console.

It is worth observing that the operating system itself has no built-in drivers for input/output from various devices. Data are simply produced

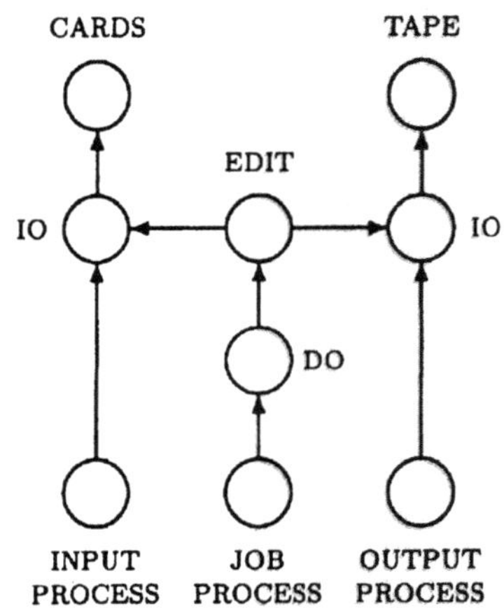

Figure 2 Concurrent processes and sequential programs.

and consumed by Sequential Pascal programs stored on disk. The operating system only contains the mechanism to call these. This gives the user complete freedom to supplement the system with new devices and simulate complicated input/output such as the merging, splitting and formatting of files without changing the job programs.

Most important is the ability of Sequential Pascal programs to call one another recursively with arbitrary parameters. In Fig. 2, for example, the do program calls the edit program with two identifiers as parameters. This removes the need for a separate (awkward) job control language. *The job control language is Pascal.*

This is illustrated more dramatically in Fig. 3 which shows how the command:

pascal(sorttext, printer, sort)

causes the do program to call the program *pascal.* The latter in turn calls seven compiler passes one at a time, and (if the compiled program is correct) *pascal* finally calls the filing system to store the generated code.

A program does not know whether it is being called by another program or directly from the console. In Fig. 3 the program *pascal* calls the filing system. The user, may, however, also call the file system directly, for example, to protect his program against accidental deletion:

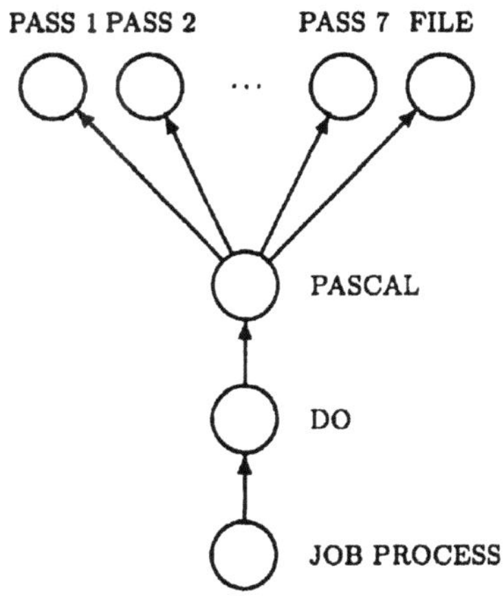

Figure 3 Compilation.

file(protect, sort, true)

The Pascal *pointer* and *heap* concepts give programs the ability to pass arbitrarily complicated data structures among each other, such as symbol tables during compilation (Jensen 1974). In most cases, however, it suffices to be able to use identifiers, integers, and booleans as program parameters.

STORE ALLOCATION

The run-time environment of Sequential and Concurrent Pascal is a kernel of 4 K words. This is the only program written in machine language. The user loads the kernel from disk into core by means of the operator's panel. The kernel then loads the Solo system and starts it. The Solo system consists of a fixed number of processes. They occupy fixed amounts of core store determined by the compiler.

All other programs are written in Sequential Pascal. Each process stores the code of the currently executed program in a fixed core segment. After termination of a program called by another, the process reloads the previous program from disk and returns to it. The data used by a process and the programs called by it are all stored in a core resident stack of fixed length.

FILE SYSTEM

The backing store is a slow *disk* with removable packs. Each user has his own disk pack containing the system and his private files. So there is no need for a hierarchical file system.

A disk pack contains a *catalog* of all files stored on it. The catalog describes itself as a file. A *file* is described by its name, type, protection and disk address. Files are looked up by hashing.

All system programs check the *types* of their input files before operating on them and associate types with their output files. The Sequential Pascal compiler, for example, will take input from an ascii file (but not from a scratch file), and will make its output a sequential code file. The possible file types are scratch, ascii, seqcode and concode.

Since each user has his own disk pack, files need only be *protected* against accidental overwriting or deletion. All files are initially unprotected. To protect one the user must call the file system from the console as described in Section 4.

To avoid compacting of files (lasting several minutes), file pages are scattered on disk and addressed indirectly through a *page map* (Fig. 4). A file is opened by looking it up in the catalog and bringing its page map into core.

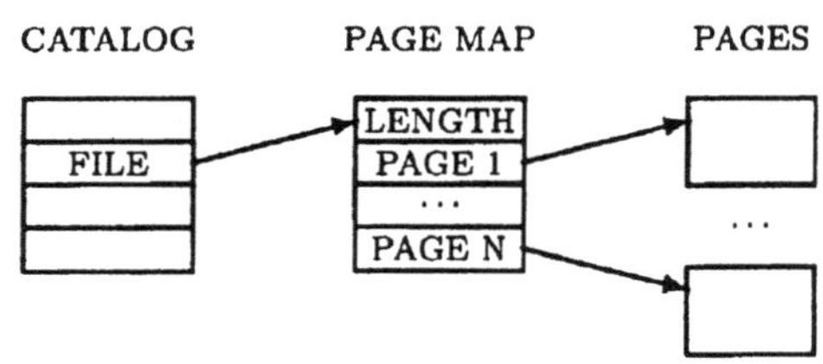

Figure 4 File system.

The resident part of the Solo system implements only the most frequently used file operations: lookup, open, close, get and put. A nonresident, sequential program, called *file*, handles the more complicated and less frequently used operations: create, replace, rename, protect, and delete file.

DISK ALLOCATION

The disk always contains a scratch file of 255 pages called *next*. A program creates a new file by outputting data to this file. It then calls the file system to associate the data with a new name, a type, and a length (≤ 255). Having done this the file system creates a new instance of *next*.

This scheme has two advantages:

1. All files are initialized with typed data.
2. A program creating a file need only call the nonresident file system once (after producing the file). Without the file *next* the file system would have to be called at least twice: before output to create the file, and after output to define its final length.

The disadvantages of having a single file *next* is that a program can only create one file at a time.

Unused disk pages are defined by a powerset of page indices stored on the disk.

On a slow disk special care must be taken to make *program loading* fast. If program pages were randomly scattered on the disk it would take 16 seconds to load the compiler and its input/output drivers. An algorithm described in Brinch Hansen (1976c) reduces this to 5 seconds. When the system creates the file *next* it tries to place it on consecutive pages within neighboring cylinders as far as possible (but will scatter the pages somewhat if it has to). It then rearranges the page indices within the page map to minimize the number of disk revolutions and cylinder movements needed to load the file. Since this is done before a program is compiled and stored on disk it is called *disk scheduling at compile time.*

The system uses a different allocation technique for the two temporary files used during compilation. Each pass of the compiler takes input from a file produced by its predecessor and delivers output to its successor on another file. A program *maketemp* creates these files and interleaves their page indices (making every second page belong to one file and every second one to the other). This makes the disk head sweep slowly across both files during a pass instead of moving wildly back and forth between them.

OPERATOR COMMUNICATION

The user communicates with the system through a console. Since a task (such as editing) usually involves several programs executed by concurrent processes these programs must identify themselves to the user before asking for input or making output:

```
do:
edit(cards, tape)
edit:
...
do:
...
```

Program identity is only displayed every time the user starts talking to a different program. A program that communicates several times with the user without interruption (such as the editor) only identifies itself once.

Normally only one program at a time tries to talk to the user (the current program executed by the job process). But an input/output error may cause a message from another process:

```
tape:
inspect
```

Since processes rarely compete for the console, it is sufficient to give a process *exclusive access* to the user for input or output of a single line. A conversation of several lines will seldom be interrupted.

A Pascal program only calls the operating system once with its identification. The system will then automatically display it when necessary.

SIZE AND PERFORMANCE

The Solo system consists of an operating system written in Concurrent Pascal and a set of system programs written in Sequential Pascal:

Program	Pascal lines	Machine words
operating system	1,300	4 K
do, io	700	4 K
file system	900	5 K
concurrent compiler	8,300	42 K
sequential compiler	8,300	42 K
editor	400	2 K
input/output programs	600	3 K
others	1,300	8 K
	21,800	110 K

(The two Pascal compilers can be used under different operating systems written in Concurrent Pascal—not just Solo.)

The amount of code written in different programming languages is:

Language	%
machine language	4
Concurrent Pascal	4
Sequential Pascal	92

This clearly shows that a good sequential programming language is more important for operating system design than a concurrent language. But although a concurrent program may be small it still seems worthwhile to write it in a high-level language that enables a compiler to do thorough checking of data types and access rights. Otherwise, it is far too easy to make time-dependent programming errors that are extremely difficult to locate.

The kernel written in machine language implements the process and monitor concepts of Concurrent Pascal and responds to interrupts. It is independent of the particular operating system running on top of it.

The Solo system requires a core store of 39 K words for programs and data:

Programs	K words
kernel	4
operating system	11
input/output programs	6
job programs	18
core store	39

This amount of space allows the Pascal compiler to compile itself.

The speed of text processing using disk input and tape output is:

Program	char/sec
copy	11,600
edit	3,300–6,200
compile	240

All these tasks are 60–100 per cent disk limited. These figures do not distinguish between time spent waiting for peripherals and time spent executing operating system or user code since this distinction is irrelevant to the user. They illustrate an overall performance of a system written in a high-level language using straightforward code generation without any optimization.

FINAL REMARKS

The compilers for Sequential and Concurrent Pascal were designed and implemented by Al Hartmann and me in half a year. I wrote the operating system and its utility programs in 3 months. In machine language this would have required 20–30 man-years and nobody would have been able to understand the system fully. The use of an efficient, abstract programming language reduced the development cost to less than 2 man-years and produced a system that is completely understood by two programmers.

The low cost of programming makes it acceptable to throw away awkward programs and rewrite them. We did this several times: An early 6-pass compiler was never released (although it worked perfectly) because we found its structure too complicated. The first operating system written in Concurrent Pascal (called *Deamy*) was used only to evaluate the expressive power of the language and was never built (Brinch Hansen 1974). The second one (called *Pilot*) was used for several months but was too slow.

From a manufacturer's point of view it is now realistic and attractive to replace a huge ineffective "general-purpose" operating system with a range of small, efficient systems for special purposes.

The kernel, the operating system, and the compilers were tested very systematically initially and appear to be correct.

Acknowledgements

The work of Bob Deverill and Al Hartmann in implementing the kernel and compiler of Concurrent Pascal has been essential for this project. I am also grateful to Gilbert McCann for his encouragement and support.

Stoy and Strachey (1972) recommend that one should learn to build good operating systems for single-users before trying to satisfy many users simultaneously. I have found this to be very good advice. I have also tried to follow the advice of Lampson (1974) and make both high- and low-level abstractions available to the user programmer.

The Concurrent Pascal project is supported by the National Science Foundation under grant number DCR74–17331.

P. Brinch Hansen 1974. Deamy—A structured operating system. Information Science, California Institute of Technology, (May), (out of print).

P. Brinch Hansen 1975. The programming language Concurrent Pascal. *IEEE Trans. on Software Engineering*, **1**, 2 (June).

P. Brinch Hansen 1976a. The Solo operating system: job interface. *Software—Practice and Experience*, **6**, 2 (April–June).

P. Brinch Hansen 1976b. The Solo operating system: processes, monitors and classes. *Software—Practice and Experience*, **6**, 2 (April–June).

P. Brinch Hansen 1976c. Disk scheduling at compile-time. *Software—Practice and Experience 6*, 2 (April–June), 201–205.

K. Jensen and N. Wirth 1974. Pascal–User manual and report. *Lecture Notes in Computer Science*, **18**, Springer-Verlag, New York.

B. W. Lampson 1974. An open operating system for a single-user machine. In *Operating Systems, Lecture Notes in Computer Science*, **16**, Springer Verlag, 208–217.

J. E. Stoy and C. Strachey 1972. OS6—an experimental operating system for a small computer. *Comput. J.*, **15**, 2.

12

THE SOLO OPERATING SYSTEM: PROCESSES, MONITORS AND CLASSES

PER BRINCH HANSEN

(1976)

This paper describes the implementation of the Solo operating system written in Concurrent Pascal. It explains the overall structure and details of the system in which concurrent processes communicate by means of a hierarchy of monitors and classes. The concurrent program is a sequence of nearly independent components of less than one page of text each. The system has been operating since May 1975.

INTRODUCTION

This is a description of the program structure of the Solo operating system. Solo is a single-user operating system for the PDP 11/45 computer written in the programming language Concurrent Pascal (Brinch Hansen 1976a, 1976b).

The main idea in Concurrent Pascal is to divide the global data structures of an operating system into small parts and define the meaningful operations on each of them. In Solo, for example, there is a data structure, called a resource, that is used to give concurrent processes exclusive access to a disk. This data structure can only be accessed by means of two procedures that request and release access to the disk. The programmer specifies that these are the only operations one can perform on a resource, and the compiler

P. Brinch Hansen, The Solo operating system: processes, monitors and classes. *Software—Practice and Experience 6*, 2 (April–June 1976), 165–200.

checks that this rule is obeyed in the rest of the system. This approach to program reliability has been called *resource protection at compile-time* (Brinch Hansen 1973). It makes programs more reliable by detecting incorrect interactions of program components before they are put into operation. It makes them more efficient by reducing the need for hardware protection mechanisms.

The combination of a data structure and the operations used to access it is called an *abstract data type*. It is abstract because the rest of the system need only know what operations one can perform on it but can ignore the details of how they are carried out. A Concurrent Pascal program is constructed from three kinds of abstract data types: processes, monitors and classes. *Processes* perform concurrent operations on data structures. They use *monitors* to synchronize themselves and exchange data. They access private data structures by means of *classes*. Brinch Hansen (1975a) is an overview of these concepts and their use in concurrent programming.

Solo is the first major example of a hierarchical concurrent program implemented in terms of abstract data types. It has been in use since May 1975. This is a complete, annotated program listing of the system. It also explains how the system was tested systematically.

PROGRAM STRUCTURE

Solo consists of a hierarchy of *program layers*, each of which controls a particular kind of computer resource, and a set of concurrent processes that use these resources (Fig. 1):

- *Resource management* controls the scheduling of the operator's console and the disk among concurrent processes.

- *Console management* lets processes communicate with the operator after they have gained access to the console.

- *Disk management* gives processes access to the disk files and a catalog describing them.

- *Program management* fetches program files from disk into core on demand from processes that wish to execute them.

- *Buffer management* transmits data among processes.

These facilities are used by seven concurrent processes:

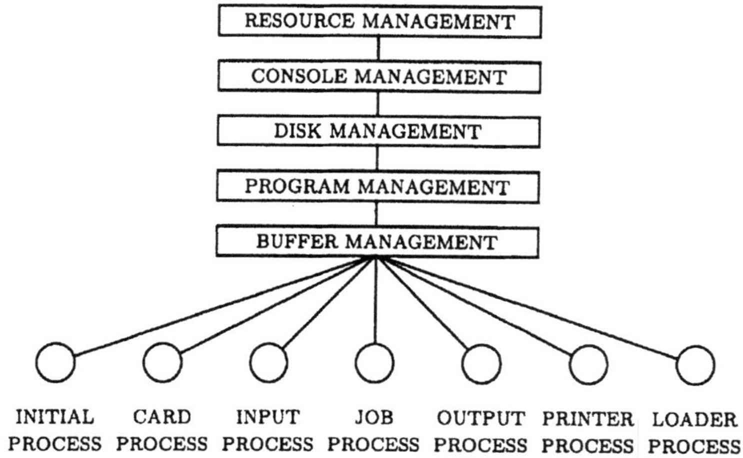

Figure 1 Program layers and processes.

- A *job process* executes Pascal programs upon request from the operator.
- Two *input/output processes* produce and consume the data of the job process.
- A *card process* feeds punched cards to the input process which then removes trailing blanks from them and packs the text into blocks.
- A *printer process* prints lines that are unpacked from blocks and sent to it by the output process.
- A *loader process* preempts and reinitializes the operating system when the operator pushes the bell key on the console.
- An *initial process* starts up the rest of the system after system loading.

The term *program layer* is only used as a convenient way of explaining the gross division of labor within the system. It cannot be represented by any language notation in Concurrent Pascal.

ABSTRACT DATA TYPES

Each program layer consists of one or more abstract data types (monitors and classes).

Resource management

A *fifo* class implements a first-in, first-out queue that is used to maintain multiprocess queues and message buffers.

A *resource* monitor gives processes exclusive access to a computer resource. It is used to control disk access.

A *typewriter resource* monitor gives processes exclusive access to a console and tells them whether they need to identify themselves to the operator.

Console management

A *typewriter* class transmits a single line between a process and a console (but does not give a process exclusive access to it).

A *terminal* class gives a process the illusion that it has its own private console by giving it exclusive access to the operator for input or output of a single line.

A *terminal stream* makes a terminal look character oriented.

Disk management

A *disk* class can access a page anywhere on disk (but does not give a process exclusive access to it). It uses a terminal to report disk failure.

A *disk file* can access any page belonging to a particular file. The file pages, which may be scattered on disk, are addressed indirectly through a page map. The disk address of the page map identifies the file. It uses a disk to access the map and its pages.

A *disk table* class makes a disk catalog of files look like an array of entries, some of which describe files, and some of which are empty. The entries are identified by numeric indices. It uses a disk file to access the catalog page by page.

A *disk catalog* monitor can look up files in a disk catalog by means of their names. It uses a resource to get exclusive acess to the disk and a disk table to scan the catalog.

A *data file* class gives a process access to a named disk file. It uses a resource, a disk catalog, and a disk file to access the disk.

Program management

A *program file* class can load a named disk file into core when a process wishes to execute it. It uses a resource, a disk catalog, and a disk file to do this.

A *program stack* monitor keeps track of nested program calls within a process.

Buffer management

The *buffer* monitors transmit various kinds of messages between processes: arguments (scalars or identifiers), lines, and pages.

The following defines the purpose, specification, and implementation of each of these abstract data types.

INPUT/OUTPUT

The following data types are used in elementary input/output operations:

```
type iodevice =
  (typedevice, diskdevice, tapedevice, printdevice, carddevice);

type iooperation = (input, output, move, control);

type ioarg = (writeeof, rewind, upspace, backspace);

type ioresult =
  (complete, intervention, transmission, failure,
  endfile, endmedium, startmedium);

type ioparam =
  record
    operation: iooperation;
    status: ioresult;
    arg: ioarg
  end;

const nl = '(:10:)'; ff = '(:12:)'; cr = '(:13:)'; em = '(:25:)';

const linelength = 132;
```

type line = **array** [1..linelength] **of** char;

const pagelength = 512;
type page = **array** [1..pagelength] **of** char;

They define the identifiers of peripheral devices, input/output operations and their results as well as the data types to be transferred (printer lines or disk pages). The details of input/output operations are explained in Brinch Hansen (1975b).

FIFO QUEUE

type fifo = class(limit: integer)

A fifo keeps track of the length and the head and tail indices of an array used as a first-in, first-out queue (but does not contain the queue elements themselves). A fifo is initialized with a constant that defines its range of queue indices 1..limit. A user of a fifo must ensure that the length of the queue remains within its physical limit:

$$0 \leq \text{arrivals} - \text{departures} \leq \text{limit}$$

The routines of a fifo are:

function arrival: integer

Returns the index of the next queue element in which an arrival can take place.

function departure: integer

Returns the index of the next queue element from which a departure can take place.

function empty: boolean

Defines whether the queue is empty (arrivals = departures).

function full: boolean

Defines whether the queue is full (arrivals = departures + limit).

Implementation:

A fifo queue is represented by its head, tail and length. The Concurrent Pascal compiler will ensure that these variables are only accessed by the routines of the class. In general, a class variable can only be accessed by calling one of the routines associated with it (Brinch Hansen 1975a). The final statement of the class is executed when an instance of a fifo queue is declared and initialized.

```
type fifo =
class(limit: integer);

var head, tail, length: integer;

function entry arrival: integer;
begin
  arrival := tail;
  tail := tail mod limit + 1;
  length := length + 1;
end;

function entry departure: integer;
begin
  departure := head;
  head := head mod limit + 1;
  length := length - 1;
end;

function entry empty: boolean;
begin empty := (length = 0) end;

function entry full: boolean;
begin full := (length = limit) end;

begin head := 1; tail := 1; length := 0 end;
```

RESOURCE

type resource = monitor

A resource gives exclusive access to a computer resource (but does not perform any operations on the resource itself). A user of a resource must request it before using it and release it afterwards. If the resource is released within a finite time it will also become available to any process requesting it within a finite time. In short, the resource scheduling is fair.

procedure request

Gives the calling process exclusive access to the resource.

procedure release

Makes the resource available for other processes.

Implementation:

A resource is represented by its state (free or used) and a queue of processes waiting for it. The multiprocess queue is represented by two data structures: an array of single-process queues and a fifo to keep track of the queue indices.

The initial statement at the end of the monitor sets the resource state to free and initializes the fifo variable with a constant defining the total number of processes that can wait in the queue.

The compiler will ensure that the monitor variables only can be accessed by calling the routine entries associated with it. The generated code will ensure that at most one process at a time is executing a monitor routine (Brinch Hansen 1975a). The monitor can delay and (later) continue the execution of a calling process.

A routine associated with a class or monitor is called by mentioning the class or monitor variable followed by the name of the routine. As an example

next.arrival

will perform an arrival operation on the fifo variable next.

```
const processcount = 7;
type processqueue = array [1..processcount] of queue;

type resource =
```

```
monitor

var free: boolean; q: processqueue; next: fifo;

procedure entry request;
begin
  if free then free := false
  else delay(q[next.arrival]);
end;

procedure entry release;
begin
  if next.empty then free := true
  else continue(q[next.departure]);
end;

begin free := true; init next(processcount) end;
```

TYPEWRITER RESOURCE

type typeresource = monitor

A typewriter resource gives processes exclusive access to a typewriter console. A calling process supplies an identification of itself and is told whether it needs to display it to the operator. The resource scheduling is fair as explained in the definition of the *resource* monitor.

procedure request(text: line; var changed: boolean)

Gives the calling process exclusive access to the resource. The process identifies itself by a text line. A boolean changed defines whether this is the same identification that was used in the last call of request (in which case there is no need to display it to the operator again).

procedure release

Makes the resource available again for other processes.

Implementation:

```
type typeresource =
monitor

var free: boolean; q: processqueue; next: fifo; header: line;

procedure entry request(text: line; var changed: boolean);
begin
  if free then free := false
  else delay(q[next.arrival]);
  changed := (header <> text);
  header := text;
end;

procedure entry release;
begin
  if next.empty then free := true
  else continue(q[next,departure]);
end;

begin
  free := true; header[1] := nl;
  init next(processcount);
end;
```

TYPEWRITER

type typewriter = class(device: iodevice)

A typewriter can transfer a text line to or from a typewriter console. It does not identify the calling process on the console or give it exclusive access to it. A typewriter is initialized with the identifier of the device it controls.

A newline character (nl) terminates the input or output of a line. A line that exceeds 73 characters is forcefully terminated by a newline character.

procedure write(text: line)

Writes a line on the typewriter.

procedure read(var text: line)

Rings the bell on the typewriter and reads a line from it. Single characters or the whole line can be erased and retyped by typing *control c* or *control l*. The typewriter responds to erasure by writing a question mark.

Implementation:

The procedure writechar is not a routine entry; it can only be called within the typewriter class. The standard procedure io delays the calling process until the transfer of a single character is completed.

```
type typewriter =
class(device: iodevice);

const linelimit = 73;
  cancelchar = '(:3:)'; "control c"
  cancelline = '(:12:)'; "control l"

procedure writechar(x: char);
var param: ioparam; c: char;
begin
  param.operation := output;
  c := x;
  io(c, param, device);
end;

procedure entry write(text: line);
var param: ioparam; i: integer; c: char;
begin
  param.operation := output;
  i := 0;
  repeat
    i := i + 1; c := text[i];
    io(c, param, device);
  until (c = nl) or (i = linelimit);
  if c <> nl then writechar(nl);
end;

procedure entry read(var text: line);
```

```
const bel = '(:7:)';
var param: ioparam; i: integer; c: char;
begin
  writechar(bel);
  param.operation := input;
  i := 0;
  repeat
    io(c, param, device);
    if c = cancelline then
      begin
        writechar(nl);
        writechar('?');
        i := 0;
      end
    else if c = cancelchar then
      begin
        if i > 0 then
          begin
            writechar('?');
            i := i - 1;
          end
      end
    else
      begin i := i + 1; text[i] := c end
  until (c = nl) or (i = linelimit);
  if c <> nl then
    begin
      writechar(nl);
      text[linelimit + 1] := nl;
    end;
end;

begin end;
```

TERMINAL

type terminal = class(access: typeresource)

A terminal gives a single process exclusive access to a typewriter, identifies the process to the operator and transfers a line to or from the device. The terminal uses a typewriter resource to get exclusive access to the device.

procedure read(header: line; var text: line)

Writes a header (if necessary) on the typewriter and reads a text line from it.

procedure write(header, text: line)

Writes a header (if necessary) followed by a text line on the typewriter.

The header identifies the calling process. It is only output if it is different from the last header output on the typewriter.

Implementation:

A class or monitor can only call other classes or monitors if they are declared as variables within it or passed as parameters during initialization (Brinch Hansen 1975a). So a terminal can only call the monitor *access* and the class *unit*. These access rights are checked during compilation.

```
type terminal =
class(access: typeresource);

var unit: typewriter;

procedure entry read(header: line; var text: line);
var changed: boolean;
begin
  access.request(header, changed);
  if changed then unit.write(header);
  unit.read(text);
  access.release;
end;

procedure entry write(header, text: line);
```

```
var changed: boolean;
begin
  access.request(header, changed);
  if changed then unit.write(header);
  unit.write(text);
  access.release;
end;

begin init unit(typedevice) end;
```

TERMINAL STREAM

type terminalstream = class(operator: terminal)

A terminal stream enables a process to identify itself once and for all and then proceed to read and write single characters on a terminal. A terminal stream uses a terminal to input or output a line at a time.

procedure read(var c: char)

Reads a character from the terminal.

procedure write(c: char)

Writes a character on the terminal.

procedure reset(text: line)

Identifies the calling process.

Implementation:

The terminal stream contains two line buffers for input and output.

```
type terminalstream =
class(operator: terminal);

const linelimit = 80;

var header: line; endinput: boolean;
  inp, out: record count: integer; text: line end;
```

```
procedure initialize(text: line);
begin
  header := text;
  endinput := true;
  out.count := 0;
end;

procedure entry read(var c: char);
begin
  with inp do
    begin
      if endinput then
        begin
          operator.read(header, text);
          count := 0;
        end;
      count := count + 1;
      c := text[count];
      endinput := (c = nl);
    end;
end;

procedure entry write(c: char);
begin
  with out do
    begin
      count := count + 1;
      text[count] := c;
      if (c = nl) or (count = linelimit) then
        begin
          operator.write(header, text);
          count := 0;
        end;
    end;
end;

procedure entry reset(text: line);
```

```
begin initialize(text) end;

begin initialize('unidentified:(:10:)') end;
```

DISK

type disk = class(typeuse: typeresource)

A disk can transfer any page to or from a disk device. A disk uses a typewriter resource to get exclusive access to a terminal to report disk failure. After a disk failure, the disk writes a message to the operator and repeats the operation when he types a newline character.

procedure read(pageaddr: integer; var block: univ page)

Reads a page identified by its absolute disk address.

procedure write(pageaddr: integer; var block: univ page)

Writes a page identified by its absolute disk address.

A page is declared as a universal type to make it possible to use the disk to transfer pages of different types (and not just text).

Implementation:

The standard procedure io delays the calling process until the disk transfer is completed (Brinch Hansen 1975b).

```
type disk =
class(typeuse: typeresource);

var operator: terminal;

procedure transfer(command: iooperation;
  pageaddr: univ ioarg; var block: page);
var param: ioparam; response: line;
begin
  with param, operator do
    begin
      operation := command;
```

```
          arg := pageaddr;
          io(block, param, diskdevice);
          while status <> complete do
            begin
              write('disk:(:10:)', 'error(:10:)');
              read('push return(:10:)', response);
              io(block, param, diskdevice);
            end;
      end;
  end;

  procedure entry read(pageaddr: integer; var block: univ page);
  begin transfer(input, pageaddr, block) end;

  procedure entry write(pageaddr: integer; var block; univ page);
  begin transfer(output, pageaddr, block) end;

  begin init operator(typeuse) end;
```

DISK FILE

type diskfile = class(typeuse: typeresource)

A disk file enables a process to access a disk file consisting of a fixed number of pages ($\leq$ 255). A disk file uses a typewriter resource to get exclusive access to the operator after a disk failure.

The disk file is identified by the absolute address of a page map that defines the length of the file and the disk addresses of its pages. To a calling process the pages of a file are numbered 1, 2, ..., length.

Initially, the file is closed (inaccessible). A user of a file must open it before using it and close it afterwards. Read and write have no effect if the file is closed or if the page number is outside the range 1..length.

procedure open(mapaddr: integer)

Makes a disk file with a given page map accessible.

procedure close

Makes the disk file inaccessible.

function length: integer

Returns the length of the disk file (in pages). The length of a closed file is zero.

procedure read(pageno: integer; **var** *block:* **univ** *page)*

Reads a page with a given number from the disk file.

procedure write(pageno: integer; **var** *block:* **univ** *page)*

Writes a page with a given number on the disk file.

Implementation:

The variable *length* is prefixed with the word *entry.* This means that its value can be used directly outside the class. It can, however, only be changed within the class. So a *variable entry* is similar to a function entry. Variable entries can only be used within classes.

```
const maplength = 255;
type filemap =
  record
    filelength: integer;
    pageset: array [1..maplength] of integer
  end;

type diskfile =
class(typeuse: typeresource);

var unit: disk; map: filemap; opened: boolean;

entry length: integer;

function includes(pageno: integer): boolean;
begin
  includes := opened &
    ( 1 <= pageno) & (pageno <= length);
end;

procedure entry open(mapaddr: integer);
```

```
begin
  unit.read(mapaddr, map);
  length := map.filelength;
  opened := true;
end;

procedure entry close;
begin
  length := 0;
  opened := false;
end;

procedure entry read(pageno: integer; var block: univ page);
begin
  if includes(pageno) then
    unit.read(map.pageset[pageno], block);
end;

procedure entry write(pageno: integer; var block: univ page);
begin
  if includes(pageno) then
    unit.write(map.pageset[pageno], block);
end;

begin
  init unit(typeuse);
  length := 0;
  opened := false;
end;
```

CATALOG STRUCTURE

The disk contains a catalog of all files. The following data types define the structure of the catalog:

```
const idlength = 12;
type identifier = array [1..idlength] of char;

type filekind = (empty, scratch, ascii, seqcode, concode);
```

```
type fileattr =
  record
    kind: filekind;
    addr: integer;
    protected: boolean;
    notused: array [1..5] of integer
  end;

type catentry =
  record
    id: identifier;
    attr: fileattr;
    key, searchlength: integer
  end;

const catpagelength = 16;
type catpage = array [1..catpagelength] of catentry;

const cataddr = 154;
```

The catalog is itself a file defined by a page map stored at the *catalog address*. Every *catalog page* contains a fixed number of catalog entries. A *catalog entry* describes a file by its identifier, attributes and hash key. The search length defines the number of files that have a hash key equal to the index of this entry. It is used to limit the search for a non-existing file name.

The *file attributes* are its kind (empty, scratch, ascii, sequential or concurrent code), the address of its page map, and a boolean defining whether it is protected against accidental deletion or overwriting. The latter is checked by all system programs operating on the disk, but not by the operating system. Solo provides a mechanism for protection, but does not enforce it.

DISK TABLE

type disktable = class(typeuse: typeresource; cataddr: integer)

A disk table makes a disk catalog look like an array of catalog entries identified by numeric indices 1, 2, ..., length. A disk table uses a typewriter resource to get exclusive access to the operator after a disk failure and a catalog address to locate a catalog on disk.

function length: integer

Defines the number of entries in the catalog.

procedure read(i: integer; var elem: catentry)

Reads entry number *i* in the catalog. If the entry number is outside the range 1..length the contents of the entry is undefined.

Implementation:

A disk table stores the most recently used catalog page to make a sequential search of the catalog fast.

```
type disktable =
class(typeuse: typeresource; cataddr: integer);

var file: diskfile; pageno: integer; block: catpage;

entry length: integer;

procedure entry read(i: integer; var elem: catentry);
var index: integer;
begin
  index := (i - 1) div catpagelength + 1;
  if pageno <> index then
    begin
      pageno := index;
      file.read(pageno, block);
    end;
  elem := block[(i - 1) mod catpagelength + 1];
end;

begin
  init file(typeuse);
  file.open(cataddr);
  length := file.length * catpagelength;
  pageno := 0;
end;
```

DISK CATALOG

type diskcatalog =
monitor(typeuse: typeresource; diskuse: resource; cataddr: integer)

The disk catalog describes all disk files by means of a set of named entries that can be looked up by processes. A disk catalog uses a resource to get exclusive access to the disk during a catalog lookup and a typewriter resource to get exclusive access to the operator after a disk failure. It uses a catalog address to locate the catalog on disk.

procedure lookup(id: identifier; var attr: fileattr; var found: boolean)

Searches for a catalog entry describing a file with a given identifier and indicates whether it found it. If so, it also returns the file attributes.

Implementation:

A disk catalog uses a disk table to make a cyclical search for an identifier. The initial catalog entry is selected by hashing. The search stops when the identifier is found or when there are no more entries with the same hash key. The disk catalog has exclusive access to the disk during the lookup to prevent competing processes from causing disk arm movement.

```
type diskcatalog =
monitor(typeuse: typeresource; diskuse: resource; cataddr: integer);

var table: disktable;

function hash(id: identifier): integer;
var key, i: integer; c: char;
begin
  key := 1; i := 0;
  repeat
    i := i + 1; c := id[i];
    if c <> ' ' then
      key := key * ord(c) mod table.length + 1;
  until (c = ' ') or (i = idlength);
  hash := key;
end;
```

```
procedure entry lookup(id: identifier;
  var attr: fileattr; var found: boolean);
var key, more, index: integer; elem: catentry;
begin
  diskuse.request;
  key := hash(id);
  table.read(key, elem);
  more := elem.searchlength;
  index := key; found := false;
  while not found & (more > 0) do
    begin
      table.read(index, elem);
      if elem.id = id then
        begin attr := elem.attr; found := true end
      else
        begin
          if elem.key = key then more := more - 1;
          index := index mod table.length + 1;
        end;
    end;
  diskuse.release;
end;

begin init table(typeuse, cataddr) end;
```

DATA FILE

type datafile =
class(typeuse: typeresource; diskuse: resource; catalog: diskcatalog)

A data file enables a process to access a disk file by means of its name in a diskcatalog. The pages of a data file are numbered 1, 2, ..., length. A data file uses a resource to get exclusive access to the disk during a page transfer and a typewriter resource to get exclusive access to the operator after disk failure. It uses a catalog to look up the the file.

Initially a data file is inaccessible (closed). A user of a data file must open it before using it and close it afterwards. If a process needs exclusive access to a data file while using it, this must be ensured at higher levels of programming.

procedure open(id: identifier; var found: boolean)

Makes a file with a given identifier accessible if it is found in the catalog.

procedure close

Makes the file inaccessible.

procedure read(pageno: integer; var block: univ page)

Reads a page with a given number from the file. It has no effect if the file is closed or if the page number is outside the range 1..length.

procedure write(pageno: integer; var block: univ page)

Writes a page with a given number on the file. It has no effect if the file is closed or if the page number is outside the range 1..length.

function length: integer

Defines the number of pages in the file. The length of a closed file is zero.

Implementation:

```
type datafile =
class(typeuse: typeresource; diskuse: resource; catalog: diskcatalog);

var file: diskfile; opened: boolean;

entry length: integer;

procedure entry open(id: identifier; var found: boolean);
var attr: fileattr;
begin
  catalog.lookup(id, attr, found);
  if found then
    begin
      diskuse.request;
      file.open(attr.addr);
      length := file.length;
```

```
          diskuse.release;
        end;
      opened := found;
    end;

    procedure entry close;
    begin
      file.close;
      length := 0;
      opened := false;
    end;

    procedure entry read(pageno: integer; var block: univ page);
    begin
      if opened then
        begin
          diskuse.request;
          file.read(pageno, block);
          diskuse.release;
        end;
    end;

    procedure entry write(pageno: integer; var block: univ page);
    begin
      if opened then
        begin
          diskuse.request;
          file.write(pageno, block);
          diskuse.release;
        end;
    end;

    begin
      init file(typeuse);
      length := 0;
      opened := false;
    end;
```

PROGRAM FILE

type progfile =
class(typeuse: typeresource; diskuse: resource; catalog: diskcatalog)

A program file can transfer a sequential program from a disk file into core. The program file is identified by its name in a disk catalog. A program file uses a resource to get exclusive access to the disk during program loading and a typewriter resource to get exclusive access to the operator after disk failure. It uses a disk catalog to look up the file.

procedure open(id: identifier; var state: progstate)

Loads a program with a given identifier from disk and returns its state. The program state is one of the following: ready for execution, not found, the disk file is not sequential code, or the file is too big to be loaded into core.

function store: progstore

Defines the variable in which the program file is stored. A program store is an array of disk pages.

Implementation:

A program file has exclusive access to the disk until it has loaded the entire program. This is to prevent competing processes from slowing down program loading by causing disk arm movement.

```
type progstate = (ready, notfound, notseq, toobig);

const storelength1 = 40;
type progstore1 = array [1..storelength1] of page;

type progfile1 =
class(typeuse: typeresource; diskuse: resource; catalog: diskcatalog);

var file: diskfile;

entry store: progstore1;

procedure entry open(id: identifier; var state: progstate);
```

```
var attr: fileattr; found: boolean; pageno: integer;
begin
  catalog.lookup(id, attr, found);
  with diskuse, file, attr do
    if not found then state := notfound
    else if kind <> seqcode then state := notseq
    else
      begin
        request;
        open(addr);
        if length <= storelength1 then
          begin
            for pageno := 1 to length do
              read(pageno, store[pageno]);
            state := ready;
          end
        else state := toobig;
        close;
        release;
      end;
end;

begin init file(typeuse) end;
```

Solo uses two kinds of program files (progfile1 and progfile2); one for large programs and another one for small ones. They differ only in the dimension of the program store used. The need to repeat the entire class definition to handle arrays of different lengths is an awkward inheritance from Pascal.

PROGRAM STACK

type progstack = monitor

A program stack maintains a last-in, first-out list of identifiers of programs that have called one another. It enables a process to keep track of nested calls of sequential programs.

For historical reasons a program stack was defined as a monitor. In the present version of the system it might as well have been a class.

function space: boolean

Tells whether there is more space in the program stack.

function any: boolean

Tells whether the stack contains any program identifiers.

procedure push(id: identifier)

Puts an identifier on top of the stack. It has no effect if the stack is full.

procedure pop(var line, result: univ integer)

Removes a program identifier from the top of the stack and defines the line number at which the program terminated as well as its result. The result either indicates normal termination or one of several run-time errors as explained in the Concurrent Pascal report (Brinch Hansen 1975b).

procedure get(var id: identifier)

Defines the identifier stored in the top of the stack (without removing it). It has no effect if the stack is empty.

Implementation:

A program stack measures the extent of the heap of the calling process before pushing an identifier on the stack. If a pop operation shows abnormal program termination, the heap is reset to its original point to prevent the calling process from crashing due to lack of data space.

The standard routines, *attribute* and *setheap*, are defined in the Concurrent Pascal report.

```
type resulttype =
  (terminated, overflow, pointererror, rangeerror, varianterror,
  heaplimit, stacklimit, codelimit, timelimit, callerror);

type attrindex =
  (caller, heaptop, progline, progresult, runtime);

type progstack =
```

```
monitor

const stacklength = 5;

var stack:
  array [1..stacklength] of
    record progid: identifier; heapaddr: integer end;
  top: 0..stacklength;

function entry space: boolean;
begin space := (top < stacklength) end;

function entry any: boolean;
begin any := (top > 0) end;

procedure entry push(id: identifier);
begin
  if top < stacklength then
    begin
      top := top + 1;
      with stack[top] do
        begin
          progid := id;
          heapaddr := attribute(heaptop);
        end;
    end;
end;

procedure entry pop(var line, result: univ integer);
const terminated = 0;
begin
  line := attribute(progline);
  result := attribute(progresult);
  if result <> terminated then
    setheap(stack[top].heapaddr);
  top := top - 1;
end;
```

```
procedure entry get(var id: identifier);
begin
  if top > 0 then id := stack[top].progid;
end;

begin top := 0 end;
```

PAGE BUFFER

type pagebuffer = monitor

A page buffer transmits a sequence of data pages from one process to another. Each sequence is terminated by an end of file mark.

procedure read(var text: page; var eof: boolean)

Receives a message consisting of a text page and an end of file indication.

procedure write(text: page; eof: boolean)

Sends a message consisting of a text page and an end of file indication.

If the end of file is true then the text page is empty.

Implementation:

A page buffer stores a single message at a time. It will delay the sending process as long as the buffer is full and the receiving process until it becomes full ($0 \leq \text{writes} - \text{reads} \leq 1$).

```
type pagebuffer =
monitor

var buffer: page; last, full: boolean;
  sender, receiver: queue;

procedure entry read(var text: page; var eof: boolean);
begin
  if not full then delay(receiver);
  text := buffer; eof := last; full := false;
  continue(sender);
```

```
end;

procedure entry write(text: page; eof: boolean);
begin;
  if full then delay(sender);
  buffer := text; last := eof; full := true;
  continue(receiver);
end;

begin full := false end;
```

Solo also implements buffers for transmission of arguments (enumerations and identifiers) and lines. They are similar to the page buffer (but use no end of file marks). The need to duplicate routines for each message type is an inconvenience caused by the fixed data types of Pascal.

CHARACTER STREAM

type charstream = class(buffer: pagebuffer)

A character stream enables a process to communicate with another process character by character. A character stream uses a page buffer to transmit one page of characters at a time from one process to another.

A sending process must open its stream for writing before using it. The last character transmitted in a sequence should be an end of medium (em).

A receiving process must open its stream for reading before using it.

procedure initread

Opens a character stream for reading.

procedure initwrite

Opens a character stream for writing.

procedure read(var c: char)

Reads the next character from the stream. The effect is undefined if the stream is not open for reading.

procedure write(c: char)

Writes the next character in the stream. The effect is undefined if the stream is not open for writing.

Implementation:

```
type charstream =
class(buffer: pagebuffer);

var text: page; count: integer; eof: boolean;

procedure entry read(var c: char);
begin
  if count = pagelength then
    begin
      buffer.read(text, eof);
      count := 0;
    end;
  count := count + 1;
  c := text[count];
  if c = em then
    begin
      while not eof do buffer.read(text, eof);
      count := pagelength;
    end;
end;

procedure entry initread;
begin count := pagelength end;

procedure entry write(c: char);
begin
  count := count + 1;
  text[count] := c;
  if (count = pagelength) or (c = em) then
    begin
      buffer.write(text, false); count := 0;
      if c = em then buffer.write(text, true);
```

```
    end;
  end;

  procedure entry initwrite;
  begin count := 0 end;

  begin end;
```

TASKS AND ARGUMENTS

The following data types are used by several processes:

```
type taskkind = (inputtask, jobtask, outputtask);

type argtag = (niltype, booltype, inttype, idtype, ptrtype);
  argtype = record tag: argtag; arg: identifier end;

const maxarg = 10;
type arglist = array [1..maxarg] of argtype;

type argseq = (inp, out);
```

The *task kind* defines whether a process is performing an input task, a job task, or an output task. It is used by sequential programs to determine whether they have been loaded by the right kind of process. As an example, a program that controls card reader input can only be called by an input process.

A process that executes a sequential program can pass a list of arguments to it. A program *argument* consists of a tag field defining its type (boolean, integer, identifier, or pointer) and another field defining its value. (Since Concurrent Pascal does not include the variant records of Sequential Pascal one can only represent a program argument by the largest one of its variants—an identifier.)

A job process is connected to two input and output processes by *argument buffers* called its input and output sequences.

JOB PROCESS

type jobprocess =
process
(typeuse: typeresource; diskuse: resource;
catalog: diskcatalog; inbuffer, outbuffer: pagebuffer;
inrequest, inresponse, outrequest, outresponse: argbuffer;
stack: progstack)
"program data space" +16000

A job process executes Sequential Pascal programs that can call one another recursively. Initially, it executes a program called *do* with console input. A job process also implements the interface between sequential programs and the Solo operating system as defined in Brinch Hansen (1976b).

A job process needs access to the operator's console, the disk, and its catalog. It is connected to an input and an output process by two page buffers and four argument buffers as explained in Brinch Hansen (1976a). It uses a program stack to handle nested calls of sequential programs.

It reserves a data space of 16,000 bytes for user programs and a code space of 20,000 bytes. This enables the Pascal compiler to compile itself.

Implementation:

The private variables of a job process give it access to a terminal stream, two character streams for input and output, and two data files. It uses a large program file to store the currently executed program. These variables are inaccessible to other processes.

The job process contains a declaration of a sequential program that defines the types of its arguments and the variable in which its code is stored (the latter is inaccessible to the program). It also defines a list of interface routines that can be called by a program. These routines are implemented within the job process. They are defined in Brinch Hansen (1976b).

Before a job process can call a sequential program it must load it from disk into a program store and push its identifier onto a program stack. After termination of the program, the job process pops its identifier, line number, and result from the program stack, reloads the previous program from disk and returns to it.

A process can only interact with other processes by calling routines within monitors that are passed as parameters to it during initialization (such as the catalog declared at the beginning of a job process). These access rights are checked at compile-time (Brinch Hansen 1975a).

```
type jobprocess =
process
  (typeuse: typeresource; diskuse: resource;
  catalog: diskcatalog; inbuffer, outbuffer: pagebuffer;
  inrequest, inresponse, outrequest, outresponse: argbuffer;
  stack: progstack);
"program data space" +16000

const maxfile = 2;
type file = 1..maxfile;

var operator: terminal; opstream: terminalstream;
  instream, outstream: charstream;
  files: array [file] of datafile;
  code: progfile1;

program job(var param: arglist; store: progstore1);
entry read, write, open, close, get, put, length,
  mark, release, identify, accept, display, readpage,
  writepage, readline, writeline, readarg, writearg,
  lookup, iotransfer, iomove, task, run;

procedure call(id: identifier; var param: arglist;
  var line: integer; var result: resulttype);
var state: progstate; lastid: identifier;
begin
  with code, stack do
    begin
      line := 0;
      open(id, state);
      if (state = ready) & space then
        begin
          push(id);
          job(param, store);
          pop(line, result);
        end
```

```
        else if state = toobig then result := codelimit
        else result := callerror;
        if any then
          begin get(lastid); open(lastid, state) end;
      end;
  end;

  procedure entry read(var c: char);
  begin instream.read(c) end;

  procedure entry write(c: char);
  begin outstream.write(c) end;

  procedure entry open(f: file; id: identifier; var found: boolean);
  begin files[f].open(id, found) end;

  procedure entry close(f: file);
  begin files[f].close end;

  procedure entry get(f: file; p: integer; var block: page);
  begin files[f].read(p, block) end;

  procedure entry put(f: file; p: integer; var block: page);
  begin files[f].write(p, block) end;

  function entry length(f: file): integer;
  begin length := files[f].length end;

  procedure entry mark(var top: integer);
  begin top := attribute(heaptop) end;

  procedure entry release(top: integer);
  begin setheap(top) end;

  procedure entry identify(header: line);
  begin opstream.reset(header) end;

  procedure entry accept(var c: char);
```

```
begin opstream.read(c) end;

procedure entry display(c: char);
begin opstream.write(c) end;

procedure entry readpage(var block: page; var eof: boolean);
begin inbuffer.read(block, eof) end;

procedure entry writepage(block: page; eof: boolean);
begin outbuffer.write(block, eof) end;

procedure entry readline(var text: line);
begin end;

procedure entry writeline(text: line);
begin end;

procedure entry readarg(s: argseq; var arg: argtype);
begin
  if s = inp then inresponse.read(arg)
  else outresponse.read(arg);
end;

procedure entry writearg(s: argseq; arg: argtype);
begin
  if s = inp then inrequest.write(arg)
  else outrequest.write(arg);
end;

procedure entry lookup(id: identifier;
  var attr: fileattr; var found: boolean);
begin catalog.lookup(id, attr, found) end;

procedure entry iotransfer(device: iodevice;
  var param: ioparam; var block: page);
begin
  if device = diskdevice then
    begin
```

```
      diskuse.request;
      io(block, param, device);
      diskuse.release;
    end
  else io(block, param, device);
end;

procedure entry iomove(device: iodevice; var param: ioparam);
begin io(param, param, device) end;

function entry task: taskkind;
begin task := jobtask end;

procedure entry run(id: identifier; var param: arglist;
  var line: integer; var result: resulttype);
begin call(id, param, line, result) end;

procedure initialize;
var i: integer; param: arglist; line: integer; result: resulttype;
begin
  init operator(typeuse), opstream(operator),
    instream(inbuffer), outstream(outbuffer);
  instream.initread; outstream.initwrite;
  for i := 1 to maxfile do
    init files[i](typeuse, diskuse, catalog);
  init code(typeuse, diskuse, catalog);
  with param[2] do
    begin tag := idtype; arg := 'console     ' end;
  call( 'do          ', param, line, result);
  operator.write('jobprocess:(:10:)', 'terminated (:10)');
end;

begin initialize end;
```

IO PROCESS

type ioprocess =
process
  (typeuse: typeresource; diskuse: resource;
  catalog: diskcatalog; slowio: linebuffer;
  buffer: pagebuffer; request, response: argbuffer;
  stack: progstack; iotask: taskkind)
"program data space" +2000

An io process executes Sequential Pascal programs that produce or consume data for a job process. It also implements the interface between these programs and the Solo operating system.

An io process needs access to the operator, the disk, and the catalog. It is connected to a card reader (or a line printer) by a line buffer and to a job process by a page buffer and two argument buffers. It uses a program stack to handle nested calls of sequential programs.

It reserves a data space of 2,000 bytes for input/output programs and a code space of 4,000 bytes.

Initially, it executes a program called *io*

Implementation:

The implementation details are similar to a job process.

```
type ioprocess =
process
  (typeuse: typeresource; diskuse: resource;
  catalog: diskcatalog; slowio: linebuffer;
  buffer: pagebuffer; request, response: argbuffer;
  stack: progstack; iotask: taskkind);
"program data space" +2000

type file = 1..1;

var operator: terminal; opstream: terminalstream;
  iostream: charstream; iofile: datafile;
  code: progfile2;

program driver(var param: arglist; store: progstore2);
```

```
entry read, write, open, close, get, put, length,
  mark, release, identify, accept, display, readpage,
  writepage, readline, writeline, readarg, writearg,
  lookup, iotransfer, iomove, task, run;

procedure call(id: identifier; var param: arglist;
  var line: integer; var result: resulttype);
var state: progstate; lastid: identifier;
begin
  with code, stack do
    begin
      line := 0;
      open(id, state);
      if (state = ready) & space then
        begin
          push(id);
          driver(param, store);
          pop(line, result);
        end
      else if state = toobig then result := codelimit
      else result := callerror;
      if any then
        begin get(lastid); open(lastid, state) end;
    end;
end;

procedure entry read(var c: char);
begin iostream.read(c) end;

procedure entry write(c: char);
begin iostream.write(c) end;

procedure entry open(f: file; id: identifier; var found: boolean);
begin iofile.open(id, found) end;

procedure entry close(f: file);
begin iofile.close end;
```

```
procedure entry get(f: file; p: integer; var block: page);
begin iofile.read(p, block) end;

procedure entry put(f: file; p: integer; var block: page);
begin iofile.write(p, block) end;

function entry length(f: file): integer;
begin length := iofile.length end;

procedure entry mark(var top: integer);
begin top := attribute(heaptop) end;

procedure entry release(top: integer);
begin setheap(top) end;

procedure entry identify(header: line);
begin opstream.reset(header) end;

procedure entry accept(var c: char);
begin opstream.read(c) end;

procedure entry display(c: char);
begin opstream.write(c) end;

procedure entry readpage(var block: page; var eof: boolean);
begin buffer.read(block, eof) end;

procedure entry writepage(block: page; eof: boolean);
begin buffer.write(block, eof) end;

procedure entry readline(var text: line);
begin slowio.read(text) end;

procedure entry writeline(text: line);
begin slowio.write(text) end;

procedure entry readarg(s: argseq; var arg: argtype);
begin request.read(arg) end;
```

```
procedure entry writearg(s: argseq; arg: argtype);
begin response.write(arg) end;

procedure entry lookup(id: identifier;
  var attr: fileattr; var found: boolean);
begin catalog.lookup(id, attr, found) end;

procedure entry iotransfer(device: iodevice;
  var param: ioparam; var block: page);
begin
  if device = diskdevice then
    begin
      diskuse.request;
      io(block, param, device);
      diskuse.release;
    end
  else io(block, param, device);
end;

procedure entry iomove(device: iodevice; var param: ioparam);
begin io(param, param, device) end;

function entry task: taskkind;
begin task := iotask end;

procedure entry run(id: identifier; var param: arglist;
  var line: integer; var result: resulttype);
begin call(id, param, line, result) end;

procedure initialize;
var param: arglist; line: integer; result: resulttype;
begin
  init operator(typeuse), opstream(operator),
    iostream(buffer), iofile(typeuse, diskuse, catalog),
    code(typeuse, diskuse, catalog);
  if iotask = inputtask then iostream.initwrite
  else iostream.initread;
```

```
    call( 'io          ', param, line, result);
    operator.write('ioprocess:(:10:)', 'terminated (:10)');
  end;

  begin initialize end;
```

CARD PROCESS

type cardprocess =
process(typeuse: typeresource; buffer: linebuffer)

A card process transmits cards from a card reader through a line buffer to an input process. The card process can access the operator to report device failure and a line buffer to transmit data. It is assumed that the card reader is controlled by a single card process. As long as the card reader is turned off or is empty the card process waits. It begins to read cards as soon as they are available in the reader. After a transmission error the card process writes a message to the operator and continues the input of cards.

Implementation:

The standard procedure *wait* delays the card process one second (Brinch Hansen 1975b). This reduces the processor time spent waiting for operator intervention.

```
type cardprocess =
process(typeuse: typeresource; buffer: linebuffer);

var operator: terminal; param: ioparam;
  text: line; ok: boolean;
begin
  init operator(typeuse);
  param.operation := input;
  cycle
    repeat
      io(text, param, carddevice);
      case param.status of
        complete:
          ok := true;
        intervention:
```

```
          begin ok := false; wait end;
        transmission, failure:
          begin
            operator.write('cards:(:10:)', 'error(:10:)');
            ok := false;
          end
      end
    until ok;
    buffer.write(text);
  end;
end;
```

PRINTER PROCESS

type printerprocess =
process(typeuse: typeresource; buffer: linebuffer)

A printer process transmits lines from an output process to a line printer. The printer process can access the operator to report device failure and a line buffer to receive data. It is assumed that the line printer is controlled only by a single printer process. After a printer failure the printer process writes a message to the operator and repeats the output of the current line until it is successful.

Implementation:

```
type printerprocess =
process(typeuse: typeresource; buffer: linebuffer);

var operator: terminal; param: ioparam; text: line;
begin
  init operator(typeuse);
  param.operation := output;
  cycle
    buffer.read(text);
    io(text, param, printdevice);
    if param.status <> complete then
      begin
        operator.write('printer:(:10:)', 'inspect(:10:)');
```

```
          repeat
            wait;
            io(text, param, printdevice);
          until param.status = complete;
        end;
    end;
  end;
```

LOADER PROCESS

type loaderprocess =
process(diskuse: resource)

A loader process preempts the operating system and reinitializes it when the operator pushes the *bell* key (*control g*) on the console. A loader process needs access to the disk to be able to reload the system.

Implementation:

A control operation on the typewriter delays the loader process until the operator pushes the bell key (Brinch Hansen 1975b).

The operating system is stored on consecutive disk pages starting at the *Solo address.* It is loaded by means of a control operation on the disk as defined in Brinch Hansen (1975b). Consecutive disk pages are used to make the system kernel of Concurrent Pascal unaware of the structure of a particular filing system (such as the one used by Solo). The disk contains a sequential program *start* that can copy the Solo system from a concurrent code file into the consecutive disk segment defined above.

```
type loaderprocess =
process(diskuse: resource);

const soloaddr = 24;
var param: ioparam;

procedure initialize(pageno: univ ioarg);
begin
  with param do
    begin
      operation := control;
```

```
      arg := pageno;
    end;
end;

begin
  initialize(soloaddr);
  "await bel signal"
  io(param, param, typedevice);
  "reload solo system"
  diskuse.request;
  io(param, param, diskdevice);
  diskuse.release;
end;
```

INITIAL PROCESS

The initial process initializes all other processes and monitors and defines their access rights to one another. After initialization the operating system consists of a fixed set of components: a card process, an input process, a job process, an output process, a printer process, and a loader process. They have access to an operator, a disk, and a catalog of files. Process communication takes place by means of two page buffers, two line buffers and four argument buffers (see also Fig. 1).

Implementation:

When a process, such as the initial process, terminates its execution, its variables continue to exist (because they may be used by other processes).

```
var
  typeuse: typeresource;
  diskuse: resource; catalog: diskcatalog;
  inbuffer, outbuffer: pagebuffer;
  cardbuffer, printerbuffer: linebuffer;
  inrequest, inresponse, outrequest, outresponse: argbuffer;
  instack, outstack, jobstack: progstack;
  reader: cardprocess; writer: printerprocess;
  producer, consumer: ioprocess; master: jobprocess;
  watchdog: loaderprocess;
begin
```

```
  init
    typeuse, diskuse,
    catalog(typeuse, diskuse, cataddr),
    inbuffer, outbuffer,
    cardbuffer, printerbuffer,
    inrequest, inresponse, outrequest, outresponse,
    instack, outstack, jobstack,
    reader(typeuse, cardbuffer),
    writer(typeuse, printerbuffer),
    producer(typeuse, diskuse, catalog, cardbuffer,
      inbuffer, inrequest, inresponse, instack, inputtask),
    consumer(typeuse, diskuse, catalog, printerbuffer),
      outbuffer, outrequest, outresponse, outstack, outputtask),
    master(typeuse, diskuse, catalog, inbuffer, outbuffer,
      inrequest, inresponse, outrequest, outresponse,
      jobstack),
    watchdog(diskuse);
end;
```

CONCLUSION

The Solo system consists of 22 line printer pages of Concurrent Pascal text divided into 23 component types (10 classes, 7 monitors, and 6 processes). A typical component is less than one page long and can be studied in isolation as an (almost) independent piece of program. All program components called by a given component are explicitly declared within that component (either as permanent variables or a parameters to it). To understand a component it is only necessary to know *what* other components called by it do, but *how* they do it is irrelevant.

The entire system can be studied component by component as one would read a book. In that sense, Concurrent Pascal supports *abstraction* and *hierarchical structuring* of concurrent programs very nicely.

It took 4 compilations to remove the formal programming errors from the Solo system. It was then tested systematically from the bottom up by adding one component type at a time and trying it by means of short test processes. The whole program was tested in 27 runs (or about 1 run per component type). This revealed 7 errors in the test processes and 2 trivial ones in the system itself. Later, about one third of it was rewritten to speed up program loading. This took about one week. It was then compiled and put into operation in one day and has worked ever since.

I can only suggest two plausible explanations for this unusual testing experience. It seems to be vital that the compiler prevents new components from destroying old ones (since old components cannot call new ones, and new ones can only call old ones through routines that have already been tested). This strict checking of hierarchical access rights makes it possible for a large system to evolve gradually through a sequence of intermediate, stable subsystems.

I am also convinced now that the use of abstract data types which hide implementation details within a fixed set of routines encourages a clarity of design that makes programs practically correct before they are even tested. The slight inconvenience of strict type checking is of minor importance compared to the advantages of instant program reliability.

Although Solo is a small concurrent program of only 1,300 lines it does implement a virtual machine that is very convenient to use for program development (Brinch Hansen 1976a). The availability of cheap microprocessors will put increasing pressure on software designers to develop special-purpose operating systems at very low cost. Concurrent Pascal is one example of a programming tool that may make this possible.

P. Brinch Hansen 1973. *Operating System Principles*, Chapter 7, Resóurce Protection. Prentice-Hall, Englewood Cliffs, NJ.

P. Brinch Hansen 1975a. The programming language Concurrent Pascal. *IEEE Trans. on Software Engineering*, **1**, 2.

P. Brinch Hansen 1975b. *Concurrent Pascal Report.* Information Science, California Institute of Technology, (June).

P. Brinch Hansen 1976a. The Solo operating system: a Concurrent Pascal program. *Software—Practice and Experience*, **6**, 2 (April–June).

P. Brinch Hansen 1976b. The Solo operating system: job interface. *Software—Practice and Experience*, **6**, 2 (April–June),.

Acknowledgements

The development of Concurrent Pascal and Solo has been supported by the National Science Foundation under grant number DCR74–17331.

13

DESIGN PRINCIPLES

PER BRINCH HANSEN

(1977)

This is the opening chapter of the author's book on concurrent programming. The essay describes the fundamental principles of programming which guided the design and implementation of the programming language Concurrent Pascal and the model operating systems written in that language.

This book describes a method for writing concurrent programs of high quality. Since there is no common agreement among programmers about the qualities a good program should have, I will begin by describing my own requirements.

Program Quality

A good program must be *simple*, *reliable*, and *adaptable*. Without simplicity one cannot expect to understand the purpose and details of a large program. Without reliability one cannot seriously depend on it. And without adaptability to changing requirements a program eventually becomes a fossil.

Fortunately, these essential requirements go hand in hand. Simplicity gives one the confidence to believe that a program works and makes it clear how it can be changed. Simplicity, reliability, and adaptability make programs *manageable*.

In addition, it is desirable to make programs that can work efficiently on several different computers for a variety of similar applications. But *efficiency*, *portability*, and *generality* should never be sought at the expense

P. Brinch Hansen, *The Architecture of Concurrent Programs*, Chapter 1 Design Principles, Prentice Hall, Englewood Cliffs, NJ, (July 1977), 3–14.

of simplicity, reliability, and adaptability, for only the latter qualities make it possible to understand what programs do, depend on them, and extend their capabilities.

The poor quality of much existing software is, to a large extent, the result of turning these priorities upside down. Some programmers justify extremely complex and incomprehensible programs by their high efficiency. Others claim that the poor reliability and efficiency of their huge programs are outweighed by their broad scope of application.

Personally I find the efficiency of a tool that nobody fully understands irrelevant. And I find it difficult to appreciate a general-purpose tool which is so slow that it cannot do anything well. But these are matters of taste and style and are likely to remain so.

Whenever program qualities appear to be in conflict with one another I shall consistently settle the issue by giving first priority to manageability, second priority to efficiency, and third priority to generality. This boils down to the simple rule of limiting our computer applications to those which programmers fully understand and which machines can handle well. Although this is too narrow a view for experimental computer usage it is sound advice for professional programming.

Let us now look more closely at these program qualities to see how they can be achieved.

Simplicity

We will be writing concurrent programs which are so large that one cannot understand them all at once. So we must reason about them in smaller *pieces*. What properties should these pieces have? Well, they should be so small that any one of them is trivial to understand in itself. It would be ideal if they were no more than *one page* of text each so that they can be comprehended at a glance.

Such a program could be studied page by page as one reads a book. But in the end, when we have understood what all the pieces do, we must still be able to see what their combined effect *as a whole* is. If it is a program of many pages we can only do this by ignoring most of our detailed knowledge about the pieces and relying on a much simpler description of what they do and how they work together.

So our program pieces must allow us to make a clear separation of their detailed behavior and that small part of it which is of interest when we consider combinations of such pieces. In other words, we must distinguish between the *inner and outer behavior* of a program piece.

Program pieces will be built to perform well-defined, simple functions. We will then combine program pieces into larger *configurations* to carry out more complicated functions. This design method is effective because it splits a complicated task into simpler ones: First you convince yourself that the pieces work individually, and then you think about how they work together. During the second part of the argument it is essential to be able to forget how a piece works in detail—otherwise, the problem becomes too complicated. But in doing so one makes the fundamental assumption that the piece always will do the same when it carries out its function. Otherwise, you could not afford to ignore the detailed behavior of that piece in your reasoning about the whole system.

So *reproducible behavior* is a vital property of program pieces that we wish to build and study in small steps. We must clearly keep this in mind when we select the kind of program pieces that large concurrent programs will be made of. The ability to repeat program behavior is taken for granted when we write sequential programs. Here the sequence of events is completely defined by the program and its input data. But in a concurrent program simultaneous events take place at rates not fully controlled by the programmer. They depend on the presence of other jobs in the machine and the scheduling policy used to execute them. This means that a conscious effort must be made to design concurrent programs with reproducible behavior.

The idea of reasoning first about *what* a piece does and then studying *how* it does it in detail is most effective if we can repeat this process by explaining each piece in terms of simpler pieces which themselves are built from still simpler pieces. So we shall confine ourselves to *hierarchical structures* composed of *layers* of program pieces.

It will certainly simplify our understanding of hierarchical structures if each part only depends on a small number of other parts. We will therefore try to build structures that have *minimal interfaces* between their parts.

This is extremely difficult to do in *machine language* since the slightest programming mistake can make an instruction destroy any instruction or variable. Here the *whole store* can be the interface between any two instructions. This was made only too clear in the past by the practice of printing the contents of the entire store just to locate a single programming error.

Programs written in *abstract languages* (such as Fortran, Algol, and Pascal) are unable to modify themselves. But they can still have broad interfaces in the form of *global variables* that can be changed by every statement (by intention or mistake).

We will use a programming language called *Concurrent Pascal*, which makes it possible to divide the global variables into smaller parts. Each of these is accessible to a small number of statements only.

The main contribution of a good programming language to simplicity is to provide an abstract *readable notation* that makes the parts and structure of a program obvious to a reader. An abstract programming language *suppresses machine detail* (such as addresses, registers, bit patterns, interrupts, and sometimes even the number of processors available). Instead the language relies on *abstract concepts* (such as variables, data types, synchronizing operations, and concurrent processes). As a result, program texts written in abstract languages are often an order of magnitude shorter than those written in machine language. This *textual reduction* simplifies program engineering considerably.

The fastest way to discover whether or not you have invented a simple program structure is to try to *describe* it in completely readable terms—adopting the same standards of clarity that are required of a survey paper published by a journal. If you take pride in your description you have probably invented a good program structure. But if you discover that there is no simple way of describing what you intend to do, then you should probably look for some other way of doing it.

Once you appreciate the value of description as an early warning signal of unnecessary complexity it becomes self-evident that program structures should be described (without detail) *before* they are built and should be described by the *designer* (and not by anybody else). *Programming is the art of writing essays in crystal clear prose and making them executable.*

Reliability

Even the most readable language notation cannot prevent programmers from making mistakes. In looking for these in large programs we need all the help we can get. A whole range of techniques is available

correctness proofs
proofreading
compilation checks
execution checks
systematic testing

With the exception of correctness proofs, all these techniques played a vital role in making the concurrent programs described in this book work.

Formal proofs are still at an experimental stage, particularly for concurrent programs. Since my aim is to describe techniques that are immediately useful in professional software development, I have omitted proofs here.

Among the useful verification techniques, I feel that those that reveal errors at the earliest possible time during the program development should be emphasized to achieve reliability as soon as possible.

One of the primary goals of Concurrent Pascal is to push the role of *compilation checks* to the limit and reduce the use of *execution checks* as much as possible. This is not done just to make compiled programs more efficient by reducing the overhead of execution checks. In program engineering, compilation and execution checks play the same roles as preventive maintenance and flight recorders do in aviation. The latter only tell you why a system crashed; the former prevents it. This distinction seems essential to me in the design of real-time systems that will control vital functions in society. Such systems must be highly reliable *before* they are put into operation.

Extensive compilation checks are possible only if the language notation is *redundant*. The programmer must be able to specify important properties in at least two different ways so that a compiler can look for possible inconsistencies. An example is the use of declarations to introduce variables and their types before they are used in statements. The compiler could easily derive this information from the statements—provided these statements were always correct.

We shall also follow the crucial principle of language design suggested by Hoare: *The behavior of a program written in an abstract language should always be explainable in terms of the concepts of that language and should never require insight into the details of compilers and computers.* Otherwise, an abstract notation has no significant value in reducing complexity.

This principle immediately rules out the use of machine-oriented features in programming languages. So I shall assume that *all programming will take place in abstract programming languages.*

Dijkstra has remarked that *testing* can be used only to show the presence of errors but never their absence. However true that may be, it seems very worthwhile to me to show the presence of errors and remove them one at a time. In my experience, the combination of careful proofreading, extensive compilation checks, and systematic testing is a very effective way to make a program so dependable that it can work for months without problems. And that is about as reliable as most other technology we depend on. I do not know of better methods for verifying large programs at the moment.

I view programming as the art of building *program pyramids* by adding one brick at a time to the structure and making sure that it does not collapse in the process. The pyramid must remain *stable* while it is being built. I will regard a (possibly incomplete) program as being stable as long as it behaves in a predictable manner.

Why is program testing so often difficult? Mainly, I think, because the addition of a new program piece can spread a burst of errors throughout the rest of a program and make previously tested pieces behave differently. This clearly violates the sound principle of being able to assume that when you have built and tested a part of a large program it will continue to behave correctly *under all circumstances.*

So we will make the strong requirement that *new program pieces added on top of old ones must not be able to make the latter fail.* Since this property must be verified before program testing takes place, it must be done by a compiler. We must therefore use a language notation that makes it clear what program pieces can do to one another. This strong *confinement of program errors* to the part in which they occur will make it much easier to determine from the behavior of a large program where its errors are.

Adaptability

A large program is so expensive to develop that it must be used for several years to make the effort worthwhile. As time passes the users' needs change, and it becomes necessary to modify the program somewhat to satisfy them. Quite often these modifications are done by people who did not develop the program in the first place. Their main difficulty is to find out how the program works and whether it will still work after being changed.

A small group of people can often succeed in developing the first version of a program in a low-level language with little or no documentation to support them. They do it by talking to one another daily and by sharing a mental picture of a simple structure.

But later, when the same program must be extended by other programmers who are not in frequent contact with the original designers, it becomes painfully clear that the "simple" structure is not described anywhere and certainly is not revealed by the primitive language notation used. It is important to realize that *for program maintenance a simple and well-documented structure is even more important than it is during program development.* I will not talk about the situation in which a program that is neither simple nor well documented must be changed.

There is an interesting relationship between programming errors and changing user requirements. Both of them are sources of *instability* in the program construction process that make it difficult to reach a state in which you have complete confidence in what a program does. They are caused by our inability to fully comprehend at once what a large program is supposed to do in detail.

The relative frequencies of program errors and changing requirements are of crucial importance. If programming introduces numerous errors that are difficult to locate, many of them may still be in the program when the user requests changes of its function. And when an engineer constantly finds himself changing a system that he never succeeded in making work correctly in the first place, he will eventually end up with a very unstable product.

On the other hand, if program errors can be located and corrected at a much faster rate than the system develops, then the addition of a new piece (or a change) to the program will soon lead to a stable situation in which the current version of the program works reliably and predictably. The engineer can then, with much greater confidence, adapt his product to slowly changing needs. This is a strong incentive to make program verification and testing fast.

A hierarchical structure consists of program pieces that can be studied one at a time. This makes it easier to read the program and get an initial understanding of what it does and how it does it. Once you have that insight, the consequences of changing a hierarchical program become clear. When you change a part of a program pyramid you must be prepared to inspect and perhaps change the program parts that are on top of it (for they are the only ones that can possibly depend on the one you changed).

Portability

The ability to use the same program on a variety of computers is desirable for economic reasons: Many users have different computers; sometimes they replace them with new ones; and quite often they have a common interest in sharing programs developed on different machines.

Portability is only practical if programs are written in abstract languages that hide the differences between computers as much as possible. Otherwise, it will require extensive rewriting and testing to move programs from one machine to another. Programs written in the same language can be made portable in several ways:

1. by having *different compilers* for different machines. This is only practical for the most widespread languages.

2. by having a *single compiler* that can be modified to generate code for different machines. This requires a clear separation within the compiler of those parts that check programs and those that generate code.

3. by having a *single computer* that can be simulated efficiently on different machines.

The Concurrent Pascal compiler generates code for a simple machine tailored to the language. This machine is simulated by an assembly language program of 4 K words on the PDP 11/45 computer. To move the language to another computer one rewrites this interpreter. This approach sacrifices some efficiency to make portability possible. The loss of efficiency can be eliminated on a microprogrammable machine.

Efficiency

Efficient programs save time for people waiting for results and reduce the cost of computation. The programs described here owe their efficiency to

special-purpose algorithms
static store allocation
minimal run-time checking

Initially the loading of a large program (such as a compiler) from disk took about 16 sec on the PDP 11/45 computer. This was later reduced to 5 sec by a disk allocation algorithm that depends on the special characteristics of program files (as opposed to data files). A scheduling algorithm that tries to reduce disk head movement in general would have been useless here. The reasons for this will be made clear later.

Dynamic store algorithms that move programs and data segments around during execution can be a serious source of inefficiency that is not under the programmer's control. The implementation of Concurrent Pascal does not require garbage collection or demand paging of storage. It uses static allocation of store among a fixed number of processes. The store requirements are determined by the compiler.

When programs are written in assembly language it is impossible to predict what they will do. Most computers depend on hardware mechanisms to prevent such programs from destroying one another or the operating system.

In Concurrent Pascal most of this protection is guaranteed by the compiler and is not supported by hardware mechanisms during execution. This drastic reduction of run-time checking is only possible because all programs are written in an abstract language.

Generality

To achieve simplicity and reliability we will depend exclusively on a machine-independent language that makes programs readable and extensive compilation checks possible. To achieve efficiency we will use the simplest possible store allocation.

These decisions will no doubt reduce the usefulness of Concurrent Pascal for some applications. But I see no way of avoiding that. To impose *structure* upon yourself is to impose *restrictions* on your freedom of programming. You can no longer use the machine in any way you want (because the language makes it impossible to talk directly about some machine features). You can no longer delay certain program decisions until execution time (because the compiler checks and freezes things much earlier). But the freedom you lose is often illusory anyhow, since it can complicate programming to the point where you are unable to cope with it.

This book describes a range of small operating systems. Each of them provides a special service in the most efficient and simple manner. They show that Concurrent Pascal is a useful programming language for minicomputer operating systems and dedicated real-time applications. I expect that the language will be useful (but not sufficient) for writing large, general-purpose operating systems. But that still remains to be seen. I have tried to make a programming tool that is very convenient for many applications rather than one which is tolerable for all purposes.

Conclusion

I have discussed the programming goals of

simplicity
reliability
adaptability
efficiency
portability

and have suggested that they can be achieved by careful design of program structure, language notation, compiler, and code interpreter. The properties that we must look for are the following:

structure:	hierarchical structure small parts minimal interfaces reproducible behavior readable documentation
notation:	abstract and readable structured and redundant
compiler:	reliable and fast extensive checking portable code
interpreter:	reliable and fast minimal checking static store allocation

This is the philosophy we will follow in the design of concurrent programs.

Literature

For me the most enjoyable thing about computer programming is the insight it gives into problem solving and design. The search for simplicity and structure is common to all intellectual disciplines.

Here are a historian and a biologist talking about the importance of recognizing structure:

"It is a matter of some importance to link teaching and research, even very detailed research, to an acceptable architectonic vision of the whole. Without such connections, detail becomes mere antiquarianism. Yet while history without detail is inconceivable, without an organizing vision it quickly becomes incomprehensible ... What cannot be understood becomes meaningless, and reasonable men quite properly refuse to pay attention to meaningless matters."

William H. McNeill (1974)

"There have been a number of physicists who suggested that biological phenomena are related to the finest aspects of the constitution of matter, in a manner of speaking below the chemical level. But the evidence, which is almost too abundant, indicates that biological phenomena operate on the 'systems' level, that is, above chemistry."

Walter M. Elsasser (1975)

A linguist, a psychologist, and a logician have this to say about writing and notation:

"Omit needless words. Vigorous writing is concise. A sentence should contain no unnecessary words, a paragraph no unnecessary sentences, for the same reason that a drawing should have no unnecessary lines and a machine no unnecessary parts. This requires not that the writer make all his sentences short, or that he avoid all detail and treat his subject only in outline, but that every word tell."

William Strunk, Jr. (1959)

"How complex or simple a structure is depends critically upon the way in which we describe it. Most of the complex structures found in the world are enormously redundant, and we can use this redundancy to simplify their description. But to use it, to achieve the simplification, we must find the right representation."

Herbert A. Simon (1969)

"There is something uncanny about the power of a happily chosen ideographic language; for it often allows one to express relations which have no names in natural language and therefore have never been noticed by anyone. Symbolism, then, becomes an organ of discovery rather than mere notation."

Susanne K. Langer (1967)

An engineer and an architect discuss the influence of human errors and cultural changes on the design process:

"First, one must perform perfectly. The computer resembles the magic of legend in this respect, too. If one character, one pause, of the incantation is not strictly in proper form, the magic doesn't work. Human beings are not accustomed to being perfect, and few areas of human activity demand it. Adjusting to the requirement for perfection is, I think, the most difficult part of learning to program."

Frederick P. Brooks, Jr. (1975)

"Misfit provides an incentive to change ... However, for the fit to occur in practice, one vital condition must be satisfied. It must have time to happen. The process must be able to achieve its equilibrium before the next culture change upsets it again. It must actually have time to reach its equilibrium

every time it is disturbed—or, if we see the process as continous rather than intermittent, the adjustment of forms must proceed more quickly than the drift of the culture context."

Christopher Alexander (1964)

Finally, here are a mathematician and a physicist writing about the beauty and joy of creative work:

"The mathematician's patterns, like the painter's or the poet's, must be beautiful; the ideas, like the colours or the words, must fit together in a harmonious way. Beauty is the first test: there is no permanent place in the world for ugly mathematics."

G.H. Hardy (1967)

"The most powerful drive in the ascent of man is his pleasure in his own skill. He loves to do what he does well and, having done it well, he loves to do it better. You see it in his science. You see it in the magnificence with which he carves and builds, the loving care, the gaiety, the effrontery. The monuments are supposed to commemorate kings and religions, heroes, dogmas, but in the end the man they commemorate is the builder."

Jacob Bronowski (1973)

References

Alexander, C. 1964. *Notes on the Synthesis of Form.* Harvard University Press, Cambridge, MA.

Bronowski, J. 1973. *The Ascent of Man.* Little, Brown and Company, Boston, MA.

Brooks, F.P. 1975. *The Mythical Man-Month. Essays on Software Engineering.* Addison-Wesley, Reading, MA.

Elsasser, W.M. 1975. *The Chief Abstractions of Biology.* American Elsevier, New York.

Hardy, G.H. 1967. *A Mathematician's Apology.* Cambridge University Press, New York.

Langer, S.K. 1967. *An Introduction to Symbolic Logic.* Dover Publications, New York.

McNeill, W.H. 1974. *The Shape of European History.* Oxford University Press, New York.

Simon, H.A. 1969. *The Sciences of the Artificial.* The MIT Press, Cambridge, MA.

Strunk, W., and White, E.B. 1959. *The Elements of Style.* Macmillan, New York.

PART V

DISTRIBUTED COMPUTING

14

A SYNTHESIS EMERGING?

EDSGER W. DIJKSTRA

(1975)

Author's comment (added 1982): In retrospect this text is not without historical interest: it records the highlights of a discussion mentioned [as "Verbal communication" (Dijkstra 1975)] in C. A. R. Hoare's "Communicating sequential processes", Comm. ACM 21, 8 (Aug. 1978), 666-677. The text was evidently written in a state of some excitement; in retrospect we may conclude that this excitement was not entirely unjustified. Seeing Hoare keenly interested in the topic, I left that arena.

Introduction

This document does not contain language proposals; at a later stage they may be inspired by it. It has no other purpose than to record discussions and programming experiments. It is exciting because it seems to open the possibility of writing programs that could be implemented

(a) either by normal sequential techniques
(b) or by elephants built from mosquitoes
(c) or by a data-driven machine.

That programs intended for the second or third implementation could be "inefficient" when regarded as sequential programs is here irrelevant. The important result would be that the same mathematical technique for the intellectual mastery of sequential programs can be taken over—hopefully lock, stock and barrel—for the intellectual mastery of those, as yet less familiar, designs. Finally, and this seems the most important promise, it introduces the possibility of concurrent execution in a non-operational manner.

E. W. Dijkstra, A synthesis emerging? In E. W. Dijkstra, *Selected Writings on Computing: A Personal Perspective*, (1982), 147–160.

From the past, terms as "sequential programming" and "parallel programming" are still with us, and we should try to get rid of them, for they are a great source of confusion. They date from the period that it was the purpose of our programs to instruct our machines: now it is the purpose of the machines to execute our programs. Whether the machine does so sequentially, one thing at a time, or with a considerable amount of concurrency, is a matter of implementation and should *not* be regarded as a property of the programming language. In the years behind us we have carried out this program of non-operational definition of semantics for a simple programming language that admits (trivially) a sequential implementation; our ultimate goal is a programming language that admits (highly?) concurrent implementations equally trivially. The experiments described in this report are a first step towards that goal.

27th and 31st July, 1975

It all started on Sunday 27th of July 1975, when Tony Hoare explained to me in the garden of Hotel Sepp in Marktoberdorf (Western Germany) upon my request the class-concept of SIMULA (including the so-called inner-concept); at least he explained his version of it. I had always stayed away from it as far as possible, in order to avoid contamination with the extremely operational point of view as practised by Dahl et al., and, after some time I could not even (under)stand their mechanistic descriptions anymore; they just made me shudder. In late 1974, Tony sent me a paper that looked better, but still made me shudder; I read it once, but, doubting whether I could endure the exposure, I consciously refused to study it at that moment. On Saturday 26th I decided that the moment to be courageous had come and asked Tony to explain to me what he was considering. He was a tolerant master, allowing me to change terminology, notation and a way of looking at it, things I had to do in order to make it all fit within my frame of mind. To begin with, I shall record how our discussions struck root in my mind. I don't know whether a real SIMULA fan will still recognize the class-concept; he may get the impression that I am writing about something totally different. My descriptions are definitely still more operational and mechanistic than I would like them to be; it is hard to get rid of old habits!

* *
*

Suppose that we consider a natural number, which can be introduced with the initial value zero, and can be decreased and increased by 1, provided it remains non-negative. A nondeterministic, never-ending program that may generate *any* history of a natural number is then

```
nn begin privar x; x vir int := 0;
         do true → x := x + 1
          ▯ x > 0 → x := x - 1
         od
   end
```

Suppose we want to write a main program operating on two natural numbers y and z, a main program that "commands" these values to be increased and decreased as it pleases. In that case we can associate with each of the two natural numbers y and z a nondeterministic program of the above type, be it that the nondeterminacy of each of these two program executions has to be resolved ("settled", if you prefer) in such a way that the two histories are in accordance with the "commands" in the main program. For this purpose we consider the following program. (Please remember that the chosen notations are not a proposal: they have been introduced only to make the discussion possible!)

```
nn gen begin privar x; x vir int : = 0;
             do ?inc → x := x + 1
              ▯ x > 0 cand ?dec → x := x - 1
             od
       end
```

main program:

```
begin privar y, z; y vir nn; z vir nn;
         .
         .
         .
         y.inc; ...; y.dec; ...; z.inc; ...; z.dec; ...
end
```

NOTES

1) We have written two programs. Eventually we shall have three sequential processes, two of type *nn*—one for y and one for z—and one of type "main program". The fact that the first one can be regarded as a kind of "template" I have indicated by writing **gen** (suggesting "generator") in front of its **begin**.

2) The main program is the only one to start with; upon the initialization y **vir** nn the second one is started—and remains idling in the repetitive construct—, upon the initialization z **vir** nn, the last one is introduced in an identical fashion. It is assumed—e.g because the "main program" is written after nn—that the main program is within the lexical scope of the identifier nn.

3) The two identifiers *inc* and *dec*—preceded in the text of nn by a question mark—are subordinate to the type nn; i.e. if y is declared and initialized as a variable of type nn, the operations *inc* and *dec*—invoked by $y.inc$ and $y.dec$ respectively—are defined on it and can be implemented by suitably synchronizing and sequencing the execution of the y-program with that of the main program.

4) When in the main program $y.inc$ is commanded, this is regarded in the y-program as the guard *?inc* being true (once). Otherwise guards (or guard components) with the question mark are regarded as undefined. Only a true guard makes the guarded statement eligible for execution.

5) The block exit of the main program, to which the variables y and z are local, implies that all the "query-guards" are made false: when *?inc* and *?dec* are false for the y-program, the repetitive construct terminates and that local block exit is performed: the x local to the y-program may cease to exist. It is sound to view the implicit termination of the blocks associated with the variables y and z to be completed before the exit of the block to which they are local—the main program—is completed. (End of Notes.)

* *
*

In the preceding section we have assumed that the main program was somehow within the scope of nn. But one can ask what funny kind of identifier this is; it is the name of a program text, however, there are as many *nns* as the main program introduces natural numbers. The decent way to overcome this is to introduce a fourth program, a "natural number maker", say *peano*. Suppose that the purpose of *peano* is not only to provide—i.e. to create and to destroy—natural numbers, but also to print at the end of its life the maximum natural number value that has ever existed.

```
peano
begin privar totalmax; totalmax vir int := 0;
  do ?nn → gen begin privar x, localmax;
                 x vir int, localmax vir int := 0, 0;
               (//do ?inc → x := x + 1;
                          do localmax < x → localmax := x od
                 [] x > 0 cand ?dec → x := x − 1
                 od//);
                 do totalmax < localmax → totalmax := localmax od
               end
  od;
  print(totalmax)
end
```

main program

```
begin privar y, z; y vir peano.nn; z vir peano.nn;
        .
        .
        .
        y.inc; ...; y.dec; ...; z.inc; ...; z.dec
end
```

The idea was, that the program called *peano* is read in and executed, until it gets stuck at the repetitive construct with the (undefined) query *?nn*. With the knowledge of the identifier *peano* (and its subordinate *peano.nn*) the main program is read in and executed, and because *inc* is subordinate to *peano.nn*, it becomes subordinate to *y* by the initializing declaration *y* **vir** *peano.nn*.

NOTES

1) In the above it has not been indicated when *peano* will terminate and print the value of *totalmax*.

2) The generator describing the natural number exists of three parts:

its opening code;
(//its local code//)
; its closing code.

Access to the local variable *totalmax* of *peano* is permitted only in the opening code—here the facility is not used and in *nn* the "(//" could have been moved forward—and in the closing code. Different natural numbers may *inc* simultaneously, only their opening and closing codes are assumed to be performed in mutual exclusion.

3) If the main program is a purely sequential one, immediately after initialization *y.dec* will cause the main program to get stuck. If the main program consists of a number of concurrent ones, the one held up in *y.dec* may proceed after another process has performed *y.inc*. Our natural numbers would then provide an implementation for semaphores!

4) It is now possible to introduce, besides the *peano* given above, a *peanodash* that, for instance, omits the recording of maximum values. The main program could then begin with

begin privar y, z; y **vir** peano.nn; z **vir** peanodash.nn; ...

The importance of the explicitly named *maker* in the declaration/initialization lies in the fact that it allows us to provide alternative implementations for variables of the same (abstract) type. (End of Notes.)

The above records the highlights of Sunday's discussion as I remember them. Many of the points raised have been recorded for the sake of completeness: we may pursue them later, but most of them not in this report, as the discussion took another turn on the next Thursday.

* *
*

On Thursday, a couple of hours were wasted by considering how also in the local code instances of generated processes—natural numbers—could be granted mutually exclusive access to the local variables of their maker. Although we came up with a few proposals of reasonable consistency, Tony became suddenly disgusted, and I had to agree. The whole effort had been "to separate", and now we were re-introducing a tool for fine-grained interference! Our major result that day was the coding of a recursive data structure of type *sequence*. The coding was as follows (omitting the type of parameters and of function procedures). It is not exactly the version coded on that Thursday afternoon, but the differences are minor.

```
sequencemaker begin
  do ?sequence → gen begin
  (//do ?empty → result := true
       ▯ ?has(i) → result := false
       ▯ ?truncate → result := false
       ▯ ?back → result := nil
       ▯ ?remove(i) → skip
       ▯ ?insert(i) → begin privar first, rest; first vir nint := i;
           rest vir sequencemaker.sequence;
           do first ≠ nil cand ?empty → result := false
             ▯ first ≠ nil cand ?has(i) → if first = i →
               result := true ▯ first ≠ i → result := rest.has(i) fi
             ▯ first ≠ nil cand ?truncate → result := true;
               begin pricon absorbed;
                 absorbed vir bool := rest.truncate;
                 if absorbed → skip ▯ non absorbed → first := nil fi
               end
             ▯ first ≠ nil cand ?back → result := first; first := rest.back
             ▯ first ≠ nil cand ?remove(i) → if i ≠ first → rest.remove(i)
               ▯ i = first → first := rest.back fi
             ▯ first ≠ nil cand ?insert(i) → if i ≠ first → rest.insert(i)
               ▯ i = first → skip fi
           od end
     od//) end
od end
```

It is a recursive definition of a sequence of different integers. Let s be a variable of type sequence.

s.empty	is a boolean function, *true* if the sequence s is empty, otherwise false
s.has(i)	is a boolean function with an argument i of type integer; it is *true* if i occurs in the sequence, otherwise *false*
s.truncate	is an operator upon s, which also returns a boolean value; if s is nonempty, the last value is removed and the value *true* is returned; if s is empty, it remains so and the value *false* is returned
s.back	is an operator upon s, which returns a value of type *nint* (i.e. the integers, extended with the value *nil*); if s is nonempty, the first value is returned and removed from s; if s is empty, it remains so and the value *nil* is returned

s.remove(i)	is an operator upon s with an argument i of type integer; if i does not occur in s, s is left unchanged; otherwise the value i is removed from the sequence s without changing the order of the remaining elements in the sequence
s.insert(i)	is an operator upon s with an argument i of type integer; if i does occur in s, s is left unchanged, otherwise s is extended at the far end with the value i.

(The above is a set of rather crazy specifications: they grew in an alternation of simplifications—we started with a binary tree—in order to reduce the amount of writing we had to do, and complications, when we became more ambitious, and wanted to show what we could do.)

NOTE. I am aware of the lousiness of the notation of an operator upon s that returns a value. I apologize for this lack of good taste. (End of Note.)

The *sequencemaker* is very simple: it can only provide as many sequences as it is asked to provide; the storage requirements for a sequence are very simple, viz. a stack. (In our rejected example of the binary tree, although lifetimes are, in a fashion, nested, life is not so simple.) The *sequencemaker* has no local variables (like *peano*); accordingly, each sequence is simple: its opening and closing codes are empty. The outer repetitive construct describes the behaviour of the empty sequence: all its actions are simple with the exception of *?insert(i)*, as a result of which the sequence becomes nonempty. In an inner block, which describes the behaviour of a sequence that contains at least one element, two local variables are declared: the integer *first* for that one element, and the sequence *rest* for any remaining ones.

It is illuminating to follow the execution of the call *remove(i)*. Suppose that i does not occur in the sequence. Then we constantly have $i \neq \mathit{first}$, and the task of removing i is constantly delegated to the rest, until it is delegated to an empty rest, for which *remove(i)* reduces to a *skip*. If, however, the value i occurs in the sequence, it occurs in a nonempty sequence, and $i = \mathit{first}$ is discovered; the command then propagates in the form $\mathit{first} := \mathit{rest.back}$. The last nonempty sequence that performs $\mathit{first} := \mathit{rest.back}$ gets the value *nil* from its successor and establishes for itself $\mathit{first} = \mathit{nil}$. As a result, the repetitive construct in its inner block is terminated, an inner block exit is performed, prior to the completion of which all query-guards for its successor are set *false*, and its successor performs an exit from its outer block and ceases to exist.

It is also instructive to follow how, upon exit from block

begin privar s; s **vir** sequencemaker.sequence; ... **end**

at a moment that *s* may contain many elements, the sequence *s* disappears. All query-guards to *s* are set to *false*, which forces termination of the inner repetitive construct for *s*, which results in a block exit from its inner block (which first requires deletion of its *rest*); upon completion of this block exit, the query-guards still being *false*, termination of the outer repetitive construct and block exit from the outer block of *s* are forced. This is very beautiful: the hint to delete itself, given to the head of the sequence, propagates up to its end, reflects there, travels back, folding up the sequence in a nice stack-wise fashion, as, of course, it should. In its elegance— or should I say: completeness?—it had a great appeal to us.

*   *
*

It was at this stage, that I realized that the same program could be visualized as a long sequence—long enough, to be precise—of mosquitoes:

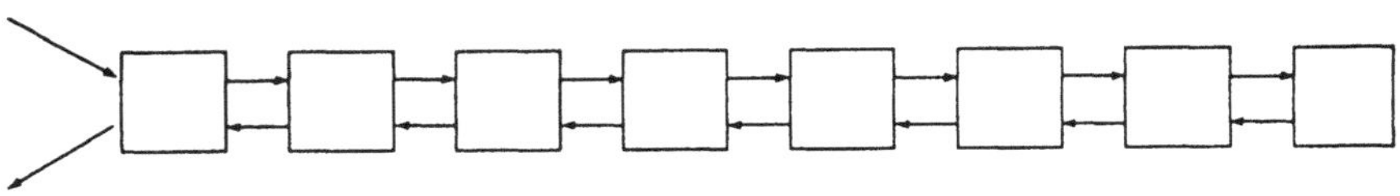

where each mosquito is essentially a copy of the text between (// and //), and each mosquito is the *rest* for its left-hand neighbour. Execution of the declaration *rest* **vir** *sequencemaker.sequence* can be interpreted as a command to one's right-hand neighbour to initialize its instruction counter to the beginning of the program. Each mosquito is ready to accept a next command from the left as soon as it has nothing more to do, i.e. its control has successfully returned to one of the sets of query-guards. Giving a command to the right lasts until the command has been accepted when no answer is required and until the answer has been returned when an answer is required.

It is instructive to follow the propagation of activity for the various commands.

?empty is immediately reflected.

?has(i) propagates up the sequence until *i* has been detected or the sequence has been exhausted, and from there the boolean value (*true* or *false*,

respectively) is reflected and travels to the left until it leaves the sequence at the front end. All the time the sequence is busy and cannot accept another command. The time it takes to return the answer *true* depends on the distance of i from the beginning of the sequence; the time it takes to return the answer *false* is the longest one, and depends on the actual length of the sequence (not on the number of mosquitoes available).

?truncate and *?back* propagate at practically full speed to the right; at each mosquito, there is a reflection one place back to absorb the answer. Note that *?truncate* (in the inner block) starts with **result** := *true* and *?back* starts with **result** := *first*—actions, which can be taken to be completed when the mosquito to the left has absorbed the value. This is done in order to allow the mosquito to the left to continue as quickly as possible.

?remove(i) propagates still more simply (until it becomes a *?back*).

?insert(i) propagates also quite simply, until the wave is either absorbed—because i = *first* is encountered—or the sequence is extended with one element. The fascinating observation is that any sequence of *?remove(i)*, *?insert(i)*, *?back*, and *?truncate* may enter the sequence at the left: they will propagate with roughly the same speed along the sequence; if the sequence is long, a great number of such commands will travel along the sequence to the right. It is guaranteed to be impossible that one command "overtakes" the other, and we have introduced the possibility of concurrency in implementation in an absolutely safe manner.

NOTE. Originally *?truncate* was coded differently. It did not return a boolean value, and was in the outer guarded command set

```
?truncate → skip
```

and in the inner guarded command set

```
first ≠ nil cand ?truncate →
  if rest.empty → first := nil
  [] non rest.empty → rest.truncate
  fi
```

As soon as we started to consider the implementation by a sequence of mosquitoes, however, we quickly changed the code, because the earlier version had awkward propagation properties: two steps forward, one step backward. The version returning the boolean was coded when we had not yet introduced the type *nint*; after we had done so, we could also have coded truncate with a parameter of type integer: in the outer guarded command set

?truncate(i) → **result** := nil

and in the inner guarded command set

first ≠ nil **cand** ?truncate(i) →
  result := i; first := rest.truncate(first)

The last part of this note is rather irrelevant. (End of Note.)

This was the stage at which we were when we left Marktoberdorf. As I wrote in my trip report EWD506 "A surprising discovery, the depth of which is—as far as I am concerned—still unfathomed.".

*　　　*
*

What does one do with "discoveries of unfathomed depth"? Well, I decided to let it sink in and not to think about it for a while—the fact that we had a genuine heatwave when I returned from Marktoberdorf helped to take that decision!. The discussion was only taken up again last Tuesday afternoon in the company of Martin Rem and the graduate student Poirters, when we tried to follow the remark, made in my trip report, that it would be nice to do away with von Neumann's instruction counter. (This morning I found a similar suggestion in "Recursive Machines and Computing Technology", by V.M. Gluskov, M.B. Ignatyev, V.A. Myasnikov, and V.A. Torgashev, IFIP 1974; this morning I received a copy of that article from Philip H. Enslow, who had drawn my attention to it.)

We had, of course, observed that the propagation properties of *has(i)* are very awkward. It can keep a whole sequence of mosquitoes occupied, all of them waiting for the boolean value to be returned. As long as this boolean value has not been returned to the left-most mosquito, no new command can be accepted by the first mosquito, and that is sad. The string of mosquitoes, as shown above, is very much different from the elephant structure that we have already encountered very often, viz. all mosquitoes in a ring.

Nice propagation properties would be displayed by a string of mosquitoes that send the result as soon as found to the right, instead of back to the left! Before we pursue that idea, however, I must describe how I implemented (recursive) function procedures in 1960—a way, which, I believe, is still the standard one.

Upon call of a function procedure the stack was extended with an "empty element", an as yet undefined anonymous intermediate result. On top of that the procedure's local variables would be allocated, and during the activation of the procedure body, that location—named **result**—would be treated as one of the local variables of the procedure. A call

$$\begin{array}{ll} ?\mathrm{has(i)} \rightarrow & \mathbf{if}\ \mathrm{i} = \mathrm{first} \rightarrow \mathbf{result} := \mathrm{true} \\ & [\!]\ \mathrm{i} \neq \mathrm{first} \rightarrow \mathbf{result} := \mathrm{rest.has(i)} \\ & \mathbf{fi} \end{array}$$

could result in 9 times the second alternative and once the first, so that the answer is found at a moment of dynamic depth of nesting equal to 10. In the implementation technique described, the boolean result is then handed down the stack in ten successive steps: the anonymous result at level $n + 1$ becomes at procedure return the anonymous result at level n, which is assigned to the anonymous result of level n, etc.: a sequence of alternating assignments and procedure returns. Under the assumption that assignment is not an expensive operation, this implementation technique can be defended very well.

But it is an implementation choice! When implementing

result := rest.has(i)

no one forces us to manipulate the value of *rest.has(i)* as an intermediate result that subsequently can be assigned! An alternative interface with the function procedure would have been to give it an additional implicit parameter, viz. the destination of the result—e.g. in a sufficiently global terminology, such as distance from stack bottom. In that case the implementation of

result := rest.has(i)

would consist of a recursive call on *has* in which the implicit destination parameter received would just be handed over to the next activation. When, at dynamic depth 10, the boolean value would become known, it would instantaneously be placed at its final destination, after which the stack could collapse. In the case of a fixed number of mosquitoes, always present, needed or not—that is the simplification I am thinking about now—there is not much stack collapse, and the configuration that now suggests itself is the following

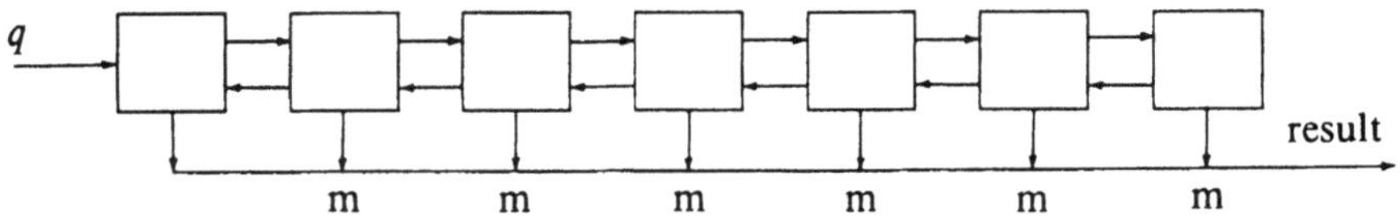

The mosquitoes still have the same mutual interconnection pattern, but I assume that each request for a value that enters the network at the left at the question mark is accompanied by "a destination" for the result. The reason that I have added the line at the bottom is the following. A sequence is a very simple arrangement, and in that case also the "external result", as soon as known, could be handed to the right-hand neighbour for further transmission. If, however, we consider the tree that would correspond to a variable of the type "binary tree", the result would then finally arrive in one of the many leaves. If we associate a real copper wire with each connection between two mosquitoes, and we wish the result to appear at a single point, then we must introduce some connecting network so that the various paths of the results can merge. Hence the additional line. The points marked m are binary merge points. We have arranged them linearly, we could have arranged them logarithmically, logically—and perhaps even physically—we can think of them as "multi-entry merges".

I am not now designing in any detail the appropriate mechanism for collecting the external result as soon as it has been formed somewhere in the network. My point is that there are many techniques possible, which all can be viewed as different implementation techniques for the same (recursive) program. Their only difference is in "propagation characteristics". The reason that I draw attention to the difference in implementation technique for the sequential machine (without and with implicit destination parameter) is the following. In the case of the linear arrangement of mosquitoes, each mosquito only being able to send to its right-hand neighbour when its right hand neighbour is ready to accept, we have a pipeline that, by the nature of its construction, produces results in the order in which they have been requested. This, in general, seems too severe a restriction, and for that purpose each request is accompanied by a "destination" that as a kind of tag accompanies the corresponding result when finally produced. Obviously, the environment driving the network must be such that never two requests with the same destination could reside simultaneously in the network.

* *

*

True to our principle that about everything sensible that can be said about computing can be illustrated with Euclid's Algorithm, we looked at good old Euclid's Algorithm with our new eyes. We also took a fairly recent version that computes the greatest common divisor of three positive numbers. It is

```
x, y, z := X, Y, Z;
  do x > y → x := x − y
  ▯ y > z → y := y − z
  ▯ z > x → z := z − x
  od
```

with the obvious invariant relation

gcd(x, y, z) = gcd(X, Y, Z) **and** x > 0 **and** y > 0 **and** z > 0

Our next version was semantically equivalent, but written down a little bit differently, in an effort to represent that in each repetition we were really operating on a triple x, y, z. That is, we regarded the above program as an abbreviation of

```
x, y, z := X, Y, Z;
  do x > y → x, y, z := x − y, y, z
  ▯ y > z → x, y, z := x, y − z, z
  ▯ z > x → x, y, z := x, y, z − x
  od
```

We then looked at it and said, why only change one value? This, indeed, is not necessary, and we arrived at the following similar, but mathematically different, program:

```
x, y, z := X, Y, Z;                                          (program 3)
do non x = y = z → x, y, z := f(x, y), f(y, z), f(z, x) od
```

with

```
f(u, v): if u > v → result := u − v
         ▯ u ≤ v → result := u
         fi
```

or, if we want to go one step further for the sake of argument, with

```
f(u, v): if u > v → result := dif(u, v)
         ▯ u ≤ v → result := u
         fi
```

and

dif(u, v): **result** := u − v

How do we implement this? We can look at program 3 with our traditional sequential eyes, which means that at each repetition the function f is invoked three times, each next invocation only taking place when the former one has returned its answer. We can also think of three different f-networks, which can be activated simultaneously. We can also think of a *single* f-network that is activated three times in succession, but where the comparison of the next pair of arguments can coincide in time with forming the difference of the preceding pair. To be quite honest, we should rewrite program 3 in the form

```
x, y, z := X, Y, Z;                                              (program 4)
do non x = y = z → tx, ty, tz := f(x, y), f(y, z), f(z, x);
                   x, y, z := tx, ty, tz
od
```

The reason is simple: we want to make quite clear that always the old values of x, y, z are sent as arguments to the f-network, and we want to code our cycle without making any assumptions about the information capacity of the f-network. The above program works also if we have an f-network without pipelining capacity.

*　　　*
*

I was considering a mosquito that would have six local variables, x, y, z, tx, ty, and tz; it would first "open" tx, ty, and tz, i.e. make them ready to receive the properly tagged results, then send the argument pairs in any order to either one or three f-networks, and finally, as a merge node, wait until all three values had been received. When I showed this to C. S. Scholten, he pointed out to me that the same result could be obtained by two, more sequential mosquitoes: one only storing the x, y, z values, and another storing the tx, ty, tz values, waiting for the three values to be delivered by the f-network. This is right.

Some remarks, however, are in order. I can now see networks of mosquitoes, implementing algorithms that I can also interpret sequentially and for which, therefore, all the known mathematical techniques should be applicable. Each mosquito represents a nondeterministic program that will be activated by its "query-guards" when it is ready to be so addressed and is so addressed, and where the act of addressing in the addressing mosquito is only completed by the time that the mosquito addressed has honoured the request. We should realize, however, that these synchronization rules are more for safety than for "scheduling", because dynamically such networks may have awkward macroscopic properties when overloaded. Take the long string of mosquitoes that, together, form a bounded buffer, each of them alternatingly waiting for a value from the left and then trying to transmit this value to the right. If this is to be a transmission line, it has the maximum throughput when, with n mosquitoes, it contains $n/2$ values. Its capacity, however, is n. If we allow its contents to grow—because new values are pumped in at the left while no values are taken out at the right—it gets stuck: taking out values from the sequence filled to the brim empties the buffer, but this effect only propagates slowly to the left and the danger of awkward macroscopic oscillations seems not excluded.

The next remark is that I have now considered elephants built from mosquitoes, but the design becomes very similar to that of a program for a data-driven machine. The programs I have seen for data-driven machines were always pictorial ones—and I don't like pictures with arrows, because they tend to become very confusing—and their semantics were always given in an operational fashion. Both characteristics point to the initial stage of unavoidable immaturity. I now see a handle for separating the semantics from the (multi-dimensional, I am tempted to add) computational histories envisaged. In a sense we don't need to envisage them anymore, and the whole question of parallelism and concurrency has been pushed a little bit more into the domain where it belongs: implementation. This is exciting.

* *
*

A sobering remark is not misplaced either, and that is that we have already considered highly concurrent engines—e.g. the hyperfast Fourier transform via the perfect shuffle—that seem to fall as yet outside the scope of constructs considered here. And so does apparently the on-the-fly garbage collection. We can only conclude that there remains enough work to be done!

PS. For other reasons forced to go to town, I combine that trip with a visit to the Eindhoven Xerox branch. The time to reread my manuscript for typing errors is lacking and I apologize for their higher density.

15

COMMUNICATING SEQUENTIAL PROCESSES

C. A. R. HOARE

(1978)

This paper suggests that input and output are basic primitives of programming and that parallel composition of communicating sequential processes is a fundamental program structuring method. When combined with a development of Dijkstra's guarded command, these concepts are surprisingly versatile. Their use is illustrated by sample solutions of a variety of familiar programming exercises.

1 Introduction

Among the primitive concepts of computer programming, and of the high-level languages in which programs are expressed, the action of assignment is familiar and well understood. In fact, any change of the internal state of a machine executing a program can be modelled as an assignment of a new value to some variable part of that machine. However, the operations of input and output, which affect the external environment of a machine, are not nearly so well understood. They are often added to a programming language only as an afterthought.

Among the structuring methods for computer programs, three basic constructs have received widespread recognition and use: A repetitive construct (e.g. the **while** loop), an alternative construct (e.g. the conditional **if**. . .**then**. . .**else**), and normal sequential program composition (often denoted by a semicolon). Less agreement has been reached about the design of other important program structures, and many suggestions have

C. A. R. Hoare, Communicating sequential processes. *Communications of the ACM 21*, 8 (August) 1978, 666–677.

been made: Subroutines (Fortran), procedures (Algol 60 (Naur 1960)), entries (PL/I), coroutines (UNIX (Thompson 1976)), classes (SIMULA 67 (Dahl et al. 1967)), processes and monitors (Concurrent Pascal (Brinch Hansen 1975)), clusters (CLU (Liskov 1974)), forms (ALPHARD (Wulf et al. 1976)), actors (Atkinson and Hewitt 1976).

The traditional stored-program digital computer has been designed primarily for deterministic execution of a single sequential program. Where the desire for greater speed has led to the introduction of parallelism, every attempt has been made to disguise this fact from the programmer, either by hardware itself (as in the multiple function units of CDC 6600) or by the software (as in an I/O control package, or a multiprogrammed operating system). However, developments of processor technology suggest that a multiprocessor machine, constructed from a number of similar self-contained processors (each with its own store), may become more powerful, capacious, reliable, and economical than a machine which is disguised as a monoprocessor.

In order to use such a machine effectively on a single task, the component processors must be able to communicate and to synchronize with each other. Many methods of achieving this have been proposed. A widely adopted method of communication is by inspection and updating of a common store (as in Algol 68 (van Wijngaarden 1969), PL/I, and many machine codes). However, this can create severe problems in the construction of correct programs and it may lead to expense (e.g. crossbar switches) and unreliability (e.g. glitches) in some technologies of hardware implementation. A greater variety of methods has been proposed for synchronization: semaphores (Dijkstra 1968), events (PL/I), conditional critical regions (Hoare 1972a), monitors and queues (Concurrent Pascal (Brinch Hansen 1975)), and path expressions (Campbell 1974). Most of these are demonstrably adequate for their purpose, but there is no widely recognized criterion for choosing between them.

This paper makes an ambitious attempt to find a single simple solution to all these problems. The essential proposals are:

(1) Dijkstra's guarded commands (1975a) are adopted (with a slight change of notation) as sequential control structures, and as the sole means of introducing and controlling nondeterminism.

(2) A parallel command, based on Dijkstra's *parbegin* (1968), specifies concurrent execution of its constituent sequential commands (processes). All the processes start simultaneously, and the parallel command ends only when

they are all finished. They may not communicate with each other by updating global variables.
(3) Simple forms of input and output command are introduced. They are used for communication between concurrent processes.
(4) Such communication occurs when one process names another as destination for output *and* the second process names the first as source for input. In this case, the value to be output is copied from the first process to the second. There is *no* automatic buffering: In general, an input or output command is delayed until the other process is ready with the corresponding output or input. Such delay is invisible to the delayed process.
(5) Input commands may appear in guards. A guarded command with an input guard is selected for execution only if and when the source named in the input command is ready to execute the corresponding output command. If several input guards of a set of alternatives have ready destinations, only one is selected and the others have *no* effect; but the choice between them is arbitrary. In an efficient implementation, an output command which has been ready for a long time should be favoured; but the definition of a language cannot specify this since the relative speed of execution of the processes is undefined.
(6) A repetitive command may have input guards. If all the sources named by them have terminated, then the repetitive command also terminates.
(7) A simple pattern-matching feature, similar to that of Reynolds (1965), is used to discriminate the structure of an input message, and to access its components in a secure fashion. This feature is used to inhibit input of messages that do not match the specified pattern.

The programs expressed in the proposed language are intended to be implementable both by a conventional machine with a single main store, and by a fixed network of processors connected by input/output channels (although very different optimizations are appropriate in the different cases). It is consequently a rather static language: The text of a program determines a fixed upper bound on the number of processes operating concurrently; there is no recursion and no facility for process-valued variables. In other respects also, the language has been stripped to the barest minimum necessary for explanation of its more novel features.

The concept of a communicating sequential process is shown in Sections 3–5 to provide a method of expressing solutions to many simple programming exercises which have previously been employed to illustrate the use of various proposed programming-language features. This suggests that the process may constitute a synthesis of a number of familar and new programming ideas. The reader is invited to skip the examples which do not interest him.

However, this paper also ignores many serious problems. The most serious is that it fails to suggest any proof method to assist in the development and verification of correct programs. Secondly, it pays no attention to the problems of efficient implementation, which may be particularly serious on a traditional sequential computer. It is probable that a solution to these problems will require (1) imposition of restrictions in the use of the proposed features; (2) re-introduction of distinctive notations for the most common and useful special cases; (3) development of automatic optimization techniques; and (4) the design of appropriate hardware.

Thus the concepts and notations introduced in this paper (although described in the next section in the form of a programming language fragment) should not be regarded as suitable for use as a programming language, either for abstract or for concrete programming. They are at best only a partial solution to the problems tackled. Further discussion of these and other points will be found in Section 7.

2 Concepts and notations

The style of the following description is borrowed from Algol 60 (Naur 1960). Types, declarations, and expressions have not been treated; in the examples, a Pascal-like notation (Wirth 1971) has usually been adopted. The curly braces { } have been introduced into BNF to denote none or more repetitions of the enclosed material. (Sentences in parentheses refer to an implementation: they are not strictly part of a language definition.)

<command> ::= <simple command> | <structured command>
<simple command> ::= <null command> | <assignment command>
    | <input command> | <output command>
<structured command> ::= <alternative command>
    | <repetitive command> | <parallel command>
<null command> ::= skip
<command list> ::= {<declaration>;| <command>;}<command>

A command specifies the behaviour of a device executing the command. It may succeed or fail. Execution of a simple command, if successful, may have an effect on the internal state of the executing device (in the case of assignment), or on its external environment (in the case of output), or on both (in the case of input). Execution of a structured command involves execution of some or all of its constituent commands, and if any of these fail, so does the structured command. (In this case, whenever possible, an implementation should provide some kind of comprehensible error diagnostic message.)

A null command has no effect and never fails.

A command list specifies sequential execution of its constituent commands in the order written. Each declaration introduces a fresh variable with a scope which extends from its declaration to the end of the command list.

2.1 Parallel commands

<parallel command> ::= [<process>{|| <process>}]
<process> ::= <process label><command list>
<process label> ::= <empty> | <identifier> ::
    | <identifier>(<label subscript>{,<label subscript>}) ::
<label subscript> ::= <integer constant> | <range>
<integer constant> ::= <numeral> | <bound variable>
<bound variable> ::= <identifier>
<range> ::= <bound variable>:<lower bound>..<upper bound>
<lower bound> ::= <integer constant>
<upper bound> ::= <integer constant>

Each process of a parallel command must be *disjoint* from every other process of the command, in the sense that it does not mention any variable which occurs as a target variable (see Sections 2.2 and 2.3) in any other process.

A process label without subscripts, or one whose label subscripts are all integer constants, serves as a name for the command list to which it is prefixed; its scope extends over the whole of the parallel command. A process whose label subscripts include one or more ranges stands for a series of processes, each with the same label and command list, except that each has a different combination of values substituted for the bound variables. These values range between the lower bound and the upper bound inclusively. For example, `X(i:1..n) :: CL` stands for

$\texttt{X(1) :: CL}_1 \| \texttt{X(2) :: CL}_2 \| \ldots \| \texttt{X(n) :: CL}_n$

where each $\texttt{CL}_j$ is formed from `CL` by replacing every occurrence of the bound variable `i` by the numeral `j`. After all such expansions, each process label in a parallel command must occur only once and the processes must be well formed and disjoint.

A parallel command specifies concurrent execution of its constituent processes. They all start simultaneously and the parallel command terminates successfully only if and when they have all successfully terminated. The relative speed with which they are executed is arbitrary.

Examples:

(1) `[cardreader?cardimage||lineprinter!lineimage]`

Performs the two constituent commands in parallel, and terminates only when both operations are complete. The time taken may be as low as the longer of the times taken by each constituent process, i.e. the sum of its computing, waiting, and transfer times.

(2) `[west :: DISASSEMBLE||X :: SQUASH||east :: ASSEMBLE]`

The three processes have the names `west`, `X`, and `east`. The capitalized words stand for command lists which will be defined in later examples.

(3) `[room :: ROOM||fork(i:0..4) :: FORK||phil(i:0..4) :: PHIL]`

There are eleven processes. The behaviour of `room` is specifed by the command list `ROOM`. The behaviour of the five processes `fork(0)`, `fork(1)`, `fork(2)`, `fork(3)`, `fork(4)`, is specifed by the command list `FORK`, within which the bound variable `i` indicates the identity of the particular fork. Similar remarks apply to the five processes `PHIL`.

2.2 Assignment commands

<assignment command> ::= <target variable> := <expression>
<expression> ::= <simple expression> | <structured expression>
<structured expression> ::= <constructor>(<expression list>)
<constructor> ::= <identifier> | <empty>
<expression list> ::= <empty> | <expression>{,<expression>}
<target variable> ::= <simple variable> | <structured target>
<structured target> ::= <constructor>(<target variable list>)
<target variable list> ::= <empty> | <target variable>
{,<target variable>}

An expression denotes a value which is computed by an executing device by application of its constituent operators to the specified operands. The value of an expression is undefined if any of these operations are undefined. The value denoted by a simple expression may be simple or structured. The value denoted by a structured expression is structured; its constructor is that of the expression, and its components are the list of values denoted by the constituent expressions of the expression list.

An assignment command specifies evaluation of its expression, and assignment of the denoted value to the target variable. A simple target variable may have assigned to it a simple or a structured value. A structured target variable may have assigned to it a structured value, with the same constructor. The effect of such assignment is to assign to each constituent simpler variable of the structured target the value of the corresponding component of the structured value. Consequently, the value denoted by the target variable, if evaluated *after* a successful assignment, is the same as the value denoted by the expression, as evaluated *before* the assignment.

An assignment fails if the value of its expression is undefined, or if that value does not *match* the target variable, in the following sense: A *simple* target variable matches any value of its type. A *structured* target variable matches a structured value, provided that: (1) they have the same constructor, (2) the target variable list is the same length as the list of components of the value, (3) each target variable of the list matches the corresponding component of the value list. A structured value with no components is known as a "signal".

Examples:

(1)	`x := x + 1`	the value of `x` after the assignment is the same as the value of `x + 1` before.
(2)	`(x, y) := (y, x)`	exchanges the values of `x` and `y`.
(3)	`x:= cons(left, right)`	constructs a structured value and assigns it to `x`.
(4)	`cons(left, right) := x`	fails if `x` does not have the form `cons(y, z)`; but if it does, then `y` is assigned to left, and `z` is assigned to right.
(5)	`insert(n) := insert(2*x + 1)`	equivalent to `n:= 2*x + 1`.

(6)	`c:= P()`	assigns to `c` a "signal" with constructor `P`, and no components.
(7)	`P():= c`	fails if the value of `c` is not `P()`; otherwise has no effect.
(8)	`insert(n) := has(n)`	fails, due to mismatch.

Note: Successful execution of both (3) and (4) ensures the truth of the postcondition `x = cons(left, right)`; but (3) does so by changing `x` and (4) does so by changing left and right. Example (4) will fail if there is *no* value of left and right which satisfes the postcondition.

2.3 Input and output commands

<input command> ::= <source>?<target variable>
<output command> ::= <destination>!<expression>
<source> ::= <process name>
<destination> ::= <process name>
<process name> ::= <identifier> | <identifier>(<subscripts>)
<subscripts> ::= <integer expression>{,<integer expression>}

Input and output commands specify communication between two concurrently operating sequential processes. Such a process may be implemented in hardware as a special-purpose device (e.g. cardreader or line printer), or its behaviour may be specified by one of the constituent processes of a parallel command. Communication occurs between two processes of a parallel command whenever (1) an input command in one process specifies as its source the process name of the other process; (2) an output command in the other process specifies as its destination the process name of the first process; and (3) the target variable of the input command matches the value denoted by the expression of the output command. On these conditions, the input and output commands are said to *correspond.* Commands which correspond are executed simultaneously, and their combined effect is to assign the value of the expression of the output command to the target variable of the input command.

An input command fails if its source is terminated. An output command fails if its destination is terminated or if its expression is undefined.

(The requirement of synchronization of input and output commands means that an implementation will have to delay whichever of the two commands happens to be ready first. The delay is ended when the corresponding command in the other process is also ready, or when the other process terminates. In the latter case the first command fails. It is also possible that the delay will never be ended, for example, if a group of processes are attempting communication but none of their input and output commands correspond with each other. This form of failure is known as a deadlock.)

Examples:

(1) `cardreader?cardimage` — from cardreader, read a card and assign its value (an array of characters) to the variable cardimage.

(2) `lineprinter!lineimage` — to lineprinter, send the value of lineimage for printing.

(3) `X?(x,y)` — from process named `X`, input a pair of values and assign them to `x` and `y`.

(4) `DIV!(3*a + b, 13)` — to process `DIV`, output the two specifed values.

Note: If a process named `DIV` issues command (3), and a process named `X` issues command (4), these are executed simultaneously, and have the same effect as the assignment: `(x, y):= (3*a + b, 13)` (≡ `x:= 3*a + b; y:= 13`).

(5) `console(i)?c` — from the `i`th element of an array of consoles, input a value and assign it to `c`.

(6) `console(j - 1)!“A”` — to the `(j - 1)`th console, output character `‘‘A’’`.

(7) `X(i)?V()` — from the `i`th of an array of processes `X`, input a signal `V()`; refuse to input any other signal.

(8) `sem!P()` — to sem output a signal `P()`.

2.4 Alternative and repetitive commands

<repetitive command> ::= * <alternative command>
<alternative command> ::= [<guarded command>
  {▯<guarded command>}]
<guarded command> ::= <guard>→<command list>
  |(<range>{,<range>}) <guard>→<command list>
<guard> ::= <guard list> | <guard list>;<input command>
  | <input command>
<guard list> ::= <guard element> {;<guard element>}
<guard element> ::= <boolean expression> | <declaration>

A guarded command with one or more ranges stands for a series of guarded commands, each with the same guard and command list, except that each has a different combination of values substituted for the bound variables. The values range between the lower bound and upper bound inclusive. For example, `(i:1..n)G → CL` stands for

$G_1 \rightarrow CL_1 \,\square\, G_2 \rightarrow CL_2 \,\square \ldots \square\, G_n \rightarrow CL_n \,\square$

where each $G_j \rightarrow CL_j$ is formed from `G → CL` by replacing every occurrence of the bound variable `i` by the numeral `j`.

A guarded command is executed only if and when the execution of its guard does not fail. First its guard is executed and then its command list. A guard is executed by execution of its constituent elements from left to right. A Boolean expression is evaluated: If it denotes false, the guard fails, but an expression that denotes true has no effect. A declaration introduces a fresh variable with a scope that extends from the declaration to the end of the guarded command. An input command at the end of a guard is executed only if and when a corresponding output command is executed. (An implementation may test whether a guard fails simply by trying to execute it, and discontinuing execution if and when it fails. This is valid because such a discontinued execution has no effect on the state of the executing device.)

An alternative command specifies execution of exactly one of its constituent guarded commands. Consequently, if all guards fail, the alternative command fails. Otherwise an arbitrary one with successfully executable guard is selected and executed. (An implementation should take advantage of its freedom of selection to ensure efficient execution and good response. For example, when input commands appear as guards, the command which corresponds to the earliest ready and matching output command should in general be preferred; and certainly, no executable and ready output command should be passed over unreasonably often.)

A repetitive command specifies as many iterations as possible of its constituent alternative command. Consequently, when all guards fail, the repetitive command terminates with no effect. Otherwise, the alternative command is executed once and then the whole repetitive command is executed again. (Consider a repetitive command when all its true guard lists end in an input guard. Such a command may have to be delayed until either (1) an output command corresponding to one of the input guards becomes ready, or (2) all the sources named by the input guards have terminated. In case (2), the repetitive command terminates. If neither event ever occurs, the process fails (in deadlock).)

Examples:

(1) `[x ≥ y → m:= x □ y ≥ x → m:= y]`

If x ≥ y, assign x to m; if y ≥ x assign y to m; if both x ≥ y and y ≥ x, either assignment can be executed.

(2) `i:=0;*[i < size; content(i) ≠ n → i:= i + 1]`

The repetitive command scans the elements `content(i)`, for i = 0, 1, ..., until either `i ≥ size`, or a value equal to `n` is found.

(3) `*[c: character; west?c → east!c]`

This reads all the characters output by west, and outputs them one by one to east. The repetition terminates when the process west terminates.

(4)
```
*[(i:1..10)continue(i); console(i)?c → X!(i, c);
console(i)!ack(); continue(i):= (c ≠ sign off)]
```

This command inputs repeatedly from any of ten consoles, provided that the corresponding element of the Boolean array continue is true. The bound variable i identifies the originating console. Its value, together with the character just input, is output to X, and an acknowledgment signal is sent back to the originating console. If the character indicated `sign off`, `continue(i)` is set false, to prevent further input from that console. The repetitive command terminates when all ten elements of continue are false. (An implementation should ensure that no console which is ready to provide input will be ignored unreasonably often.)

(5)
```
*[n:integer; X?insert(n) → INSERT
□n:integer; X?has(n) → SEARCH; X!(i<size)
]
```

(Here, and elsewhere, capitalized words INSERT and SEARCH stand as abbreviations for program text defined separately.)

On each iteration this command accepts from X *either* (a) a request to `insert(n)`, (followed by INSERT) *or* (b) a question `has(n)`, to which it outputs an answer back to X. The choice between (a) and (b) is made by the next output command in X. The repetitive command terminates when X does. If X sends a non-matching message, deadlock will result.

(6)
```
*[X?V() → val:= val + 1
□val > 0; Y?P() → val:= val - 1
]
```

On each iteration, accept *either* a V() signal from X and increment val, *or* a P() signal from Y, and decrement val. But the second alternative cannot be selected unless val is positive (after which val will remain invariantly nonnegative). (When val > 0, the choice depends on the relative speeds of X and Y, and is not determined.) The repetitive command will terminate when both X and Y are terminated, or when X is terminated and val ≤ 0.

3 Coroutines

In parallel programming coroutines appear as a more fundamental program structure than subroutines, which can be regarded as a special case (treated in the next section).

3.1 Copy

Problem: Write a process X to copy characters output by process west to process east.
Solution:

```
X::  *[c:character; west?c → east!c]
```

Notes: (1) When west terminates, the input `west?c` will fail, causing termination of the repetitive command, and of process X. Any subsequent input command from east will fail. (2) Process X acts as a single-character buffer between west and east. It permits west to work on production of the next character, before east is ready to input the previous one.

3.2 Squash

Problem: Adapt the previous program to replace every pair of consecutive asterisks ** by an upward arrow ↑. Assume that the final character input is not an asterisk.
Solution:

```
X::  *[c:character; west?c →
  [c ≠ asterisk → east!c
  □c = asterisk → west?c;
       [c ≠ asterisk → east!asterisk; east!c
       □c = asterisk → east!upward arrow
  ]] ]
```

Notes: (1) Since west does not end with asterisk, the second `west?c` will not fail. (2) As an exercise, adapt this process to deal sensibly with input which ends with an odd number of asterisks.

3.3 Disassemble

Problem: To read cards from a cardfile and output to process X the stream of characters they contain. An extra space should be inserted at the end of each card.
Solution:

```
*[cardimage:(1..80)character; cardfile?cardimage →
    i:integer; i:= 1;
    *[i≤80 → X!cardimage(i); i:= i + 1]
    X!space
]
```

Notes: (1) `(1..80)character` declares an array of 80 characters, with subscripts ranging between 1 and 80. (2) The repetitive command terminates when the cardfile process terminates.

3.4 Assemble

Problem: To read a stream of characters from process X and print them in lines of 125 characters on a lineprinter. The last line should be completed with spaces if necessary.
Solution:

```
lineimage:(1..125)character;
i:integer; i:=1;
*[c:character; X?c →
    lineimage(i):= c;
    [i≤124 → i:= i + 1
    □i = 125 → lineprinter!lineimage; i:= 1
]   ];
[i=1 → skip
□i>1 → *[i≤125 → lineimage(i):= space; i:= i + 1];
    lineprinter!lineimage
]
```

Note: When X terminates, so will the first repetitive command of this process. The last line will then be printed, if it has any characters.

3.5 Reformat

Problem: Read a sequence of cards of 80 characters each, and print the characters on a line printer at 125 characters per line. Every card should be

followed by an extra space, and last line should be completed with space if necessary.
Solution:

```
[west::DISASSEMBLE||X::COPY||east::ASSEMBLE]
```

Notes: (1) The capitalized names stand for program text defined in previous sections. (2) The parallel command is designed to terminate after the card file has terminated. (3) This elementary problem is difficult to solve elegantly without coroutines.

3.6 Conway's problem (1963)

Problem: Adapt the above program to replace every pair of consecutive asterisks by an upward arrow.
Solution:

```
[west::DISASSEMBLE||X::SQUASH||east::ASSEMBLE]
```

4 Subroutines and data representations

A conventional nonrecursive subroutine can be readily implemented as a coroutine, provided that (1) its parameters are called "by value" and "by result", and (2) it is disjoint from its calling program. Like a Fortran subroutine, a coroutine may retain the values of local variables (*own* variables, in Algol terms) and it may use input commands to achieve the effect of "multiple entry points" in a safer way than PL/I. Thus a coroutine can be used like a SIMULA class instance as a concrete representation for abstract data.

A coroutine acting as a subroutine is a process operating concurrently with its user process in a parallel command: `[subr::SUBROUTINE||X::USER]`. The `SUBROUTINE` will contain (or consist of) a repetitive command:

```
*[X?(value params) → ...; X!(result params)]
```

where ... computes the results from the values input. The subroutine will terminate when its user does. The `USER` will call the subroutine by a pair of commands: `subr!(arguments); ...; subr?(results)`. Any commands between these two will be executed concurrently with the subroutine.

A multiple-entry subroutine, acting as a representation for data (Hoare 1972b), will also contain a repetitive command which represents each entry by an alternative input to a structured target with the entry name as constructor. For example,

```
*[X?entry1(value params) → ...
□X?entry2(value params) → ...
]
```

The calling process X will determine which of the alternatives is activated on each repetition. When X terminates, so does this repetitive command. A similar technique in the user program can achieve the effect of multiple exits.

A recursive subroutine can be simulated by an array of processes, one for each level of recursion. The user process is level zero. Each activation communicates its parameters and results with its predecessor and calls its successor if necessary:

```
[recsub(0)::USER||recsub(i:1..reclimit)::RECSUB]
```

The user will call the first element of

```
recsub: recsub(1)!(arguments); ...; recsub(1)?(results);
```

The imposition of a fixed upper bound on recursion depth is necessitated by the "static" design of the language.

This clumsy simulation of recursion would be even more clumsy for a mutually recursive algorithm. It would not be recommended for conventional programming; it may be more suitable for an array of microprocessors for which the fixed upper bound is also realistic.

In this section, we assume each subroutine is used only by a *single* user process (which may, of course, itself contain parallel commands).

4.1 Function: division with remainder

Problem: Construct a process to represent a function-type subroutine, which accepts a positive dividend and divisor, and returns their integer quotient and remainder. Efficiency is of no concern.
Solution:

```
[DIV::*[x,y:integer; X?(x,y) →
      quot,rem:integer;quot:= 0; rem:= x;
      *[rem ≥ y → rem:= rem − y; quot:= quot + 1];
      X!(quot,rem)
      ]
||X::USER
]
```

4.2 Recursion: factorial

Problem: Compute a factorial by the recursive method, to a given limit.
Solution:

```
[fac(i:1..limit)::
*[n:integer;fact(i − 1)?n →
  [n = 0 → fac(i − 1)!1
  □n > 0 → fac(i + 1)!n − 1;
    r:integer;fac(i + 1)?r; fac(i − 1)!(n ∗ r)
  ]]
||fac(0)::USER
]
```

Note: This unrealistic example introduces the technique of the "iterative array" which will be used to better effect in later examples.

4.3 Data representation: small set of integers (Hoare 1972b)

Problem: To represent a set of not more than 100 integers as a process, S, which accepts two kinds of instruction from its calling process X: (1) `S!insert(n)`, insert the integer `n` in the set, and (2) `S!has(n); ...; S?b`, `b` is set true if `n` is in the set, and false otherwise. The initial value of the set is empty.

Solution:

```
S::
content:(0..99)integer; size:integer; size:= 0;
*[n:integer; X?has(n) → SEARCH;X!(i < size)
□n:integer; X?insert(n) → SEARCH;
    [i < size → skip
    □i = size; size < 100 →
        content(size):= n; size:= size + 1
]   ]
```

where `SEARCH` is an abbreviation for:

```
i:integer; i:= 0;
*[i < size; content(i) ≠ n → i:= i + 1]
```

Notes: (1) The alternative command with guard `size` < `100` will fail if an attempt is made to insert more than 100 elements. (2) The activity of insertion will in general take place concurrently with the calling process. However, any subsequent instruction to S will be delayed until the previous insertion is complete.

4.4 Scanning a set

Problem: Extend the solution to 4.3 by providing a fast method for scanning all members of the set without changing the value of the set. The user program will contain a repetitive command of the form:

```
S!scan(); more:boolean; more:= true;
*[more;x:integer; S?next(x) → ... deal with x ...
□more; S?noneleft() → more:= false
]
```

where `S!scan()` sets the representation into a scanning mode. The repetitive command serves as a `for` statement, inputting the successive members of x from the set and inspecting them until finally the representation sends a signal that there are no members left. The body of the repetitive command is not permitted to communicate with S in any way.

Solution: Add a third guarded command to the outer repetitive command of S:

```
...□X?scan → i:integer; i:= 0;
             *[i < size → X!next(content(i)); i:= i + 1];
             X!noneleft()
```

4.5 Recursive data representation: small set of integers

Problem: Same as above, but an array of processes is to be used to achieve a high degree of parallelism. Each process should contain at most one number. When it contains no number, it should answer *false* to all inquiries about membership. On the first insertion, it changes to a second phase of behaviour, in which it deals with instructions from its predecessor, passing some of them on to its successor. The calling process will be named S(0). For efficiency, the set should be sorted, i.e. the ith process should contain the ith largest number.

Solution:

```
S(i:1..100)::
*[n:integer; S(i - 1)?has(n) → S(0)!false
□n:integer; S(i - 1)?insert(n) →
  *[m:integer; S(i - 1)?has(m) →
    [m ≤ n → S(0)!(m = n)
    □m > n → S(i + 1)!has(m)
    ]
  □m:integer; S(i - 1)?insert(m) →
    [m < n → S(i + 1)!insert(n); n:= m
    □m = n → skip
    □m > n → S(i + 1)!insert(m)
] ] ]
```

Notes: (1) The user process `S(0)` inquires whether `n` is a member by the commands `S(1)!has(n); ...; [(i:1...100)S(i)?b → skip]`. The appropriate process will respond to the input command by the output command in line 2 or line 5. This trick avoids passing the answer back "up the chain". (2) Many insertion operations can proceed in parallel, yet any subsequent `has` operation will be performed correctly. (3) All repetitive commands and all processes of the array will terminate after the user process `S(0)` terminates

4.6 Multiple exits: remove the least member

Exercise: Extend the above solution to respond to a command to yield the least member of the set and to remove it from the set. The user program will invoke the facility by a pair of commands:

```
S(1)!least(); [x:integer;S(1)?x → deal with x ...
              □S(1)?noneleft() → ...
              ]
```

or, if he wishes to scan and empty the set, he may write:

```
S(1)!least();more:boolean; more:= true;
  *[more; x:integer; S(1)?x → ... deal with x ...; S(1)!least()
  □more; S(1)?noneleft() → more:= false
  ]
```

Hint: Introduce a Boolean variable, `b`, initialized to true, and prefix this to all the guards of the inner loop. After responding to a `!least()` command from its predecessor, each process returns its contained value `n`, asks its successor for its least, and stores the response in `n`. But if the successor returns `noneleft()`, `b` is set false and the inner loop terminates. The process therefore returns to its initial state (solution due to David Gries).

5 Monitors and scheduling

This section shows how a monitor can be regarded as a single process which communicates with more than one user process. However, each user process must have a different name (e.g. producer, consumer) or a different subscript (e.g. `X(i)`) and each communication with a user must identify its source or destination uniquely.

Consequently, when a monitor is prepared to communicate with any of its user processes (i.e. whichever of them calls first) it will use a guarded command with a range. For example: `*[(i:1..100)X(i)?(value parameters) → ... ;X(i)!(results)]`. Here, the bound variable `i` is used to send the results back to the calling process. If the monitor is not prepared to accept input from some particular user (e.g. `X(j)`) on a given occasion, the input command may be preceded by a Boolean guard. For example, two successive inputs from the same process are inhibited by `j = 0; *[(i:1..100)i ≠ j; X(i)?(values) → ...; j:= i]`. Any attempted output from `X(j)` will be delayed until a subsequent iteration, after the output of some process `X(i)` has been accepted and dealt with.

Similarly, conditions can be used to delay acceptance of inputs which would violate scheduling constraints—postponing them until some later occasion when some other process has brought the monitor into a state in which the input can validly be accepted. This technique is similar to a conditional critical region (Hoare 1972a) and it obviates the need for special synchronizing variables such as events, queues, or conditions. However, the absence of these special facilities certainly makes it more difficult or less efficient to solve problems involving priorities—for example, the scheduling of head movement on a disk.

5.1 Bounded buffer

Problem: Construct a buffering process `X` to smooth variations in the speed of output of portions by a producer process and input by a consumer process. The consumer contains pairs of commands `X!more(); X?p`, and the producer contains commands of the form `X!p`. The buffer should contain up to ten portions.

Solution:

```
X::
buffer:(0..9)portion;
in,out:integer; in:= 0; out:= 0;
comment 0 ≤ out ≤ in ≤ out + 10;
  *[in < out + 10; producer?buffer(in mod 10) → in:= in + 1
  □out < in; consumer?more() → consumer!buffer(out mod 10);
      out:= out + 1
   ]
```

Notes: (1) When `out < in < out + 10`, the selection of the alternative in the repetitive command will depend on whether the producer produces before the consumer consumes, or vice versa. (2) When `out = in`, the buffer is empty and the second alternative cannot be selected even if the consumer is ready with its command `X!more()`. However, after the producer has produced its next portion, the consumer's request can be granted on the next iteration. (3) Similar remarks apply to the producer, when `in = out + 10`. (4) `X` is designed to terminate when `out = in` and the producer has terminated.

5.2 Integer semaphore

Problem: To implement an integer semaphore, `S`, shared among an array `X(i:1..100)` of client processes. Each process may increment the semaphore by `S!V()` or decrement it by `S!P()`, but the latter command must be delayed if the value of the semaphore is not positive.
Solution:

```
S::val:integer; val:= 0;
  *[(i:1..100)X(i)?V() → val:= val + 1
  □(i:1..100)val > 0; X(i)?P() → val:= val − 1
  ]
```

Notes: (1) In this process, no use is made of knowledge of the subscript `i` of the calling process. (2) The semaphore terminates only when all hundred processes of the process array `X` have terminated.

5.3 Dining philosophers (Problem due to E.W. Dijkstra)

Problem: Five philosophers spend their lives thinking and eating. The philosophers share a common dining room where there is a circular table surrounded by five chairs, each belonging to one philosopher. In the centre of the table there is a large bowl of spaghetti, and the table is laid with five forks (see Figure 1). On feeling hungry, a philosopher enters the dining room, sits in his own chair, and picks up the fork on the left of his place. Unfortunately, the spaghetti is so tangled that he needs to pick up and use the fork on his right as well. When he has finished, he puts down both forks, and leaves the room. The room should keep a count of the number of philosophers in it.

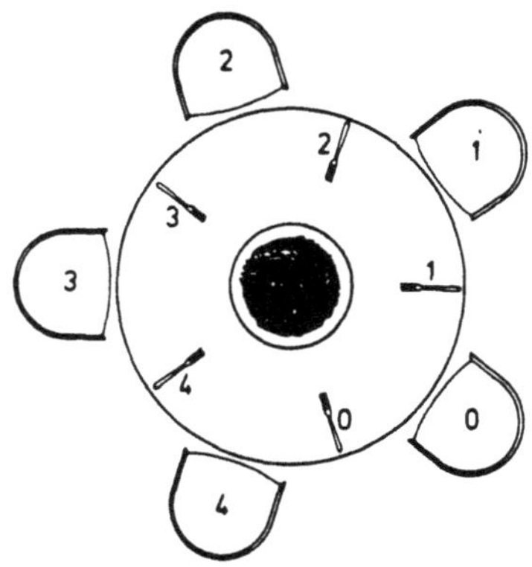

Fig. 1

Solution: The behaviour of the ith philosopher may be described as follows:

```
PHIL = *[... during ith lifetime ... →
        THINK;
        room!enter();
        fork(i)!pickup(); fork((i + 1) mod 5)!pickup();
        EAT;
        fork(i)!putdown(); fork((i + 1) mod 5)!putdown();
        room!exit()
        ]
```

The fate of the ith fork is to be picked up and put down by a philosopher sitting on either side of it:

```
FORK =
  *[phil(i)?pickup() → phil(i)?putdown ()
  □phil((i − 1) mod 5)?pickup() → phil((i − 1) mod 5)?putdown()
  ]
```

The story of the room may be simply told:

```
ROOM = occupancy:integer; occupancy:= 0;
  *[(i:0..4)phil(i)?enter() → occupancy:= occupancy + 1
  □(i:0..4)phil(i)?exit() → occupancy:= occupancy − 1
  ]
```

All these components operate in parallel:

```
[room::ROOM||fork(i:0..4)::FORK||phil(i:0..4)::PHIL]
```

Notes: (1) The solution given above does not prevent all five philosophers from entering the room, each picking up his left fork and starving to death because he cannot pick up his right fork. (2) Exercise: Adapt the above program to avert this sad possibility. Hint: Prevent more than four philosophers from entering the room. (Solution due to E.W. Dijkstra.)

6 Miscellaneous

This section contains further examples of the use of communicating sequential processes for the solution of some less familiar problems; a parallel version of the sieve of Eratosthenes, and the design of an iterative array. The proposed solutions are even more speculative than those of the previous sections, and in the second example, even the question of termination is ignored.

6.1 Prime numbers: the sieve of Eratosthenes (McIlroy 1968)

Problem: To print in ascending order all primes less than 10000. Use an array of processes, SIEVE, in which each process inputs a prime from its predecessor and prints it. The process then inputs an ascending stream of numbers from its predecessor and passes them on to its successor, suppressing any that are multiples of the original prime.

Solution

```
[SIEVE(i:1..100)::
  p,mp:integer;
  SIEVE(i - 1)?p;
  print!p;
  mp:= p; comment mp is a multiple of p;
  *[m:integer; SIEVE(i - 1)?m →
    *[m > mp → mp:= mp + p];
    [m = mp → skip
    □m < mp → SIEVE(i + 1)!m
] ]
||SIEVE(0)::print!2; n:integer; n:= 3;
      *[n < 10000 → SIEVE(1)!n; n:= n + 2]
||SIEVE(101)::*[n:integer;SIEVE(100)?n → print!n]
||print::*[(i:0..101) n:integer; SIEVE(i)?n → ...]
]
```

Note: (1) This beautiful solution was contributed by David Gries. (2) It is algorithmically similar to the program developed in (Dijkstra 1972, pp. 27–32).

6.2 An iterative array: matrix multiplication

Problem: A square matrix `A` of order 3 is given. Three streams are to be input, each stream representing a column of an array `IN`. Three streams are to be output, each representing a column of the product matrix `IN` × `A`. After an initial delay, the results are to be produced at the same rate as the input is consumed. Consequently, a high degree of parallelism is required. The solution should take the form shown in Figure 2. Each of the nine nonborder nodes inputs a vector component from the west and a partial sum from the north. Each node outputs the vector component to its east, and an updated partial sum to the south. The input data is produced by the west border nodes, and the desired results are consumed by south border nodes. The north border is a constant source of zeros and the east border is just a sink. No provision need be made for termination nor for changing the values of the array `A`.

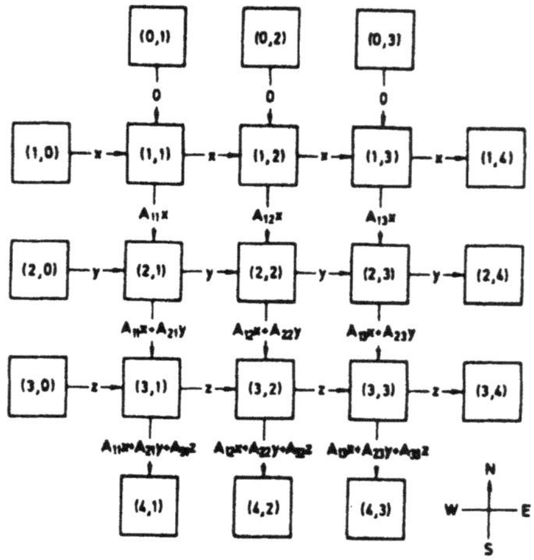

Fig. 2

Solution: There are twenty-one nodes, in five groups, comprising the central square and the four borders:

```
[M(i:1..3,0)::WEST
||M(0,j:1..3)::NORTH
||M(i:1..3,4)::EAST
||M(4,j:1..3)::SOUTH
||M(i:1..3,j:1..3)::CENTRE
]
```

The `WEST` and `SOUTH` borders are processes of the user program; the the remaining processes are:

```
NORTH = *[true → M(1,j)!0]
EAST = *[x:real; M(i,3)?x → skip]
CENTER = *[x:real; M(i,j − 1)?x →
    M(i,j + 1)!x; sum:real;
    M(i − 1,j)?sum; M(i + 1,j)!(A(i,j)*x + sum)
  ]
```

7 Discussion

A design for a programming language must necessarily involve a number of decisions which seem to be fairly arbitrary. The discussion of this section is intended to explain some of the underlying motivation and to mention some unresolved questions.

7.1 Notations

I have chosen single-character notations (e.g. !,?) to express the primitive concepts, rather than the more traditional boldface or underlined English words. As a result, the examples have an APL-like brevity, which some readers find distasteful. My excuse is that (in contrast to APL) there are only a very few primitive concepts and that it is standard practice of mathematics (and also good coding practice) to denote common primitive concepts by brief notations (e.g. $+,\times$). When read aloud, these are replaced by words (e.g. plus, times).

Some readers have suggested the use of assignment notation for input and output:

<target variable> := <source>
<destination> := <expression>

I find this suggestion misleading: it is better to regard input and output as distinct primitives, justifying distinct notations.

I have used the same pair of brackets (`[...]`) to bracket all program structures, instead of the more familiar variety of brackets (**if**..**fi**, **begin**..**end**, **case**..**esac**, etc.). In this I follow normal mathematical practice, but I must also confess to a distaste for the pronunciation of words like **fi**, **od**, or **esac**.

I am dissatisfed with the fact that my notation gives the same syntax for a structured expression and a subscripted variable. Perhaps tags should be distinguished from other identifers by a special symbol (say #).

I was tempted to introduce an abbreviation for combined declaration and input, e.g. `X?(n:integer)` for `n:integer; X?n`.

7.2 Explicit naming

My design insists that every input or output command must name its source or destination explicitly. This makes it inconvenient to write a library of processes which can be included in subsequent programs, independent of the process names used in that program. A partial solution to this problem is to allow one process (the *main* process) of a parallel command to have an empty label, and to allow the other processes in the command to use the empty process name as source or destination of input or output.

For construction of large programs, some more general technique will also be necessary. This should at least permit substitution of program text for names defined elsewhere—a technique which has been used informally throughout this paper. The Cobol COPY verb also permits a substitution for formal parameters within the copied text. But whatever facility is introduced, I would recommend the following principle: Every program, after assembly with its library routines, should be printable as a text expressed wholly in the language, and it is this printed text which should describe the execution of the program, independent of which parts were drawn from a library.

Since I did not intend to design a complete language, I have ignored the problem of libraries in order to concentrate on the essential semantic concepts of the program which is actually executed.

7.3 Port names

An alternative to explicit naming of source and destination would be to name a *port* through which communication is to take place. The port names would be local to the processes, and the manner in which pairs of ports are to be connected by channels could be declared in the head of a parallel command.

This is an attractive alternative which could be designed to introduce a useful degree of syntactically checkable redundancy. But it is semantically equivalent to the present proposal, provided that each port is connected to exactly one other port in another process. In this case each channel can be identifed with a tag, together with the name of the process at the other end. Since I wish to concentrate on semantics, I preferred in this paper to use the simplest and most direct notation, and to avoid raising questions about the possibility of connecting more than two ports by a single channel.

7.4 Automatic buffering

As an alternative to synchronization of input and output, it is often proposed that an outputting process should be allowed to proceed even when the inputting process is not yet ready to accept the output. An implementation would be expected automatically to interpose a chain of buffers to hold output messages that have not yet been input.

I have deliberately rejected this alternative, for two reasons: (1) It is less realistic to implement in multiple disjoint processors, and (2) when buffering is required on a particular channel, it can readily be specified using the given primitives. Of course, it could be argued equally well that synchronization can be specifed when required by using a pair of buffered input and output commands.

7.5 Unbounded process activation

The notation for an array of processes permits the same program text (like an Algol recursive procedure) to have many simultaneous "activations"; however, the exact number must be specifed in advance. In a conventional single-processor implementation, this can lead to inconvenience and wastefulness, similar to the fixed-length array of Fortran. It would therefore be attractive to allow a process array with no a priori bound on the number of elements; and to specify that the exact number of elements required for a particular execution of the program should be determined dynamically, like the maximum depth of recursion of an Algol procedure or the number of iterations of a repetitive command.

However, it is a good principle that every actual run of a program with unbounded arrays should be identical to the run of some program with all its arrays bounded in advance. Thus the unbounded program should be defined as the "limit" (in some sense) of a series of bounded programs with increasing bounds. I have chosen to concentrate on the semantics of the bounded case—which is necessary anyway and which is more realistic for implementation on multiple microprocessors.

7.6 Fairness

Consider the parallel command:

```
[X::Y!stop()||Y::continue:boolean;continue:= true;
    *[continue; X?stop() → continue := false
      □continue → n:= n + 1
      ]
]
```

If the implementation always prefers the second alternative in the repetitive command of Y, it is said to be *unfair*, because although the output command in X could have been executed on an infinite number of occasions, it is in fact always passed over.

The question arises: Should a programming language definition specify that an implementation must be *fair*? Here, I am fairly sure that the answer is NO. Otherwise, the implementation would be obliged to successfully complete the example program shown above, in spite of the fact that its nondeterminism is unbounded. I would therefore suggest that it is the programmer's responsibility to prove that his program terminates correctly—without relying on the assumption of fairness in the implementation. Thus the program shown above is incorrect, since its termination cannot be proved.

Nevertheless, I suggest that an efficient implementation should try to be reasonably fair and should ensure that an output command is not delayed unreasonably often after it first becomes executable. But a proof of correctness must not rely on this property of an efficient implementation. Consider the following analogy with a sequential program: An efficient implementation of an alternative command tends to favour the alternative which can be most efficiently executed, but the programmer must ensure that the logical correctness of his program does not depend on this property of his implementation.

This method of avoiding the problem of fairness does not apply to programs such as operating systems which are intended to run forever, because in this case termination proofs are not relevant. But I wonder whether it is ever advisable to write or to execute such programs. Even an operating system should be designed to bring itself to an orderly conclusion reasonably soon after it inputs a message instructing it to do so. Otherwise, the only way to stop it is to "crash" it.

7.7 Functional coroutines

It is interesting to compare the processes described here with those proposed in Kahn (1974); the differences are most striking. There, coroutines are strictly deterministic: No choice is given between alternative sources of input. The output commands are automatically buffered to any required degree. The output of one process can be automatically fanned out to any number of processes (including itself!) which can consume it at differing rates. Finally, the processes there are designed to run forever, whereas my proposed parallel command is normally intended to terminate. The design in Kahn (1974) is based on an elegant theory which permits proof of the properties of programs. These differences are not accidental—they seem to be natural consequences of the difference between the more abstract applicative (or functional) approach to programming and the more machine-oriented imperative (or procedural) approach, which is taken by communicating sequential processes.

7.8 Output guards

Since input commands may appear in guards, it seems more symmetric to permit output commands as well. This would allow an obvious and useful simplification in some of the example programs, for example, in the bounded buffer (5.1). Perhaps a more convincing reason would be to ensure that the externally visible effect and behaviour of every parallel command can be modelled by some sequential command. In order to model the parallel command

```
Z::[X!2||Y!3]
```

we need to be able to write the sequential alternative command:

```
Z::[X!2 → Y!3□Y!3 → X!2]
```

Note that this cannot be done by the command

```
Z::[true → X!2; Y!3□true → Y!3; X!2]
```

which can fail if the process Z happens to choose the first alternative, but the processes Y and X are synchronized with each other in such a way that Y must input from Z before X does, e.g.

```
 Y::Z?y; X!go()
||X::Y?go();Z?x
```

7.9 Restriction: Repetitive command with input guard

In proposing an unfamiliar programming-language feature, it seems wiser at first to specify a highly restrictive version rather than to propose extensions—especially when the language feature claims to be primitive. For example, it is clear that the multidimensional process array is not primitive, since it can readily be constructed in a language which permits only single-dimensional arrays. But I have a rather more serious misgiving about the repetitive command with input guards.

The automatic termination of a repetitive command on termination of the sources of all its input guards is an extremely powerful and convenient feature but it also involves some subtlety of specification to ensure that it is implementable; and it is certainly not primitive, since the required effect can be achieved (with considerable inconvenience) by explicit exchange of end() signals. For example, the subroutine DIV (4.1) could be rewritten:

```
  [DIV::continue:boolean; continue:= true;
  *[continue; X?end() → continue:= false
  □continue; x,y:integer; X?(x,y) → ...; X!(quot,rem)
||X::USER PROG; DIV!end()
  ]
```

Other examples would be even more inconvenient.

But the dangers of convenient facilities are notorious. For example the repetitive commands with input guards may tempt the programmer to write them without making adequate plans for their termination; and if it turns out that the automatic termination is unsatisfactory, reprogramming for explicit termination will involve severe changes, affecting even the interfaces between the processes.

8 Conclusion

This paper has suggested that input, output, and concurrency should be regarded as primitives of programming, which underlie many familiar and less familiar programming concepts. However, it would be unjustified to conclude that these primitives can wholly replace the other concepts in a programming language. Where a more elaborate construction (such as a procedure or monitor) is frequently useful, has properties which are more simply provable, and can be implemented more efficiently than the general case, there is a strong reason for including in a programming language a special notation for that construction. The fact that the construction can be defined in terms of simpler underlying primitives is a useful guarantee that its inclusion is logically consistent with the remainder of the language.

Acknowledgments. The research reported in this paper has been encouraged and supported by a Senior Fellowship of the Science Research Council of Great Britain. The technical inspiration was due to Edsger W. Dijkstra (1975b), and the paper has been improved in presentation and content by valuable and painstaking advice from D. Gries, D. Q. M. Fay, E. W. Dijkstra, N. Wirth, R. Milne, M. K. Harper, and its referees. The role of IFIP W.G.2.3 as a forum for presentation and discussion is acknowledged with pleasure and gratitude.

References

Atkinson, R., and Hewitt, C. 1976. Synchronisation in actor systems. Working Paper 83, M.I.T., Cambridge, Mass., Nov.

Brinch Hansen, P. 1975. The programming language Concurrent Pascal. *IEEE Trans. Software Eng. 1*, 2 (June), 199–207.

Campbell, R.H., and Habermann, A.N. 1974. The specification of process synchronisation by path expressions. *Lecture Notes in Computer Science 16*, Springer, 89–102.

Conway, M.E. 1963. Design of a separable transition-diagram compiler. *Comm. ACM 6*, 7 (July), 396–408.

Dahl, O.-J., et al. 1967. SIMULA 67, common base language. Norwegian Computing Centre, Forskningveien, Oslo.

Dijkstra, E.W. 1968. Co-operating sequential processes. In *Programming Languages*, F. Genuys, Ed., Academic Press, New York, 43–112.

Dijkstra, E.W. 1972. Notes on structured programming. In *Structured Programming*, Academic Press, New York, 1–82.

Dijkstra, E.W. 1975a. Guarded commands, nondeterminacy, and formal derivation of programs. *Comm. ACM 18*, 8 (Aug.), 453–457.

Dijkstra, E.W. 1975b. Verbal communication, Marktoberdorf, Aug.

Hoare, C.A.R. 1972a. Towards a theory of parallel programming. In *Operating Systems Techniques*, Academic Press, New York, 61–71.

Hoare, C.A.R. 1972b. Proof of correctness of data representations. *Acta Informatica 1*, 4, 271–281.

Kahn, G. 1974. The semantics of a simple language for parallel programming. In *Proc. IFIP Congress 74*, North Holland.

Liskov, B.H. 1974. A note on CLU. Computation Structures Group Memo. 112, M.I.T., Cambridge, Mass.

McIlroy, M.D. 1968. Coroutines. Bell Laboratories, Murray Hill, N.J.

Naur, P., Ed. 1960. Report on the algorithmic language ALGOL 60. *Comm. ACM 3*, 5 (May), 299–314.

Reynolds, J.C. 1965. COGENT. ANL-7022, Argonne Nat. Lab., Argonne, Ill.

Thompson, K. 1976. The UNIX command language. In *Structured Programming*, Infotech, Nicholson House, Maidenhead, England, 375–384.

van Wijngaarden, A., Ed. 1969. Report on the algorithmic language ALGOL 68. *Numer. Math. 14*, 79–218.

Wulf, W.A., London, R.L., and Shaw, M. 1976. Abstraction and verification in ALPHARD. Dept. of Comptr. Sci., Carnegie-Mellon U., Pittsburgh, Pa., June.

Wirth, N. 1971. The programming language PASCAL. *Acta Informatica 1*, 1, 35–63.

16

DISTRIBUTED PROCESSES: A CONCURRENT PROGRAMMING CONCEPT

PER BRINCH HANSEN

(1978)

A language concept for concurrent processes without common variables is introduced. These processes communicate and synchronize by means of procedure calls and guarded regions. This concept is proposed for real-time applications controlled by microcomputer networks with distributed storage. The paper gives several examples of distributed processes and shows that they include procedures, coroutines, classes, monitors, processes, semaphores, buffers, path expressions, and input/output as special cases.

1 INTRODUCTION

This paper introduces *distributed processes*—a new language concept for concurrent programming. It is proposed for real-time applications controlled by microcomputer networks with distributed storage. The paper gives several examples of distributed processes and shows that they include procedures, coroutines, classes, monitors, processes, semaphores, buffers, path expressions and input/output as special cases.

Real-time applications push computer and programming technology to its limits (and sometimes beyond). A real-time system is expected to monitor simultaneous activities with critical timing constraints continuously and reliably. The consequences of system failure can be serious.

P. Brinch Hansen, Distributed processes: A concurrent programming concept, *Communications of the ACM 21*, 11 (November 1978), 934–941.

Real-time programs must achieve the ultimate in simplicity, reliability, and efficiency. Otherwise one can neither understand them, depend on them, nor expect them to keep pace with their environments. To make real-time programs manageable it is essential to write them in an abstract programming language that hides irrelevant machine detail and makes extensive compilation checks possible. To make real-time programs efficient at the same time will probably require the design of computer architectures tailored to abstract languages (or even to particular applications).

From a language designer's point of view, real-time programs have these characteristics:

1. A real-time program interacts with an environment in which many things happen simultaneously at high speeds.

2. A real-time program must respond to a variety of *nondeterministic requests* from its environment. The program cannot predict the order in which these requests will be made but must respond to them within certain time limits. Otherwise, input data may be lost or output data may lose their significance.

3. A real-time program controls a computer with a fixed configuration of processors and peripherals and performs (in most cases) a fixed number of concurrent tasks in its environment.

4. A real-time program never terminates but continues to serve its environment as long as the computer works. (The occasional need to stop a real-time program, say at the end of an experiment, can be handled by ad hoc mechanisms, such as turning the machine off or loading another program into it.)

What is needed then for real-time applications is the ability to specify a fixed number of concurrent tasks that can respond to nondeterministic requests. The programming languages *Concurrent Pascal* and *Modula* come close to satisfying the requirements for abstract concurrent programming (Brinch Hansen 1975, 1977; Wirth 1977). Both of them are based on the *monitor* concept (Brinch Hansen 1973; Hoare 1974). Modula, however, is primarily oriented towards multiprogramming on a single processor. And a straightforward implementation of Concurrent Pascal requires a single processor or a multiprocessor with a common store. In their present form, these languages are not ideal for a microcomputer network with distributed storage only.

It may well be possible to modify Concurrent Pascal to satisfy the constraints of distributed storage. The ideas proposed here are more attractive, however, because they unify the monitor and process concepts and result in more elegant programs. The new language concepts for real-time applications have the following properties:

1. A real-time program consists of a fixed number of concurrent processes that are started simultaneously and exist forever. Each process can access its *own variables* only. There are no common variables.

2. A process can call *common procedures* defined within other processes. These procedures are executed when the other processes are waiting for some conditions to become true. This is the only form of process communication.

3. Processes are synchronized by means of nondeterministic statements called *guarded regions* (Hoare 1972; Brinch Hansen 1978).

These processes can be used as program modules in a multiprocessor system with common or distributed storage. To satisfy the real-time constraints each processor will be dedicated to a single process. When a processor is waiting for some condition to become true then its processor is also waiting until an external procedure call makes the condition true. This does not represent a waste of resources but rather a temporary lack of useful work for that processor. Parameter passing between processes can be implemented either by copying within a common store or by input/output between separate stores.

The problems of designing verification rules and computer architectures for distributed processes are currently being studied and are not discussed. This paper also ignores the serious problems of performance evaluation and fault tolerance.

2 LANGUAGE CONCEPTS

A concurrent program consists of a fixed number of sequential processes that are executed simultaneously. A *process* defines its own variables, some common procedures, and an initial statement

```
process name
own variables
common procedures
initial statement
```

A process may only access its *own variables.* There are no common variables. But a process may call *common procedures* defined either within itself or within other processes. A procedure call from one process to another is called an *external request.*

A process performs two kinds of *operations* then: the *initial statement* and the *external requests* made by other processes. These operations are executed one at a time by *interleaving.* A process begins by executing its initial statement. This continues until the statement either terminates or waits for a condition to become true. Then another operation is started (as the result of an external request). When this operation in turn terminates or waits the process will either begin yet another operation (requested by another process) or it will resume an earlier operation (as the result of a condition becoming true). This interleaving of the initial statement and the external requests continues forever. If the initial statement terminates, the process continues to exist and will still accept external statements.

So the interleaving is controlled by the program (and *not* by clock signals at the machine level). A process switches from one operation to another only when an operation terminates or waits for a condition within a guarded region (introduced later).

A process continues to execute operations except when all its current operations are delayed within guarded regions or when it makes a request to another process. In the first case, the process is idle until another process calls it. In the second case, the process is idle until the other process has completed the operation requested by it. Apart from this nothing is assumed about the order in which a process performs its operations.

A process guarantees only that it will perform *some* operations as long as there are any unfinished operations that can proceed. But only the programmer can ensure that *every* operation is performed within a finite time.

A *procedure* defines its input and output parameters, some local variables perhaps, and a statement that is executed when it is called.

proc name(input param#output param)
local variables
statement

A process P can call a procedure R defined within another process Q as follows:

call $Q.R$(expressions, variables)

Before the operation R is performed the expression values of the call are assigned to the *input* parameters. When the operation is finished the values of the *output* parameters are assigned to the variables of the call. Parameter passing between processes can therefore be implemented either by copying within a common store or by input/output between processors that have no common store.

In this paper processes can call procedures within one another without any restrictions. In a complete programming language additional notation would be added to limit the access rights of individual processes. It may also be necessary to eliminate recursion to simplify verification and implementation. But these are issues that will not concern us here.

Nondeterminism will be controlled by two kinds of statements called *guarded commands* and *guarded regions*. A guarded region can delay an operation, but a guarded command cannot.

A guarded command (Dijkstra 1975) enables a process to make an arbitrary choice among several statements by inspecting the current state of its variables. If none of the alternatives are possible in the current state the guarded command cannot be executed and will either be skipped or cause a program exception.

The guarded commands have the following syntax and meaning:

$$\textbf{if } B_1\text{: } S_1 \mid B_2\text{: } S_2 \mid \dots \textbf{ end}$$

$$\textbf{do } B_1\text{: } S_1 \mid B_2\text{: } S_2 \mid \dots \textbf{ end}$$

If statement: If some of the conditions B_1, B_2, ..., are true then select one of the true conditions B_i and execute the statement S_i that follows it; otherwise, stop the program.

(If the language includes a mechanism whereby one process can detect the failure of another process, it is reasonable to let an exception in one process stop that process only. But, if recovery from programming errors is not possible then it is more consistent to stop the whole program. This paper does not address this important issue.)

Do statement: While some of the conditions are true, select one of them arbitrarily and execute the corresponding statement.

A guarded region (Hoare 1972; Brinch Hansen 1978) enables a process to wait until the state of its variables makes it possible to make an arbitrary choice among several statements. If none of the alternatives are possible in the current state the process postpones the execution of the guarded region.

The guarded regions have the following syntax and meaning:

when B_1: S_1 | B_2: S_2 | ... **end**

cycle B_1: S_1 | B_2: S_2 | ... **end**

When statement: Wait until one of the conditions is true and execute the corresponding statement.

Cycle statement: Endless repetition of a when statement.

If several conditions are true within a guarded command or region it is unpredictable which one of the corresponding statements the machine will select. This uncertainty reflects the nondeterministic nature of real-time applications.

The *data types* used are either integers, booleans, or characters, or they are finite sets, sequences, and arrays with at most n elements of some type T:

int bool char **set**$[n]T$ **seq**$[n]T$ **array**$[n]T$

The following statement enumerates all the elements in a data structure:

for x **in** y: S **end**

For statement: For each element x in the set or array y execute the statement S. A for statement can access and change the values of array elements but can only read the values of set elements.

Finally, it should be mentioned that the empty statement is denoted *skip* and the use of semicolons is optional.

3 PROCESS COMMUNICATION

The following presents several examples of the use of these language concepts in concurrent programming. We will first consider communication between processes by means of procedure calls.

Example: Semaphore

A general semaphore initialized to zero can be implemented as a process *sem* that defines *wait* and *signal* operations.

```
process sem
s: int
proc wait when s > 0: s := s - 1 end
proc signal; s := s + 1
s := 0
```

The initial statement assigns the value zero to the semaphore and terminates. The process, however, continues to exist and can now be called by other processes

call sem.wait   **call** sem.signal

Example: Message buffer

A buffer process stores a sequence of characters transmitted between processes by means of *send* and *receive* operations.

```
process buffer
s: seq[n]char
proc send(c: char) when not s.full: s.put(c) end
proc rec(#v: char) when not s.empty: s.get(v) end
s := [ ]
```

The initial statement makes the buffer empty to begin with. The buffer operations are called as follows:

call buffer.send(x)   **call** buffer.rec(y)

The semaphore and buffer processes are similar to *monitors* (Brinch Hansen 1973; Hoare 1974): They define the representation of a shared data structure and the meaningful operations on it. These operations take place one at a time. After initialization, a monitor is idle between external calls.

Example: Character stream

A process inputs punched cards from a card reader and outputs them as a sequence of characters through a buffer process. The process deletes *spaces* at the end of each card and terminates it by a *newline* character.

```
process stream
b: array[80]char; n, i: int
do true:
  call cardreader.input(b)
  if b = blankline: skip |
    b ≠ blankline: i := 1; n := 80;
      do b[n] = space: n := n - 1 end
      do i ≤ n: call buffer.send(b[i]); i := i + 1 end
  end
  call buffer.send(newline)
end
```

This use of a process is similar to the traditional *process* concept: the process executes an initial statement only. It calls common procedures within other processes, but does not define any within itself. Such a process does not contain guarded regions because other processes are unable to call it and make the conditions within it true.

The example also illustrates how *peripheral devices* can be controlled by distributed processes. A device (such as the card reader) is associated with a single process. Other processes can access the device only through common procedures. So a peripheral device is just another process.

While a process is waiting for input/output, no other operations can take place within it. This is a special case of a more general rule: When a process P calls a procedure R within another process Q then R is considered an indivisible operation within process P, and P will not execute any other operation until R is finished (see Section 2).

Notice, that there is no need for *interrupts* even in a real-time language. Fast response to external requests is achieved by dedicating a processor to each critical event in the environment and by making sure that these processors interact with a small number of neighboring processors only (to prevent them from being overloaded with too many requests at a time).

Exercise: Write a process that receives a sequence of characters from a buffer process and outputs them line by line to a printer. The process should output a *formfeed* after every 60 lines.

4 RESOURCE SCHEDULING

We will now look at a variety of scheduling problems solved by means of guarded regions. It should perhaps be mentioned that resource schedulers are by nature *bottlenecks*. It would therefore be wise in a real-time program to make sure that each resource either is used frequently by a small number of processes or very infrequently by a larger number of processes. In many applications it is possible to avoid resource scheduling altogether and dedicate a resource to a single process (as in the card reader and line printer examples).

Example: Resource scheduler

A set of user processes can obtain exclusive access to an abstract resource by calling request and release operations within a scheduling process.

```
process resource
free: bool
proc request when free: free := false end
proc release if not free: free := true end
free := true

call resource.request ... call resource.release
```

The use of the boolean *free* forces a strict alternation of request and release operations. The program stops if an attempt is made to release a resource that is already free.

In this example, the scheduler does not know the identity of individual user processes. This is ideal when it does not matter in which order the users are served. But, if a scheduler must enforce a particular scheduling policy (such as *shortest job next*) then it must know the identity of its users to be able to grant the resource to a specific user. The following example shows how this can be done.

Example: Shortest job next scheduler

A scheduler allocates a resource among *n* user processes in shortest job next order. A request enters the identity and service time of a user process in a queue and waits until that user is selected by the scheduler. A release makes the resource available again.

The scheduler waits until one of two situations arises:

1. A process enters or leaves the queue: The scheduler will scan the queue and select the next user (but will not grant the resource to it yet).

2. The resource is not being used and the next user has been selected: The scheduler will grant the resource to that user and remove it from the queue.

User processes identify themselves by unique indices 1, 2, ..., *n*. The constant *nil* denotes an undefined process index.

The scheduler uses the following variables:

queue	the indices of waiting processes
rank	the service times of waiting processes
user	the index of the current user (if any)
next	the index of the next user (if any)

```
process sjn
queue: set[n]int; rank: array[n]int
user, next, min: int

proc request(who, time: int)
begin queue.include(who); rank[who] := time
  next := nil; when user = who: next := nil end
end

proc release; user := nil

begin queue := [ ]; user := nil; next := nil
  cycle
    not queue.empty & (next = nil):
      min := maxinteger
      for i in queue:
        if rank[i] > min: skip |
          rank[i] ≤ min: next := i; min := rank[i]
        end
      end|
    (user = nil) & (next ≠ nil):
      user := next; queue.exclude(user)
  end
end
```

In a microprocessor network where each processor is dedicated to a single process it is an attractive possibility to let a process carry out computations *between* external calls of its procedures. The above scheduler takes advantage of this capability by selecting the next user while the resource is being used by the present user. It would be simpler (but less efficient) to delay the selection of the next user until the previous one has released the resource.

The scheduling of individual processes is handled completely by means of guarded regions without the use of synchronizing variables, such as semaphores or event queues.

The periodic reevaluation of a synchronizing condition, such as

user = who

might be a serious load on a *common* store shared by other processors. But it is quite acceptable when it only involves the *local* store of a single processor that has nothing else to do. This is a good example of the influence of hardware technology on abstract algorithms.

Exercise: Write a first-come, first-served scheduler.

Example: Readers and writers

Two kinds of processes, called readers and writers, share a single resource. The readers can use the resource simultaneously, but each writer must have exclusive access to it. The readers and writers behave as follows:

call resource.startread	**call** resource.startwrite
read	write
call resource.endread	**call** resource.endwrite

A variable *s* defines the current resource *state* as one of the following:

s = 0	1 writer uses the resource
s = 1	0 processes use the resource
s = 2	1 reader uses the resource
s = 3	2 readers use the resource
...	...

This leads to the following solution (Brinch Hansen 1978):

```
process resource
s: int
proc startread when s ≥ 1: s := s + 1 end
proc endread if s > 1: s := s - 1 end
proc startwrite when s = 1: s := 0 end
proc endwrite if s = 0: s := 1 end
s := 1
```

Exercise: Solve the same problem with the additional constraint that further reader requests should be delayed as long as some writers are either waiting for or are using the resource.

Example: Alarm clock

An alarm clock process enables user processes to wait for different time intervals. The alarm clock receives a signal from a timer process after each time unit. (The problems of representing a clock with a finite integer are ignored here.)

```
process alarm
time: int

proc wait(interval: int)
due: int
begin due := time + interval
  when time = due: skip end
end

proc tick; time := time + 1

time := 0
```

5 PROCESS ARRAYS

So far we have only used one instance of each process. The next example uses an array of n identical processes (Hoare 1978):

process name[n]

A standard function *this* defines the identity of an individual process within the array ($1 \leq \text{this} \leq n$).

Example: Dining philosophers

Five philosophers alternate between thinking and eating. When a philosopher gets hungry, he joins a round table and picks up two forks next to his plate and starts eaiting. There are, however, only five forks on the table. So a philosopher can eat only when none of his neighbors are eating. When a philosopher has finished eating he puts down his two forks and leaves the table again.

```
process philosopher[5]
do true: think
  call table.join(this); eat; call table.leave(this)
end

process table
eating: set[5]int
proc join(i: int)
when([i ⊖ 1, i ⊕ 1] & eating) = [ ]: eating.include(i) end
proc leave(i: int); eating.exclude(i)
eating := [ ]
```

This solution does not prevent two philosophers from starving a philosopher between them to death by eating alternately.

Exercise: Solve the same problem without starvation.

Example: Sorting array

A process array sorts m data items in order $O(m)$. The items are input through sort process 1 that stores the smallest item input so far and passes the rest to its successor sort process 2. The latter keeps the second smallest item and passes the rest to its successor sort process 3, and so on. When the m items have been input they will be stored in their natural order in sort processes 1, 2, ..., m. They can now be output in increasing order through sort process 1. After each output the processes receive the remaining items from their successors.

A user process behaves as follows:

```
A: array[m]int
for x in A: call sort[1].put(x) end
for x in A: call sort[1].get(x) end
```

The sorting array can sort n elements or less ($m \leq n$). A sorting process is in equilibrium when it holds one item only. When the equilibrium is disturbed by its predecessor, a process takes the following action:

1. If the process holds two items, it will keep the smallest one and pass the largest one to its successor.

2. If the process holds no items, but its successor does, then the process will fetch the smallest item from its successor.

A sorting process uses the following variables:

here	the items stored in this process (0 ≤ here.length ≤ 2)
rest	the number of items stored in its successors

A standard function *succ* defines the index of the successor process (succ = this + 1).

```
process sort[n]
here: seq[2]int; rest, temp: int
proc put(c: int) when here.length < 2: here.put(c) end
proc get(#v: int) when here.length = 1: here.get(v) end

begin here := [ ]; rest := 0
  cycle
    here.length = 2:
      if here[1] ≤ here[2]: temp := here[2]; here := [here[1]] |
        here[1] > here[2]: temp := here[1]; here := [here[2]]
      end
      call sort[succ].put(temp); rest := rest + 1 |
    (here.length = 0) & (rest > 0):
      call sort[succ].get(temp); rest := rest − 1
      here := [temp]
  end
end
```

A hardware implementation of such a sorting array could be used as a very efficient form of priority scheduling queue.

Exercise: Program a process array that contains $N = 2^n$ numbers to begin with and which will add them in time $O(\log_2 N)$.

Since a process can define a common procedure it obviously includes the *procedure* concept as a special case. Hoare (1978) shows that a process array also can simulate a *recursive* procedure with a fixed maximum depth of recursion.

Exercise: Write a process array that computes a Fibonacci number by recursion.

6 ABSTRACT DATA TYPES

A process combines a data structure and all the possible operations on it into a single program module. Since other processes can perform these operations only on the data structure, but do not have direct access to it, it is called an *abstract* data structure.

We have already seen that a process can function as a *monitor*—an abstract data type that is shared by several processes. The next example shows that a process also can simulate a *class*—an abstract data type that is used by a single process only.

Example: Vending machine

A vending machine accepts one coin at a time. When a button is pushed the machine returns an item with change provided there is at least one item left and the coins cover the cost of it; otherwise, all the coins are returned.

```
process vending_machine
items, paid, cash: int
proc insert(coin: int) paid := paid + coin
proc push(#change, goods: int)
if (items > 0) & (paid ≥ price)
      change := paid − price; cash := cash + price
      goods := 1; items := items − 1; paid := 0 |
   (items = 0) or (paid < price):
      change := paid; goods := 0; paid := 0
end
begin items := 50; paid := 0; cash := 0 end
```

7 COROUTINES

Distributed processes can also function as coroutines. In a coroutine relationship between two processes P and Q only one of them is running at a time. A resume operation transfers control from one process to the other. When a process is resumed it continues at the point where it has transferred control to another process.

```
process P
go: bool
proc resume; go := true

begin go := false
   ...
   call Q.resume
   when go: go := false end
   ...
end
```

Process Q is very similar.

8 PATH EXPRESSIONS

Path expressions define meaningful *sequences* of operations P, Q, ..., (Campbell 1974). A path expression can be implemented by a scheduling process that defines the operations P, Q, ..., as procedures and uses a state variable s to enforce the sequence in which other processes may invoke these procedures.

Suppose, for example, that the operation P only can be followed by the operation Q as shown by the graph below:

To implement this path expression one associates a distinct state a, b, and c with each arrow in the graph and programs the operations as follows:

proc P **if** $s = a$: ... $s := b$ **end**

proc Q **if** $s = b$: ... $s := c$ **end**

If P is called in the state $s = a$ it will change the state to $s = b$ and make Q possible. Q, in turn, changes the state from b to c. An attempt to perform P or Q in a state where they are illegal will cause a program exception (or a delay if a *when* statement is used within the operation).

The next path expression specifies that either P or Q can be performed. This is enforced by means of two states a and b.

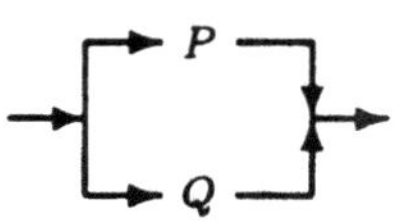

proc P **if** $s = a$: ... $s := b$ **end**

proc Q **if** $s = a$: ... $s := b$ **end**

If an operation P can be performed zero or more times then the execution of P leaves the state $s = a$ unchanged as shown below.

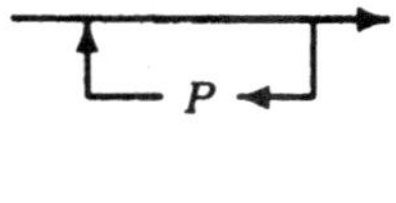

proc P **if** $s = a$: ... **end**

The simple resource scheduler in Section 4 implements a composite path expression in which the sequence *request* ... *release* is repeated zero or more times.

The readers and writers problem illustrates the use of a state variable to permit some operations to take place *simultaneously* while other operations are temporarily *excluded* (in this case, simultaneous reading by several processes excludes writing). Each simultaneous operation P is surrounded by a pair of scheduling operations, *startP* and *endP*. The state variable counts the number of P operations in progress.

9 IMPLEMENTATION HINTS

The following outlines the general nature of an implementation of distributed processes but ignores the details which are currently being studied.

In a well-designed concurrent program one may assume that each process communicates with a small number of neighboring processes only. For if the interactions are not strongly localized one cannot expect to gain much from concurrency. (A few resource schedulers may be an exception to this rule.)

Each processor will contain a distributed process P and a small, fixed number of anonymous processes which are the *representatives* of those distributed processes that can call process P. Additional notation in the language should make it possible for a compiler to determine the number of processes which call a particular process.

Whenever a processor is idle it activates a local representative which then waits until it receives a request with input data from another processor. The representative now calls the local procedure requested with the available input. When the procedure terminates, its output data are returned to the other processor and the representative becomes passive again. The switching from one *quasiconcurrent* process to another within a processor takes place as described in Section 2.

Since processes are permanent and procedures are nonrecursive, a compiler can determine the maximum storage required by a distributed process and the local representatives of its environment. So the storage allocation is *static* within each processor.

The parameter passing between two processors requires a single *input* operation before a procedure is executed and a single *output* operation when it terminates.

The speed of process switching within a single processor will probably be crucial for its real-time response.

The technique of representing the environment of a processor by local processes synchronized with external processes seems conceptually attractive. Although these processes are anonymous in this proposal one could design a language in which the store of a single process is shared by quasiconcurrent processes which communicate with nonlocal processes by input/output only.

10 FINAL REMARKS

It would certainly be feasible to adapt the processes and monitors of Concurrent Pascal to multiprocessor networks with distributed storage by restricting the parameter passing mechanism as proposed here. All the examples discussed here could then be programmed in that language—but not nearly as elegantly!

What then are the merits of distributed processes? Primarily, that they are a combination of *well-known* programming concepts (processes, procedures, and conditional critical regions) which *unify* the class, monitor, and process concepts. They include a surprising number of basic programming concepts as special cases:

procedures
coroutines
classes
monitors
processes
semaphores
buffers
path expressions
input/output

Since there is a common denominator for all these concepts, it may well be possible to develop common proof rules for them. The use of a single concept will certainly simplify the language implementation considerably.

The Concurrent Pascal machine distinguishes between 15 virtual instructions for classes, monitors, and processes. This number would be reduced by a factor of three for distributed processes. In addition, numerous special cases would disappear in the compiler.

It is also encouraging that distributed processes can be used to write elegant algorithms both for the more well-known concurrent problems and for some new ones that are nontrivial.

A recent proposal by Hoare (1978) has the same pleasant properties. Both proposals attack the problem of concurrency without shared variables and recognize the need for nondeterminacy within a single process.

Hoare's *communicating sequential processes* can be created and terminated dynamically. A single data transfer from one process to another is the communication mechanism. A process synchronizes itself with its environment by guarded input commands which are executed when a boolean expression is true *and* input is available from another process. The relationships between two communicating processes is symmetrical and requires both of them to name the other. The brief and nonredundant notation does not require declarations of communication channels but depends (conceptually) on dynamic type checking to recognize matching input and output commands in two processes.

In their present form communicating sequential processes seem well-suited to a theoretical investigation of concurrency and as a concise specification language that suppresses minor details, However, as Hoare points out, the language concepts and the notation would have to be modified to make them practical for program implementation.

The proposal for *distributed processes* is intended as a first step toward a practical language for networks. The proposal recognizes that the exchange of input and output in one operation is a frequent case, particularly for peripheral devices which return a result after each operation. The notation is redundant and enables a compiler to determine the number of processes and their storage requirements. The relationship between two communicating processes is asymmetrical and requires only that the caller of an operation name the process that performs it. This asymmetry is useful in hierarchical systems in which servants should be unaware of the identities of their masters.

Distributed processes derive much of their power from the ability to delay process interactions by means of boolean expressions which may involve both the global variables of a process *and* the input parameters from other processes (as illustrated by the *sjn* scheduler and the alarm clock). The price for this flexibility is the need for quasiconcurrent processes in the implementation. A more restricted form of Hoare's proposal might be able to implement process synchronization by the simpler method of polling a number of data channels until one of them transmits data.

But more work remains to be done on verification rules and network architectures for these new concepts. And then the ideas must be tested in *practice* before a final judgment can be made.

Acknowledgements

I am grateful to Nissim Francez, Wolfgang Franzen, Susan Gerhart, Charles Hayden, John Hennessy, Tony Hoare, David Lomet, David MacQueen, Johannes Madsen, David Musser, Michel Sintzoff, Jørgen Staunstrup and the referees for their constructive comments.

References

Brinch Hansen, P. 1973. *Operating System Principles.* Prentice Hall, Englewood Cliffs, NJ.

Brinch Hansen, P. 1975. The programming language Concurrent Pascal. *IEEE Transactions on Software Engineering 1*, 2 (June), 199–207.

Brinch Hansen, P. 1977. *The Architecture of Concurrent Programs.* Prentice Hall, Englewood Cliffs, NJ.

Brinch Hansen, P., and Staunstrup, J. 1978. Specification and implementation of mutual exclusion. *IEEE Transactions on Software Engineering 4*, 4 (September), 365–370.

Campbell, R.H., and Habermann, A.N. 1974. The specification of process synchronization by path expressions. *Lecture Notes in Computer Science 16*, 89–102.

Dijkstra, E.W. 1975. Guarded commands, nondeterminacy, and formal derivation of programs. *Communications of the ACM 18*, 8 (August), 453–457.

Hoare, C.A.R. 1972. Towards a theory of parallel programming. In *Operating Systems Techniques*, C.A.R. Hoare and R.H. Perrott, Eds., Academic Press, New York.

Hoare, C.A.R. 1974. Monitors: An operating system structuring concept. *Communications of the ACM 17*, 10 (October), 549–557.

Hoare, C.A.R. 1978. Communicating sequential processes. *Communications of the ACM 21*, 8 (August), 666–677.

Wirth, N. 1977. Modula: A programming language for modular multiprogramming. *Software—Practice and Experience 7*, 1 (January), 3–35.

17

JOYCE—A PROGRAMMING LANGUAGE FOR DISTRIBUTED SYSTEMS

PER BRINCH HANSEN

(1987)

This paper describes a secure programming language called Joyce based on CSP and Pascal. Joyce permits unbounded (recursive) activation of communicating agents. The agents exchange messages through synchronous channels. A channel can transfer messages of different types between two or more agents. A compiler can check message types and ensure that agents use disjoint sets of variables only. The use of Joyce is illustrated by a variety of examples.

1 INTRODUCTION

Two years after the invention of the monitor concept (Brinch Hansen 1973; Hoare 1974), Concurrent Pascal had been developed (Brinch Hansen 1975) and used for operating system design (Brinch Hansen 1976). Within ten years, half a dozen production-quality languages were monitor-based, among them Modula (Wirth 1977), Pascal-Plus (Welsh 1979), Mesa (Lampson 1980) and Concurrent Euclid (Holt 1982).

Eight years after the CSP proposal (Hoare 1978), several CSP-based languages have been developed: these include CSP80 (Jazayeri 1980), RBCSP (Roper 1981), ECSP (Baiardi 1984), Planet (Crookes 1984) and the low-level language occam (Inmos 1984). But no experience has been reported on the use of these languages for non-trivial system implementation. Although CSP has been highly successful as a notation for theoretical work

P. Brinch Hansen, Joyce—A programming language for distributed systems. *Software—Practice and Experience 17*, 1 (January 1987), 29–50.

(Hoare 1985), it has probably been too far removed from the requirements of a secure programming language.

This paper describes a secure programming language called Joyce for the design and implementation of distributed systems. Joyce is based on CSP and Pascal (Wirth 1971).

A Joyce program consists of nested procedures which define communicating agents. Joyce permits unbounded (recursive) activation of agents. The execution of a program activates an initial agent. Agents may dynamically activate subagents which run concurrently with their creators. The variables of an agent are inaccessible to other agents.

Agents communicate by means of symbols transmitted through channels. Every channel has an alphabet—a fixed set of symbols that can be transmitted through the channel. A symbol has a name and may carry a message of a fixed type.

Two agents match when one of them is ready to output a symbol to a channel and the other is ready to input the same symbol from the same channel. When this happens, a communication takes place in which a message from the sending agent is assigned to a variable of the receiving agent.

The communications on a channel take place one at a time. A channel can transfer symbols in both directions between two agents.

A channel may be used by two or more agents. If more than two agents are ready to communicate on the same channel, it may be possible to match them in several different ways. The channel arbitrarily selects two matching agents at a time and lets them communicate.

A polling statement enables an agent to examine one or more channels until it finds a matching agent. Both sending and receiving agents may be polled.

Agents create channels dynamically and access them through local port variables. When an agent creates a channel, a channel pointer is assigned to a port variable. The agent may pass the pointer as a parameter to subagents.

When an agent reaches the end of its defining procedure, it waits until all its subagents have terminated before terminating itself. At this point, the local variables and any channels created by the agent cease to exist.

This paper defines the concepts of Joyce and illustrates the use of the language to implement a variety of well-known programming concepts and algorithms.

2 LANGUAGE CONCEPTS

Joyce is based on a minimal Pascal subset: type integer, boolean, char and real; enumerated, array and record types; constants, variables and expressions; assignment, if, while, compound and empty statements.

This subset is extended with concurrent programming concepts called agent procedures, port types and channels, agent, port, input/output and polling statements.

The Joyce grammar is defined in extended BNF notation: $[E]$ denotes an E sentence (or none). $\{E\}$ denotes a finite (possibly empty) sequence of E sentences. Tokens are enclosed in quotation marks, e.g. "**begin**".

This paper concentrates on the concurrent aspects of Joyce.

Port types

```
TypeDefinition = TypeName "=" NewType ";" .
NewType = PascalType | PortType .
PortType = "[" Alphabet "]" .
Alphabet = SymbolClass { "," SymbolClass } .
SymbolClass = SymbolName [ "(" MessageType ")" ] .
MessageType = TypeName .
```

A Joyce program defines abstract concurrent machines called agents. The agents communicate by means of values called symbols transmitted through entities called channels. The set of possible symbols that can be transmitted through a channel is called its alphabet.

Agents create channels dynamically and access them through variables known as port variables. The types of these variables are called port types.

A type definition

$$T = [s_1(T_1), s_2(T_2), \ldots, s_n(T_n)];$$

defines a port type named T. The port value *nil* T is of type T and denotes a non-existing channel. All other port values of type T denote distinct channels with the given alphabet. The port values (also known as channel pointers) are unordered.

The alphabet is the union of a fixed number of disjoint symbol classes named $s_1, s_2, \ldots, s_n$.

A symbol class $s_i(T_i)$ consists of every possible value of type T_i prefixed with the name s_i. The T_i values are called messages.

A symbol class s_j consists of a single symbol named s_j without a message. The symbol is called a signal.

The symbol names $s_1, s_2, \ldots, s_n$ must be distinct, and $T_1, T_2, \ldots, T_n$ must be names of known types. (Every type has a name and is said to be known within its scope.) The message types cannot be (or include) port types.

Examples:

1. A port type named *stream* with two symbol classes named *int* and *eos*. Every *int* symbol includes a message of type integer. The *eos* symbol is a signal:

   stream = [int(integer), eos];

2. A port type named *PV* with two signals *P* and *V*:

   PV = [P, V];

Note. Symbols of the same alphabet must have distinct names. Symbols of different alphabets may have the same names. Different symbols of the same alphabet may carry messages of the same type.

Port variables

PortAccess = VariableAccess .

A variable $v : T$ of a port type T holds a port value. If the value of v is *nil* T, a port access v denotes a non-existing channel; otherwise, it denotes a channel with the alphabet given by T. (The channel itself is not a variable, but a communication device shared by agents.)

Examples:

1. Access a port variable named *inp*:

   inp

2. Access the *i*th element of an array of port variables named *ring*:

   ring[i]

Port statements

Statement = PascalStatement | PortStatement |
  InputOutputStatement | PollingStatement |
  AgentStatement .
PortStatement = "+" PortAccess .

The creation of a new channel is called the activation of the channel. A port statement $+c$ denotes activation of a new channel. The variable access c must be of a known port type T.

When an agent executes the port statement, a new channel with the alphabet given by T is created and a pointer to the channel is assigned to the port variable c. The agent is called the creator of the channel. The channel itself is known as an internal channel of the agent. The channel ceases to exist when its creator terminates.

Examples:

1. Create a new channel and assign the pointer to the port variable *inp*:

+inp

2. Create a new channel and assign the pointer to the port variable *ring[i]*:

+ring[i]

Input/output statements

InputOutputCommand = OutputCommand | InputCommand .
OutputCommand = PortAccess "!" OutputSymbol .
OutputSymbol = SymbolName ["(" OutputExpression ")"] .
OutputExpression = Expression .
InputCommand = PortAccess "?" InputSymbol .
InputSymbol = SymbolName ["(" InputVariable ")"] .
InputVariable = VariableAccess .
InputOutputStatement = InputOutputCommand .

A communication is the transfer of a symbol from one agent to another through a channel. The sending agent is said to output the symbol, and the receiving agent is said to input the symbol. The agents access the channel through local port variables.

Consider an agent p which accesses a channel through a port variable b, and another agent q which accesses the same channel through a different port variable c. The port variables must be of the same type:

$$T = [s_1(T_1), s_2(T_2), \ldots, s_n(T_n)];$$

An output command $b!s_i(e_i)$ denotes output of a symbol $s_i(e_i)$ through the channel denoted by the port variable b. s_i must be the name of one of the symbol classes of T, and the expression e_i must be of the corresponding message type T_i.

An input command $c?s_i(v_i)$ denotes input of a symbol $s_i(v_i)$ through the channel denoted by the port variable c. s_i must be the name of one of the symbol classes of T, and the variable access v_i must be of the corresponding message type T_i.

When an agent p is ready to output the symbol s_i on a channel, and another agent q is ready to input the same symbol from the same channel, the two agents are said to match and a communication between them is said to be feasible. If and when this happens, the two agents execute the output and input commands simultaneously. The combined effect is defined by the following sequence of actions:

1. p obtains a value by evaluating the output expression e_i.
2. q assigns the value to its input variable v_i.

(If the symbol s_i is a signal, steps 1 and 2 denote empty actions.)

After a communication, the agents proceed concurrently.

When an agent reaches an input/output command which denotes a communication that is not feasible, the behavior of the agent depends on whether the command is used as an input/output statement or as a polling command (defined in the next section).

The effect of an input/output statement is to delay an agent until the communication denoted by the statement has taken place.

The communications on a channel take place one at a time. A channel can transfer symbols in both directions between two agents.

A channel may be used by two or more agents. If more than two agents are ready to communicate on the same channel, it may be possible to match them in several different ways. The channel arbitrarily selects two matching agents at a time and lets them communicate.

Examples:

1. Use the port variable *out* to output an *int* symbol with the message $x + 1$:

   out!int(x + 1)

2. Use the port variable *inp* to input an *int* symbol and assign the message to y:

   inp?int(y)

3. Use the port variable *out* to output an *eos* signal:

   out!eos

4. Use the port variable *inp* to input an *eos* signal:

   inp?eos

5. Use the port variable *ring[i]* to output a *token* signal:

   ring[i]!token

Polling statements

PollingStatement =
  "**poll**" GuardedStatementList "**end**" .
GuardedStatementList =
  GuardedStatement { "|" GuardedStatement } .
GuardedStatement = Guard "->" StatementList .
Guard = PollingCommand ["&" PollingExpression] .
PollingCommand = InputOutputCommand .
PollingExpression = BooleanExpression .

A polling statement

poll
  C_1 & B_1 -> SL_1 |
  C_2 & B_2 -> SL_2 |
  ...
  C_n & B_n -> SL_n
end

denotes execution of exactly one of the guarded statements

$$C_i \ \& \ B_i \ {-}{>} \ SL_i$$

An agent executes a polling statement in two phases, known as the polling and completion phases:

1. Polling: the agent examines the guards $C_1 \& B_1$, $C_2 \& B_2$, ..., $C_n \& B_n$ cyclically until finds one with a polling command C_i that denotes a feasible communication and a polling expression B_i that denotes true (or is omitted).

2. Completion: the agent executes the selected polling command C_i followed by the corresponding statement list SL_i.

While an agent is polling, it can be matched only by another agent that is ready to execute an input/output statement. Two agents polling at the same time do not match.

Example:

Use a port variable named *user* to either (1) input a P signal (provided an integer $x > 0$) and decrement x, or (2) input a V signal and increment x:

```
poll
  user?P & x > 0 -> x := x - 1 |
  user?V -> x := x + 1
end
```

Note. Polling has no side-effects, but may cause program failure if the expression evaluation causes a range error (or overflow).

Agent statements

AgentStatement =
  AgentName ["(" ActualParameterList ")"] .
ActualParameterList =
  ActualParameter { "," ActualParameter } .
ActualParameter = Expression .

An agent procedure P defines a class of agents. The creation and start of an agent is called its activation. The activation of a P agent creates a new instance of every variable defined in procedure P. These variable instances are called the own variables of the new agent. When the agent refers to a variable x in P, it refers to its own instance of x. The own variables of an agent are inaccessible to other agents.

An agent is always activated by another agent (called its creator). The new agent is called a subagent of its creator. After the creation, the subagent and its creator run concurrently.

An agent statement

$$P(e_1, e_2, \ldots, e_m)$$

denotes activation of a new agent. P must be the name of a known agent procedure (defined in the next section). The actual parameter list must contain an actual parameter e_i for every formal parameter a_i defined by P. e_i must be an expression of the same type as a_i.

When an agent executes an agent statement, a subagent is created in two steps:

1. The own variables of the subagent are created as follows:
   (a) The formal parameters of P are created one at a time in the order listed. Every formal parameter a_i is assigned the value denoted by the corresponding actual parameter e_i.
   (b) The variables defined in the procedure body of P are created with unpredictable initial values.
2. The subagent is started.

A port operand used as an actual parameter denotes a channel which is accessible to both the subagent and its creator. It is known as an external channel of the subagent.

An agent defined by a procedure P may activate P recursively. Every activation creates a new P agent with its own variables.

Example:

Activate a semaphore agent with two actual parameters: the integer 1 and a port value named *user*:

semaphore(1, user)

Agent procedures

AgentProcedure = "**agent**" AgentName ProcedureBlock ";" .
ProcedureBlock =
  ["(" FormalParameterList ")"] ";" ProcedureBody .
FormalParameterList =
  ParameterDefinition { ";" ParameterDefinition } .
ParameterDefinition =
  VariableName { "," VariableName } ":" TypeName .
ProcedureBody =
  [ConstantDefinitionPart] [TypeDefinitionPart]
  { AgentProcedure } [VariableDefinitionPart]
  CompoundStatement .

An agent procedure P defines a class of agents. Every formal parameter is a local variable that is assigned the value of an expression when a P agent is activated.

After its activation, a P agent executes the corresponding procedure body in two steps:

1. The agent executes the compound statement of P.
2. The agent waits until all its subagents (if any) have terminated. At this point, the own variables and internal channels of the agent cease to exist, and the agent terminates.

Example: semaphore

An agent procedure that defines a semaphore which accepts P and V signals:

```
agent semaphore(x: integer; user: PV);
begin
  while true do
    poll
      user?P & x > 0 -> x := x - 1|
      user?V -> x := x + 1
    end
end;
```

Programs

Program =
  [ConstantDefinitionPart][TypeDefinitionPart]
  AgentProcedure .

A program defines an agent procedure *P*. The program is executed by activating and executing a single *P* agent (the initial agent). The activation of the initial agent is the result of executing an agent statement in another program (an operating system). A program communicates with its operating system through the external channels of the initial agent (the system channels).

3 PROGRAM EXAMPLES

The following examples illustrate the use of Joyce to implement stream processing, functions, data representations, monitors and ring nets. The examples have been compiled and run on an IBM PC using a Joyce compiler and interpreter written in Pascal.

Stream processing

First, we look at agents that input and output bounded data streams. Every stream is a (possibly empty) sequence of integers ending with an *eos* signal:

```
type stream = [int(integer), eos];
```

Example: generate

An agent that generates an arithmetic progression $a_0, a_1, \ldots, a_{n-1}$, where $a_i = a + i \times b$:

```
agent generate(out: stream;
  a, b, n: integer);
```

```
var i: integer;
begin
  i := 0;
  while i < n do
    begin
      out!int(a + i*b); i := i + 1
    end;
  out!eos
end;
```

Example: copy

An agent that copies a stream:

```
agent copy(inp, out: stream);
var more: boolean; x: integer;
begin
  more := true;
  while more do
    poll
      inp?int(x) -> out!int(x)|
      inp?eos -> more := false
    end;
  out!eos
end;
```

Example: merge

An agent that outputs an arbitrary interleaving of two input streams:

```
agent merge(inp1, inp2, out: stream);
var n, x: integer;
begin
  n := 0;
  while n < 2 do
    poll
      inp1?int(x) -> out!int(x)|
      inp1?eos -> n := n + 1|
      inp2?int(x) -> out!int(x)|
      inp2?eos -> n := n + 1
```

```
    end;
    out!eos
  end;
```

A value input from one of the streams inp_1 and inp_2 is immediately output. The agent terminates when both input streams have been exhausted ($n = 2$).

Example: suppress duplicates

An agent that outputs a stream derived from an ordered input stream by suppressing duplicates:

```
agent suppress(inp, out: stream);
var more: boolean; x, y: integer;
begin
  poll
    inp?int(x) -> more := true|
    inp?eos -> more := false
  end;
  while more do
    poll
      inp?int(y) ->
        if x <> y then
          begin out!int(x); x := y end|
      inp?eos -> out!int(x); more := false
    end;
  out!eos
end;
```

Example: iterative buffer

A buffer implemented as a pipeline of 10 copy agents:

```
agent buffer(inp, out: stream);
const n = 9;
type net = array [1..n] of stream;
use copy;
var a: net; i: integer;
begin
  +a[1]; copy(inp, a[1]); i := 2;
```

```
    while i <= n do
      begin
        +a[i]; copy(a[i-1], a[i]); i := i + 1
      end;
    copy(a[n], out)
  end;
```

The buffer agent is a composite agent which activates an array of copy agents and channels by iteration. The length $n+1$ of the iterative array is specified by a constant n. During compilation, the *use* sentence is replaced by the text of the copy agent.

This algorithm is an example of "information hiding". A user agent may regard the copy and buffer agents as different implementations of the same mechanism: a copying agent with an input and an output channel. The subagents and internal channels of the buffer agent are therefore made invisible to its environment.

Example: recursive buffer

A recursive version of the previous buffer:

```
agent buffer(n: integer; inp, out: stream);
use copy;
var succ: stream;
begin
  if n = 1 then copy(inp, out)
  else
    begin
      +succ; copy(inp, succ);
      buffer(n - 1, succ, out)
    end
end;
```

The length n of the recursive array is specified when it is activated. If $n = 1$, the buffer consists of a single copy agent only; otherwise, it consists of a copy agent followed by a buffer of length $n - 1$.

The next two examples illustrate the use of a programming paradigm known as a dynamic accumulator. This is a pipeline which uses an input stream to compute another stream. The pipeline accumulates the new stream while it is being computed and outputs it as a whole when it is complete. Every agent (except the last one) in the pipeline holds one element of the new stream. The last agent is empty. Each time the pipeline has computed another element, the last agent receives an element and extends the pipeline with a new empty agent. Since the length of the computed stream is not known *a priori*, the pipeline begins as a single empty agent. At the end of the input stream, the pipeline outputs the elements of the computed stream one at a time and terminates.

Example: recursive sorting

A dynamic accumulator that inputs a (possibly empty) stream and outputs the elements in non-decreasing order:

```
agent sort(inp, out: stream);
var more: boolean; x, y: integer;
  succ: stream;
begin
  poll
    inp?int(x) -> +succ;
      sort(succ, out); more := true;|
    inp?eos -> out!eos; more := false
  end;
  while more do
    poll
      inp?int(y) ->
        if x > y then
          begin succ!int(x); x := y end
        else succ!int(y)|
      inp?eos -> out!int(x);
        succ!eos; more := false
    end
end;
```

The sorting agents share a common output channel. Initially, an agent is the last one in the chain and is empty. After receiving the first value from its predecessor, the agent creates a successor and becomes non-empty. The agent now inputs the rest of the stream from its predecessor and keeps the smallest value x received so far. The rest it sends to its successor. When the agent inputs an *eos* signal it terminates as follows: if it is empty, the agent sends *eos* through the common channel; otherwise it outputs x on the common channel and sends *eos* to its successor.

As an example, while sorting the sequence

$$3, 1, 2, \mathit{eos}$$

the accumulator s starts as a single empty agent denoted by $< \phi >$ and is extended by a new agent for every value input:

Initially:	$s =< \phi >$
After inputting 3:	$s =< 3 >, < \phi >$
After inputting 1:	$s =< 1 >, < 3 >, < \phi >$
After inputting 2:	$s =< 1 >, < 2 >, < 3 >, < \phi >$

The sorting accumulator may be tested by means of a pipeline with three agents:

```
agent pipeline1;
use generate, sort, print;
var a, b: stream;
begin
  +a; +b; generate(a, 10, -1, 10);
  sort(a, b); print(b)
end;
```

The print agent accepts a stream and prints it.

The next pipeline merges two unordered streams, sorts the results, suppresses duplicates and prints the rest:

```
agent pipeline2;
use generate, merge, sort, suppress, print;
var a, b, c, d, e: stream;
begin
  +a; +b; +c; +d; +e;
  generate(a, 1, 1, 10);
  generate(b, 10, -1, 10);
  merge(a, b, c); sort(c, d);
  suppress(d, e); print(e)
end;
```

Example: prime sieve

A dynamic accumulator that inputs a finite sequence of natural numbers 1, 2, 3, ..., n and outputs those that are primes:

```
agent sieve(inp, out: stream);
var more: boolean; x, y: integer;
  succ: stream;
begin
  poll
    inp?int(x) -> +succ;
      sieve(succ, out); more := true|
    inp?eos -> out!eos; more := false
  end;
  while more do
    poll
      inp?int(y) ->
        if y mod x <> 0 then succ!int(y)|
      inp?eos -> out!int(x);
        succ!eos; more := false
    end;
end;
```

Initially, a sieve agent inputs a prime x from its predecessor and activates a successor. The agent then skips all further input which is divisible by x and sends the rest to its successor. At the end, the agent sends x through the common channel and sends *eos* either to its successor (if any) or through the output channel.

The sieve can be optimized somewhat by letting every agent output its prime as soon as it has been input. The present form of the algorithm was chosen to show that the sort and sieve agents are almost identical variants of the same programming paradigm. (They differ in one statement only!)

Since 2 is the only even prime, we may as well feed the sieve with odd numbers 3, 5, 7, ... only. The following pipeline prints all primes between 3 and 9999:

```
agent primes;
use generate, sieve, print;
var a, b: stream;
begin
  +a; +b; generate(a, 3, 2, 4999);
  sieve(a, b); print(b)
end;
```

Function evaluation

A function $f(x)$ can be evaluated by activating an agent with two parameters denoting the argument x and a channel. The agent evaluates $f(x)$, outputs the result on the channel and terminates.

A procedure can be implemented similarly.

Example: recursive Fibonacci

An agent that computes a Fibonacci number recursively by means of a tree of subagents:

```
type func = [val(integer)];

agent fibonacci(f: func; x: integer);
var g, h: func; y, z: integer;
begin
  if x <= 1 then f!val(x)
  else
    begin
      +g; fibonacci(g, x - 1);
      +h; fibonacci(h, x - 2);
      g?val(y); h?val(z); f!val(y + z)
    end
end;
```

Data representation

An agent can also implement a set of operations on a data representation.

Example: recursive set

Problem. Represent a set of integers as an agent with an input and an output channel. Initially, the set is empty. The set agent accepts three kinds of commands from a single user agent only:

1. Insert an integer n in the set:

   inp!insert(n)

2. Return a boolean b indicating if n is in the set:

```
inp!has(n); out?return(b)
```

3. Delete the set:

```
inp!delete
```

Solution.

```
type
  setinp = [insert(integer), has(integer), delete];
  setout = [return(boolean)];

agent intset(inp: setinp; out: setout);
type state = (empty, nonempty, deleted);
var s: state; x, y: integer; succ: setinp;
begin
  s := empty;
  while s = empty do
    poll
      inp?insert(x) -> +succ;
        intset(succ, out); s := nonempty|
      inp?has(x) -> out!return(false)|
      inp?delete -> s := deleted
    end;
  while s = nonempty do
    poll
      inp?insert(y) ->
        if x > y then
          begin succ!insert(x); x := y end
        else if x < y then succ!insert(y)|
      inp?has(y) ->
        if x >= y then out!return(x = y)
          else succ!has(y)|
      inp?delete -> succ!delete; s := deleted
    end
end;
```

The set agent is very similar to the sort and sieve agents. It contains either one member of the set or none. Initially, the agent is empty and answers false to all membership queries. After the first insertion, it activates an empty successor to which it passes any command it cannot handle. To speed up processing, the set is ordered. Many insertions can proceed simultaneously in the pipeline. Insertion of an already existing member has no effect. A delete signal propagates through all the set agents and makes them terminate.

Monitors

A monitor is a scheduling agent that enables two or more user agents to share a resource. The user agents can invoke operations on the resource one at a time only. A monitor may use boolean expressions to delay operations until they are feasible.

Example: ring buffer

A monitor that implements a non-terminating ring buffer which can hold up to ten messages:

```
agent buffer(inp, out: stream);
const n = 10;
type contents = array [1..n] of integer;
var head, tail, length: integer;
  ring: contents;
begin
  head := 1; tail := 1; length := 0;
  while true do
    poll
      inp?int(ring[tail]) & length < n ->
        tail := tail mod n + 1;
        length := length + 1|
      out!int(ring[head]) & length > 0 ->
        head := head mod n + 1;
        length := length - 1
    end
end;
```

An empty buffer may input a message only. A full buffer may output only. When the buffer contains at least one and at most nine values, it is ready either to input or to output a message.

Example: scheduled printer

A monitor that gives one user agent at a time exclusive access to a printer during a sequence of write operations. The user agent must open the printer before writing and close it afterwards:

```
type printsym = [open, write(char), close];

agent printer(user: printsym);
var more: boolean; x: char;
begin
  while true do
    begin
      user?open; more := true;
      while more do
        poll
          user?write(x) -> print(x)|
          user?close -> more := false
        end
    end
end;
```

When the printer has received an open symbol from a user agent, it accepts only a (possibly empty) sequence of write symbols followed by a close symbol. This protocol prevents other agents from opening the printer and using it simultaneously. (The details of printing are ignored.)

Ring nets

So far, we have only considered agents connected by acyclic nets of channels. In the final example, the agents are connected by a cyclic net of channels.

Example: nim players

From a pile of 20 coins, three players take turns picking one, two or three coins from the pile. The player forced to pick the last coin loses the game.

The game is simulated by three agents connected by a ring of three channels. When the game begins, one of the agents receives all the coins:

```
agent nim;
use player;
var a, b, c: stream;
```

```
begin
  +a; +b; +c; player(20, a, b);
  player(0, b, c); player(0, c, a);
end;
```

The players behave as follows:

```
agent player(pile: integer;
  pred, succ: stream);
var more: boolean;
begin
  if pile > 0 then succ!int(pile - 1);
  more := true;
  while more do
    poll
      pred?int(pile) ->
        if pile > 1 then succ!int(pile - 1)
        else { loser }
          begin
            succ!eos; pred?eos; more := false
          end|
      pred!eos -> succ!eos; more := false
    end
end;
```

When an agent receives the pile from its predecessor, it reduces it and sends the rest (if any) to its successor. (To simplify the algorithm slightly, an agent always removes a single coin). The agent that picks the last coin sends *eos* to its successor and waits until the signal has passed through the other two agents and comes back from its predecessor. At that point, the loser terminates. When a non-losing agent receives *eos* instead of a pile, it passes the signal to its successor and terminates.

The dining philosophers problem (Hoare 1978) is another example of a ring net. It is left as an exercise to the reader.

4 DESIGN ISSUES

The following motivates some of the design decisions of Joyce.

Terminology and notation

In the literature, the word "process" often denotes a sequential process. Since a composite agent is not sequential, I prefer to use another word for communicating machines (namely, "agents").

It was tempting to use the notation of CSP (Hoare 1978) or one of the successors of Pascal, for example Modula-2 (Wirth 1982). However, in spite of its limitations, Pascal has a readable notation which is familiar to everyone. Chosing a pure Pascal subset has enabled me to concentrate on the concurrent aspects of Joyce.

Indirect naming

One of the major advantages of monitors is their ability to communicate with processes and schedule them without being aware of process names. Joyce agents also refer indirectly to one another by means of port variables.

In CSP, an input/output command must name the source or destination process directly. The text of a process must therefore be modified when it is used in different contexts. This complicates the examples in (Hoare 1978): the user of a process array $S(1..n)$ is itself named $S(0)$! And the prime sieve is composed of three different kinds of processes to satisfy the naming rules.

Direct process naming also makes it awkward to write a server with multiple clients of different kinds (such as the scheduled printer). If the clients are not known *a priori*, it is in fact impossible.

ECSP and RBCSP use process variables for indirect naming. CSP80, occam, Planet and a theoretical variant of CSP, which I shall call TCSP (Hoare 1985), use ports or channels.

Message declarations

So far, the most common errors in Joyce programs have been type errors in input/output commands. I am therefore convinced that any CSP language must include message declarations which permit complete type checking during compilation. In this respect, CSP and occam are insecure languages. Although ECSP does not include message declarations, the compiler performs type checking of messages after recognizing (undeclared) channels by statement analysis.

The simplest idea is to declare channels which can transfer messages of a single type only (as in CSP80 or Planet). But this does not even work well for a simple agent that copies a bounded stream. Such an agent needs two channels, both capable of transferring two different kinds of symbols. Otherwise, four channels are required: two for stream values and two for *eos* signals.

As a modest increase in complexity, I considered a channel which can transfer messages of a finite number of distinct types $T_1, T_2, \ldots, T_n$. But this proposal is also problematic since (1) it is necessary to treat signals as distinct data types, and (2) an agent still needs multiple channels to distinguish between different kinds of messages of the same type (such as the *has* and *insert* symbols in the *intset* example).

To avoid a confusing proliferation of channels, the ability to define channel alphabets with named symbols seems essential. The symbol names play the same role as the (undeclared) "constructors" of CSP or the procedure names of monitors: they describe the nature of an event in which a process participates.

Channel sharing

The *intset* pipeline is made simpler and more efficient by the use of a single output channel shared by all the agents. A set agent which receives a query about the member it holds can immediately output the answer through the common channel instead of sending it through all its successors. This improvement was suggested in (Dijkstra 1982).

Channel sharing also simplifies the scheduled printer. If every channel can be used by two processes only, it is necessary to connect a resource process to multiple users by means of a quantifier called a "replicator."

I expect channel sharing to work well for lightly used resources. But, if a shared resource is used heavily, some user agents may be bypassed by others and thus prevented from using the resource. In such cases, it may be necessary to introduce separate user channels to achieve fairness.

Output polling

In CSP, ECSP, RBCSP and occam, polling is done by input commands only. This restriction prevents a sender and receiver from polling the same channel simultaneously. Unfortunately, it also makes the input and output of a ring buffer asymmetric (Hoare 1978).

Like CSP80 and TCSP, Joyce permits both input and output polling. It is the programmer's responsibility to ensure that a polling agent is always matched by an agent that executes an input/output statement. This property is automatically satisfied in a hierarchical system in which every agent polls its masters only (Silberschatz 1979).

Polling loops

CSP includes a polling loop that terminates when all the processes polled have terminated. Hoare (1985) remarks: "The trouble with this convention is that it is complicated to define and implement."

In RBCSP, a process waiting for input from a terminated process is terminated only when all processes are waiting or terminated.

A Joyce agent terminates when it reaches the end of its procedure. This is a much more flexible mechanism which enables an agent to send a termination signal to another agent without terminating itself.

I resisted the temptation to include polling loops, such as

```
do inp?int(x) -> out!int(x)
until inp?eos -> out!eos end
```

Although this simplifies the copy and printer agents, it cannot be used directly in the other examples. It may even complicate programs, if it is used where it is inappropriate.

Unbounded activation

In CSP one can activate only a fixed number of processes simultaneously. If these processes terminate, they do it simultaneously. A process cannot activate itself recursively. It is, however, possible to activate a fixed-length array of indexed processes which can imitate the behavior (but not quite the elegance) of a recursive process.

Joyce supports unbounded (recursive) agent activation. The beauty of the recursive algorithms is sufficient justification for this feature. The ability to activate identical agents by iteration and recursion removes the need for indexed agents (as in CSP, RBCSP, Planet and occam). The rule that an agent terminates only when all its subagents have terminated was inspired by the task concept of Ada (Roubine 1980).

Procedures and functions

To force myself to make agents as general as possible, I excluded ordinary procedures and functions from Joyce. As a result, I felt obliged to design an agent concept which includes the best features of Pascal procedures: value parameters, recursion and efficient implementation. Although agent procedures may be recursive, every agent has one instance only of its own variables. Consequently, a compiler can determine the lengths of agent activation records. This simplifies storage allocation considerably.

Security

A programming language is secure if its compiler and run-time support can detect all violations of the language rules (Hoare 1973). Programs written in an insecure language may cause obscure system-dependent errors which are inexplicable in terms of the language report. Such errors can be extremely difficult to locate and correct.

Joyce is a far more secure language than Pascal (Welsh 1977). A compiler can check message types and ensure that agents use disjoint sets of variables only. (The disjointness is automatically guaranteed by the syntax and scope rules.)

When an agent is activated, every word of its activation record may be set to nil. Afterwards a simple run-time check can detect unitialized port variables.

There are no dangling references, either, to channels that have ceased to exist. Every port variable of an agent is either nil or points to an internal or external channel of the agent. Now, an internal channel exists as long as the agent and its port variables exist. And an external channel exists as long as the ancestor that created it. This ancestor, in turn, exists at least as long as the given agent. So, a port variable is either nil or points to an existing channel.

Implementability

The first Joyce compiler is a Pascal program of 3300 lines which generates P-code. The code is currently interpreted by a Pascal program of 1000 lines. (Reals are not implemented yet.) The surprisingly simple implementation of agents and channels will be described in a future paper.

Proof rules

The problems of finding proof rules for Joyce are currently being studied and are not discussed here. However, the algorithms shown have a convincing simplicity that makes me optimistic in this respect.

Language comparison

Table 1 summarizes the key features of the CSP languages (except TCSP).

Table 1

	CSP	occam	ECSP	Planet	RBCSP	CSP80	Joyce
Indirect naming	−	+	+	+	+	+	+
Message declaration	−	−	−	+	+	+	+
Input polling	+	+	+	−	+	+	+
Output polling	−	−	−	−	−	+	+
Recursion	−	−	−	−	−	−	+

Hoare (1978) emphasized that CSP should not be regarded as suitable for use as a programming language but only as a partial solution to the problems tackled. However, all that remained to be done was to modify these concepts. CSP is still the foundation for the new generation of concurrent programming languages discussed here.

5 FINAL REMARKS

This paper has presented a secure programming language which removes several restrictions of the original CSP proposal by introducing:

1. port variables
2. channel alphabets
3. output polling
4. channel sharing
5. recursive agents

The language has been implemented on a personal computer.

More work remains to be done on verification rules and implementation of the language on a parallel computer. The language needs to be used extensively for the design of parallel algorithms before a final evaluation can be made.

Acknowledgements

It is a pleasure to acknowledge the helpful comments of Birger Andersen, Peter T. Andersen, Lotte Bangsborg, Peter Brinch, Niels Christian Juul and Bo Salomon.

References

Baiardi, F., Ricci, L., and Vanneschi, M. 1984. Static checking of interprocess communication in ECSP. *ACM SIGPLAN Notices 19*, 6 (June), 290–299.

Brinch Hansen, P. 1973. *Operating System Principles.* Prentice-Hall, Englewood Cliffs, NJ.

Brinch Hansen, P. 1975. The programming language Concurrent Pascal. *IEEE Transactions on Software Engineering 1*, 2 (June), 199–205.

Brinch Hansen, P. 1976. The Solo operating system. *Software—Practice and Experience 6*, 2 (April–June), 141–205.

Crookes, D., and Elder, J.W.G. 1984. An experiment in language design for distributed systems. *Software-Practice and Experience 14*, 10 (October), 957–971.

Dijkstra, E.W. 1982. *Selected Writings on Computing: A Personal Perspective.* Springer-Verlag, New York, 147–160.

Hoare, C.A.R. 1973. Hints on programming language design. Computer Science Department, Stanford University, Stanford, CA, (December).

Hoare, C.A.R. 1974. Monitors: An operating system structuring concept. *Communications of the ACM 17*, 10 (October), 549–557.

Hoare, C.A.R. 1978. Communicating sequential processes. *Communications of the ACM 21*, 8 (August), 666–677.

Hoare, C.A.R. 1985. *Communicating Sequential Processes.* Prentice-Hall, Englewood Cliffs, NJ.

Holt, R.C. 1982. A short introduction to Concurrent Euclid. *ACM SIGPLAN Notices 17*, (May), 60–79.

Inmos, Ltd. 1984. *occam Programming Manual.* Prentice-Hall, Englewood Cliffs, NJ.

Jazayeri, M., Ghezzi, C., Hoffman, D., Middleton, D., and Smotherman, M. 1980. CSP/80: A language for communicating sequential processes. *IEEE Compcon Fall*, (September), 736–740.

Lampson, B.W., and Redell, D.D. 1980. Experience with processes and monitors in Mesa. *Communications of the ACM 23*, 2 (February), 105–117.

Roper, T.J., and Barter, C.J. 1981. A communicating sequential process language and implementation. *Software—Practice and Experience 11*, 11 (November), 1215–1234.

Roubine, O., and Heliar, J.-C. 1980. Parallel processing in Ada. In *On the Construction of Programs*, R.M. McKeag, and A.M. Macnaghten, Eds. Cambridge University Press, Cambridge, 193–212.

Silberschatz, A. 1979. Communication and synchronization in distributed systems. *IEEE Transactions on Software Engineering 5*, 6 (November), 542–546.

Welsh, J., Sneeringer, W.J., and Hoare, C.A.R. 1977. Ambiguities and insecurities in Pascal. *Software—Practice and Experience 7*, 6 (November–December), 685–696.

Welsh, J., and Bustard, D.W. 1979. Pascal-Plus—Another language for modular multiprogramming. *Software—Practice and Experience 9*, 11 (November), 947–957.

Wirth, N. 1971. The programming language Pascal. *Acta Informatica 1*, 35–63.

Wirth, N. 1977. Modula—A language for modular multiprogramming. *Software—Practice and Experience 7*, 1 (January–February), 3–35.

Wirth, N. 1982. *Programming in Modula-2.* Springer-Verlag, New York.

PART VI

IMPLEMENTATION ISSUES

18

SUPERPASCAL: A PUBLICATION LANGUAGE FOR PARALLEL SCIENTIFIC COMPUTING

PER BRINCH HANSEN

(1994)

Parallel computers will not become widely used until scientists and engineers adopt a common programming language for publication of parallel scientific algorithms. This paper describes the publication language SuperPascal by examples. SuperPascal extends Pascal with deterministic statements for parallel processes and synchronous message communication. The language permits unrestricted combinations of recursive procedures and parallel statements. SuperPascal omits ambiguous and insecure features of Pascal. Restrictions on the use of variables enable a single-pass compiler to check that parallel processes are disjoint, even if the processes use procedures with global variables. A portable implementation of SuperPascal has been developed on a Sun workstation under Unix.

1 INTRODUCTION

One of the major challenges in computer science today is to develop effective programming tools for the next generation of parallel computers. It is equally important to design educational programming tools for the future users of parallel computers. Since the 1960s, computer scientists have recognized the distinction between *publication languages* that emphasize clarity of concepts, and *implementation languages* that reflect pragmatic concerns and historical traditions (Forsythe 1966; Perlis 1966). I believe that parallel computers

P. Brinch Hansen, SuperPascal—A publication language for parallel scientific computing. *Concurrency—Practice and Experience 6*, 5 (August 1994), 461–483.

will not become widely used until scientists and engineers adopt a common programming language for publication of parallel scientific algorithms.

It is instructive to consider the historical role of Pascal as a publication language for sequential computing. The first paper on Pascal appeared in 1971 (Wirth 1971). At that time, there were not very many textbooks on computer science. A few years later, universities began to use Pascal as the standard programming language for computer science courses. The spreading of Pascal motivated authors to use the language in textbooks for a wide variety of computer science courses: introductory programming (Wirth 1973), operating systems (Brinch Hansen 1973), program verification (Alagić 1978), compilers (Welsh 1980), programming languages (Tennent 1981), and algorithms (Aho 1983). In 1983, IEEE acknowledged the status of Pascal as the *lingua franca* of computer science by publishing a Pascal standard (IEEE 1983). Pascal was no longer just another programming tool for computer users. It had become a thinking tool for researchers exploring new fields in computer science.

We now face a similar need for a common programming language for students and researchers in computational science. To understand the requirements of such a language, I spent three years developing a collection of *model programs* that illustrate the use of structured programming in parallel scientific computing (Brinch Hansen 1993a). These programs solve regular problems in science and engineering: linear equations, n-body simulation, matrix multiplication, shortest paths in graphs, sorting, fast Fourier transforms, simulated annealing, primality testing, Laplace's equation, and forest fire simulation. I wrote these programs in *occam* and tested their performance on a *Computing Surface* configured as a pipeline, a tree, a cube, or a matrix of *transputers* (Inmos 1988; McDonald 1991).

This practical experience led me to the following conclusions about the future of parallel scientific computing (Forsythe 1966; Dunham 1982; May 1989; Brinch Hansen 1993a):

1. A *general-purpose parallel computer* of the near future will probably be a multicomputer with tens to thousands of processors with local memories only. The computer will support automatic routing of messages between any pair of processors. The hardware architecture will be transparent to programmers, who will be able to connect processors arbitrarily by virtual communication channels. Such a parallel computer will enable programmers to think in terms of problem-oriented process configurations. There will be no need to map these configura-

tions onto a fixed architecture, such as a hypercube.

2. The regular problems in computational science can be solved efficiently by *deterministic parallel computations.* I have not found it necessary to use a statement that enables a parallel process to poll several channels until a communication takes place on one of them. Nondeterministic communication is necessary at the hardware level in a routing network, but appears to be of minor importance in parallel programs for computational science.

3. Parallel scientific algorithms can be developed in an *elegant publication language* and tested on a sequential computer. When an algorithm works, it can easily be moved to a particular multicomputer by rewriting the algorithm in another programming language chosen for pragmatic rather than intellectual reasons. Subtle parallel algorithms should be published in their entirety as executable programs written in a publication language. Such programs may serve as models for other scientists, who wish to study them with the assurance that every detail has been considered, explained, and tested.

A publication language for computational science should, in my opinion, have the following properties:

1. The language should extend a widely used standard language with *deterministic parallelism* and *message communication.* The extensions should be defined in the spirit of the standard language.

2. The language should make it possible to program *arbitrary configurations* of parallel processes connected by communication channels. These configurations may be defined iteratively or recursively and created dynamically.

3. The language should enable a single-pass compiler to check that parallel processes do not interfere in a time-dependent manner. This check is known as *syntactic interference control.*

The following describes SuperPascal—a publication language for parallel scientific computing. SuperPascal extends Pascal with deterministic statements for parallel processes and synchronous communication. The language permits unrestricted combinations of recursive procedures and parallel statements. SuperPascal omits ambiguous and insecure features of Pascal.

Restrictions on the use of variables permit a single-pass compiler to check that parallel processes are disjoint, even if the processes use procedures with global variables.

Since the model programs cover a broad spectrum of algorithms for scientific computing, I have used them as a guideline for language design. SuperPascal is based on well-known language features (Dijkstra 1968; Hoare 1971, 1972, 1985; Ambler 1977; Lampson 1977; IEEE 1983; Brinch Hansen 1987; Inmos 1988). My only contribution has been to select the smallest number of concepts that enable me to express the model programs elegantly. This paper illustrates the parallel features of SuperPascal by examples. The SuperPascal language report defines the syntax and semantics concisely and explains the differences between SuperPascal and Pascal (Brinch Hansen 1994a). The interference control is further discussed in (Brinch Hansen 1994b).

A *portable implementation* of SuperPascal has been developed on a Sun workstation under Unix. It consists of a compiler and an interpreter written in Pascal. The SuperPascal compiler is based on the Pascal compiler described and listed in (Brinch Hansen 1985). The compiler and interpreter are in the public domain. You can obtain the SuperPascal software by using anonymous FTP from the directory *pbh* at *top.cis.syr.edu.* The software has been used to rewrite the model programs for computational science in SuperPascal.

2 A PROGRAMMING EXAMPLE

I will use pieces of a model program to illustrate the features of SuperPascal. The Miller-Rabin algorithm is used for *primality testing* of a large integer (Rabin 1980). The model program performs p probabilistic tests of the same integer simultaneously on p processors. Each test either proves that the integer is composite, or it fails to prove anything. However, if, say, 40 trials of a 160-digit decimal number all fail, the number is prime with virtual certainty (Brinch Hansen 1992a, 1992b).

The program performs multiple-length arithmetic on natural numbers represented by arrays of w digits (plus an overflow digit):

```
type number = array [0..w] of integer;
```

A single trial is defined by a procedure with the heading

```
procedure test(a: number; seed: real;
  var composite: boolean)
```

Each trial initializes a random number generator with a distinct seed.

The parallel computation is organized as a ring network consisting of a master process and a pipeline connected by two communication channels (Fig. 1).

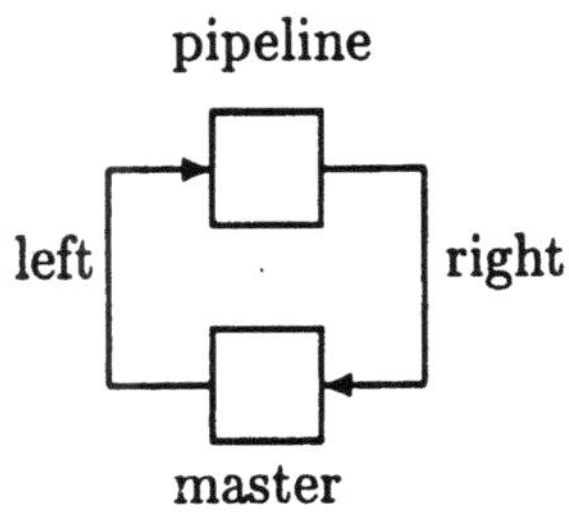

Figure 1 A ring network.

The pipeline consists of p identical, parallel nodes connected by $p+1$ communication channels (Fig. 2).

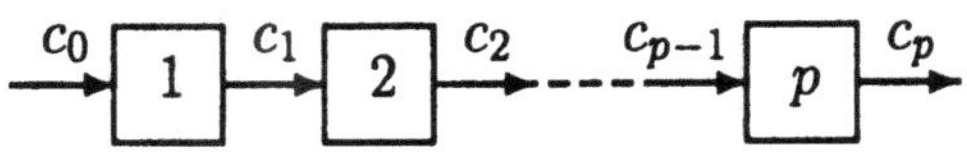

Figure 2 A pipeline.

The master sends a number through the pipeline and receives p boolean values from the pipeline. The booleans are the results of p independent trials performed in parallel by the nodes.

3 MESSAGE COMMUNICATION

3.1 Communication channels

The communication channels of SuperPascal are *deterministic synchronous channels:*

1. A channel can transmit one message at a time in either direction between two parallel processes.

2. Before a communication, a process makes a deterministic selection of a communication channel, a communication direction, and a message type.

3. A communication takes place when one process is ready to send a message of some type through a channel, and another process is ready to receive a message of the same type through the same channel.

3.2 Channel and message types

A channel is not a variable, but a communication medium shared by two parallel processes. Each channel is created dynamically and identified by a distinct value, known as a *channel reference*. A variable that holds a channel reference is called a *channel variable*. An expression that denotes a channel reference is called a *channel expression*. These concepts are borrowed from *Joyce* (Brinch Hansen 1987).

As an example, the declarations

```
type channel = *(boolean, number);
var left: channel;
```

define a new type, named *channel*, and a variable of this type, named *left*. The value of the variable is a reference to a channel that can transmit messages of types *boolean* and *number* only.

In general, a type definition of the form

$$\textbf{type } T = *(T_1, T_2, \ldots, T_n);$$

introduces a new *channel type* T. The values of type T are an unordered set of channel references created dynamically. Each channel reference of type T denotes a distinct channel that can transmit messages of types $T_1, T_2, \ldots, T_n$ only (the *message types*).

3.3 Channel creation

The effect of an *open* statement

$$\text{open}(v)$$

is to create a new channel and assign the corresponding channel reference to a channel variable v. The channel reference is of the same type as the channel variable.

The abbreviation

$$\text{open}(v_1, v_2, \ldots, v_n)$$

is equivalent to

$$\textbf{begin}\ \text{open}(v_1);\ \text{open}(v_2, \ldots, v_n)\ \textbf{end}$$

As an example, two channels, *left* and *right*, can be opened as follows

open(left, right)

or as shown below

begin open(left); open(right) **end**

A channel exists until the program execution ends.

3.4 Communication procedures

Consider a process that receives a number a through a channel, *left*, and sends it through another channel, *right:*

```
var left, right: channel; a: number;
receive(left, a); send(right, a)
```

The message communication is handled by two required procedures, *send* and *receive.*

In general, a *send* statement

send(b, e)

denotes *output* of the value of an expression e through the channel denoted by an expression b. The expression b must be of a channel type T, and the type of the expression e must be a message type of T.

A *receive* statement

receive(c, v)

denotes *input* of the value of a variable v through the channel denoted by an expression c. The expression c must be of a channel type T, and the type of the variable v must be a message type of T.

The send and receive operations defined by the above statements are said to *match* if they satisfy the following conditions:

1. The channel expressions b and c are of the same type T and denote the same channel.

2. The output expression e and the input variable v are of the same type, which is a message type of T.

The execution of a send operation delays a process until another process is ready to execute a matching receive operation (and vice versa). If and when this happens, a *communication* takes place as follows:

1. The sending process obtains a value by evaluating the output expression e.

2. The receiving process assigns the value to the input variable v.

After the communication, the sending and receiving processes proceed independently.

The abbrevation

$$\text{send}(b, e_1, e_2, \ldots, e_n)$$

is equivalent to

$$\textbf{begin } \text{send}(b, e_1); \text{send}(b, e_2, \ldots, e_n) \textbf{ end}$$

Similarly,

$$\text{receive}(c, v_1, v_2, \ldots, v_n)$$

is equivalent to

$$\textbf{begin } \text{receive}(c, v_1); \text{receive}(c, v_2, \ldots, v_n) \textbf{ end}$$

The following *communication errors* are detected at run-time:

1. *Undefined channel reference:* A channel expression does not denote a channel.

2. *Channel contention:* Two parallel processes both attempt to send (or receive) through the same channel at the same time.

3. *Message type error:* Two parallel processes attempt to communicate through the same channel, but the output expression and the input variable are of different message types.

Message communication is illustrated by two procedures in the primality testing program. The *master* process, shown in Fig. 1, sends a number a through its left channel, and receives p booleans through its right channel. If at least one of the booleans is true, the number is composite; otherwise, it is considered to be prime (Algorithm 1).

```
procedure master(
  a: number; var prime: boolean;
  left, right: channel);
var i: integer; composite: boolean;
begin
  send(left, a); prime := true;
  for i := 1 to p do
    begin
      receive(right, composite);
      if composite then
        prime := false
    end
end;
```

Algorithm 1 Master.

The pipeline *nodes*, shown in Fig. 2, are numbered 1 through p. Each node receives a number a through its left channel, and sends a through its right channel (unless the node is the last one in the pipeline). The node then tests the number for primality using the node index i as the seed of its random number generator. Finally, the node outputs the boolean result of its own trial, and copies the results obtained by its $i - 1$ predecessors (if any) in the pipeline (Algorithm 2).

3.5 Channel arrays

Since channel references are typed values, it is possible to define an array of channel references. A variable of such a type represents an array of channels.

The pipeline nodes in Fig. 2 are connected by a row of channels created as follows:

```
procedure node(i: integer;
  left, right: channel);
var a: number; j: integer;
  composite: boolean;
begin
  receive(left, a);
  if i < p then send(right, a);
  test(a, i, composite);
  send(right, composite);
  for j := 1 to i - 1 do
    begin
      receive(left, composite);
      send(right, composite)
    end
end;
```

Algorithm 2 Node.

```
type channel = *(boolean, number);
  row = array [0..p] of channel;
var c: row; i: integer;
for i := 0 to p do open(c[i])
```

Later, I will program a matrix of processes connected by a horizontal and a vertical matrix of channels. The channel matrices, h and v, are defined and initialized as follows:

```
type
  row = array [0..q] of channel;
  net = array [0..q] of row;
var h, v: net; i, j: integer;
for i := 0 to q do
  for j := 0 to q do
    open(h[i,j], v[i,j])
```

3.6 Channel variables

The value of a channel variable v of a type T is undefined, unless a channel reference of type T has been assigned to v by executing an open statement

$$\text{open}(v)$$

or an assignment statement

$$v := e$$

If the value of the expression e is a channel reference of type T, the effect of the assignment statement is to make the values of v and e denote the same channel.

If e and f are channel expressions of the same type, the boolean expression

$$e = f$$

is true, if e and f denote the same channel, and is false otherwise. The boolean expression

$$e <> f$$

is equivalent to

$$\textbf{not } (e = f)$$

In the following example, the references to two channels, *left* and *right*, are assigned to the first and last elements of a channel array c:

c[0] := left; c[p] := right

After the first assignment, the value of the boolean expression

c[0] = left

is *true*.

4 PARALLEL PROCESSES

4.1 Parallel statements

The effect of a *parallel statement*

$$\textbf{parallel } S_1|S_2|\ldots|S_n \textbf{ end}$$

```
procedure ring(a: number;
  var prime: boolean);
var left, right: channel;
begin
  open(left, right);
  parallel
    pipeline(left, right)|
    master(a, prime, left, right)
  end
end;
```

Algorithm 3 Ring.

is to execute the *process statements* $S_1, S_2, \ldots, S_n$ as parallel processes until all of them have terminated.

Algorithm 3 defines a *ring net* that determines if a given integer a is prime. The ring, shown in Fig. 1, consists of two parallel processes, a master and a pipeline, which share two channels. The master and the pipeline run in parallel until both of them have terminated.

A parallel statement enables you to run different kinds of algorithms in parallel. This idea is useful only for a small number of processes. It is impractical to write thousands of process statements, even if they are identical.

4.2 Forall statements

To exploit parallel computing with many processors, we need the ability to run multiple instances of the same algorithm in parallel.

As an example, consider the *pipeline* for primality testing. From the abstract point of view, shown in Fig. 1, the pipeline is a single process with two external channels. At the more detailed level, shown in Fig. 2, the pipeline consists of an array of identical, parallel nodes connected by a row of channels.

Algorithm 4 defines the pipeline.

The first and last elements of the channel array c

$$\text{c[0]} = \text{left} \qquad \text{c[p]} = \text{right}$$

refer to the external channels of the pipeline. The remaining elements

```
procedure pipeline(left, right: channel);
type row = array [0..p] of channel;
var c: row; i: integer;
begin
  c[0] := left; c[p] := right;
  for i := 1 to p - 1 do
    open(c[i]);
  forall i := 1 to p do
    node(i, c[i-1], c[i])
end;
```

Algorithm 4 Iterative pipeline.

```
c[1], c[2], ..., c[p-1]
```

denote the internal channels.

For $p \geq 1$, the statement

```
forall i := 1 to p do
  node(i, c[i-1], c[i])
```

is equivalent to the following statement (which is too tedious to write out in full for a pipeline with more than, say, ten nodes):

```
parallel
  node(1, c[0], c[1])|
  node(2, c[1], c[2])|
    ...
  node(p, c[p-1], c[p])
end
```

The variable i used in the *forall* statement is not the same variable as the variable i declared at the beginning of the pipeline procedure.

In the *forall* statement, the clause

```
i := 1 to p
```

is a *declaration* of an *index variable* i that is local to the procedure statement

```
node(i, c[i-1], c[i])
```

Each node process has its own instance of this variable, which holds a distinct index in the range from 1 to p.

It is a coincidence that the control variable of the *for* statement and the index variable of the *forall* statement have the same identifier in this example. However, the scopes of these variables are different.

In general, a *forall* statement

$$\textbf{forall } i := e_1 \textbf{ to } e_2 \textbf{ do } S$$

denotes a (possibly empty) array of parallel processes, called *element processes*, and a corresponding range of values, called *process indices*. The lower and upper bounds of the index range are denoted by two expressions, e_1 and e_2, of the same simple type. Every index value corresponds to a separate element process defined by an *index variable* i and an *element statement* S.

The *index variable declaration*

$$i := e_1 \textbf{ to } e_2$$

introduces the variable i that is local to S.

A *forall* statement is executed as follows:

1. The expressions, e_1 and e_2, are evaluated. If $e_1 > e_2$, the execution of the *forall* statement terminates; otherwise, step 2 takes place.

2. $e_2 - e_1 + 1$ element processes run in parallel until all of them have terminated. Every element process creates a local instance of the index variable i, assigns the corresponding process index to the variable, and executes the element statement S. When an element process terminates, its local instance of the index variable ceases to exist.

A model program for solving *Laplace's equation* uses a *process matrix* (Brinch Hansen 1993b). Figure 3 shows a $q \times q$ matrix of parallel nodes connected by two channel matrices, h and v.

Each node process is defined by a procedure with the heading:

```
procedure node(i, j: integer;
  up, down, left, right: channel)
```

A node has a pair of indices (i, j) and is connected to its four nearest neighbors by channels, *up, down, left*, and *right*.

The process matrix is defined by nested *forall* statements:

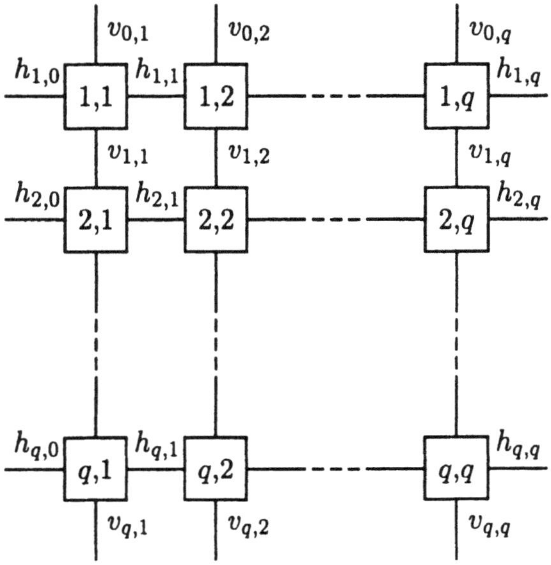

Figure 3 A process matrix.

```
forall i := 1 to q do
  forall j := 1 to q do
    node(i, j, v[i-1,j], v[i,j], h[i,j-1], h[i,j])
```

4.3 Recursive parallel processes

SuperPascal supports the beautiful concept of recursive parallel processes. Figure 4 illustrates a recursive definition of a *pipeline* with p nodes:

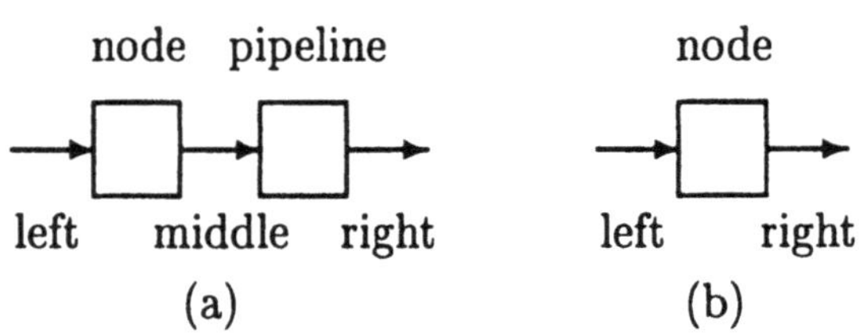

Figure 4 A recursive pipeline.

1. If $p > 1$, the pipeline consists of a single node followed by a shorter pipeline of $p - 1$ nodes (Fig. 4a).

2. If $p = 1$, the pipeline consists of a single node only (Fig. 4b).

The pipeline is defined by combining a recursive procedure with a parallel statement (Algorithm 5).

```
procedure pipeline(min, max: integer;
  left, right: channel);
var middle: channel;
begin
  if min < max then
    begin
      open(middle);
      parallel
        node(min, left, middle)|
        pipeline(min + 1, max,
          middle, right)
      end
    end
  else node(min, left, right)
end;
```

Algorithm 5 Recursive pipeline.

The pipeline consists of nodes with indices in the range from *min* to *max* (where $min \leq max$). The pipeline has a left and a right channel. If $min < max$, the pipeline opens a middle channel, and splits into a single node and a smaller pipeline running in parallel; otherwise, the pipeline behaves as a single node.

The effect of the procedure statement

```
pipeline(1, p, left, right)
```

is to activate a pipeline that is equivalent to the one shown in Fig. 2.

The recursive pipeline has a *dynamic length* defined by parameters. The nodes and channels are created by recursive parallel activations of the pipeline procedure. The iterative pipeline programmed earlier has a fixed length because it uses a channel array of fixed length (Algorithm 4).

A model program for *divide and conquer* algorithms uses a binary *process tree* (Brinch Hansen 1991a). Figure 5 shows a tree of seven parallel processes connected by seven channels.

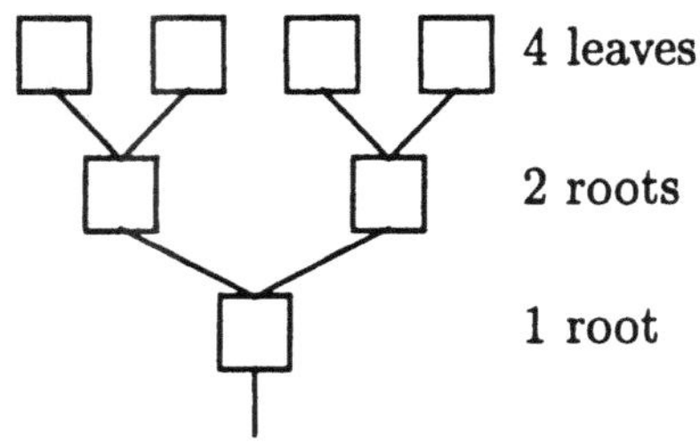

Figure 5 A specific process tree.

The bottom process of the tree inputs data from the bottom channel, and sends half of the data to its left child process, and the other half to its right child process. The splitting of data continues in parallel higher up in the tree, until the data are evenly distributed among the leaf processes at the top. Each leaf transforms its own portion of the data, and outputs the results to its parent process. Each parent combines the partial results of its children, and outputs them to its own parent. The parallel combination of results continues at lower levels in the tree, until the final results are output through the bottom channel.

A process tree can be defined recursively as illustrated by Fig. 6.

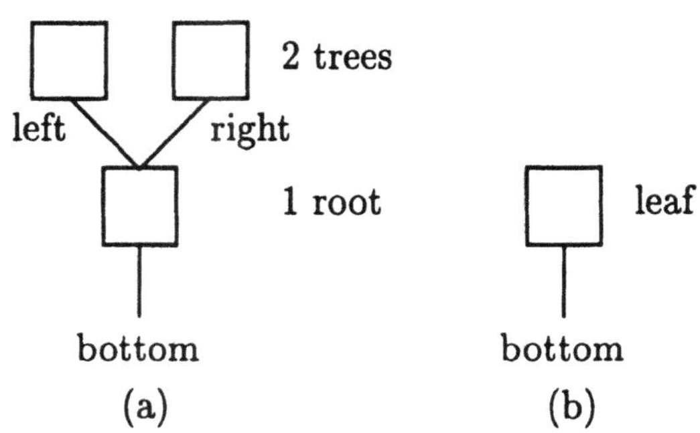

Figure 6 A recursive tree.

A binary tree is connected to its environment by a single bottom channel. A closer look reveals that the tree takes one of two forms:

1. A tree with more than one node consists of a root process and two smaller trees running in parallel (Fig. 6a).

2. A tree with one node only is a leaf process (Fig. 6b).

The process *tree* is defined by a recursive procedure (Algorithm 6). The *depth* of the tree is the number of process layers above the bottom process. Figure 5 shows a tree of depth 2.

```
procedure tree(depth: integer;
  bottom: channel);
var left, right: channel;
begin
  if depth > 0 then
    begin
      open(left, right);
      parallel
        tree(depth - 1, left)|
        tree(depth - 1, right)|
        root(bottom, left, right)
      end
    end
  else leaf(bottom)
end;
```

Algorithm 6 Recursive tree.

The behavior of *roots* and *leaves* is defined by two procedures of the form:

procedure root(bottom, left, right: channel)

procedure leaf(bottom: channel)

These procedures vary from one application of the tree to another.

The effect of the procedure statement

tree(2, bottom)

is to activate a binary tree of depth 2.

A notation for recursive processes is essential in a parallel programming language. The reason is simple. It is impractical to formulate thousands of processes with different behaviors. We must instead rely on repeated use of a small number of behaviors. The simplest problems that satisfy this requirement are those that can be reduced to smaller problems of the same kind and solved by combining the partial results. Recursion is the natural programming tool for these *divide and conquer* algorithms.

5 INTERFERENCE CONTROL

5.1 Disjoint processes

The relative speeds of asynchronous, parallel processes are generally unknown. If parallel processes update the same variables at unpredictable times, the combined effect of the processes is time-dependent. Similarly, if two parallel processes both attempt to send (or receive) messages through the same channel at unpredictable times, the net effect is time-dependent. Processes with *time-dependent errors* are said to *interfere* with one another due to *variable* or *channel conflicts.*

When a program with a time-dependent error is executed repeatedly with the same input, the output usually varies in an unpredictable manner from one run to another. The irreproducible behavior makes it difficult to locate interference by systematic program testing. The most effective remedy is to introduce additional restrictions, which make process interference impossible. These restrictions must be checked by a compiler before a parallel program is executed.

In the following, I concentrate on syntactic detection of variable conflicts. The basic requirement is simple: Parallel processes can only update disjoint sets of variables. A variable that is updated by a process may only be used by that process. Parallel processes may, however, share variables that are not updated by any of them. Parallel processes that satisfy this requirement are called *disjoint processes.*

5.2 Variable contexts

I will illustrate the issues of interference control by small examples only. The problem is discussed concisely in (Brinch Hansen 1994b).

In theory, syntactic detection of variable conflicts is a straightforward process. A single-pass compiler scans a program text once. For every statement S, the compiler determines the set of variables that may be updated and the set of variables that may be used as expression operands during the execution of S. These sets are called the *target* and *expression variables* of S. Together they define the *variable context* of S. If we know the variable context of every statement, it is easy to check if parallel statements define disjoint processes.

As an example, the *open* statement

open(h[i,j])

denotes creation of a component $h_{i,j}$ of a channel array h. Since the index values i and j are known during execution only, a compiler is unable to distinguish between different elements of the same array. Consequently, the entire array h is regarded as a target variable (the only one) of the open statement. The expression variables of the statement are i and j.

An *entire variable* is a variable denoted by an identifier only, such as h, i, or j above. During compilation, any operation on a component of a *structured variable* is regarded as an operation on the entire variable. The target and expression variables of a statement are therefore sets of entire variables.

A compiler cannot predict if a component of a conditional statement will be executed or skipped. To be on the safe side, the variable context of a *structured statement* is defined as the union of the variable contexts of its components.

Consider the conditional statement

if i < p **then** send(right, a)

It has no target variables, but uses three expression variables, i, *right* and a (assuming that p is a constant).

5.3 Parallel statements

The choice of a notation for parallel processes is profoundly influenced by the requirement that a compiler must be able to detect process interference. The syntax of a parallel statement

$$\textbf{parallel}\ S_1|S_2|\ldots|S_n\ \textbf{end}$$

clearly shows that the process statements $S_1, S_2, \ldots, S_n$ are executed in parallel.

The following restriction ensures that a parallel statement denotes disjoint processes: *A target variable of one process statement cannot be a target or an expression variable of another process statement.* This rule is enforced by a compiler.

Let me illustrate this restriction with three examples. The parallel statement

```
parallel open(h[i,j])|open(v[i,j]) end
```

defines two *open* statements executed simultaneously. The target variable h of the first process statement does not occur in the second process statement. Similarly, the target variable v of the second process statement is not used in the first process statement. Consequently, the parallel statement defines disjoint processes.

However, the parallel statement

```
parallel
  receive(left, a)|
  if i < p then send(right, a)
end
```

is incorrect, because the target variable a of the first process statement is also an expression variable of the second process statement.

Finally, the parallel statement

```
parallel c[0] := left|c[p] := right end
```

is incorrect, since the process statements use the same target variable c.

Occasionally, a programmer may wish to override the interference control of parallel statements. This is useful when it is obvious that parallel processes update distinct elements of the same array. The previous restriction does not apply to a parallel statement prefixed by the clause [*sic*]. This is called an *unrestricted statement.* The programmer must prove that such a statement denotes disjoint processes.

The following example is taken from a model program that uses the process matrix shown in Fig. 3:

```
[sic] { 1 <= k <= m }
parallel
  receive(up, u[0,k])|
  send(down, u[m,k])|
  receive(left, u[k,0])|
  send(right, u[k,m])
end
```

This statement enables a node process to simultaneously exchange four elements of a local array u with its nearest neighbors. The initial comment implies that the two input elements are distinct and are not used as output elements.

The programmer should realize that the slightest mistake in an unrestricted statement may introduce a subtle time-dependent error. The incorrect statement

```
[sic] { 1 <= k <= m }
parallel
  receive(up, u[1,k])|
  send(down, u[m,k])|
  receive(left, u[k,1])|
  send(right, u[k,m])
end
```

is time-dependent, but only if $k = 1$.

5.4 Forall statements

The following restriction ensures that the statement

forall $i := e_1$ **to** e_2 **do** S

denotes disjoint processes: *In a forall statement, the element statement S cannot use target variables.* This is checked by a compiler.

This restriction implies that a process array must output its final results to another process or a file. Otherwise, the results will be lost when the element processes terminate and their local variables disappear. For technological reasons, the same restriction is necessary if the element processes run on separate processors in a parallel computer with distributed memory.

In the primality testing program, a pipeline is defined by the statement

```
forall i := 1 to p do node(i, c[i-1], c[i])
```

Since the node procedure has value parameters only, the procedure statement

```
node(i, c[i-1], c[i])
```

uses expression variables only (i and c).

The incorrect statement

```
forall i := 1 to p - 1 do open(c[i])
```

denotes element processes that attempt to update the same variable c in parallel.

If it is desirable to use the above statement, it must be turned into an *unrestricted statement*:

```
[sic] { distinct elements c[i] }
forall i := 1 to p - 1 do open(c[i])
```

The initial comment shows that the node processes are disjoint, since they update distinct elements of the channel array c.

Again, it needs to be said that a programming error in an unrestricted statement may cause time-dependent behavior. The incorrect statement

```
[sic] forall i := 1 to p - 1 do open(c[1])
```

denotes parallel assignments of channel references to the same array element c_1.

Needless to say, syntactic interference control is of limited value if it is frequently overridden. A programmer should make a conscientious effort to limit the use of unrestricted statements as much as possible. The thirteen model programs, that I wrote, include five unrestricted statements only; all of them denote operations on distinct array elements.

5.5 Variable parameters

To enable a compiler to recognize distinct variables, a language should have the property that distinct variable identifiers occurring in the same statement denote distinct entire variables. Due to the scope rules of Pascal, this assumption is satisfied by all entire variables except variable parameters.

The following procedure denotes parallel creation of a pair of channels:

```
procedure pair(var c, d: channel);
begin
  parallel open(c)|open(d) end
end;
```

The parallel processes are disjoint only if the formal parameters, c and d, denote distinct actual parameters.

The procedure statement

```
pair(h[i,j], v[i,j])
```

is valid, since the actual parameters are elements of different arrays, h and v.

However, the procedure statement

```
pair(left, left)
```

is incorrect, because it makes the identifiers, c and d, *aliases* of the same variable, *left*.

Aliasing of variable parameters is prevented by the following restriction: *The actual variable parameters of a procedure statement must be distinct entire variables (or components of such variables).*

An *unrestricted statement* is not subject to this restriction. A model program for *n-body simulation* computes the gravitational forces between a pair of bodies, p_i and p_j, and adds each force to the total force acting on the corresponding body (Brinch Hansen 1991b). This operation is denoted by a procedure statement

```
{ i <> j } [sic] addforces(p[j], p[i])
```

with two actual variable parameters. The initial comment shows that the parameters, p_i and p_j, are distinct elements of the same array variable p.

5.6 Global variables

Global variables used in procedures are another source of aliasing. Consider a procedure that updates a global seed and returns a random number (Algorithm 7).

The procedure statement

```
random(x)
```

```
var seed: real;

procedure random(var number: real);
var temp: real;
begin
  temp := a*seed;
  seed := temp - m*trunc(temp/m);
  number := seed/m
end;
```

Algorithm 7 Random number generator.

denotes an operation that updates two distinct variables, x and *seed.*

On the other hand, the procedure statement

random(seed)

turns the identifier *number* into an alias for *seed.*

To prevent aliasing, it is necessary to regard the global variable as an *implicit parameter* of both procedure statements. Since the procedure uses the global variable as a target *and* an expression variable, it is both an *implicit variable parameter* and an *implicit value parameter* of the procedure statements.

The rule that actual variable parameters cannot be aliases applies to all variable parameters of a procedure statement, explicit as well as implicit parameters. However, since implicit value parameters can also cause trouble, we need a stronger restriction defined as follows (Brinch Hansen 1994b): The *restricted actual parameters* of a procedure statement are the explicit variable parameters that occur in the statement and the implicit parameters of the corresponding procedure block. *The restricted actual parameters of a procedure statement must be distinct entire variables (or components of such variables).*

In the primality testing program, the pipeline nodes use a random number generator. If the seed variable is global to the node procedure, then the seed is also an implicit variable parameter of the procedure statement

node(i, c[i–1], c[i])

Consequently, the statement

```
forall i := 1 to p do node(i, c[i-1], c[i])
```

denotes parallel processes that (indirectly) update the same global variable at unpredictable times. The concept of implicit parameters enables a compiler to detect this variable conflict. The problem is avoided by making the procedure, *random*, and its global variable, *seed*, local to the node procedure. The node processes will then be updating different instances of this variable.

The parallel statement

```
parallel write(x)|writeln end
```

is invalid because the required textfile *output* is an implicit variable parameter of both *write* statements.

Similarly, the parallel statement

```
parallel
  read(x)|
  if eof then writeln
end
```

is incorrect because the required textfile *input* is an implicit variable parameter of the *read* statement and an implicit value parameter of the *eof* function designator.

5.7 Functions

Functions may use global variables as implicit value parameters only. The following rules ensure that functions have no side-effects:

1. Functions cannot use implicit or explicit variable parameters.
2. Procedure statements cannot occur in the statement part of a function block.

The latter restriction implies that functions cannot use the required procedures for message communication and file input/output. This rule may seem startling at first. I introduced it after noticing that my model programs include over 40 functions, none of which violate this restriction.

Since functions have no side-effects, expressions cannot cause process interference.

5.8 Further restrictions

Syntactic detection of variable conflicts during single-pass compilation requires additional language restrictions:

1. *Pointer types* are omitted.
2. *Goto statements* and *labels* are omitted.
3. *Procedural* and *functional parameters* are omitted.
4. *Forward declarations* are omitted.
5. *Recursive functions* and *procedures* cannot use implicit parameters.

These design decisions are discussed in (Brinch Hansen 1994b).

5.9 Channel conflicts

Due to the use of channel references, a compiler is unable to detect process interference caused by channel conflicts. From a theoretical point of view, I have serious misgivings about this flaw. In practice, I have found it to be a minor problem only. Some channel conflicts are detected by the run-time checking of communication errors mentioned earlier. For regular process configurations, such as pipelines, trees, and matrices, the remaining channel conflicts are easy to locate by proofreading the few procedures that define how parallel processes are connected by channels.

6 SUPERPASCAL VERSUS OCCAM

occam2 is an admirable implementation language for transputer systems (Inmos 1988). It achieves high efficiency by relying on static allocation of processors and memory. The occam notation is somewhat bulky and not sufficiently general for a publication language:

1. Key words are capitalized.
2. A real constant requires eight additional characters to define the length of its binary representation.
3. Simple statements must be written on separate lines.
4. An *if* statement requires two additional lines to describe an empty *else* statement.

5. Array types cannot be named.

6. Record types cannot be used.

7. Process arrays must have constant lengths.

8. Functions and procedures cannot be recursive.

occam3 includes type definitions, but is considerably more complicated than occam2 (Kerridge 1993).

occam was an invaluable source of inspiration for SuperPascal. Years ahead of its time, occam set a standard of simplicity and security against which future parallel languages will be measured. The parallel features of SuperPascal are a subset of occam2 with the added generality of dynamic process arrays and recursive parallel processes. This generality enables you to write parallel algorithms that cannot be expressed in occam.

7 FINAL REMARKS

Present multicomputers are quite difficult to program. To achieve high performance, each program must be tailored to the configuration of a particular computer. Scientific users, who are primarily interested in getting numerical results, constantly have to reprogram new parallel architectures and are getting increasingly frustrated at having to do this (Sanz 1989).

As educators, we should ignore this short-term problem and teach our students to write programs for the next generation of parallel computers. These will probably be general-purpose multicomputers that can run portable scientific programs written in parallel programming languages.

In this paper, I have suggested that universities should adopt a common programming language for publication of papers and textbooks on parallel scientific algorithms. The language Pascal has played a major role as a publication language for sequential computing. Building on that tradition, I have developed SuperPascal as a publication language for computational science. SuperPascal extends Pascal with deterministic statements for parallel processes and message communication. The language enables you to define arbitrary configurations of parallel processes, both iteratively and recursively. The number of processes may vary dynamically.

I have used the SuperPascal notation to write portable programs for regular problems in computational science. I found it easy to express these programs in three different programming languages (SuperPascal, Joyce, and occam2) and run them on three different architectures (a Unix workstation, an Encore Multimax, and a Meiko Computing Surface).

Acknowledgements

While writing this paper, I have benefited from the perceptive comments of James Allwright, Jonathan Greenfield and Peter O'Hearn.

References

Aho, A.V., Hopcroft, J.E., and Ullman, J.D. 1983. *Data Structures and Algorithms.* Addison-Wesley, Reading, MA.

Alagić, S., and Arbib, M.A. 1978. *The Design of Well-Structured and Correct Programs.* Springer-Verlag, New York.

Ambler, A.L., Good, D.I., Browne, J.C., Burger, W.F., Cohen, R.M., and Wells, R.E. 1977. Gypsy: a language for specification and implementation of verifiable programs. *ACM SIGPLAN Notices 12*, 2, 1–10.

Brinch Hansen, P. 1973. *Operating System Principles.* Prentice-Hall, Englewood Cliffs, NJ.

Brinch Hansen, P. 1985. *Brinch Hansen on Pascal Compilers.* Prentice-Hall, Englewood Cliffs, NJ.

Brinch Hansen, P. 1987. Joyce—A programming language for distributed systems. *Software Practice and Experience 17*, 1 (January), 29–50.

Brinch Hansen, P. 1991a. Parallel divide and conquer. School of Computer and Information Science, Syracuse University, Syracuse, NY.

Brinch Hansen, P. 1991b. The n-body pipeline. School of Computer and Information Science, Syracuse University, Syracuse, NY.

Brinch Hansen, P. 1992a. Primality testing. School of Computer and Information Science, Syracuse University, Syracuse, NY.

Brinch Hansen, P. 1992b. Parallel Monte Carlo trials. School of Computer and Information Science, Syracuse University, Syracuse, NY.

Brinch Hansen, P. 1993a. Model programs for computational science: A programming methodology for multicomputers. *Concurrency—Practice and Experience 5*, 5 (August), 407–423.

Brinch Hansen, P. 1993b. Parallel cellular automata: A model program for computational science. *Concurrency—Practice and Experience 5*, 5 (August) 425–448.

Brinch Hansen, P. 1994a. The programming language SuperPascal. *Software—Practice and Experience 24*, 5 (May), 467–483.

Brinch Hansen, P. 1994b. Interference control in SuperPascal—A block-structured parallel language. *Computer Journal 37*, 5, 399–406.

Dijkstra, E.W. 1968. Cooperating sequential processes. In *Programming Languages*, F. Genuys, Ed. Academic Press, New York, 43–112.

Dunham, C.B. 1982. The necessity of publishing programs. *Computer Journal 25*, 1, 61–62.

Forsythe, G.E. 1966. Algorithms for scientific computing. *Communications of the ACM 9*, 4 (April), 255–256.

Hoare, C.A.R. 1971. Procedures and parameters: an axiomatic approach. *Lecture Notes in Mathematics 188*, 102–171.

Hoare, C.A.R. 1972. Towards a theory of parallel programming. In *Operating Systems Techniques*, C.A.R. Hoare and R.H. Perrott, Eds. Academic Press, New York, 61–71.

Hoare, C.A.R. 1985. *Communicating Sequential Processes.* Prentice Hall, Englewood Cliffs, NJ.

IEEE 1983. *IEEE Standard Pascal Computer Programming Language*, Institute of Electrical and Electronics Engineers, New York.

Inmos, Ltd. 1988. *occam 2 Reference Manual*, Prentice Hall, Englewood Cliffs, NJ.

Kerridge, J. 1993. Using occam3 to build large parallel systems: Part 1, occam3 features. *Transputer Communications 1* (to appear).

Lampson, B.W., Horning, J.J., London, R.L., Mitchell, J.G., and Popek, G.J. 1977. Report on the programming language Euclid. *ACM SIGPLAN Notices 12*, 2 (February).

McDonald, N. 1991. Meiko Scientific, Ltd. In *Past, Present, Parallel: A Survey of Available Parallel Computing Systems*, A. Trew and G. Wilson, Eds. Springer-Verlag, New York, 165–175.

May, D. 1989. Discussion. In *Scientific Applications of Multiprocessors*, R. Elliott and C.A.R. Hoare, Eds. Prentice-Hall, Englewood Cliffs, NJ, 54.

Perlis, A.J. 1966. A new policy for algorithms? *Communications of the ACM 9*, 4 (April), 255.

Rabin, M.O. 1980. Probabilistic algorithms for testing primality. *Journal of Number Theory 12*, 128–138.

Sanz, J.L.C., Ed. 1989. *Opportunities and Constraints of Parallel Computing*, Springer-Verlag, New York.

Tennent, R.D. 1981. *Principles of Programming Languages*, Prentice-Hall, Englewood Cliffs, NJ.

Welsh, J., and McKeag, M. 1980. *Structured System Programming*, Prentice-Hall, Englewood Cliffs, NJ.

Wirth, N. 1971. The programming language Pascal. *Acta Informatica 1*, 35–63.

Wirth, N. 1973. *Systematic Programming: An Introduction.* Prentice-Hall, Englewood Cliffs, NJ.

19

EFFICIENT PARALLEL RECURSION

PER BRINCH HANSEN

(1995)

A simple mechanism is proposed for dynamic memory allocation of a parallel recursive program with Algol-like scope rules. The method is about as fast as the traditional stack discipline for sequential languages. It has been used to implement the parallel programming language SuperPascal.

1 Introduction

I will describe a memory allocation scheme for block structured programming languages that support unbounded activation of parallel processes and recursive procedures. This technique has been used to implement the parallel programming language SuperPascal (Brinch Hansen 1994).

Three decades ago, Dijkstra (1960) proposed the standard method of dynamic memory allocation for recursive procedures in block structured, sequential languages, such as Algol 60 (Naur 1963), Pascal (Wirth 1971) and C (Kernighan 1978).

The scope rules of Algol-like languages support stack allocation of memory for sequential programs. All variables are kept in a single stack. When a block is activated, an *activation record* (a data segment of fixed length) is pushed on the stack. The activation record holds a fresh instance of every local variable of the block. At the end of the activation, the activation record is popped from the stack. Since each activation creates a new instance of the local variables, stack allocation works for both recursive and nonrecursive procedures. The crucial assumption behind stack allocation is that dynamically nested block activations always terminate in last-in, first-out order.

P. Brinch Hansen, Efficient parallel recursion, *SIGPLAN Notices 30*, 12 (December 1995), 9–16.

After two decades of research in parallel programming languages, there is still no efficient standard method for dynamic memory allocation of parallel recursion. When you add parallelism to a block structured language, the variable instances form a tree structured stack with branches that grow and shrink simultaneously. If dynamic parallelism is combined with unbounded recursion, the number and extent of the stack branches are unpredictable.

In a parallel recursive program, there is no simple relationship between the order in which blocks are entered and exited. So, you cannot use the traditional last-in, first-out allocation. This makes it more difficult to reclaim and reuse the memory space of activation records efficiently.

With few exceptions, language designers have ignored the thorny problems of parallel memory allocation by outlawing recursion and restricting parallelism to the point where it is possible to use static memory allocation.

In many languages, it is impossible to reclaim the memory space of parallel processes. These include Concurrent Pascal (Brinch Hansen 1975), Simone (Kaubisch 1976), Modula (Wirth 1977), Distributed Processes (Brinch Hansen 1978), Pascal Plus (Welsh 1979), StarMod (Cook 1980), SR (Andrews 1981), Concurrent Euclid (Holt 1983), Planet (Crookes 1984) and Pascal-FC (Davies 1990).

CSP (Hoare 1978), Edison (Brinch Hansen 1981), and occam (Inmos 1988) support process activation and termination, but only of a fixed number of parallel nonrecursive processes determined during compilation.

Static memory allocation is adequate for many parallel computations (Fox 1988). However, parallel recursion is the natural programming tool for parallel versions of divide-and-conquer algorithms, such as quicksort, the fast Fourier transform and the Barnes-Hut algorithm for n-body simulation (Fox 1994).

Parallel recursion requires dynamic allocation and release of activation records in a tree structured stack. B6700 Algol (Organick 1973) and Mesa (Lampson, 1980) demonstrate that it is possible to support both parallelism and recursion in systems programming languages. The substantial overhead of parallel processes in these languages is acceptable in operating systems, which support slowly changing configurations of user processes. It is, however, too inefficient for highly parallel computations.

Is there a memory allocation method that makes parallel recursion as efficient as sequential recursion for all systems and user programs? I don't know any. Parallel recursion can probably only be implemented efficiently at the expense of some generality.

As a reasonable compromise, I will confine myself to the problem of allocating activation records of different lengths for a single parallel program in a memory of fixed size. The proposed technique is more ambitious than previous methods in the following sense: *it succeeds in making the activation and termination of parallel processes and recursive procedures equally fast!*

Joyce (Brinch Hansen 1989) was my first attempt to simplify memory allocation for parallel recursion. The multiprocessor implementation of Joyce uses a stack-like scheme for parallel block activation in a single memory heap. On entry to a block, an activation record is allocated at the top of the heap. On exit from the block, the activation record is marked as free. Free space is reclaimed only when it is at the top of the heap. This method works well for many parallel recursive programs. However, it fails if a program continues to demand space for parallel block activations before previously released space can be reclaimed. In that situation, the heap grows until it runs out of memory.

The occasional failure of the Joyce heap made me look for a more robust memory allocation for SuperPascal. After solving this problem, I found that I had reinvented a simplified version of the *Quick Fit* allocator, which was used for heap management in the sequential programming language Bliss (Weinstock 1988).

The main contribution of this paper is the discovery that Quick Fit is an efficient memory allocator for a parallel recursive language that requires an *unbounded, tree structured stack* of activation records. The consistent omission of efficient parallel recursion in previous block structured languages shows that this insight only seems obvious once you know the solution.

2 Assumptions

I will state the assumptions behind the method in general terms. However, I will use the implementation of block structured parallel languages to motivate the assumptions.

The general problem is to allocate and release segments of different lengths in a memory of fixed size under the following assumptions:

- *Each segment occupies a contiguous memory area of fixed length.*

In a block structured program, the unit of memory allocation is an activation record of fixed length that holds the local variable instances of a single activation of a block.

- *A segment is never relocated in memory.*

During program execution, the activation records in use are linked by pointers representing variable parameters, nested blocks, and activation sequences. Dynamic relocation of linked activation records would be complicated and time-consuming.

- *A segment is released only when no other segment in use points to it.*

The scope rules enable a compiler to check that the local variable instances of a block activation are accessed only during the activation. Consequently, the corresponding activation record can safely be released on exit from the block.

- *Segments are generally allocated and released in unpredictable order.*

The nondeterministic nature of parallel recursion complicates the dynamic memory allocation considerably.

- *There is a fixed number of segment lengths.*

A block structured program consists of a fixed number of blocks. (In SuperPascal, a block is either a process statement or a procedure.) Each activation of the same block allocates an activation record of the same fixed length.

- *A program tends to use segments of the same lengths repeatedly.*

This is a plausible hypothesis about any program that uses the same procedures numerous times to transform different parts of large data structures sequentially or in parallel. The measurements in Section 4 strongly support this assumption.

The above assumptions are satisfied by a single block structured program that runs in a fixed memory area. However, they are not realistic for an operating system, which allocates an unbounded number of segments, most of which are unique to particular user jobs.

```
var pool: array [1..limit] of integer;
  memory: array [min..max] of integer;
  top: integer;

procedure initialize;
var index: integer;
begin
  for index := 1 to limit do
     pool[index] := empty;
  top := min - 1
end;

procedure allocate( index, length: integer;
  var address: integer);
begin
  address := pool[index];
  if address <> empty then
    pool[index] := memory[address]
  else
    begin
      address := top + 1;
      top := top + length;
      assume top <= max
    end
end;

procedure release( index, address: integer);
begin
  memory[address] := pool[index];
  pool[index] := address
end;
```

Algorithm 1 Memory allocation.

3 Implementation

Algorithm 1 defines the allocation of activation records for a parallel program that runs on a single processor in a memory area of fixed size. On a multicomputer with distributed memory, each processor must manage its own memory for local processes. On a multiprocessor with shared memory, the allocation and release of activation records must be indivisible operations.

I assume that an operating system allocates a fixed amount of memory for the execution of a parallel program. The allocation method used by the operating system is beyond the scope of this discussion. My only concern is the algorithms used by a running program to allocate activation records within its own memory.

A dynamic boundary divides the program memory into two contiguous parts. One part is the heap, which holds all past and present activation records. The rest is free space. During program execution, the heap can only grow, and the free space can only shrink. A register holds the current top address of the heap.

The blocks in a program have consecutive indices and fixed activation record lengths determined by a compiler. For each block, a running program maintains a pool consisting of all free activation records reclaimed after previous activations of the block. Each pool is represented by an address, which either denotes an empty pool or is the first link in a list of free activation records of the same length.

Initially, the entire memory is free and every pool is empty.

On entry to a block with a given index and length, an attempt is made to allocate a free activation record from the corresponding pool. If the pool is empty, a new activation record of the given length is allocated in the free space, which is reduced accordingly.

On exit from the block, the activation record is released and added to the corresponding pool.

The algorithms for allocating and releasing an activation record are not intended to be implemented as separate procedures. They are part of the machine code executed at the beginning and end of every process statement and procedure. An activation record is allocated or released in constant time. Most processors can perform these simple operations by executing three or four machine instructions.

When the execution of a program ends, its memory area is still divided into pools of free activation records and the remaining free space. However, that does not matter, since the operating system will reclaim the entire memory area as a single unit.

4 Performance

The heap allocation method described here has been used to implement the block structured parallel language SuperPascal. So far, I have written parallel SuperPascal programs for a dozen standard problems in computational science (Brinch Hansen 1995).

Table 1 shows the ability of the heap allocator to recycle previous activation records during the execution of three parallel programs on a single processor.

Table 1 Measurements.

Parallel program	Quicksort tree	N-body pipeline	Laplace matrix
Number of blocks	16	24	28
Process activations	11	300	25,609
Procedure activations	18,120	513,553	67,156
New activation records	51	27	64
Reused activation records	18,080	513,826	92,701

The quicksort tree uses both parallel recursion (to create a binary tree of processes) and sequential recursion (to quicksort in parallel). The program consists of 16 blocks which are activated a total of 18,131 times (eleven process activations plus 18,120 procedure activations). These block activations create 51 new activation records, which are reused 18,080 times.

The n-body pipeline is a parallel nonrecursive program that repeatedly recreates a pipeline to perform force calculation for n gravitational bodies. During an n-body simulation the program activates parallel processes 300 times and procedures 513,553 times. These activations are handled by reusing the same 27 activation records over and over again.

The Laplace matrix is a highly parallel nonrecursive program. It creates parallel processes 25,609 times and calls procedures 67,156 times. These 92,765 block activations require only 64 activation records.

When these parallel program solve larger problems, the two nonrecursive programs run longer, but do not require more activation records. The number of activation records used by the quicksort tree increases slightly when the depth of the sequential recursion increases.

If no procedure is activated recursively or in parallel, the heap allocation uses the same amount of memory as static allocation (one activation record per block). In general, each block requires separate activation records for all activations of the block that may be in progress simultaneously (due to recursion or parallelism, or both).

5 Conclusions

I have described a simple heap mechanism for dynamic memory allocation of a parallel recursive program with Algol-like scope rules.

The mechanism has the following *advantages*:

- The heap allocation supports unbounded dynamic activation and termination of parallel processes and recursive procedures.
- The activation and termination of parallel processes and recursive procedures are equally fast.
- The heap allocation for parallel recursion is as efficient in reusing memory as the traditional stack discipline for sequential recursion.
- On a multicomputer with distributed memory, heap allocation is about as fast as stack allocation.

In its simplest form (presented here), the method has only two *limitations*:

- An activation record used to activate a block can only be reused by activating the same block again. This compromise makes it easy to release and reallocate the memory space of block activations.
- On a multiprocessor with shared memory, the need to lock and unlock the heap twice during a block activation makes the method less attractive.

Both limitations can probably be removed by more complicated variants of the basic idea. I leave that as an exercise for the reader.

Acknowledgements

It is a pleasure to acknowledge the comments of Art Bernstein, Ole-Johan Dahl, Ric Holt, Butler Lampson, Peter O'Hearn, Ron Perrott, and Jørgen Staunstrup.

References

Andrews, G.R. 1981. Synchronizing resources. *ACM Transactions on Programming Languages and Systems 3*, 4 (October), 405–430.

Brinch Hansen, P. 1975. The programming language Concurrent Pascal. *IEEE Transactions on Software Enginering 1*, 2 (June), 199–207.

Brinch Hansen, P. 1978. Distributed processes: A concurrent programming concept. *Communications of the ACM 21*, 11 (November), 934-941.

Brinch Hansen, P. 1981. Edison—a multiprocessor language. *Software—Practice and Experience 11*, 4 (April), 325–361.

Brinch Hansen, P. 1989. A multiprocessor implementation of Joyce. *Software—Practice and Experience 9*, 6 (June), 579–592.

Brinch Hansen, P. 1994. The programming language SuperPascal. *Software—Practice and Experience 24*, 5 (May), 467–483.

Brinch Hansen, P. 1995. *Studies in Computational Science: Parallel Programming Paradigms.* Prentice Hall, Englewood Cliffs, NJ, (March).

Cook, R. 1980. *Mod—a language for distributed programming. *IEEE Transactions on Software Engineering 6*, 6 (November), 563–571.

Crookes, D. and Elder, J.W.G. 1984. An experiment in language design for distributed systems. *Software—Practice and Experience 14*, 10 (October), 957–971.

Davies G.L. and Burns, A. 1990. The teaching language Pascal-FC. *Computer Journal 33*, 147–154.

Dijkstra, E.W. 1960. Recursive programming. *Numerische Mathematik 2*, 312–318.

Fox, G.C., Johnson, M.A., Lyzenga, G.A., Otto, S.W., Salmon, J.K. and Walker, D.W. 1988. *Solving Problems on Concurrent Processors*, Vol. I. Prentice Hall, Englewood Cliffs, NJ.

Fox, G.C., Messina, P.C. and Williams, R.D. 1994. *Parallel Computing Works!* Morgan Kaufman, San Francisco, CA.

Hoare, C.A.R. 1978. Communicating sequential processes. *Communications of the ACM 21*, 8 (August), 666–677.

Holt, R.C. 1983. *Concurrent Euclid, the Unix Operating System and Tunis.* Addison-Wesley, Reading, MA.

Inmos Ltd. 1988. *occam 2 Reference Manual.* Prentice Hall, Englewood Cliffs, NJ.

Kaubisch, W.H., Perrott, R.H. and Hoare, C.A.R. 1976. Quasiparallel programming. *Software—Practice and Experience 6*, 3 (July–September), 341–356.

Kernighan, B.W. and Ritchie, D.M. 1978. *The C Programming Language.* Prentice Hall, Englewood Cliffs, NJ.

Lampson, B.W. and Redell, D.D. 1980. Experience with processes and monitors in Mesa. *Communications of the ACM 23*, 2 (February), 105–117.

Naur, P. 1963. Revised report on the algorithmic language Algol 60. *Communications of the ACM 6*, 1 (January), 1–17.

Organick, E.I. 1973. *Computer System Organization: The B5700/B6700 Series.* Academic Press, New York.

Weinstock, C.B., and Wulf, W.A. 1988. Quick Fit: an efficient algorithm for heap storage management. *SIGPLAN Notices 23*, 10 (October), 141–148.

Welsh, J. and Bustard, D.W. 1979. Pascal-Plus—another language for modular multiprogramming. *Software—Practice and Experience 9*, 11 (November), 947–957.

Wirth, N. 1971. The programming language Pascal. *Acta Informatica 1*, 1, 35–63.

Wirth, N. 1977. Modula: a programming language for modular multiprogramming. *Software—Practice and Experience 7*, 1 (January–February), 3–35.

MIX
Papier aus verantwortungsvollen Quellen
Paper from responsible sources
FSC® C105338

If you have any concerns about our products,
you can contact us on
ProductSafety@springernature.com

In case Publisher is established outside the EU,
the EU authorized representative is:
Springer Nature Customer Service Center GmbH
Europaplatz 3, 69115 Heidelberg, Germany

Printed by Libri Plureos GmbH
in Hamburg, Germany